Participatory Literacy Practices for P-12 Classrooms in the Digital Age

Jessica S. Mitchell
University of North Alabama, USA

Erin N. Vaughn
University of North Alabama, USA

A volume in the Advances in Early Childhood and K-12 Education (AECKE) Book Series

IGI Global
DISSEMINATOR OF KNOWLEDGE

Published in the United States of America by
IGI Global
Information Science Reference (an imprint of IGI Global)
701 E. Chocolate Avenue
Hershey PA, USA 17033
Tel: 717-533-8845
Fax: 717-533-8661
E-mail: cust@igi-global.com
Web site: http://www.igi-global.com

Library of Congress Cataloging-in-Publication Data

Names: Mitchell, Jessica S., 1984- editor. | Vaughn, Erin N., 1982- editor.

Title: Participatory literacy practices for P-12 classrooms in the digital age / Jessica S. Mitchell and Erin N. Vaughn, Editors.
Description: Hershey, PA : Information Science Reference, [2020] | Includes bibliographical references. | Summary: “”This book explores the role of participatory literacy in P-12 student learning through digital instruction. It also addresses current issues in teacher education which can be applied to a broad educational context”--Provided by publisher”-- Provided by publisher.
Identifiers: LCCN 2019015741 | ISBN 9781799800002 (hardcover) | ISBN 9781799800019 (paperback) | ISBN 9781799800026 (ebook)
Subjects: LCSH: Computer-assisted instruction. | Information literacy--Study and teaching. | Computer literacy--Study and teaching. | Teachers--Training of.
Classification: LCC LB1028.43 .P367 2020 | DDC 371.33--dc23
LC record available at https://lccn.loc.gov/2019015741

This book is published in the IGI Global book series Advances in Early Childhood and K-12 Education (AECKE) (ISSN: 2329-5929; eISSN: 2329-5937)

British Cataloguing in Publication Data
A Cataloguing in Publication record for this book is available from the British Library.

All work contributed to this book is new, previously-unpublished material. The views expressed in this book are those of the authors, but not necessarily of the publisher.

For electronic access to this publication, please contact: eresources@igi-global.com.

Advances in Early Childhood and K-12 Education (AECKE) Book Series

Jared Keengwe
University of North Dakota, USA

ISSN:2329-5929
EISSN:2329-5937

Mission

Early childhood and K-12 education is always evolving as new methods and tools are developed through which to shape the minds of today's youth. Globally, educational approaches vary allowing for new discussions on the best methods to not only educate, but also measure and analyze the learning process as well as an individual's intellectual development. New research in these fields is necessary to improve the current state of education and ensure that future generations are presented with quality learning opportunities.

The **Advances in Early Childhood and K-12 Education (AECKE)** series aims to present the latest research on trends, pedagogies, tools, and methodologies regarding all facets of early childhood and K-12 education.

Coverage

- Pedagogy
- Performance Assessment
- Individualized Education
- K-12 Education
- Standardized Testing
- Common Core State Standards
- Reading and Writing
- Literacy Development
- Learning Outcomes
- Urban K-12 Education

IGI Global is currently accepting manuscripts for publication within this series. To submit a proposal for a volume in this series, please contact our Acquisition Editors at Acquisitions@igi-global.com or visit: http://www.igi-global.com/publish/.

The Advances in Early Childhood and K-12 Education (AECKE) Book Series (ISSN 2329-5929) is published by IGI Global, 701 E. Chocolate Avenue, Hershey, PA 17033-1240, USA, www.igi-global.com. This series is composed of titles available for purchase individually; each title is edited to be contextually exclusive from any other title within the series. For pricing and ordering information please visit http://www.igi-global.com/book-series/advances-early-childhood-education/76699. Postmaster: Send all address changes to above address.

Titles in this Series

For a list of additional titles in this series, please visit:
https://www.igi-global.com/book-series/advances-early-childhood-education/76699

Narrative Thinking and Storytelling for Problem Solving in Science Education
John Thomas Riley (The Big Moon Dig, USA) and Luisa dall'Acqua (Scientific Lyceum TCO, Italy)
Information Science Reference • copyright 2019 • 271pp • H/C (ISBN: 9781522584018) • US $175.00 (our price)

Critical Essays on the New Moral Imperative for Supporting Marginalized Students in PK-20 Education
Rebecca J. Blankenship (Florida Agricultural and Mechanical University, USA)
Information Science Reference • copyright 2019 • 268pp • H/C (ISBN: 9781522577874) • US $175.00 (our price)

Cyberbullying and the Critical Importance of Educational Resources for Prevention and Intervention
Gilberto Marzano (Rezekne Academy of Technologies, Latvia) and Joanna Lizut (Janusz Korczak Pedagogical University in Warsaw, Poland)
Information Science Reference • copyright 2019 • 323pp • H/C (ISBN: 9781522580768) • US $175.00 (our price)

K-12 STEM Education in Urban Learning Environments
Jillian L. Wendt (University of the District of Columbia, USA) and Danielle L. Apugo (University of the District of Columbia, USA)
Information Science Reference • copyright 2019 • 309pp • H/C (ISBN: 9781522578147) • US $190.00 (our price)

Cases on Kyosei Practice in Music Education
Richard Keith Gordon (Seisa University, Japan & California State University, USA) and Taichi Akutsu (Shujitsu University, Japan & Seisa University, Japan)
Information Science Reference • copyright 2019 • 296pp • H/C (ISBN: 9781522580423) • US $175.00 (our price)

Cultivating a Culture of Nonviolence in Early Childhood Development Centers and Schools
Simon George Taukeni (University of Namibia, Namibia)
Information Science Reference • copyright 2019 • 322pp • H/C (ISBN: 9781522574767) • US $185.00 (our price)

Advanced Strategies and Models for Integrating RTI in Secondary Schools
Pam L. Epler (Grand Canyon University, USA)
Information Science Reference • copyright 2019 • 356pp • H/C (ISBN: 9781522583226) • US $185.00 (our price)

Handbook of Research on Emerging Practices and Methods for K-12 Online and Blended Learning
Tina Lane Heafner (University of North Carolina at Charlotte, USA) Richard Hartshorne (University of Central Florida, USA) and Richard Thripp (University of Central Florida, USA)

IGI Global
DISSEMINATOR OF KNOWLEDGE

701 East Chocolate Avenue, Hershey, PA 17033, USA
Tel: 717-533-8845 x100 • Fax: 717-533-8661
E-Mail: cust@igi-global.com • www.igi-global.com

Table of Contents

Detailed Table of Contents

Embracing a culturally responsive teaching pedagogy in classrooms is one means for addressing literacy inequities with students of color. Afterschool literacy tutoring is another means of addressing these inequities, but little is known about implementing culturally responsive teaching in afterschool environments. This qualitative case study explored how cultural differences impacted an urban elementary afterschool literacy tutoring program. Grounded in participatory literacy theory, the authors conclude that it is normal for cultural differences to occur and cause disruptions during tutoring; however, culturally responsive teaching can mitigate these interruptions through developing caring relationships, creating a safe learning environment, implementing a participatory student-centered curriculum using online resources, and critiquing social inequalities. The discussion offers seven principles of culturally responsive teaching to use in literacy instructional environments.

This chapter explores the varied participatory practices that were triggered during the Spring 2016 iteration of the Digital Dialogue Project (DDP), an initiative that connected different age groups in distinct subject-area classes within contrasting schools embedded inside divergent communities. During the project, youth (from 3rd grade to 12th grade) engaged in three phases: (1) producing multimodal products connected to curricular goals, (2) virtually sharing/viewing/commenting on the digital product with small groups of 3-5 youth from different schools, and (3) meeting face to face at a culminating field trip to engage in collaborative theater exercises to dramatically embody the groups' digital stories. Authors provide concrete examples of the kinds of participation that the DDP evoked as well as key pedagogical commitments to literacies that were central to designing and implementing the project. Throughout the chapter, real talk for practicing teachers is provided in order to offer guidance for those interested in imagining similar participatory projects for youth.

Engaging in artifactual literacy as a collective in a teacher education seminar class gives space for objects and texts to bring forth reimagined and alternative ways to be "teacher." An elementary teacher education program utilizes a seminar space to invite teachers to write from artifacts to analyze, deconstruct, and reconstruct their teacher identities. The analysis and discussions of the reconstructed narratives that define, contest, or shape identities give needed distance from traditional and often constricting narratives of "teacher" and "teaching." The investment of this critical identity work in teacher education is depicted in the analysis of two preservice teachers' collective writing in a digital space.

Participatory literacy practices include the ways in which individuals interpret, make, and share as a way of connecting in our digitally mediated culture. This chapter is a culmination of an across-university partnership created between the two authors and the pre-service teachers that collaborated online about teaching and learning. Three threads of participatory literacy practices are shared within the chapter including 1) the use of blogging across university settings, 2) the implementation of digital professional learning communities (PLCs) to connect and collaborate with other pre-service teachers, and 3) the formation and participation in digital literature circles to co-construct meaning from children's literature. This chapter includes the authors' attempts at collaboration across university settings using different tools, platforms, and resources. This work is an example for other teachers and teacher educators to consider how we can help pre-service teachers be part of the participatory culture and provide an even wider community of learners.

This chapter addresses the need to make time and space for transliteracy practices in the classroom. University pre-service teachers are used as the primary example as the chapter documents how these students made meaning across a range of platforms, while reading the acclaimed young adult novel The Hate U Give. The university course, titled Language and Literacy, focuses on methods of literacy instruction in the classroom. A lesson plan framework is included in the chapter that is especially user friendly for educator preparation classrooms as well as high school and middle school teachers. The chapter explores the experiences of the college students while reading The Hate U Give, while detailing how the students created meaning through a variety of traditional and modern teaching practices.

Foreword

Literacy and literacies are often standardized within educational systems to be fixed, standard and acquirable, creating a binary between those who have acquired it and those for whom it eludes. Due to intra and transnational-migration, educational and language policies have economized literacy as countable and fixed, assessing schools by this narrow standard and thereby, its students, families, and educators. Such a narrow definition suggests that schools are the primary experts and arbitrators of literacy acquisition, yet literacies are creatively negotiated and performed in multiple places. Participatory literacies expands and critiques this standardization of content and location, by examining the *agents* within the creation of multi-modal and multilingual literacies. More simply, multiliteracies. Individuals or agents who come from diverse identities and communities transform the literacy landscape as they create new methods and modes of expression that are translational to our diversifying world.

Participatory literacies fall at the intersection of agency, creativity, and resistance. Agency refers to the perspectives and actions taken on by individuals to show their competency and creativity. Often, agents take on these roles in resistance to institutional structures that pre-define literacy and what it takes to be regarded as literate. New participatory literacies become manifest through the hybridization of languages, creating new varieties of expression and communication. Social media allows for such expressions to expand, adapt, and transform within an audience of other agents who share the same or dissimilar interest. These relevant and creative literacies is an essential component of civic engagement as it is inclusive of creative and competent agents who have historically been marginalized or omitted from the definition of a literate person.

In this book, *Participatory Literacy Practices for P-12 Classrooms in the Digital Age*, scholars working in K-12 schools, universities, community centers, and after school programs document their definitions of participatory literacies. Scholars and practitioners working among students of color, poverty, language background, and immigration describe how their interactions with and amongst students is creating new venues and opportunities for literacy expression. Engaging with critical, digital, technological, and linguistic literacies, authors articulate how students are resisting the pre-determined, fixed and countable literacy through the production of videos, blogs, and websites. This rich compilation also demonstrates that such multiliteracies are not being generated solely in schools, but in homes, communities, and community centers, demonstrating the diverse agents committed to the creative agency of their students. Moreover, the book provides an important lens into how literacy can and is being transformed, changing the perspectives of educators to see their students as literate agents of resistance and creativity.

Patricia Morita-Mullaney
Purdue University in West Lafayette, USA

Patricia Morita-Mullaney *is an Assistant Professor of Literacy and Language at Purdue University in West Lafayette, Indiana.*

Preface

INTRODUCTION

We approached this project firmly grounded in the philosophical orientation that *literacy*, a historically contentious concept to define, denotes far more than the ability to read and write. Too often, contemporary classrooms approach literacy in this more traditional sense, restricting the experiences of its 21st century learners to the functional reading and writing of printed texts and limiting the empowering potential of literacy beyond the classroom walls. Consequently, youth in today's classrooms often internalize the purposes of literacy as nothing more than gatekeeper tasks to earn grades and pass tests (Wiggins, 2009), rather than for its transformative possibilities in a rapidly evolving democratic and multicultural society. Thus, the contents of this book seek to disrupt the boundaries of traditional literacy practices with those that more strongly reflect the social and cultural demands of the 21st century. To accomplish this aim, we align our theoretical orientation with perspectives which define literacy as dynamically situated in specific social and cultural contexts, extending traditional skills, such as multimodal receptivity and production, for full inclusivity, and serving authentic, *participatory* purposes both within and outside of the classroom (Alvermann & Moje, 2019; Olthouse, 2013; Vasquez, Janks, & Comber, 2019). We utilize Wohlwend's (2016) definition of participatory literacies as, "ways of interpreting, making, sharing, and belonging in increasingly globally and digitally mediated cultures across multiple media platforms" (p. 62), within our work, and we contend that literacy remains an inherently social practice across each space it takes place.

Participatory literacies are best understood within context-based frameworks that draw from students' funds of knowledge (Gonzalez, Moll, & Amanti, 2005) and utilize both digital and multimodal resources to scaffold the meaning-making process. Because literacy practices involve complex interactions among audiences and tasks, they change based on context (Alvermann & Moje, 2019; Olthouse, 2013), meaning that how one engages in literacy at school is likely different than at home, with friends, and via digital outlets such as social media. Not only must literacy pedagogy prepare students to participate across a variety of communicative platforms, but it also requires teachers to both recognize and build upon the pre-established and diverse literacy practices of their students. Through this approach, students' background knowledge and lived experiences are perceived as assets to the knowledge construction and production in the classroom, which can be particularly empowering for students whose communication skills are not often valued in the traditional curriculum (Olthouse, 2013). Furthermore, the use of digital and multimodal resources, such as blogs, podcasts, infographics, and many others, provide multiple entry points for students to interpret and share knowledge with audiences beyond the classroom walls

(Sang, 2017). Many of the chapters in this book highlight participatory literacy projects through which youth were encouraged to draw upon their literate backgrounds while utilizing a variety of digital and multimodal tools to make sense of new skills and concepts.

Arguably the most important aspect of participatory literacies is the empowering potential for social transformation (Brown, Schell, & Mei Ni, 2018). Rooted in the philosophies of Paulo Freire, critical literacy advocates for "understanding the relationship between texts, meaning-making, and power in order to undertake transformative social action that contributes to the achievement of a more equitable social order" (Janks & Vasquez, 2011, p. 1). Such scholars argue that literacy is inherently political, rendering political consequences in society, and thus, should be treated as such in the educational setting. Participatory literacy pedagogy with this critical bent empowers young learners to harness literacy as a vehicle for examining power relationships, addressing social issues within their communities, and ultimately dismantling inequitable ways of being (Vasquez et al., 2019). When engaged in such learning experiences, youth often develop agentive voices (Argenal & Jacquez, 2015), resulting in powerful cultural and civic identity development with the realization that they have the potential to impact social change. Hence, *literacy* rooted in this philosophical orientation extends traditional purposes for reading and writing and becomes an authentic—and vital—tool for both individual and collective social transformation. A number of chapters in this book illuminate the transformative potential of participatory literacies as youth engage in learning experiences that examine the intersectionality of social forces such as race and power while challenging the status quo.

ORGANIZATION

To meet the above calls for authentic participation across diverse populations, we invited chapter proposals from presenters at annual conferences of a variety of professional organizations such as the Literacy Research Association (LRA), National Council of Teachers of English (NCTE), and the National Council for the Social Studies (NCSS). Chapter authors were invited based on the praxis of their work as it intersected with the preparation of teacher candidates in digitally-mediated contexts and with the following recommended topics:

- Media literacy
- Digital technology
- Critical literacy; theory and praxis
- Culturally relevant literacy practice
- Promoting inclusive learning environments
- P-12 teachers and students as change agents
- Multimodal content utilizing digital literacy skills
- Literacy practices that promote civic discourse and social action

Ultimately, chapters were selected based on the following purpose statement for the scope of this work: The purpose of this interdisciplinary work is to inform perspectives in teacher education which equip future or current teachers with knowledge of the larger context of participatory literacy research where digital content is integrated to support inclusive classroom designs. Invited contributions to this work encompass a wide variety of research traditions and may include both theoretical and empirical research designs. Potential designs may draw upon field studies in education and social sciences research, theoretical contributions which examine the perception of literacy in a digital society, or niche research interests related to teacher education in specific disciplines such as English Language Arts and Social Studies.

In the following sections, we provide an overview of each of the three contexts of this book: P-12 classrooms, community-based contexts, and teacher education programs. In doing so, we not only share first-hand accounts from the field as exemplars for future classroom teachers to explore, but we also provide models of participatory practice occuring in teacher education programs across the country. As each of the three sections of this book explores a unique context for participatory literacy practices, we provide an overview of each context and relate the significance of chapter contributions in relationship to meeting the objectives for this work.

Section 1: Participatory Literacy Practices in P-12 Classrooms

The chapters in this section of the book provide direct insights into participatory literacy practices enacted in traditional classroom settings. A microcosm of democracy, the classroom is a powerful setting where youth can socially construct and produce knowledge, potentially impacting audiences beyond their immediate communities. Teachers who approach literacy through a participatory lens design authentic and collaborative learning environments and incorporate a variety of digital and multimodal tools into classroom activities to scaffold the meaning-making process. (Olthouse, 2013; Wohlwend, 2016). Additionally, pedagogy that prioritizes participatory literacy fosters individual and collective identity development, facilitates critical thinking about social issues, and encourages youth to utilize literacy practices in service of improving the communities of which they are a part.

In the chapters that follow, the authors present a variety of pedagogical practices that cultivated powerful participatory literacy learning with their students in P-12 classrooms. For example, the authors of Chapter 1 facilitated the production of short stories with their early learners by creating opportunities for students to manipulate digital images for story design, elevating a student with limited English language skills in his ability to assist his peers in their use of digital tools. The teachers highlighted in Chapter 2 fostered a student-centered writing unit in which their students engaged in investigative journalism in order to produce podcasts that illuminated multiple perspectives for understanding social issues such as income inequality. The authors of Chapter 3 explored the integrative nature of literacy and social studies as they explained how participatory literacy practices, such as the use of social media and other Web 2.0 technologies, can be used to foster civic engagement and informed social action. Finally, the authors of Chapter 4 explored the impact of reality television on the perceptions of high school students, and they addressed the need for critical media skills within today's youth that challenge the often stereotypical depictions of individuals and groups produced by sources of media. In sum, this section shares the powerful potential of participatory literacy pedagogy in P-12 spaces and illuminates strategies used to design learning environments conducive to digital contexts.

Chapter Overviews

Chapter 1 argues the need for multimodal and digital play in early childhood classrooms. More particularly, the authors highlight how children used Legos and digital tools to compose stories, fostering a creative and agentic co-construction of knowledge.

Chapter 2 shares the journey of two educators as their students investigated a variety of perspectives surrounding abstract concepts such as equity and "the American Dream." They produced student-authored podcasts while engaging a variety of multimodal formats, including e-books, local plays, oral interviews, etc.

Chapter 3 explores strategies for fostering participatory literacy practices with an emphasis on civic engagement. The authors argue the need for media literacy skills and explain how digital tools, such as social media, can be used to foster collaboration and decision-making, connecting students with the world beyond the classroom and reducing barriers to civic engagement.

Chapter 4 investigates how high school students perceived the hidden messages and their impact of reality television shows. The authors argue the need for critical literacy instruction in classrooms, through which youth learn to analyze and critique the relationships between power, identity, and the media.

Section 2: Participatory Literacy Practices in Community Contexts

The chapters in this section illuminate principles of "third space" (Bhabha, 1994; Gutierrez, 2008; Potter & McDougall, 2017) which "values and draws from the numerous meaning-making social contexts, representational modes, and tools (available de-signs) that students possess to help them extract, express, and (re)design meaning in their academic, public, and private lives" (Skerrett, 2010, pg. 67). Third space blends informal and formal spaces of learning (Gutierrez, 2008) and not only occurs in physical locations such as public libraries or after-school tutoring centers, but also exists entirely in digital contexts such as digital exchange projects that connect students to broader audiences beyond their own classroom or immediate context (Potter & McDougall, 2017). Implicit to the aims of this book, the concept of third space is particularly useful to literacy research which utilizes narrative inquiry to support social inclusion in the "digital divide" (Warschauer & Tate, 2019). As Mills and Stornaiulo (2019) contend, "writing and literacies studies must critically account for the role of interrupting subordination of marginalized groups on the basis of race, language, culture, geographic location, class, gender, ability, religion, and national origin" (p. 1). Third space holds the potential to interrupt such subordination by creating locations for new communities to emerge in critical dialogue, thereby facilitating an impetus for social inclusion.

In the chapters that follow, third space is evoked by communities of practice which emerge from the contexts presented by the authors of each chapter. For example, the authors of Chapter 5 bring attention to community-based assets as a means of connecting students to social issues in their own communities and for exploration of their own identities in relationship to their community. In Chapter 6, a literacy tutoring center provided a shared community space for both academic advancement and critical reflection across cultural orientations. In Chapter 7, digital and face-to-face communication across differing school communities further facilitated personal insights from the participants in the project. In sum, this section presents three unique spaces where participatory practices connected students to perspectives from new audiences and contexts, creating new frames of interpretation.

Chapter Overviews

Chapter 5 illuminates how teachers utilized community resources to generate interest, increase relatability, and promote social action among its students, particularly those whose lived experiences are often not reflected in pre-packaged curricula. The authors share particular instructional strategies harnessed by classroom teachers, such as neighborhood prints and artifact sharing, that encouraged the exploration of identity and place and rendered opportunities to improve the local community.

Chapter 6 chronicles an urban university in partnership with an afterschool tutoring center. Insights from this chapter include reflections of how culturally relevant instructional practices facilitated exploration of perceived differences through student-centered participatory curriculum.

Chapter 7 follows the most recent iteration of an initiative to connect students from different communities in a "mini-public" experience, scaffolded for democratic practice in a participatory culture. Facilitated through a collaboration between a local college professor and a high school teacher, students created multimodal projects, shared and commented on the projects via digital spaces, and eventually met to enact shared understandings of the project.

Section 3: Participatory Literacy Practices in Teacher Education

The chapters in this section of the book provide examples of theory and research-based practices for current consideration in the preparation of future educators, providing timely discussion for the current context of teacher education. For example, as the global call for STEM curriculum and technology-infused experiences have impacted the way teacher candidates participate in instructional activities (McCulloch, Hollebrands, Lee, Harrison, & Mutlu, 2018), there has been an increase in the discussion of the role of computer programming in both literacy instruction and teacher preparation. Similarly, shifts in content have also raised questions about how best to teach technology and/or digital literacy such as through interdisciplinary or discipline-specific approaches. The authors of Chapter 8 contribute to this discussion by providing an overview of teacher candidates working in clinical experiences to embed interdisciplinary projects which utilize literacy experiences across the curriculum. In Chapter 9, the authors explore how teacher educators approached teaching basic computer programming (coding) procedures to elementary students. Finally in Chapter 10, the authors explore the role of writing instruction in teacher education by advocating for multi-modal approaches to writing pedagogy.

In consideration of other timely discussions in teacher preparation, there is also a call for critical experiences in teacher education to deconstruct and reconstruct teacher identity. (Lensmire & Schick, 2017). By facilitating experiences in which teacher candidates explore their own identities, future educators are better equipped to tackle complex social phenomena, such as the exploration of positionality in relationship to diverse student perspectives. As Mills & Stornaiulo contend, educators should "know how to respect cultural difference in local and global contexts, and to understand the complexities of literacies against the multiplicity of identities, socio-material relations, textual practices and labor markets that cross national, state, cultural, linguistic boundaries" (p.1-2). The chapters in this section also provide examples of how teacher education programs use digital experiences to reflexively explore identity among stakeholders—from university professors and teacher candidates to cooperating teachers and P-12 students. Additionally, these chapters provide examples of how digitally-mediated communication, across a variety of platforms and for varied purposes, have served as a venue for collective meaning-making. For example, in Chapter 11, the authors provide an example of a critical approach to exploring teacher identity through the analysis of digital writing artifacts. In Chapter 12, the authors share ways in which future educators experience digital literacy culture across college campuses in response to children's literature, widening their own perspectives of how to incorporate similar experiences into their own classrooms. In Chapter 13, the authors also share how teacher education students participated in a digital discussion of a critical young adult text. Ultimately, these chapters all represent ways teacher education programs have responded to current trends in teacher education and provide timely discussions for consideration.

Chapter Overviews

Chapter 8 chronicles a teacher education program in its mission to provide digital experiences, allowing teacher candidates to transfer skills into authentic contexts. Such experiences included content-based integration with an emphasis on the creation of interdisciplinary STREAM projects, authentic student-led projects using technology, and collaboration with cooperating teachers in diverse P-6 field-based contexts.

Chapter 9 follows a study of the attitudes, interests, and experiences of teacher education candidates during a clinical practicum in which they taught elementary students how to use coding procedures. The authors trace the development of coding instruction in teacher education and conclude the chapter with appropriate examples of literacy-based coding instruction for elementary contexts.

Chapter 10 chronicles research-based practices for the incorporation of multi-modal writing experiences in teacher education programs. The authors present concrete examples of activities which support digital writing experiences for teacher education candidates and provide implications for supporting teachers in transferring digital writing experiences into classroom practice.

Chapter 11 posits a critical approach to teacher preparation through the analysis of artifacts created by elementary education teacher candidates. As a result of a writing seminar, teacher candidates explored issues of teacher identity. The authors highlight the reflections of two teacher candidates participating in digital exchanges which culminated in exploration of teacher identity.

Chapter 12 shares the experiences of university professors collaborating across campuses to create opportunities for teacher candidates to explore a variety of digital platforms and to experience a robust participatory culture. Digital experiences included the use of blogging, implementation of digital professional learning communities, and digital literature circles that co-constructed meaning from children's literature.

Chapter 13 follows the experiences of pre-service teachers participating in transliteracy practices during a literacy methods course, as they reflected on their perceptions of the meaning-making process during a shared reading of the young adult novel, *The Hate U Give*. The authors provide a lesson plan framework for middle and high school teachers interested in creating similar transliteracy experiences for students.

CONCLUSION

The social and cultural demands of the 21st century have rapidly evolved, requiring a citizenry literate in a multitude of modalities and across a vast expanse of communicative spaces. Moreover, citizens must be equipped to participate and continuously reconstruct the democratic and multicultural society in which we live. To best prepare our youth for this endeavor, literacy pedagogy must extend beyond traditional practices of reading and writing to include those that are participatory and transformative, empowering youth of all social and cultural backgrounds as co-constructors and producers of knowledge. As many of the chapters in this work illustrate, participatory literacy practices are not only a vital component of the current classroom climate, but also hold the potential to impact the realities of the students who participate in these spaces for years to come.

REFERENCES

Alvermann, D. E., & Moje, E. B. (2018). A relational model of adolescent literacy instruction: Disrupting the discourse of "every teacher a teacher of reading". In D. E. Alvermann, N. J. Unrau, M. Sailors, & R. B. Ruddell (Eds.), *Theoretical models and processes of literacy* (pp. 378–396). New York, NY: Routledge. doi:10.4324/9781315110592-22

Argenal, A., & Jacquez, T. (2015). Critical service-learning and social justice: A holistic curriculum. In O. Delano-Oriaran, M. W. Penick-Parks, & S. Fondrie (Eds.), *The Sage source- book of service-learning and civic engagement* (pp. 61–65). Thousand Oaks, CA: Sage. doi:10.4135/9781483346625.n15

Bhabha, H. K. (1994). *The location of culture*. London, UK: Routledge.

Brown, C. L., Schell, R., & Ni, M. (2018). Powerful participatory literacy for English learners. *Journal of Adolescent & Adult Literacy*, *62*(4), 369–378. doi:10.1002/jaal.913

Gonzalez, N., Moll, L. C., & Amanti, C. (2005). *Funds of knowledge: Theorizing practices in households, communities, and classrooms*. Mahwah, NJ: Lawrence Erlbaum Associates, Inc.

Gutiérrez, K. D. (2008). Developing a sociocritical literacy in the third space. *Reading Research Quarterly*, *43*(2), 148–164. doi:10.1598/RRQ.43.2.3

Janks, H., & Vasquez, V. (2011). Editorial: Critical literacy revisited: Writing as critique. *English Teaching*, *10*(1), 1–6.

Lensmire, A., & Schick, A. (Eds.). (2017). *(Re)narrating teacher identities: Telling truths and becoming teachers*. New York, NY: Peter Lang. doi:10.3726/b10687

McCulloch, A. W., Hollebrands, K., Lee, H., Harrison, T., & Mutlu, A. (2018). Factors that influence secondary mathematics teachers' integration of technology in mathematics lessons. *Computers & Education*, *123*, 26–40. doi:10.1016/j.compedu.2018.04.008

Mills, K. A., & Stornaiulo, A. (2019). Digital diversity, ideology, and the politics of a writing revolution. In K. A. Mills, A. Stornaiuolo, A. Smith, & J. Z. Pandya (Eds.), *Handbook of writing, literacies, and education in digital cultures* (pp. 1–9). New York, NY: Routledge.

Olthouse, J. M. (2013). Multiliteracies theory and gifted education: Creating "smart spaces" in the language arts classroom. *Gifted Child Today*, *36*(4), 247–253. doi:10.1177/1076217513497575

Potter, J., & McDougall, J. (2017). *Digital media, culture and education: Theorising third space literacies*. London, UK: Palgrave Macmillan. doi:10.1057/978-1-137-55315-7

Sang, Y. (2017). Expanded territories of "literacy": New literacies and multiliteracies. *Journal of Education and Practice*, *8*(8), 16–19.

Skerrett, A. (2010). Lolita, facebook, and the third space of literacy teacher education. *Educational Studies*, *46*(1), 67–84. doi:10.1080/00131940903480233

Vasquez, V. M., Janks, H., & Comber, B. (2019). Critical literacy as a way of being and doing. *Language Arts*, *96*(5), 300–311.

Warschauer, M., & Tate, T. (2018). Digital divides and social inclusion. In K. A. Mills, A. Stornaiuolo, A. Smith, & J. Z. Pandya (Eds.), *Handbook of writing, literacies, and education in digital cultures* (pp. 63–75). New York, NY: Routledge.

Wiggins, G. (2009). Real-world writing: Making purpose and audience matter. *English Journal, 98*(5), 29–37.

Wohlwend, K. E. (2016). Who gets to play? Access, popular media, and participatory literacies. *Early Years, 37*(1), 62–76. doi:10.1080/09575146.2016.1219699

Section 1

Participatory Literacy Practices in P-12 Classrooms

Chapter 1
Literacy in Early Childhood:
Multimodal Play and Text Production

Sally Brown
https://orcid.org/0000-0002-6607-7882
Georgia Southern University, USA

ABSTRACT

This chapter is based on a year-long ethnographic research study in a Title I urban classroom with 24 seven- and eight-year-olds. Using this work, the author shares ways of teaching literacy to young readers using technology and building on student interests. In particular, students' stories constructed through Lego play and digital photography are showcased. Three major themes are identified and discussed: (1) digital play as an essential tool for story, (2) multimodal storytelling as a path for learning and new language, a (3) apprenticeships for multimodal text productions. The chapter concludes with practical suggestions for educators about ways to capitalize on students' funds of knowledge as well as their passion for digital tools in the 21st century classroom.

INTRODUCTION

The world is changing and becoming technological-based in a global sense. Many opportunities for communication and learning rely on the use of digital tools. During early childhood, children are continually being exposed to more and more digital tools as they interact informally at home with peers and formally in school contexts. These digital experiences tend to involve tools like smartphones, tablets, and computers which children use to engage with social media, apps, video games, text messaging, e-books, etc. Words alone no longer are the main means by which people communicate. Instead, multimedia affordances provide multimodal formats for meaning making. For example, the use of images, sound, and animation are central in the 21st century. Given the current context, early experiences of children are being re-shaped as they engage with technology even as young as a few months of age (Guernsey, 2014; Sefton-Green, Marsh, Erstad, & Flewitt, 2016).

As educators, it makes sense to build upon early home experiences as children engage in formal reading and writing events in classrooms. Consideration should also be given to the assets children bring

DOI: 10.4018/978-1-7998-0000-2.ch001

with them in terms of cultures, languages, and histories of working with digital tools (Dyson, 2003; Souto-Manning, 2016). Educators must consider how existing classroom resources are made available to students for constructing and creating meaning while building on their strengths. It is through the formation of interactional spaces for literacy learning that students are able to be in the moment of creating, composing, doing, and becoming authors (Kuby & Rucker, 2016).

In this case, play with physical materials like Legos are mixed with paper-based experiences and digital tools to compose stories. Play in the 21st century must include not only interactions with physical materials but also digital platforms. Knowledge evolves as children experiment with digital tools and all of the affordances they offer. Play allows for a flexible approach to thinking of materials and resources in new ways (Stephen & Edwards, 2018), and as society moves forward in the digital age, young learners include technology in their play. For example, creativity is fostered through choices in the selection of clip art, digital photography, or background images and colors (Marsh, Plowman, Yamada-Rice, Bishop, & Scott, 2016).

This requires deep thinking about the social nature of learning and consideration of how cultures, backgrounds, and experiences contribute to the rich interplay that happens during classroom learning events. It also necessitates the rethinking of play concepts and ways to begin designing alternative learning opportunities where young students experiment with different modes and practice combining them for meaning-making purposes (Wohlwend, 2011). Initially, this may only be evident to the student but through conversations and questioning, teachers can begin to see how play is unfolding in ways that showcase traditional literacies. The journey of a diverse group of second graders (ages seven and eight) is detailed in the chapter.

BACKGROUND

Building on Existing Resources

We are at a time in history when schools are filled with the voices and excitement of diverse learners who come from a range of socioeconomic backgrounds, cultures, races, ethnicities, and languages. For multilingual students, this means exploring their linguistic resources as well. In order to value all of this richness, there is a need to begin by identifying the funds of knowledge children bring with them to school, including the repertoires of digital experiences (Brown, 2017; González, Moll, & Amanti, 2006; Souto-Manning, 2016). These diverse learners bring a plethora of culturally developed bodies of knowledge from home that originate from family supported activities and expertise. Knowing about these resources from home allows the teacher to build a connection to what students already know and opens up a space for continued learning while expanding to other areas. After all, we know that learning to read and write is not solely about traditional skills like decoding. It is also heavily reliant on the child's social, cultural, and linguistic practices within the particular context during which the literacy event occurs (Reyes, DaSilva Iddings, & Feller, 2016).

Given the current context of learning for many children across the world, technology is a factor influencing these funds of knowledge as they navigate digital and non-digital tools across media, home, and school. Over half of children surveyed report engaging with technology in some format seven days per week (Rideout, Foehr, & Roberts, 2010). This is even true for children as young as five where virtual worlds like Club Penguin become playgrounds for reading and writing (Marsh, 2014; Sefton-Green et al., 2016). Through participation in a 21st century environment, children develop numerous skills and resources for learning that can be capitalized on for classroom instruction. For example, early grade students come to school knowing how to crop a photo, conduct a Google search, select and watch a YouTube video, send text messages, etc.

In addition, attention must also be given to the cultural and linguistic practices surrounding funds of knowledge. This means thinking about how families interact with and around technology and for what purposes the tools are used. This may vary across cultures and individual families (Reyes et al., 2016). It is necessary to understand the language that is used for communication purposes in the home. Is this the same language used for digital interactions? Is there a mixing of languages? One must also consider that some of the traditional forms of literacy like storytelling may come to school with the child and mix with digital tools for new forms of literacy. The grandfather's oral story of fighting in a war might become a video with captions. As a result, these are resources for educators. Rather than ignoring the multimodality of children's daily lives, they can be built upon. To do this, there needs to be an understanding of multiliteracies and a new definition of literacies (Marshall & Toohey, 2010; Reyes et al., 2016).

Multiliteracies

A broad view of looking at multiple forms of literacy is the basis for the concept of multiliteracies. This involves creating a new definition of literacy that draws from various modes. According to Kress (2009), modes are "a socially and culturally given resource for meaning making." Another way to think about this is that a mode is a sign for conveying meaning with the medium being a form that carries the sign (i.e., digital screen, paper) (Sefton-Green et al., 2016). The process through which this happens may cross boundaries between online and offline formats and material/immaterial resources.

This approach values cultural and linguistic variations and validates the many forms of literacy. This involves students using available resources to make meaning through remixing and remaking. In other words, students combine print, non-print, and other physical materials in new ways to make sense of their world. Language is no longer the most powerful communication tool. Instead, other modes like images, movements, and sounds become central for communication. Within multiliteracies, students may choose to communicate in one mode or with a mixture of modes which is considered multimodality (New London Group, 1996).

Elements of newness are added to former traditional rules of literacy. Being literate in the 21st century becomes context dependent. In a public school classroom where there is access to the Internet and digital tools, students adapt many different forms of literacy based on the purpose of the text they are constructing. This causes literacy to take a plural form. Students apply flexible and fluid practices to expand this concept of multiliteracies using multiple modes. There is no longer one "right" way to communicate. Instead, students become designers of texts and ultimately their futures (The New London Group, 1996). A key element is the authenticity of learning with a focus on the process as opposed to teacher directed instruction that restricts learning for the purposes of a product that is assigned a grade. Multiliteracies create spaces for the messiness and complexities of literacy learning.

Spaces for Collaboration

One essential component of this approach relates to the social nature of learning. As students engage collaboratively and cooperatively with peers and adults in classrooms, it mimics many home interactions where collective learning occurs. Bouncing ideas off others assists in pushing the boundaries of a multimodal production. Collaboration creates space for the voices of several students to work together to co-produce a text (which can be defined as any type of production like a video, blog entry, photograph) (New London Group, 1996).

When thinking about the social aspects of learning, we know students turn to their peers (in schools) and family members (at home) in order to understand a particular skill or concept (Dyson, 2003). Often times, students are able to increase their understanding at a higher level when they interact with others instead of working independently. Essentially, each student brings his or her knowledge and skills to the interaction, and this is extended through dialogue (White, 2016). Providing an environment that supports social interactions leads to students becoming problem solvers who design creative solutions to problems (Rogoff, 1990). This also extends to problem solving related to technology. For example, a student may ask for assistance changing the font size on their story and receive assistance. This social interaction would include talking as well as physically touching the computer or tablet and clicking on the appropriate areas of the screen. Within this complexity of multiliteracies and social interactions, attention must be given to play that ensues as part of the process.

Play

Play has long since been an indispensable aspect of early learning experiences. In particular, play offers opportunities for children to develop language and literacy skills which later are applied in more formal ways in classrooms. Play builds upon the culture and funds of knowledge of students and many times bridges the home and school communities. It has the possibility to showcase what children are doing, how their lives matter, and how they contribute to society. Ultimately, upon a close examination play demonstrates the competence of children (Yayha & Wood, 2017).

Contemporary play includes digital aspects and has a few components that are essential to consider. The first of which is sharism or the ability to co-create rather than broker one's own creation. Sharism unfolds as students call out or share ideas prior to actually creating. In other words, the focus becomes collaborative as opposed to individual. There is not a need to keep ideas to one's self, and instead snippets of ideas become central to the dialogue surrounding an activity (Ackermann, Gauntlett, & Weckstrom, 2009). Shared activity becomes internalized through a process called semiotic mediation where the learner uses tools and symbols to construct or co-construct knowledge with others. Tools, like technology, toys, and drawing/images enrich cognitive activity by carrying forth sociocultural knowledge from a social to individual plane (Wohlwend, 2011). Therefore, dialogue remains central to the reconstruction and co-construction of knowledge, and exchanging ideas with others opens up spaces for intellectual interdependence (John-Steiner & Meehan, 2000).

The second is literacies beyond print. Young authors or text designers must now think about news ways of expressing their ideas. Materials, resources, and the learner change in novel ways as ideas are constructed, revised, and re-constructed (Vygotsky, 1978). Finally, there is border crossing where students move between worlds. This entails remixing the physical and the digital in ways where students are learning to belong (Ackermann, Gauntlett, & Weckstrom, 2009). The notion of belonging means being able to connect to one's global community where one feels safe to engage with trustworthy peers. Online and offline spaces are often traversed in this type of play where students engage in actions with physical materials like Legos along with cloud-based software using digital platforms. Play offers students an avenue for drawing upon students' funds of knowledge for creative development (Burnett, 2010; Marsh et al., 2016).

When these notions of play are applied to storytelling, the importance of modes comes to the surface. The multimodal nature of 21st century play means that the modes in which students engage have the power to impact the other modes being employed. There is movement beyond holding a physical object to a virtual world as in digital photography (Yayha & Wood, 2017). The telling of stories is recursive. It involves co-constructing narratives in complex ways that may include body movement, material objects, and dialogue (Wohlwend, 2011). Planning and control remain in the hands of the learner which can be referred to as student agency (Fisher, 2010). During one study (Cremin, Flewitt, Swann, Faulkner, & Kucirkova, 2018) focused on storytelling and story-acting, the children physically mimicked each other's actions during play. They were learning different roles and ways that story could unfold. The co-construction of stories led to multimodal narratives where clarity was realized through interactions and engagement with multiple forms of a story. This play afforded students a chance to try out various story elements to construct a just right text.

Playing with digital tools expands the resources available to children and opens possibilities. The child becomes free to manipulate and interpret the tools and artifacts produced in multiple ways. In thinking about play in this manner, children are active agents who use technology to determine their own outcomes. Play itself becomes one path for learning how to use digital tools and discovering the available productions (Arnott, 2016). When taking all of this into account, it makes the case for transforming traditional beliefs about play and thinking deeply about the potential of digital play.

Becoming

Through play, experimentation with digital tools, and dialogue, students are becoming young authors, writers, text designers, and artists. These literacy practices enable students to determine who they are and to see the possibilities of who they may be in the future as they navigate new ways of being (Davies, 2014). According to Jackson and Mazzei (2012), becoming includes experimentation and change, "a state of in-between-ness" (p. 722). This occurs as students engage in authentic literacy events that keep thinking moving and as a means to interrupt old ideas and make way for new transformations. In other words, students are in the process of becoming.

In one early childhood classroom, Kuby & Vaughn (2015) showcase how providing a range of multimodal materials opened spaces for agentive moves by a child to become an author and meaning maker. Additionally, the work extensive work of Wohlwend (2011; 2013) documents the process of young children becoming as they engage in literacy-based play. For example, Marshall, a kindergarten student, manipulates scissors, tape, and paper to design an original text about SpongeBob resulting in a puppet. In this case Marshall showcases his ability to become a text designer. As educators we must ask ourselves what possibilities for learning are we creating that can result in unexpected, collaborative, and collective interactions where students discover who they are and can become.

RESEARCH CONTEXT

Classroom

This ethnographic study took place in a grade two classroom in a Title 1, urban public school in the Southeastern United States. This school was an English-only school that provided English as a Second Language services to students three times per week. The 24 seven and eight-year old participants represented a variety of races, ethnicities, and languages (English, Spanish, Vietnamese, French, Wolof, and Pohnpeian). Their reading abilities, as measured by a standardized assessment (Scholastic Reading Inventory), ranged from beginning reader (a score of 0) to a grade equivalent of fourth-grade. The classroom teacher was African American with five years of teaching experience, and she implemented the school district's balanced literacy program.

Role of the Researcher

The researcher in this context served as an additional literacy teacher during the reading block. While the classroom teacher, Mrs. Green (all names are pseudonyms), taught guided reading groups, the researcher worked with small groups of children on the Lego project. The other two groups of students completed independent work like responding to books and reading passages on the computer. The students rotated groups twice during this period of an hour. The group interactions lasted approximately 30 minutes each twice per week.

Lego Project

Over the course of the school year, all of the students met with the researcher in these small groups for the Lego project. This involved several aspects which were student centered and allowed for students to be in charge of their own learning (agency). The learning sessions were open ended where students made decisions about all aspects of their multimodal stories. The project began with students reading Lego books for the first several weeks. This was to spark discussions about story elements and to talk about the ways the photographer used a camera to take photos of actual Lego creations which became book illustrations. Next, students brainstormed a story of their own through play with Legos. Each student had access to a Lego set with a large variety of Lego blocks. They created each scene (which later served as a page in their book) while engaged in conversations with the peers in their groups.

Once complete, each student used a digital camera to capture the scene. This involved the student taking multiple photos to capture various angles of their creation. Then the student moved on to the next scene using the same procedures and continued until the story was complete. Revisions took place throughout the nonlinear process. There was no rigidity in the way the story unfolded. Later, the digital photos were uploaded to Google Presentations which is similar to Microsoft PowerPoint. The final layer was adding text or written language to the images and converting it to a video if the student desired. The video conversion included the recording of student voices reading their texts. At the end of the project, students shared their texts and/or videos with members of the class and parents who attended an author's celebration.

METHODOLOGY AND ANALYSIS

Ethnography and Multimodality

An ethnographic perspective was used to capture the literacy practices of students within the specific context of this classroom. The details of this project were documented over the course of a school year using field notes, transcripts of the video recordings of small group interactions, textual products (student work samples), and transcripts of student interviews. Data was used to gather a close look at student learning, the mediation of technology, and the social interactions that ensued.

Connecting ethnography to multimodality was essential to this research because of the nature of the materials being used and the freedom of students to express their stories in a way that was personally meaningful and built upon their cultural and linguistic backgrounds. This methodology assisted in understanding literacy as a social practice and how students produced their own meanings (Jewitt, Bezemer, & O'Halloran, 2016). The texts (whether oral, based on images only, or written) were a stimulus for student dialogue that caused students to invoke a range of tools to create meaning. The meaning was embedded in the multimodal data (Flewitt, 2011). This hybrid approach provided insight into the overarching research question: What happens when students are given multimodal resources and asked to create a story?

Analysis of Data

Initially, the data were analyzed using grounded theory (Glaser & Strauss, 1967) to gain insight into the emerging data. This approach allowed for the discovery of the data that led to open coding and weekly memos. This first layer of data analysis afforded opportunities to see the overlapping of codes, the need for new codes, and eventually larger themes (Saldaña, 2015). Upon identifying themes, a multimodal transcript analysis was applied to selected transcripts (representing the larger themes) to closely examine the oral language use of children in addition to the visual, movement, and spatial forms of meaning making. Moment to moment interactions were analyzed (Baldry & Thibault, 2005). Looking at both the dialogue next to images from the video-taped interactions (like the manipulation of the Lego blocks, digital photograph, screen background, or written text) offered additional data about the meaning making process and how and when textual productions of the story unfolded and under what conditions.

FINDINGS

The findings represent three significant themes related to the research question. Each theme contributed to an overall sense of "becoming". In other words, the students opened themselves up to new encounters where discoveries were unearthed and led to experimentation and continually evolving productions of stories (Davies, 2014). In each case students made agentive moves using the available resources or materials which included communicative practices. New practices with old materials made way for disruptions that opened new avenues for meaning making (Dyson, 2003). Students' textual products and transcripts illustrate each theme.

Digital Play as an Essential Tool for Story

Digital play as a theme was defined as occasions when students experimented with digital tools at any point in literacy events. This usually took the form of students creating repeated variations of the same activity resulting in a selection. Sometimes this involved dialogue with self or others and at other times the play was silent. For example, the child may resize an image six times before coming to the conclusion that one size meets their needs.

Throughout the study, play with digital tools became indispensable for literacy learning. It occurred across groups of students, formats, and tools as students accessed Chromebook computers, digital cameras, and headphones with microphones. Below is an example of Xosha playing with the digital camera to obtain just the right angle for her photograph. This evolved in her embodied actions. Prior to this event, Xosha carefully placed multiple elements together to create her characters. For example, she selected heads, lips, hair, and clothing. She positioned each one next to the other with a line of pets (two dogs and a cat).

Xosha walked around her story board with all of the figures (people) and Lego blocks arranged just right. She spent two days placing the objects in a position that represented her story, *The Birthday Party*. Xosha grabbed a digital camera and began clicking. She tapped the back of the camera to see the images she snapped. She shook her head in a no fashion and re-opened the lens to shoot more photos. This time she stood on a chair to get a birds-eye perspective. Xosha laid on the floor in front on her base board and clicked to gain another viewpoint. She laughed and showed Keondra her pictures by pointing to the back screen. Xosha then began moving characters. She pushed them backwards so they were almost flat or level with the desk. Another photo was snapped. This time, she commented, ''I like this one. Everyone can see their faces now." (Fieldnotes, January, 2017)

Xosha used her time and tools to make meaning of her own birthday story where she introduced each of her characters in the opening scene. For her, seeing the details in the characters became essential because later she referred to these characters by name only and did not always show their faces.

Therefore, in order for her story to make sense, the reader or viewer, would need an understanding of the main characters. With the intention of providing her audience with this information, she played with the digital camera in order to locate an appropriate viewpoint (Figure 1). Each iteration of the image provided a different perspective or view of the scene. Her eyes were continually fixed on the faces and bodies of her characters.

It seemed as if Xosha understood that there are multiple interpretations to an image or mode, and she attempted to influence how her birthday event would be understood by others. Xosha can be viewed as an inventor creating a new text from available resources (Roswell & Harwood, 2015).

As noted above, Xosha snapped numerous photos until she had one that met with her storyline. She utilized the screen on the back of the camera as a resource for checking her progress. Each time she viewed her images, she thought about what she wanted to produce versus what she actually produced. The immediate feedback from the camera gave her what she needed to improve the next set of photos. It was as if she was reimagining the different angles and wondered which one would be perfect. It was a form of play and creativity and Xosha was agentive in the process (Kuby & Vaughn, 2015). Prior to this, Xosha had not used a digital camera at home or in another classroom.

When all of this did not work for Xosha, she combined other modes of meaning making by adjusting the way her characters were placed on the base. Here, Xosha was experimenting with possibilities and learning to become a photographer (Jackson & Mazzei, 2012). Bending the characters backwards and

Figure 1. Xosha's birthday party showing faces

retaking more photos ensured that her image would be perfect for the story. The shifting that Xosha did between modes and texts can be referred to as dynamic materiality (Walsh & Simpson, 2014). She was building layers of meaning as she constructed all of the different components in her text. All of these actions and tools led to a successful beginning to Xosha's story. Later, Xosha used the image, wrote text to match it, and shared the completed text production with her peers.

Multimodal Storytelling as a Path for Learning a New Language

This theme's defining characteristics are two-fold. First, it involved the use of more than one mode of communication, and second, the multiple modes worked together to form an avenue for learning English as a new language. For example, a child who did not know the English word for "robber" in their story created a Lego character dressed in black holding a gun. The student took a picture of the character and inserted it into their story. It was followed by a written text that did not include the word "robber" but inferred through the reading of the image.

The case of Omar is used to illustrate the theme of multimodal storytelling as a path for learning a new language. Part of his experience was becoming a text designer and an author of English texts (Kuby & Rucker, 2016). Omar's first language was Spanish, and he emigrated from Mexico. This was his first year in an American classroom where he learned English, and his reading performance did not register on standardized testing in English. Therefore, he received additional services to assist with English language development three times per week. Omar possessed some English communication skills that enabled him to speak with friends, but he remained quiet during most instructional activities. It appeared that Omar did not understand many of the academic tasks that his teacher assigned as they were usually completed only as he interpreted them. Through a traditional lens, his work was considered incorrect and unacceptable.

When Omar came to the group for the first time, the project was outlined for him. It was unclear what he did and did not understand. He participated in reading the Lego books through choral reading in a hushed tone of voice. Then, the Legos came out. This was all it took for Omar to engage. He did not say much and worked alone. However, Omar was busy creating his story with multiple Lego scenes. He had experience using his mother's cell phone camera, and he drew upon this to help him navigate the digital camera. There was never a call for help, not even using Google Presentation software. As time progressed, Omar said, "Done!" (He was the first student in the class to complete a story.) At first it was not clear what he meant. He physically walked over to the Chromebook, opened up his story, and said, ''See." This is one of the images Omar created and the text for his story (Figure 2 and Table 1).

This image illustrated Omar's abilities to add details to his story through his selection of available Lego tools. He placed a black hat on his brother and added a sword to his hand. The brother is seated on a brown Lego base representing a car with headlights and back up lights. His storyline as explained orally included, "My brother ride over in car to talk to me." The image highlights details of the story that Omar was not yet able to provide in the written narrative.

Figure 2. Selected photo from Omar's story: The Classic History

Table 1. Oscar's written text

Page	Oscar's Original Story	Translation to Standard English
1	Guasap men?	What's up men?
2	natin	Nothing.
3	Hawarllo	How are you?
4	An fan tenciu	I'm fine. Thank you.
5	Broter	Brother.
6	what	What?
7	I love you	I love you.
8	I love tou	I love you too.
9	Ten end	The end.

There were elements of surprise to Omar's text production. First, he drew upon existing funds of knowledge (Brown, 2017; Souto-Manning, 2016; González et al., 2006). This included his understanding of story and knowing that he needed characters with a feasible storyline. He wrote dialogue that he frequently heard in day-to-day conversations.

Omar also utilized invented spelling that capitalized on the sounds he knew in Spanish and English. Each sound was represented by letters he deemed appropriate, and he did this without any support from the teacher, researcher, or peers. In terms of traditional literacies, Omar developed the ability the write basic sight words like "what" and "you". Other instances of spelling showcase his knowledge of sound-bases or inventive spelling such as his attempt with "nothing". He wrote, "natin" indicating his understanding of the initial consonant along with some medial sounds. Because Omar was learning English in the south, there was an element of southern dialect where he heard "nothin" as opposed to "nothing", and therefore crafted his inventive attempt accordingly. In addition, Omar was learning to hear words as separate entities indicated by his one-word attempt "Hawarllo" at "how are you". His development of English was progressing. As a result, Omar fused his digital skills from home to use and manipulate the Legos, take digital photographs, and upload all of them into a Google Presentation with text.

Looking closely at the writing experience of the project for Omar highlighted his journey learning English as a new language. As stated earlier, Omar struggled with traditional assignments like worksheets where he had no freedom to show his strengths as a language user. However, in this context, he thrived without assistance from others. He demonstrated his ability to be a risk taker by writing a story entirely in English using invented spelling. He was agentive in choosing a topic, crafting a storyline, and using multimodal tools and materials to complete his story. He even knew how to use the ''shift" key to make a capital letter and make a question mark.

Omar moved on to create three more books while most students worked on their first one. Each iteration of a new storyline afforded him the opportunity to learn more English sounds, develop new vocabulary words, and spell more words using standard English. Because he was first to finish his book, this caused other students to view him in a different light. In other words, his identity changed (Kuby & Vaughn, 2015; Sakr, Connelly, & Wild, 2016). He was seen as a technology expert from which many of his peers sought assistance. His actions became embodied by others as they undertook digital tasks associated with story production. New spaces opened up for Omar. One where his creativity and knowledge were valued. One where it was okay not to write in Standard English, and one where he was considered an expert. Omar successfully used material and non-material resources to construct meaning (Sakr, Connelly, & Wild, 2016; Wohlwend, 2011).

Apprenticeships for Multimodal Text Productions

The apprenticeship theme centered around collaboration and learning from others. This theme emerged as evidenced by students engaging in dialogue that drove storylines which included both print and visual images. Students assisted each other in using and learning the digital tools in order to produce a final text. For example, one student commented, "That man is too scary. Don't use him in your story. No one will like it." The student responded by revising the look of their Lego character and changing the narrative based on the dialogic interaction.

A small group of boys were seated at desks arranged in a table format. Each of the students were in a different stage of the composing process. Peter was building with Legos. Ashton was engaged with digital photography, and the last two boys, Javon and Terris, used Chromebooks to upload their images and craft written words. Even though they worked independently, they also collaborated. Conversations flowed back and forth regarding multimodal aspects of the text construction. For example, there was a demonstration of how to put a sword in a Lego hand along with a detailed dialogue. The boys served as apprentices for one another ultimately expanding all of the knowledge each one brought to the project. The following transcripts and vignettes showcase the essence of this theme.

Terris' favorite story was Rapunzel. He read the book over and over again in class and watched the movie, *Tangled Ever After*, at home. With his extensive knowledge of the storylines, he decided to capitalize on these experiences to create a recontextualization or remix (Cremin et al., 2018; Roswell & Harwood, 2015). This began with Lego construction of a castle where Rapunzel lived. Terris snapped numerous bricks of all sizes and shapes together to make four walls. He looked puzzled and yelled out to the group, ''Hey, who knows how to make that topper thing (turret or tower)?" The following scenario unfolded after this question was posed.

Javon: *What you talking about?*

Terris: *The topper thing. You know where the princess is.* [Pointed to top of his castle wall.]

Peter: *Yeah, yeah. I know what you talking about. The tower. Let me show you. I made one before.* [Grabbed a handful of Legos. Stacked the first level in a circle. Placed another layer on top snapping them on to the first layer.]

Terris: *Oh, I see now. You have making circles. Keep going and it will get smaller.* [Moved closer to Peter and started adding bricks alongside Peter.]

Javon: *That's looking goood!!*

Here, Peter who had previous experience building a tower shaped building was the more skilled student who invited Terris to serve as his apprentice during the activity. The manipulation of Legos led to a successful background for Terris story, Tangle Before Ever After (somewhat named after the movie). Terris added a princess, Rapunzel, and a prince named Steve to that castle and proceeded to capture this event with a digital photo. The boys worked for several more weeks in this fashion.

Finally, Terris was ready to upload his images and construct a story. Initially, Terris resisted help from other students. He repeatedly stated, ''I already know what I'm writing. Don't tell me anything." However, once he finished the first two pages, he engaged the other boys in actually co-constructing his story. In the transcript below, Terris contemplated which ideas to include in his story. Each learner brought a particular aspect or skill to the process and served as an apprentice and they eventually learned from one another.

Terris: *Let me read you what I wrote so far.*

"Once opon a time their was a princess name Repusal. She is 1 year old and had lots of fun. And than some one took her 1 year later (page 1). Than their was a prins name is Steve. He said "Repuns, Repunsle, lete down her long yellow hair' and he clib the hair and than he got cot by her fake mother, He was tide to the cheir. And he got hit by a pan." What should my story say next?

Ashton: *Some of that doesn't make sense.* [Scrunched up face.]
Terris: *Like what?*
Ashton: *Where you said she was 1 year old. What? She can't be a baby. That doesn't make sense.*
Terris: *Oh, Oh.* [Smiled.] *I get it. Let me change this. How old do you think she should be?*
Ashton: *Like 15 or 20. Like she's big, not a baby.*
Terris: [Deleted 1 and typed 15.] *I fixed it. Now, I was asking, what next?*
Javon: *How about, your prince guy, yeah, have him save her.*
Terris: *He can't do it. He's tied to the chair. Remember?*
Peter: *No, no. This is better. The prince gets his legs chewed off by a bear.*
Javon: *That's dumb. There's no bear in Rapunzel. Have Rapunzel cut off her hair to free the prince.*
Terris: *Ok. Maybe. There has to be magic.*
Javon: [Passed a plastic, Lego wand.] *Use this.*
Terris: *No, something better. A rock. Magic rock. Is there a Lego rock?*
Javon: *No. You can use this.* [Held up a small, gray brick.]

An apprenticeship into effective storytelling was well underway in this event. It began when Ashton indicated that Terris's story did not make sense with a one-year old princess. Terris takes Ashton's advice and changes the story to a 15 year-old Rapunzel. Then, the boys wrestled with ideas about what happened next. They were taking on the role of meaning makers accessing their histories and experiences (Pahl, 2009). A couple of ideas were pitched which Terris considered. After some thought, he dismissed the bear, and moved more towards the magic component that Javon suggested. It appeared that the boys were all making connections to elements of story especially fairytales which they had learned about in class.

The addition of the magic rock required Terris to return to the building process. He saved his work on the Chromebook and gathered the needed materials. He proceeded to photograph Rapunzel next to the small, gray brick (magic rock). Once complete, Terris reentered the digital composing work to finish his book. The move to include the rock was considered an improvisation or a break in traditional writing styles that are more linear and less flexible (Pahl, 2009).

According to Rogoff (1990), the boys were learning from one another in this small group community within the larger classroom. Each student's actions and dialogue being mediated by the actions and dialogue of the remainder of the group. Terris and his classmates were able to change and broaden their thinking through these interactions. The collaborative talk associated with the available resources shaped the multimodal text that was eventually produced remix (Cremin, et al., 2018).

IMPLICATIONS

Instead of thinking about literacy in a very traditional manner, educators must open themselves up the possibilities that the 21st century brings with the influx of technology into the daily lives of even the youngest of children. The examples of multimodal communication practices in this chapter provide evidence for a flexible approach to literacy instruction that open doors for novel composing practices or new ways of becoming (Davies, 2014). When students become empowered through a sense of agency, they are able to produce incredible multimodal texts (Arnott, 2016). Therefore, fostering agency is a requirement in 21st century literacy classrooms and ultimately exercising agency contributes to students' successes as digital composers (Fisher, 2010).

This can start by adapting the literacy environment (e.g., student choice, flexibility, play, multimodal resources, digital tools) to allow students to think in new ways about communicating and solving problems (Kuby & Vaughn, 2015). Various Modes, formats, materials, and ways of communicating come together to inform the meaning making process for young composers. Kuby and Rucker (2016) refer to this as a pedagogy of becoming. They highlight that there is not a standard curriculum or set of procedures for teaching literacy in this way. Instead, educators should open their minds and listen to the voices of young learners in order to capture magical encounters created in newness (Davies, 2014).

This new environment must also value the knowledge, culture, and linguistic resources that students bring with them to the classroom (Brown, 2017; Souto-Manning, 2016; González et al., 2006; Reyes et al., 2016). Each student should feel appreciated for their contributions and capacities. Furthermore, educators need to spend time identifying these strengths and then honoring moments of learning (Yahya & Wood, 2017). It takes a concerted effort to gather information about the backgrounds and experiences of a classroom full of students.

This may be accomplished by interviewing students at the beginning of the year to understand their cultural and linguistic backgrounds, interests, experiences, likes, dislikes, ways of learning, use of digital tools out-of-school, etc. Teachers may also send home multilingual surveys for parents to gather additional information. Rich information may also be obtained by simply listening to students as they talk throughout the day during academic and nonacademic activities. Then, there must be determination to create lessons or learning opportunities that tie to these funds of knowledge. For example, teachers may use literature for read alouds that represents the ethnicities of their students. Finally, educators need to model and show students how to value their peers and what they have to offer within the context of the classroom.

Creativity and digital play must also be given priority in a multimodal composing curriculum. Previous examples clearly show that students need time to play and experiment to understand the resources afforded to them. Not only will they learn traditional ways of using the materials/tools, but they will also invent new techniques based on their perceptions of meaning making (Kuby & Vaughn, 2015; Vasudevan, Schultz, & Bateman, 2010). This may occur alone or in collaboration with others, and may even take on the form of an apprenticeship where one student teaches another about the possibilities a tool (Rogoff, 1990).

The apprenticeship model may overlap with a discursive co-construction of text making in a re-envisioned classroom. Student talk is powerful, and it provides avenues for fine tuning a story that in the past may have been constructed independently (Cremin et al., 2018; Roswell & Harwood, 2015). Many times, as in the example with Terris, extended dialogues offer opportunities for students to serve as decision-makers. They become empowered to make decisions about their own learning and outcomes. A role that students would not assume in a teacher-directed classroom (Arnott, 2016). This means students are active in a busy classroom that is not quiet. The teacher devotes time for students to talk to one another during literacy learning.

CONCLUSION

Within all of these complexities, the integration of digital technology into literacy instruction is necessary (Sofkova Hashemi & Cederlund, 2017). It does not serve students well to teach them how to use tools separate from instruction. There should be an authentic, valid purpose for learning how to use a tool like a digital camera or Google Presentation. Ideally, it is embedded within literacy activities. This way students experience a seamless approach between digital tools and real reasons for language and literacy use. There are real-world connections that lead students to understand communication on a global level.

Although the students in this study were limited by school district policies related to sharing beyond the classroom walls, their work illustrates the future possibilities for participatory literacies on a larger scale. For example, the Lego stories could be shared through a class website or Wiki page where parents and other peers would have access and be able to add comments. The possibilities of the new dimensions of multimodal forms of literacy help learners, "feel, think, share and connect" in ways that address contemporary realities of the 21st century (Rowsell & Wohlwend, 2016, p. 204).

The future of literacy is plural – literacies. These new literacies take multiple forms and require a variety of resources (New London Group, 1996). Each unique recontextualization of the available resources represents innovative ways to make meaning. If multimodal literacies are 21st century communication, then early childhood classrooms have an obligation to embrace the practices featured in this chapter.

FUTURE RESEARCH DIRECTIONS

The results of this research and the work of others in the field indicate a need for in-depth investigations into the early digital practices of diverse students in classroom contexts. There is a vast disparity of access to technology and the Internet across schools even within limited geographic locations, and this requires an examination of numerous sites and contexts in order to better understand the participatory learning experiences of young learners. In addition, the ways in which educators design technology embedded literacy activities vary greatly. How do teachers best utilize the resources they have access to in their classrooms? What authentic learning opportunities work well for engaging students with the available digital tools? What steps can be taken to extend the classroom walls for participatory experiences? More research is needed to discover the ways in which these practices impact students, their literacy development, and the growth of technology-based skills.

NOTE OF APPRECIATION

The author would like acknowledge the school district, principal, teacher, students, and families who all made this research possible.

REFERENCES

Ackermann, E., Gauntlett, D., & Weckstrom, C. (2009). *Defining systematic creativity: Explaining the nature of creativity and how the Lego system of play relates to it*. Billund, Denmark: The LEGO Learning Institute. Retrieved from http://www.legofoundation.com/en-us/newsroom/publications

Arnott, L. (2016). An ecological exploration of young children's digital play: Framing children's social experiences with technologies in early childhood. *Early Years*, *36*(3), 271–288. doi:10.1080/09575146.2016.1181049

Baldry, A., & Thibault, P. J. (2006). *Multimodal transcription and text analysis*. London: Equinox.

Brown, S. (2017). Building on emergent bilinguals' funds of knowledge using digital tools. In E. Ortileb & E. Cheek Jr., (Eds.), *Addressing diversity in literacy instruction* (pp. 173–193). Bingley, UK: Emerald. doi:10.1108/S2048-045820170000008018

Burnett, C. (2010). Technology and literacy in early childhood educational settings: A review of research. *Journal of Early Childhood Literacy*, *10*(3), 247–270. doi:10.1177/1468798410372154

Cremin, T., Flewitt, R., Swann, J., Faulkner, D., & Kucirkova, N. (2018). Storytelling and story-acting: Co-construction in action. *Journal of Early Childhood Research*, *16*(1), 3–17. doi:10.1177/1476718X17750205

Davies, B. (2014). *Listening to children: Being and becoming*. New York: Routledge. doi:10.4324/9781315770390

Dyson, A. (2003). *The brothers and sisters learn to write: Popular literacies in childhood and school cultures*. New York: Teachers College Press.

Fisher, R. (2010). Young writers' construction of agency. *Journal of Early Childhood Literacy*, *10*(4), 410–429. doi:10.1177/1468798410382407

Flewitt, R. (2011). Bringing ethnography to a multimodal investigation of early literacy in a digital age. *Qualitative Research*, *11*(3), 293–310. doi:10.1177/1468794111399838

Glaser, B., & Strauss, A. (1967). *The discovery of grounded theory: strategies for qualitative theory*. New Brunswick, NJ: Aldine Transaction.

González, N., Moll, L., & Amanti, C. (2016). *Funds of knowledge: Theorizing practices in households, communities, and classrooms*. New York: Routledge.

Guernsey, L. (2014). Envisioning a digital age architecture for early education. *New America-Education Policy Program,* 1-9.

Jackson, A., & Mazzei, L. (2012). *Thinking with theory in qualitative research: Viewing data across multiple perspectives*. New York: Routledge.

Jewitt, C., Bezemer, J., & O'Halloran, K. (2016). *Introducing multimodality*. New York: Routledge.

John-Steiner, V., & Meehan, T. (2000). Creativity and collaboration in knowledge construction. In C. Lee & P. Smagorinsky (Eds.), *Vygotskian perspectives on literacy research: Constructing meaning through collaborative inquiry* (pp. 31–48). New York: Cambridge University Press.

Kress, G. (2009). *Multimodality: A social semiotic approach to contemporary communication*. New York: Routledge. doi:10.4324/9780203970034

Kress, G., & van Leeuwen, T. (2001). *Multimodal discourse: The modes and media of contemporary communication*. New York: Oxford University Press.

Kuby, C., & Rucker, T. (2016). *Go be a writer: Expanding the curricular boundaries of literacy learning with children*. New York: Teachers College Press.

Kuby, C., & Vaughn, M. (2015). Young children's identities becoming: Exploring agency in the creation of multimodal literacies. *Journal of Early Childhood Literacy*, *15*(4), 433–472. doi:10.1177/1468798414566703

Marsh, J. (2014). Purposes for literacy in children's use of the online virtual world Club Penguin. *Journal of Research in Reading*, *37*(2), 179–195. doi:10.1111/j.1467-9817.2012.01530.x

Marsh, J., Plowman, L., Yamada-Rice, D., Bishop, J., & Scott, F. (2016). Digital play: A new classification. *Early Years*, *36*(3), 242–253. doi:10.1080/09575146.2016.1167675

Marshall, E., & Toohey, K. (2010). Representing family: Community funds of knowledge, bilingualism, and multimodality. *Harvard Educational Review*, *80*(2), 221–242. doi:10.17763/haer.80.2.h3446j54n608q442

New London Group. (1996). A pedagogy of multiliteracies: Designing social futures. *Harvard Educational Review*, *66*(1), 60–93. doi:10.17763/haer.66.1.17370n67v22j160u

Pahl, K. (2009). Interactions, intersections and improvisations: Studying the multimodal texts and classroom talk of six-to seven-year-olds. *Journal of Early Childhood Literacy*, *9*(2), 188–210. doi:10.1177/1468798409105586

Reyes, I., DaSilva Iddings, A., & Feller, N. (2016). Building relationships with diverse students and families: A funds of knowledge perspective. *Journal of Early Childhood Literacy*, *16*(1), 8–33. doi:10.1177/1468798415584692

Rideout, V., Foehr, U., & Roberts, D. (2010, January). *Generation M 2: Media in the Lives of 8-to 18-Year-Olds*. Retrieved from https://www.kff.org/other/event/generation-m2-media-in-the-lives-of/

Rogoff, B. (1990). *Apprenticeship in thinking: Cognitive development in social context*. New York: Oxford University Press.

Rowsell, J., & Harwood, D. (2015). "Let It Go": Exploring the Image of the Child as a Producer, Consumer, and Inventor. *Theory into Practice*, *54*(2), 136–146. doi:10.1080/00405841.2015.1010847

Rowsell, J., & Wohlwend, K. (2016). Free play or tight spaces? Mapping participatory literacies in apps. *The Reading Teacher*, *70*(2), 197–205. doi:10.1002/trtr.1490

Sakr, M., Connelly, V., & Wild, M. (2016). "Evil cats" and "jelly floods": Young children's collective constructions of digital art making in the early years classroom. *Journal of Research in Childhood Education*, *30*(1), 128–141. doi:10.1080/02568543.2015.1107156

Saldaña, J. (2015). *The coding manual for qualitative researchers*. London: Sage.

Sefton-Green, J., Marsh, J., Erstad, O., & Flewitt, R. (2017). *Establishing a Research Agenda for the Digital Literacy Practices of Young Children: A White Paper for COST Action IS1410*. doi:10.13140/RG.2.2.10896.30720

Sofkova Hashemi, S., & Cederlund, K. (2017). Making room for the transformation of literacy instruction in the digital classroom. *Journal of Early Childhood Literacy*, *17*(2), 221–253. doi:10.1177/1468798416630779

Souto-Manning, M. (2016). Honoring and building on the rich literacy practices of young bilingual and multilingual learners. *The Reading Teacher, 70*(3), 263–271. doi:10.1002/trtr.1518

Stephens, C., & Edwards, S. (2018). *Young children playing and learning in a digital age: A cultural and critical perspective*. New York: Routledge.

Vasudevan, L., Schultz, K., & Bateman, J. (2010). Rethinking composing in a digital age: Authoring literate identities through multimodal storytelling. *Written Communication, 27*(4), 442–468. doi:10.1177/0741088310378217

Vygotsky, L. (1978). *Mind in society: The development of higher psychological processes*. Cambridge, MA: Harvard University Press.

Walsh, M., & Simpson, A. (2014). Exploring literacies through touch pad technologies: The dynamic materiality of modal interactions. *Australian Journal of Language and Literacy, 37*(2), 96.

White, J. (2016). *Introducing dialogic pedagogy: Provocations for the early years*. New York: Routledge.

Wohlwend, K. (2011). *Playing their way into literacies: Reading, writing, and belonging in the early childhood classroom*. New York: Teachers College Press.

Wohlwend, K. (2013). *Literacy playshop: New literacies, popular media, and play in the early childhood classroom*. New York: Teachers College Press.

Yahya, R., & Wood, E. A. (2017). Play as third space between home and school: Bridging cultural discourses. *Journal of Early Childhood Research, 15*(3), 305–322. doi:10.1177/1476718X15616833 PMID:28867965

ADDITIONAL READING

Bhatt, I., de Roock, R., & Adams, J. (2015). Diving deep into digital literacy: Emerging methods for research. *Language and Education, 29*(6), 477–492. doi:10.1080/09500782.2015.1041972

Bjorkvall, A., & Engblom, C. (2010). Young children's exploration of semiotic resources during unofficial computer activities in the classroom. *Journal of Early Childhood Literacy, 10*(3), 271–293. doi:10.1177/1468798410372159

Brown, S. (2018). *Digital initiatives for literacy development in elementary classrooms: Engaging research and opportunities*. Hershey, PA: IGI Global. doi:10.4018/978-1-5225-3212-5

Karchmer-Klein, R., & Shinas, V. (2012). Guiding principles for supporting new literacies in your classroom. *The Reading Teacher, 65*(5), 288–293. doi:10.1002/TRTR.01044

Rowe, D., Miller, M., & Pacheco, M. (2014). Preschoolers as digital designers: Composing dual language ebooks. In R. Anderson & C. Mims (Eds.), *Handbook of research on digital tools for writing instruction in K-12 settings: Student perception and experience* (pp. 279–306). Hershey, PA: IGI Global. doi:10.4018/978-1-4666-5982-7.ch014

Vasquez, V., & Felderman, C. (2013). *Technology and critical literacy in early childhood.* New York: Routledge.

Whitebeard, D., & Basilio, M. (n.d.). *Towards a playful pedagogy in literacy: The play, learning, and narrative skills (PLaNS) project* [Pamphlet]. Retrieved from https://www.educ.cam.ac.uk/research/projects/plans/

Chapter 2
Fostering Participatory Literacies in English Language Arts Instruction Using Student-Authored Podcasts

Molly Buckley-Marudas
Cleveland State University, USA

Charles Ellenbogen
Campus International High School, USA

ABSTRACT

English language arts teachers must tend to the proliferation of easily accessible technological tools and storytelling platforms for the teaching of stories. It is critical that educators teach with and about these spaces in order to develop young people's literacies. This chapter examines an English language arts unit that required students to create an audio podcast to support students in the process of making meaning, sharing ideas, and interpreting texts. The chapter offers insights into the podcasting process for students and teachers, including ideas about technical aspects of production, lessons learned, and recommendations for future practice. The chapter discusses how this project draws on adolescents' participatory literacies and how it developed practicing teachers' participatory literacies and pedagogical approaches.

INTRODUCTION

Technology is changing the way we can tell stories and the way we can consume them. With the proliferation of easily accessible recording tools and storytelling platforms, the highly networked, immediately streamable technologies that are characteristic of today's media landscape are rewriting the rules for telling stories. Those of us in the business of teaching stories and story writing must pay attention. In this digital era, when a growing number of everyday interactions and communication channels are me-

DOI: 10.4018/978-1-7998-0000-2.ch002

diated by digital technologies, it is critical that current and future teachers acknowledge the capabilities of digital media and leverage digital media in their pedagogical designs (Hutchinson & Colwell, 2014; Leu, Kinzer, Coiro, & Cammack, 2004). National and state standards for K-12 learning and instruction, including the Common Core State Standards, place a significant emphasis on the use of digital technologies for teaching and learning (Coleman, 2011) and, according to the NCTE/IRA Standards for English Language Arts (2012), students should "Use a variety of technological and information resources to gather and synthesize information and create and communicate knowledge." Existing research suggests that teachers should teach students how to use different digital tools and help them develop multiple literacies (Lankshear & Knobel, 2007; Leu, O'Byrne, Zawlinkski, McVerry, & Everett-Cacopardo, 2009). Furthermore, with increasing awareness of the value of participatory literacies (Wohlwend, 2016) and the significance of Connected Learning (Ito, Gutierrez, Livingstone, Penuel, Rhodes, Salen, Schor, Sefton- Green, & Watkins, 2013), educators must be able to integrate digital media and technological tools in their classrooms to foster the participatory literacies that are required for young people to fully participate in today's society.

It is now well documented that digital platforms are able to create spaces of learning and offer new opportunities for interacting with others in school-based settings (Buckley-Marudas, 2016; Hull & Stornaiuolo, 2014; Ito, 2009; Mills, Ulsworth, Exley, 2018; Shanahan, 2012). A great majority of these spaces tend to be participatory in nature and offer diverse formats for sharing their ideas and intellectual work with others. It is increasingly understood that networked spaces, spaces our students are already familiar with, are creating new forms of engagement and interaction (Hutchinson & Colwell, 2014; Jenkins, 2016). Yet, despite the increase in student use of these spaces and the expansion in free or low-cost digital composing and publishing tools, much of the work that youth create in school continues to rely on traditional, alphabetic writing that is often published for the singular audience of a teacher. Although students will still develop and refine their literacies through this kind of academic writing and work, this approach elides the need for students to think multimodally and semiotically about different ways to best represent their ideas, to format material and use different texts strategically—especially the increasingly relevant audio text—to communicate their ideas and engage a variety of diverse audiences (Doerr--Stevens & Buckley-Marudas, 2019; Smith, B., 2018).

Considering the growing interest in and reliance on podcasts the past several years and the accompanying surge in podcast production and consumption, this was the year for us—a university-based English Language Arts teacher educator (Molly) and a high school English Language Arts teacher (Charles)—to pay closer attention to podcasts. Charles, in his 26th year of teaching, has never felt very comfortable with technology and, as appealing as podcasts sounded, he was reluctant to include them as a central part of an instructional unit. Molly, in her sixth year as an ELA teacher educator has researched the role of digital media and tools, including podcasting, for literacy learning in other high school classrooms and has worked to integrate podcast production into her own teacher education courses, yet had not introduced them to a high school class of her own. Both of us believed that podcasts' increasing popularity and prominence made them an important communication platform for our students to learn.

Given our roles as ELA educators, we were eager to think of podcasts both as *stories* and as *participatory literacies* in a high school Language and Literature classroom. How could we foster students' participatory literacies in and through a unit that invited students to listen to podcasts that were linked to the content of the unit and required them to publish a podcast of their own connected to one of the themes of the unit? The specific unit that we selected for this project would focus on the question of how power and money relate to the concept of the American Dream? In this chapter, we will share a range and variation of the instructional activities that were tied to this ELA unit focused on issues related to social equity, wages, economic growth, and the American Dream. The culminating performance task was a podcast produced and published by students.

We will explore this ELA unit for how it reflects and/or supports students in the process of making meaning, sharing ideas, and interpreting texts within and across multiple media platforms. We have organized our insights from this inquiry into the podcasting process we experienced with students, including ideas about technical aspects of production and approaches to assessment, as lessons learned and recommendations for future practice. We discuss some of the ways this project draws on adolescents' participatory literacies and how it developed our own participatory literacies and pedagogical approaches as educators. We hope this chapter is a guide, philosophical and practical, for fellow teachers and teacher educators who are interested in literacy practices in the digital age. We also hope that this chapter offers readers an opportunity to imagine new ways to support participatory literacies in their everyday teaching practices.

PURPOSE AND RATIONALE

We approach this work with the belief that it is critical that educators teach *with* and *about* these spaces in order to develop a robust repertoire of literacy skills for youth. There is no question that school leaders want to hire teachers who, regardless of their content area, are willing to adapt with and draw on digital media in the service of teaching academic content as well as developing young people's participatory literacies. Because technology constantly changes, our intent in this chapter is two-fold. First, we intend to offer fellow educators specific instructional approaches to support their development in this networked, participatory, and digitally driven era. Second, we describe a pedagogical stance toward evolving with technology and cultivating our own participatory literacies. This work draws on Jenkins' (2016) idea that a participatory culture is a culture with low barriers to artistic expression, support for creating and sharing one's work, and some informal mentorship between participants. Building on this, we also draw on Jenkins (2006, 2016) and Wohlwend's (2016) ideas of participatory literacies as the diverse ways of interpreting, making, sharing, and belonging in today's digitally-mediated cultures within and across different media platforms.

Although a great number of teacher preparation programs are working diligently to ensure that they prepare teachers to teach in this increasingly digital era and actively encourage in-service and pre-service teachers to tend to digital literacies and participatory literacies in their practice, many teachers have not been introduced to a range of practices that are well suited to develop and enhance participatory literacies as part of their everyday pedagogical approach. Many pre-service teachers have indicated that their educator preparation progress has not included explicit attention to how familiar technologies could be used as pedagogical tools, and they feel ill prepared to integrate digital media in their instructional approaches (Starcic, Cotic, Solomonides, & Volk, 2016). According to Hutchinson & Colwell (2014), much of the existing research on technology in the classroom is focused on the integration of technology in the classroom with little emphasis on students' literacies in relation to the technologies.

In our professional experiences, we have observed that many of today's beginning teachers finish their teacher preparation programs with a keen awareness of different digital tools and a sincere interest in their pedagogical potential, but have had little time to practice using different technologies in the service of teaching and learning. Furthermore, experienced teachers rarely have the opportunity to gain sufficient knowledge of and/or practice with different technologies to commit to using something unfamiliar in their classrooms. Based on a survey of 1,441 U.S. literacy teachers, Hutchinson & Reinking (2011) document that 81.6% of the teachers reported a lack of professional development on how to integrate technology. The same report indicates that 73% of teachers do not have time to teach students the skills needed for more complex tasks with technology. Thus, teachers often find that they are left to learn digital literacies on their own time and through their own initiative (Beach, 2012). Moreover, they are left to figure out how to use and leverage digital literacies in their instruction. Although a growing number of teachers have designed opportunities for youth to compose with digital media, including podcasts, print-based text remains the central focus when it comes to students' compositional efforts in ELA classrooms (Mills, Unsworth, & Exley, 2018). This chapter will address this shortcoming by offering specific approaches that we have used to integrate participatory literacies as a meaningful part of the curriculum. Given what we know about the value of participatory literacies for young people's interactions and ongoing learning, there is a pressing need for additional instructional materials to support teachers to design learning environments attentive to participatory literacies.

BACKGROUND AND CONCEPTUAL FRAMEWORK

Our work in classrooms and schools draws on critical literacy traditions and critical inquiry-based pedagogies, and we share the belief that networked spaces are creating new forms of engagement with others. Our work is grounded in a conceptual framework developed around participatory literacies (Jenkins, 2006; Wohlwend, 2016), sociocultural constructions of literacy (Barton & Hamilton, 2000; Gee, 1996; Scribner & Cole, 1981; Street, 1984, 1995), and conceptualizations of sound and listening as multimodal practice (Ceraso, 2014). Participatory literacies provided a useful lens to view the patterns of participation and multiple modes and forms of communication between and among students as well as between and among students and teachers. This lens was also useful in recognizing that students' digitally mediated communication allows them to participate in and contribute to learning in the classroom, but also positions them to engage and contribute to knowledge generation and learning outside the classroom. From the perspective of literacy as a social and cultural practice, we recognize that students' literacies and the texts they read and produced in these classrooms were uniquely constructed and shaped by the school context. A critical literacies perspective on listening emphasizes *how* stories are told, *who* is telling them, and for what *purpose*. A critical literacy pedagogy encourages students to examine and interrogate the texts they encounter (Janks, 2013) and compose new worlds through naming and renaming their media-rich surroundings (Stornaiuolo & Whitney, 2018). The specific concept of "situated literacies" is helpful in framing in that it suggests that literacies are always situated within certain historical, cultural, and social contexts and actively negotiated by individuals (Barton & Hamilton, 2000; Gee, 1996; Street, 1995). Finally, we adopt conceptualizations of sound as an embodied experience and listening as a multimodal practice (Ceraso, 2014). Building on critical media listening and sound studies, we also draw on the idea of listening as critical practice (Buckley-Marudas & Doerr-Stevens, in press). Listening as a critical practice is useful in that it calls attention to the ways that using sound and composing with sound as part of the intellectual work of the classroom pushes teachers and students to engage with the texts we read and the perspectives that we carry and/or encounter in new way. Finally, this work is guided by the idea that a narrow focus on the technical aspects of literacy or a strict adherence to written texts limits the potential for meaning making. Building on this, we do not think comprehension is an end in itself, but rather "a fundamental aspect of participation in endeavors shaped by the pursuit of meaning" (Wissman & Costello, 2014).

CLASSROOM CONTEXT AND RESEARCH FOCUS

We focus on building and leveraging participatory literacies in a 10th grade Language and Literature classroom in a public high school in Cleveland, Ohio. The school, in its second year as a high school, is open enrollment. Students in this class came to the high school from over 40 different middle schools. In regards to racial diversity, 83% of the student body identifies as African American. 100% of the class is identified as economically disadvantaged and 24.5% of the student body have documented disabilities. Due to the high poverty rate among students in the district, all schools in the district, including UH has universal free meals.

We will share how we arrived at podcasting in the ELA classroom and present a collection of instructional activities that are tied to a 10-week unit focused on issues related to social equity, wages, economic growth, and the American dream. The culminating project of this unit is a published podcast connected to the central themes of the unit. Although some of the students were familiar with listening to podcasts, no one in the class had prior experience creating one. Although there is no question that formal training and prior experience will bring additional depth to the teaching and learning and no doubt a greater number of high-quality final products, an important part of our chapter is to showcase that tinkering, practice, and failure are a very real part of the experience for any teacher committed to participatory literacies. In fact, being willing to embrace not knowing and not being entirely comfortable or confident with the technologies is an essential part of the pedagogical stance that is required to do this kind of work. Students are typically not accustomed to this stance; nor are they always comfortable with this approach. Although students expected us, as teachers, to *know*, we were very much learning alongside students during the course of this unit. This came with a lot of "I don't knows" and "let's try to figure it out together". As a result, the platform allowed for reciprocal teaching and learning and our encouragement for students to use their peers to help solve problems.

PEDAGOGICAL DESIGN: FOLLOW THE QUESTIONS

Arriving at Podcasts

We arrived at podcasts differently. Like many others, one of us (Charles) came to podcasts through Sarah Koenig's first season of *Serial*. He binged on the first series of *Serial* because he lived in Baltimore, where the story is set, for 3 years. One of us (Molly) came to podcasts through Krista Tippett's series, *Speaking of Faith* (now *On Being*). She was drawn to the series because it introduced a different perspective every week, but was always delivered in a consistent and straightforward format: each week the episode would offer ideas, rendered through Tippett's interview with (typically) one guest, around broad themes of humanity, spirituality, and faith. When we talked about why *Serial* in particular captured our attention and what stood out about the podcast medium, we found that in our minds a compelling podcast generally contained a similar collection of elements. Specifically, we noticed an introduction, an interview, and a conclusion that sometimes pointed forward to the next episode. We also noticed the use of music and ambient sound as emphasis or a transition.

We also found that an investigative podcast such as *Serial,* had to build audience intrigue. This resonated with an argument that a former colleague once made about why English teachers *should* teach the often-dismissed genre of mystery novels. Although there is often a dismissal of mystery novels for academic study among English teachers, this former colleague pointed out that a good mystery is often an ideal story to teach because to be successful it requires a structure. The sort of mystery and intrigue that is crafted in *Serial* is similarly helpful for teaching storytelling via podcast. Besides, students *like* mysteries. The story was being told, questions were being asked, and none of it was taking the form of the stereotypical five-paragraph essay or even a debate.

In order for investigative podcasts to work, like mystery novels, they have to have a structure. The investigator has to follow the questions. From our perspective as teachers and instructional leaders, this means that students can take them apart to see how they work. We thought about these elements at the same time we began to anticipate and plan for a unit on argument and argumentative writing. Although the podcast genre is expanding, we adopted the audio podcast as the model for this unit. Students would be expected to integrate interview material and their story using audio material.

Arriving at the Podcast Unit in English Language Arts

A key goal of the instructional unit we describe here was to support students in the process of developing an argument and using that argument to compose a compelling story. Inspired by David Bloome's words at the 2018 Virginia Hamilton Conference and in his co-authored book, *Teaching and Learning Argumentative Writing in High School ELA Classrooms* (Newell, Bloome, & Hirvela, 2015), this unit aimed to teach argument as a rhetorical tool that is less about persuasion and winning than investigation. Drawing on the work of Bloome and his colleagues, we hoped to position argument as not exclusively a binary proposition, but an opportunity for students to explore the complexities of an issue. Building on Bloome's work, we also developed the unit around the idea of "follow the questions." This is the message Ira Glass shares in the first part of a four-part storytelling series available on YouTube (KaaSerpent, 2014). In addition to this storytelling series serving as a resource for students during the course of the unit, Glass's charge to "Follow the questions" became a living framework for the podcasting project.

As part of the introduction to the unit and the podcast project, students were given an overview of the assignment, reproduced in Figure 1.

"Authors make choices for reasons" was a mantra that was central to the design of the year-long ELA course. Authors' reasons, as we hoped our students would learn, are theirs to investigate and theirs to determine. There is, within limits, no right or wrong, just that which is defensible and that which is not. That said, we often felt restrained by what we considered to be the traditional form of an argumentative essay that can often reduce the process to read the book, write the thesis, and defend it. The teacher, almost always the only audience for the work, then reads it, writes comments, and assigns a grade. At times, there are chances for revision, but the product and the process ends there. As with the traditional research paper, this approach became overly formulaic, and so did the students' writing. The students would have success, at least in terms of how it is measured by the Advanced Placement and International Baccalaureate programs, but at best, students were answering his questions, not investigating their own. At worst, they were plagiarizing. Furthermore, assigning a traditional argumentative essay did not do much to leverage digital media in the service of developing and enhancing young people's participatory

Figure 1. Investigation paper overview and description

American Dream: Power & Money → An Investigation

This is an argument paper, but I'm not going to call it that. Argument seems to imply, for most of us, the notion that you take one side and you try to win. The research is more about gathering (thank you, Internet) than genuinely researching things. In fact, I just learned that the word 'researching' means to investigate something systematically. And that's what you've been doing in preparation for producing your podcast. You are, as we practiced with the 'Slip or Trip' exercise trying to solve a problem. You may not get it right, but you are going to put forth your best argument or investigation.

So, in 950 - 1,050 words, outline the investigation of your podcast question. You should start with when you first encountered the issue you are addressing in the podcast. Maybe it was in the book you read for class, maybe it was in the news, maybe it relates to someone you know. Trace your path. Create, as Ira Glass called it, a question chain. Examples (see how you can have more than one strand in your investigation):

Should the minimum wage be raised? → What is it now? → Why is it that rate now? → When was the last time it was changed? → Why was it first created? → etc., etc. and so forth.

What's a podcast? → How do I make one? → How do I deal with the technical requirements? → How and why I should I include music? → What music should I include?

What's it like working with a partner? → Who should I choose? → Why? → What happens when the work is not divided equally?

You can even use your questions as sections for your writing. You may write in the first person (plural, if need be).

Look here for an example. Notice how the investigation includes images, short videos, graphs, graphics, etc. It is also linked to the podcast itself. This is the goal. This, too, is due December 19th and should be linked to an opportunity for me to listen to your podcast.

literacies. For more traditional written arguments, we noticed that students typically conducted online research, but their final products did not reflect the kind of networked, participatory, and interactive aspects of participatory literacies that are embedded in today's media landscape. For example, such final products are not distributed to other local or global audiences via online networks and with the teacher as the primary, if not only audience, the final products are not shared with audiences who could learn from what students find or report and students do not gain feedback from those outside audiences. In keeping with one of the central tenets of participatory literacies, the final products are a kind of reorganization and presentation of previously documented material and are not reflective of the kind of play that is possible with gathering new material and remixing it in response to a student's line of inquiry.

With our interest in podcasts as a compelling format for argument and investigation, our pedagogical commitment to expanding students' participatory literacies, and inspiration from Glass's phrase, "follow the questions," the unit began to take shape. A key text of this unit was Lynn Nottage's *Sweat* because there was a live performance at a local theatre that all students attended. In addition to watching a live production of *Sweat*, students would read Barbara Ehrenreich's *Nickel and Dimed*. Both *Sweat* and *Nickel and Dimed* address some of the struggles faced by the working poor, an increasingly pressing issue in Ohio. We also included the podcast *Grapple*, a series focused on the struggles of individuals living in the Rust Belt. As the content of this unit came to life, student-generated podcasts seemed to be an effective way for students to find their way into an argument around one of these issues. Students would be able to interpret ideas about equity, wages and economic growth through the various texts in the unit. In addition to the print, audio, and dramatic texts, students, many of whom were already working or applying for their first jobs, interviewed guests who talked about trying to manage their lives and families on minimum wage and the benefits of unions. We believed students would make meaning of all of these texts and ideas in and through the composing, production, and publishing process. The podcast was a compelling format for sharing and distributing students' ideas in a way that would honor the networked, collaborative attributes of participatory literacies.

We hoped students would choose to investigate different perspectives on the prospect of raising the minimum wage, especially as many students have or are starting to think about securing their own part-time jobs. It was also hoped that students would think about this issue from the perspectives of business owners, long-time employees, managers, and even customers. When it came to arguing for or against the issue of the minimum wage, more than a "yes" or "no" would be required. The podcast platform, with the space it offers for debate, multiple perspectives, and storytelling, was a natural fit. The culminating project would be a radio podcast addressing a central idea of the unit. Students would produce and publish a 5-minute podcast on a specific topic from the book that captured their attention. They were responsible for all steps of the production process, from pre-production to production to post-production. Podcasts could be completed individually or in pairs, but all episodes would be published to a shared web-based platform.

Even when the unit was finalized, the technical elements were daunting. We had not received any pre-service training or professional development and if we wanted to try this in conjunction with *Sweat* and *Nickel and Dimed*, there was no time for podcast training. As John Dewey (1934) advocated, we would learn by doing.

THE UNIT: FIRST STEPS

In the tradition of Wiggins and McTighe's (2005) notion of backward design, we introduced the podcast plan to the students at the beginning of the unit. All of the instructional activities, including all reading and listening, student research, and various smaller assignments, would be directed toward one thing—students' final podcasts. Prior to starting this unit, students had completed a unit that focused on oral argument and the First Amendment. The goal of students' culminating oral argument was to persuade, and indeed, to win. This podcasting unit marked a move to a more nuanced approach to argumentation and a more nuanced topic, namely the challenges faced by the working poor, particularly the working poor in the United States.

The Text Set

During the course of the unit, students would be invited to read print and digital texts, listen to audio texts, watch video texts, and attend a live theatrical performance of Lynn Nottage's *Sweat*. The majority of the students would read Barbara Ehrenreich's *Nickel and Dimed*, although some students who struggled with *Nickel and Dimed* would have the option to read Francisco Jiminez's *The Circuit* instead. Table 1 offers a description of the different texts that were included in this unit.

The Instructional Activities

To help students learn how to follow the questions to form an argument, we practiced with a variety of activities, including one that is commonly referred to as "Slip or Trip?" and one referred to as "The Lunchroom Murder" (Hillocks, 2011). Students are presented with a brief written scenario and an image of the crime scene. In the first example, there is a man lying dead at the bottom of a staircase and the

Table 1. Texts included in this ELA podcasting unit

Text	Author and Host Site	Format	Description
Sweat	Lynn Nottage	Live production	An interview-based, Pulitzer Prize (2017) winning play exploring the economic, racial and personal consequences of the gradual closing of a factory in a small Pennsylvania town.
Nickel & Dimed	Barbara Ehrenreich	Print book	Prompted by the reaction to her initial magazine article, author Barbara Ehrenreich goes 'undercover' as a low-wage worker to report on the personal and professional issues that the working poor have to confront.
Grapple	Stephanie Marudas, Keystone Crossroads (with Kouvenda Media and WHYY)	Audio-recorded, streamed podcast	A series of investigations focusing on the decline of the Rust Belt and its stumbling efforts to rise again.
Serial	Sarah Koenig, NPR	Audio-recorded, streamed podcast	Keonig et al choose a focus for each season and "follow the questions."
Podcast: Student Choice	Multiple authors	Audio-recorded, streamed podcast	Goal: To help students see a range of topics covered by podcasts (and maybe get them hooked) and for them to see that no matter what the topic, certain elements (like music) are always present.
Fight for $15 Campaign (https://fightfor15.org)	Members of a global movement of underpaid workers	Interactive website	A high-interest topic and site because so many of the students are entering the workforce for the first time,
The Circuit	Francisco Jiminez	Print Book	A text chosen for differentiation. This text was assigned to students who struggle with reading and offered as an option to those who are on the fence between struggling to read and being at grade level. Though generally considered to be fiction, it contains autobiographical elements and addresses many of the same issues as *Nickel and Dimed*, but focuses on a particular family. Though it was not intended as a specifically timely choice, it ended up being one because the family in question is not in the country legally.

students are asked whether, based on their observations of the scene and what they hear from from the one witness (the man's wife) whether he has slipped or (been) tripped. By appealing to almost every student's interest in being a classroom lawyer, students followed the questions. And one question invariably led to another. The actual answer did not matter. What did matter was the students' ability to continue to ask themselves and each other questions in order to arrive at a claim and/or a suspect that they could support with evidence. This work supported students in their research efforts, but also explicitly supported them to think about verbal and oral interactions. This would be critical for developing their podcast voice and stance and imagining an audience on the other end of the podcast stream.

Early in the unit, students were asked to find an issue they could latch onto for a short time. Since the first job Ehrenreich takes in her book is as a waitress, we talked together about the tipping economy, the living arrangements of she and her fellow workers, the particular challenges of being female in the low-wage economy, the challenges of staying healthy, the minimum wage, and several other issues that Ehrenreich raises. Though many of our students have their own experiences with growing up poor, the book helped them articulate the issues and connect them to their lives.

After naming and exploring different issues, we wanted to introduce the idea that issues are not binary. For this phase in the unit, it was important to engage students with digital content in a deliberate way. This was important for thinking about the ways digital platforms can be a powerful space to gather, showcase, and disseminate a range of ideas, but also a place that can be used to promote certain ideas and hide other ideas. Students were also introduced to the specific components that would be assessed in their podcasts. Since this was a turn from traditional culminating projects in the class and students were novices with the work, we wanted to communicate that they would not necessarily be judged solely on the technical quality of the production. See the description of the rubric in Figure 2.

Like all of the activities in this unit, this work aimed to support student intellectual engagement with the content but also to introduce them to the capacity of digitally mediated spaces for collaboration, interaction, and cross-talk. Together, the class explored the Fight for $15 campaign (https://fightfor15.org/act-now-fight-for-15-nationwide/). We considered the "fight" from a variety of perspectives, including new employees, long-time employees, managers, business owners, and customers. The goal here was to try to impress upon the students that it was not just a question of being for or against raising the minimum wage, but that it was much more complex than that. We pointed students to how the authors of the podcasts they heard worked to collect different opinions and different perspectives on an issue. With the podcast listening, students were continuing along in their books. Once they had gotten further in their books, Charles asked questions about the connections between the *Grapple* episode and what they were reading as well as about a connection between the episode they listened to and *Sweat.*

LESSONS LEARNED: SETTING THE PROJECT UP FOR SUCCESS

Given this book's explicit focus on instructional strategies for supporting and developing participatory literacies, we describe here the specific lessons we learned from our experience, including various recommendations for further development of our instructional approaches.

Figure 2. Rubric components

Rubric

Use of class time

Students are prepared to use their class time well, use it well, maintain their process journal in a timely manner and finish each class with a plan - recorded in the journal - about what needs to be completed (and who will complete it) before the next time you have time to work in class.

Understanding of Topic

Students, through the research they do and present as well as their interviews - including the questions (which should be part of your process journal) demonstrate a thorough and organized understanding of the chosen topic.

Presentation

Students speak in a manner that matches their desired audience (see planning sheet) and in a manner that their teachers can understand. The podcast demonstrates the students' creativity by including both music and sound that support the purpose of the podcast.

Lesson #1: Curating the Content

Many of the early activities in this unit were designed to support students to learn how to engage in close listening so as to help them understand different elements of a podcast and notice the various ways they could choose to structure a podcast. All of the podcasts that were pre-selected for students to listen to on their own or as a group included material from audio-recorded interviews. Since students' final podcasts for this project were required to have material from an interview, this would help students prepare for the interviews they would conduct. In order to maximize the participatory potential of podcasting, students would have to collect material from individuals who had something to say about their selected issue. We wanted students to interact with individuals who had a range and variation of perspectives on wages and working in the local economy, and learn to integrate the ideas they heard into a nuanced argument about wages and the experiences of the working poor in their community. We wanted students to learn to edit and curate the content they gathered.

Our students proved remarkably hesitant when it came to interviewing individuals outside of their friendship circles. We think this was largely due to students' lack of experience interacting with strangers or conducting formal interviews. We hoped students' confidence would increase with additional practice. Charles reached out to a community partner who recruited a number of local residents who were willing to talk with and be interviewed by students about their experiences in the low-wage workforce, in addition to community organizers. This phase of the unit included a mini lesson about using their smartphones (if available) to audio-record the interviews and tips on how to take notes as they conducted their interviews. We conducted a whole-class interview with the guests before guests were invited to interact 1-to-1 with students for individual interviews.

Ultimately, the most compelling podcasts had high-quality, relevant content from their interviews. Yet, there was a wide range in the quality of the content as well as the recording. Upon reflection, we would have created additional workshop time in the early stages before the interviews took place. Students required extensive individualized support in the first step of writing, reviewing, and rewriting their interview questions. One of the most helpful ways to support students along the pathway to a successful story and podcast was to have them consider what information they hoped each question would produce and the extent to which those answers might address or deepen understandings on the selected issue. In the second stage, students needed support testing the audio recorder and identifying a quiet space for recording. During the third stage, students needed support with logging their interviews, considering the segments that are most helpful and segments that could be cut from their script and final podcast.

To help students become more sophisticated curators of their own content, we asked students to keep notes on their podcast plan and process in a "process journal." The journal was intended to be a place for students to plan their time and reflect on what they were learning and hearing, and how it could support the argument they wanted to make in their final podcast. We also saw it as a place for students to talk about what was working and not working. It was also a pedagogical safety net. This was a new project. Students needed to be allowed to fail or not finish and this would be the evidence of their effort.

We found that the process journal got muddled and the original podcast planning sheet did not support students along the way as we hoped it would. We think the planning sheet was trying to do too many things and became unwieldy for students. In response to that realization, we changed course. The process journal morphed into a place for what we came to refer to as "Episode Notes." We also broke down the project into smaller, manageable pieces and recommended that students think in specific minutes of time for their podcast episode. See Figure 4 for breaking down the episode into a user-friendly outline.

Figure 3. Podcast planning sheet & process journal

PODCAST PLANNING SHEET – due______________

Choose a partner. If you really want to work alone, you still have to produce a 5-minute podcast.

Name(s):

Working Title of your podcast:

Topic:

Too general: being a waitress
Specific: the troubles with tipping

3 quotations from the book you're reading in class (with page numbers) to show how your topic is related to the book:

1.
2.
3.

What is the purpose for your podcast? If it helps, think of it as your thesis.

Who is your intended audience? If it helps, think of the question this way - who has the power to support what you say so it continues to happen or help make changes if that's what you recommend?

What research do you need to do in order to have the information you need for the podcast?

Who do you need to interview so it's not just you (and your partner) reading a script as your podcast? For example, if you are working on the minimum wage question, you should probably interview a person or two who makes minimum wage and someone who pays minimum wage.

How are you going to use sound (music, ambient sound) to bring your podcast to life? Don't get too hung up on this question. Don't choose music because it's cool; choose it because it supports what you're doing.

Figure 4. Podcast outline

Podcast Outline

Create an outline for your podcast. Break it into at least 3 parts:

Part I (1 minute) Who are you? What's the name of the podcast? What's the topic? (What is your theme music?) What story are you going to tell? (transition sounds, music)

Part II (3 minutes) Explain the story and your support / research for it - research, interviews, etc. What's the best order for presenting the information? (transition sounds, music, etc.)

Part III (1 minute) After your research, what are your observations, conclusions, questions about your topic? Give a preview for the next episode (though you will not have to make it). In other words, after your research, what big question are you left with that you'd want to pursue in the next episode? (Example --> Episode 1: How Living with a Minimum Wage job is very hard. Then Episode 2 → What would it take to raise the minimum wage?) Finish with theme music.

Lesson #2: Practice Listening

The original unit plan included a number of opportunities to listen to podcasts, but we found that we needed to dedicate even more time to practicing, developing, and fine-tuning students' listening capabilities. All students were assigned to listen to one of three pre-selected *Grapple* episodes and then one episode of their own choice. Each time they listened to a podcast, the students responded to a set of questions. In an era with more and more content being streamed by audio, it is critical that we develop young people's capacity for critical listening. We found that students knew very little about podcasts, particularly their internal structure or technical production. Listening became an extremely important part of the project and a critical way to connect students with other people, texts, perspectives, and voices via the podcast medium. This is important for supporting students to develop as listeners of audio content or audio-heavy content, but also, importantly, for them to be able to write for and publish in a media environment that relies heavily on audio content.

In the classroom, critical listening must be positioned as an active process. To foster and build participatory literacies, listening has to be a participatory endeavor. By that, we mean that listeners do not simply sit back and consume the audio material, but rather make sense of, question, and interact with the material. Listening is often taught as a practice of interpreting audible sounds, but critical listening is about interacting with and making sense of what is heard. We found that it is important to create additional opportunities to listen and practice critical listening together. It was a coincidence that the third season of *Serial* was released during the teaching of this unit. Better yet, it was set in our hometown of Cleveland and focused on a topic that our students were interested in—the justice system. To create additional opportunities to practice listening, the third season of *Serial* was added to the unit. As a class, we listened to the opening minutes of an episode from the third season of *Serial*. Together, we began to examine recipes for what we considered a successful podcast. How is it introduced? How is music used? How, indeed, did the author or authors follow the questions? Students were required to listen to one of four pre-selected episodes of *Grapple*, and then one episode of their choice.

Each time students listened to a new podcast episode, students responded to the same set of questions, questions that were less about the content of the podcast and more about its architecture. They needed to have the patience to listen, a skill that would also help them with their interviews. The interactions with the published podcasts coupled with the students' own interactions with their selected interviewees also required deep listening and reflected a high level of the "connected" dimension of participatory literacies. Students were almost immediately intrigued by the "to be continued" nature of the podcasts, which struck us as being akin to the adolescent fascination with book series, like Percy Jackson or the Bluford books. This work required thinking about audience and peer-to-peer interactions. Therefore, in our suggested outline for their podcasts, we asked that at the end, they indicate what the topic would be for the podcast after the one they were producing. What question did they think needed to be followed? How would this help them share their perspectives and tell the story they wanted others to hear about poverty and the working poor?

At one point in the middle of the unit, we shared an excerpt from the second episode of *Serial* and asked students to respond to the following prompts: (1) In your own words, write a short summary of what the podcast covered. (2) What storytelling techniques did the producers of the podcast use to help tell their story? (3) How did the techniques work, or if you think they were not successful, how do you think they were supposed to work? (4) What can you take from this listening experience that will help you make your podcast?

The reflection questions were deliberately designed to focus more on the actual architecture of the podcast than its content. Listening, not every adolescent's favorite task, became an incredibly important part of this project. Given the specific attributes of the podcast medium, listening became a critical way to connect students with other people, texts, perspectives, and voices.

Lesson #3: Tinker With Tools

In addition to listening, this project reflected high levels of the multimodal dimension of participatory literacies. To be successful with this project, students needed to work with multiple modes. They also needed to tinker with the tools that support distinct modes. We discovered that most students were unfamiliar or unpracticed with the various technical tools and equipment that are used to create the different elements of a podcast. To support students to develop the literacies used in the production and publication process, we found that substantial time must be dedicated to teaching them to tinker with different tools and recognize the strengths and drawbacks of different tools. We deliberately use the phrase "tinker with tools," because all participants must spend time playing with and trying out different tools and techniques. Despite the instinct to teach or introduce the one "best" tool or to offer students a very specific step by step guide or "how to" to making a podcast, that would ultimately overlook some of the critical tenets of participatory literacies. Students will become more confident with different tools by trying them out on their own. More importantly, this puts them in a position of deciding which tools are best for their purposes and their content. In the case of a classroom environment, this also creates opportunities for distributed expertise and collaborative knowledge generation.

We recommend, however, that teachers scaffold this kind of podcast assignment so to give students ample time to practice their technical skills on an assignment that has lower stakes. We should have included much more time for basic tinkering. We relied heavily on students' smartphones and occasional laptops because that is what was available to us. It would have helped to have had regular, everyday access to laptop computers for the duration of the unit. However, we found that it is possible, although not ideal, to do this without laptops in the classroom every day.

From audiotaping and voiceovers to cutting clips and integrating music, students and teachers regularly leaned on the distributed expertise in the room and accessed countless online resources and DIY videos in the process. The technical aspects created multiple challenges along the way, but we suggest that such technological and technical challenges are part of literacy learning in this digital era. When students' podcasts came in, several submitted files did not play or generated an error message. Teachers had to follow up with a number of students who had submitted a file that did not play. Part of teaching and learning in the digital era is understanding that, at times, technology will fail. Files will be corrupted, computers will crash, and systems might be shut down for routine or urgent maintenance issues. By engaging in this unit, we have learned the value of including a required test file as an early assignment. To ensure that the selected platforms are functional and that students are able to record and an audience is able to hear the recording, we recommend requiring a test file early in the unit. We will also require students to submit files a week earlier than the final due date, so to build in one final week of workshopping and troubleshooting. In the event all files are working well, this will become a place of peer review and feedback, but if technical support is needed, students can get that support before the due date.

In the future, we would seek to have someone who is experienced with podcasting or at least audio recording available to field students' questions during the middle and towards the end of the production process. This might even be a resource that we include as part of the regular workshop sessions. We

Figure 5. Technical tools and training survey

Technical Tools and Training

What technical training do you need to be successful in this project?

___ recording

___ editing

___ incorporating music, sound

___

What technical skills do you have that you can share with others?

___ recording

___ editing

___ incorporating music, sound

___

What other questions / comments / concerns do you have?

think this is important because as students tinker with the tools and become more familiar with them, they will begin to have more nuanced questions related to their project. This would also help ease the transition from project completion to file submission, being sure to honor district-based guidelines on privacy and security. We would still want to allow the distributive expertise to emerge organically. It was a delight to see students, often those who do not always shine when it comes to traditional English skills, be summoned by their peers for technical advice. We used the survey in Image 5 to gain insight into the skills students already had and the support or training they might need. We should also explore whether there is a way to acknowledge that insight in the rubric and whether formalizing something that happened naturally would undermine it.

Podcasting was a productive way for us to invite high school students into an opportunity to learn new technological tools, but most importantly, it allowed students to develop the collaborative, multimodal, and participatory literacies required to successfully complete the project. Although podcasting itself is not necessarily a new literacy practice and many adolescents and teachers are familiar with podcasts, very few have composed and published their own. As with other digital literacies, the most useful way to develop the skills associated with podcast production is through first-hand experience and trial and error.

Lesson #4: Explore Platforms

Similar to designing spaces that explicitly invite tinkering, we found that this unit required teachers to spend more time than anticipated exploring the many different platforms available not only for composing but also for publishing. In order to support the explicit intent to make students' work and ideas available for the kinds of interactions that cultivate connected, participatory learning, teachers need to examine different platforms, including features related to share-ability, affordability, and accessibility as well as any school-based guidelines on privacy and security.

We surveyed other teachers who had experience assigning podcasts and reached out to professionals in our university's Center for Instructional Technology. We reviewed all of the recommended platforms, tending to their different strengths and weaknesses, as well as possible costs. Ultimately, we recommended that students should choose a program that suited them best and worked with their device. Several chose GarageBand, some chose iMovie, and some used Spreaker. Based on a recommendation from a fellow

ELA teacher, we set up a GoogleSite to serve as a collecting place for the students' names and the titles of their podcasts, with the intent to hyperlink the podcast titles to the actual files on Soundcloud. Given our regular use of Google Suite, we ultimately chose Google Classroom and the host for the files.

For future iterations of this unit, we would seek better expertise about the production of a podcast. While the development of distributive expertise was as welcome as it was unplanned, there is no question that our future teaching will benefit from us having a stronger foundation in the technical elements of producing a podcast.

THOUGHTS MOVING FORWARD

In the process of building a classroom culture that relies on, leverages, and develops young people's participatory literacies, as well as those of the teachers, we need to pay attention to how we incorporate digitally mediated texts into our units and how we ask young people to compose with digitally mediated tools and platforms throughout the course of the entire curriculum. Moving forward, we would introduce podcasts to students earlier in the year. For example, we would include a podcast related to our exploration of the First Amendment. In this way, the platform would become part of students' prior knowledge. We would all be more familiar with the podcast genre and we would already have some shared experiences with learning to listen and practicing our listening. While audiobooks are often encouraged as a supplement for reading assignments, we recommend finding podcasts that are connected to several of the learning units. For students who are more reluctant readers, the opportunity to do homework with earphones in would be appealing. Slowly, we could give students more to think about and do, both about the form and content, as they became more experienced with podcasts. We did include a podcast episode of *99% Invisible* called "The Landlord's Game" that provided a useful connection with our later work with *The Great Gatsby*.

We need to think about the role of the Episode Notes--the redesigned process journal--and position this document as an alternative but still authentic form of writing for pre-production. This would require gathering a set of models and working from there to create a checklist indicating what should be included in a set of Episode Notes and how it will be evaluated. By removing the pressure of the word "essay" and giving students the opportunity to write with a partner, we would have every reason to anticipate more completed assignments and more purposeful writing.

We would also like to be more deliberate about the skill sets the students develop in other parts of the curriculum. In our school context, this includes their engagement with youth-led action research. In the 10th grade, all of our students are expected to be able to prepare for, conduct, and analyze an interview. In at least three cases, students were very skilled at the first two parts, but fell short or simply skipped the third part. Would it help students analyze and edit an interview if it were transcribed? As much as we tried to point it out in the model podcasts we used, students were reluctant to edit the interviews. They were fairly adept at using only relevant sections, but did not insert themselves in the middle of the interviews. This may relate to how we teach them to use dialogue in creative writing and essays. We generally advise students to use the "said" tag at the beginning or end of the quotation. Though managing the punctuation will be difficult for some of our students, if we at least introduce the idea, then we will have the common vocabulary necessary to introduce the idea of inserting their voice at appropriate points in the interview.

We want to be intentional about talking with students about the drafting and revising that goes into a podcast script. Largely tied to our own lack of experience creating and producing podcasts, it took us time to realize that we needed to include ample time for projects to be revised. Just as essays and papers should be revised, so too should podcasts. This requires using the same language —"rough" podcast, "final" podcast—and giving teachers and students sufficient time to go through the podcast publishing process. In the podcasting world, work is typically delineated into three main categories: pre-production, production, and post-production. We relied on this terminology to support students in the composition process, but we found it helpful to rely on language that was consistent with other compositions in this class. For example, a rough podcast was one that was still in draft form. In podcasting terms, the student had moved through the pre-production and production stages, and was near post-production, but might benefit from a final review. In our classroom, a "rough" podcast was not yet posted and published to the class repository. In contrast, a final podcast was used to describe students' final, polished podcasts that were ready for publication. Students' podcasts were shared with other students through the Google Classroom page, but we believe a more public, comprehensive platform would facilitate a larger audience for students and expand listenership. A goal for our second implementation of podcasting will be to expand the reach of the podcasts to relevant audiences.

Ultimately, we would like to establish a digital home for the podcasts. They can be organized by topic and serve not only as models for future students, but also as an archive that would be a resource for future students' research. Some of the topics or the people may even merit an update or sequel. During their senior year, we hope to create a Portfolio Night. This would require each 12th grader to demonstrate both his or her knowledge and skills to an audience composed of, for example, a peer, a teacher, a parent, and a community member. A sample of a podcast should be a required part of this presentation.

EXPANDING THE CANVAS FOR STORYTELLING

There is great potential for using and sharing podcasts to tell rich, nuanced stories about important and timely issues, but also simultaneously leverage digital media and participatory literacies in and through the processes of collecting, sharing, and interacting with the stories and the tools. In Ehrenreich's introduction, she wonders about whether she is the right person to tell the story of the working poor since it will require her to go undercover. Although we appreciated her acknowledging this obstacle, the students ultimately came down on the side of her not being the right person to tell it. However, Chimamanda Ngozi Adichie reminds us, "We need more stories." In addition to Adichie's call, our first novel of the year, *Haroun and the Sea of Stories,* says that all of the stories need to be told. This podcasting project did that. By the end of this unit, a collection of student-authored stories about the working poor and fair wages to add to the story that Ehrenreich tells.

We believe that podcasts and similarly networked, digitally mediated tools offer teacher educators, current teachers, and pre-service teachers useful platforms for (re)designing classrooms to support participatory literacies. We hope that this example from a high school English Language Arts classroom encourages other teachers to think deeply about the role of participatory literacies in their current and/or future classrooms. We also hope that this work urges them to identify specific strategies and instructional approaches that can be used to foster the kinds of connectivity, collaboration, and participation that are unique to literacy learning in this digital era.

REFERENCES

Barton, D., & Hamilton, M. (2000). Literacy as social practice. In D. Barton, M. Hamilton, & R. Ivanic (Eds.), *Situated literacies: Reading and writing in context* (pp. 7–15). London: Routledge.

Beach, R. (2012). Uses of digital tools and literacies in the English Language Arts Classroom. *Research in the Schools, 19*(1), 45–59.

Buckley-Marudas, M. F. (2016). Literacy learning in a digitally-rich humanities classroom. *Journal of Adolescent & Adult Literacy, 59*(5), 551–561. doi:10.1002/jaal.470

Buckley-Marudas, M. F., & Doerr-Stevens, C. (in press). Critical listening for social change: The possibility of "playback" in English Language Arts. *Ubiquity*.

Ceraso, S. (2014). (Re)Educating the senses: Multimodal listening, bodily learning, and the composition of sonic experiences. *College English, 77*(2), 102–123.

Coleman, D. (2011). *Bringing the common core to life*. Retrieved June 2019, from http://nysed.gov.rttt/resources/bringing-the-common-core-to-life.html

Dewey, J. (1934). *Art as experience*. New York, NY: Perigee.

Doerr-Stevens, C., & Buckley-Marudas, M. F. (2019). Hearing knowledge into action: Mobilizing sound for multicultural imaginaries. *International Journal of Multicultural Education, 21*(1), 105–124. doi:10.18251/ijme.v21i1.1735

Gee, J. P. (1996). *Social linguistics and literacies: Ideology in discourses / James Paul Gee*. Bristol, PA: Taylor & Francis.

Hillocks, G. Jr. (2011). *Teaching argument writing*. Portsmouth, NH: Heinemann.

Hull, G., & Stornaiuolo, A. (2014). Cosmopolitan literacies, social networks, and "proper distance": Striving to understand in a global world. *Curriculum Inquiry, 44*(1), 15–44. doi:10.1111/curi.12035

Hutchinson, A., & Colwell, J. (2014). The potential of digital technologies to support literacy instruction relevant to the Common Core State Standards. *Journal of Adolescent & Adult Literacy, 58*(2).

Hutchison, A., & Reinking, D. (2011). Teachers' perceptions of integrating information and communication technologies into literacy instruction: A national survey in the United States. *Reading Research Quarterly, 46*(4), 312–333. doi:10.1002/RRQ.002

Ito, M. (2009). *Participatory learning in a networked society: Lessons from the Digital Youth Project*. Presentation for the 2008 Annual Meeting of the American Educational Research Association Presidential Session. Retrieved August 15, 2008, from http://www.itofisher.com/mito/publications/participatory_1.html

Ito, M., Baumer, S., Bittanti, M., boyd, d., Cody, R., Herr-Stephenson, B., & Tripp, L. (2010). Hanging out, messing around, and geeking out: Kids living and learning with new media. Cambridge, MA: MIT Press.

Ito, M., Gutierrez, K., Livingstone, S., Penuel, B., Rhodes, J., Salen, K., Schor, J., Sefton-Green, J, & Watkins, S.C. (2013). Connected Learning: An Agenda for Research and Design. Irvine, CA: Digital Media and Learning Research Hub.

Janks, H. (2013). Critical literacy in teaching and research. *Education Inquiry*, *4*(2), 225–242. doi:10.3402/edui.v4i2.22071

Jenkins, H. (2006). *Convergence culture: Where old and new media collide*. New York, NY: NYU Press.

Jenkins, H. (2016). Critical literacy pedagogy. In Literacies (2nd ed.). Port Melbourne, Australia: Cambridge University Press.

KaaSerpent. (2014). *Ira Glass on storytelling, Full* (parts 1 to 4) [video]. Retrieved from https://www.youtube.com/playlist?list=PLE108783228F1E008

Koenig, S. (Host and Producer). (2014–2019). *Serial* [Audio podcast]. Retrieved from ttps://serialpodcast.org/season-one/about

Lankshear & Knobel. (2011). *New literacies: Everyday practices for classroom learning* (3rd ed.). New York, NY: Open University Press.

Leu, D. J. Jr, Kinzer, C., Coiro, J., & Cammack, D. (2004). Toward a theory of new literacies emerging from the Internet and other information and communication technologies. In R. B. Ruddell & N. Unrau (Eds.), *Theoretical models and processes of reading* (5th ed.; pp. 1568–1611). Newark, DE: International Reading Association.

Leu, D. J., O'Byrne, W. I., Zawilinki, L., McVerry, J. G., & Everett-Cacopardo, H. (2009). Expanding the new literacies conversation. *Educational Researcher*, *38*(4), 264–269. doi:10.3102/0013189X09336676

Mills, K., Ulsworth, L., & Exley, B. (2018). Sensory literacies, the body, and digital media. In K. Mills, A. Stornaiuolo, A. Smith, & J. Pandya (Eds.), *Handbook of writing, literacies and education in digital cultures*. New York, NY: Routledge.

National Council of Teachers of English/International Reading Association. (2012). *Standards for the English Language Arts*. Retrieved from: http://www2.ncte.org/resources/standards/ncte-ira-standards-for-the-english-language-arts/

Newell, G., Bloome, D., & Hirvela, A. (2015). *Teaching and learning argumentative writing in high school English language arts classrooms*. New York, NY: Routledge. doi:10.4324/9781315780498

Scribner, S., & Cole, M. (1981). *The psychology of literacy*. Cambridge, MA: Harvard University Press. doi:10.4159/harvard.9780674433014

Shanahan, L. (2012). Use of sound with digital text: Moving beyond sound as an add-on or decoration. *Contemporary Issues in Technology & Teacher Education*, *12*(3), 264–285.

Shanahan, L. (2012). Use of sound with digital text: Moving beyond sound as an add-on Or decoration. *Contemporary Issues in Technology & Teacher Education*, *12*(3), 264–285.

Smith, B. (2018). Composing for affect, audience, and identify: Toward a multidimensional understanding of adolescents' multimodal composing goals and designs. *Written Communication*, *35*(2), 182–214. doi:10.1177/0741088317752335

Starcic, A., Cotic, M., Solomonides, I., & Volk, M. (2016). Engaging preservice primary and preprimary school teachers in digital storytelling for the teaching and learning of mathematics. *British Journal of Educational Technology*, *7*(1), 29–50. doi:10.1111/bjet.12253

Stornaiuolo, A., & Whitney, E. (2018). Writing as world making. *Language Arts*, *95*(4), 205–217.

Street, B. V. (1984). *Literacy in theory and practice*. Cambridge, UK: Cambridge University Press.

Street, B. V. (1995). *Social literacies: Critical approaches to literacy in development, ethnography and education*. London, UK: Longman.

Wiggins, G., & McTighe, J. (2005) Understanding by design (2nd. ed.). Alexandria, VA: Association for Supervision and Curriculum Development (ASCD).

Wissman, K., & Costello, S. (2014). Creating digital comics in response to literature: Aesthetics, aesthetic transactions, and meaning making. *Language Arts*, *92*(2), 103–117.

Wohlwend, K. E. (2016). Who gets to play? Access, popular media and participatory literacies. *Early Years: An International Research Journal*, *37*(1), 62–76. doi:10.1080/09575146.2016.1219699

Chapter 3
Participatory Literacy and Taking Informed Action in the Social Studies

Casey Holmes
North Carolina State University, USA

Meghan McGlinn Manfra
North Carolina State University, USA

ABSTRACT

The purpose of the social studies is to prepare students for life as citizens in a democratic society, and this requires attention to the variety of digital spaces inhabited by our K-12 students in today's increasingly digitized world. Incorporating participatory technologies into structured inquiries in the social studies may help develop students' skills and abilities in critically sourcing, evaluating, sharing, and creating media, and provides the opportunity for increasingly democratic participation and civic engagement both in and out of the school setting. In this chapter, the authors suggest the integration of participatory literacy with the College, Career, and Civic Life (C3) framework as a means of supporting students in taking informed action.

INTRODUCTION

Participatory literacy has taken on new importance in the era of fake news and misinformation. Since the 2016 presidential election, educators and policymakers have been increasingly concerned with the ability of our students to navigate a complex and often deliberately misleading online landscape. In order for students to develop participatory literacy, they must have opportunities to develop the requisite skills to interpret, share, and create on digital platforms (Wohlwend, 2017), as well as to be able to discern credible information from web-based sources. This includes the ability "to contribute to blogs, wikis, social networking and sharing sites, virtual worlds, and gaming environments, which rely upon creativity, reasoning, focus, critical thinking, and capacity to collaborate" (IGI, 2019).

DOI: 10.4018/978-1-7998-0000-2.ch003

In the social studies, participatory technologies appear to provide students with more opportunities to engage in inquiry-based civic learning, while also honing their participatory literacy skills. One particular structure, the National Council for the Social Studies' *College, Career, and Civic Life (C3) Framework,* shows promise for supporting teachers in integrating civic action more explicitly into the social studies classroom in a structured manner.

In this chapter, the authors explore strategies for supporting the development of participatory literacy with a specific focus on civic engagement. The *C3 Framework* helps teachers provide the explicit scaffolding that is necessary for navigating the complex context of contemporary digital media. Integrating participatory literacy with the inquiry-based *C3 Framework* provides a structured approach for supporting student' development of deep content knowledge, critical and participatory literacy skills, and consideration of ways to impact the world beyond school.

SOCIAL STUDIES EDUCATION AND CIVIC EFFICACY

In order to truly prepare students for democratic citizenship, a key, though often overlooked, component of social studies education is supporting students as they take civic action or engage in participatory civic experiences (Levinson & Levine, 2013; Parker, 2003). Research on civic education suggests that the most effective approach to supporting students in developing their civic capacities and competencies is by providing active learning experiences focused on relevant issues, both inside and outside of the classroom (Croddy & Levine, 2014). For example, James Youniss (2012) argues that "democratic citizenship is best acquired by taking, rather than reading about, action" (p. 116). Taking action often emerges from posing and solving authentic problems that are posed through inquiry-based education, and the *C3 Framework* provides one pathway towards inquiry-driven studies.

Civic Learning in Schools

Research suggests that a lack of explicit instruction related to civic engagement is typical of student experiences in K-12 schools. A 2012 survey of young adults (18-24) conducted by the Center for Information and Research on Civic Learning and Engagement (CIRCLE) revealed that just 27% of respondents reported having participated in a project in the community as part of their high school social studies classes (Godsay et al., 2012; Levinson & Levine, 2013).

There is also evidence of markedly uneven civic engagement among young Americans (e.g., Han, 2009; Godsay et al., 2012; Levinson, 2010, 2012; Schlozman, Verba, & Brady, 2012; Swalwell, 2015); one of the primary divisions is between college-going youth and those who have never attended college. National survey data collected by CIRCLE in 2012 show that a majority of non-college youth are essentially disengaged from civic life, with 37% completely disconnected and 13.5% reporting to be "broadly engaged" (Godsay et al., 2012). Economic insecurity, family needs, financial debt, long work hours, and weak organizational connections may also contribute to low levels of civic engagement for these young adults (CIRCLE, 2013). Wealthy, well-educated citizens have traditionally had a greater voice than less advantaged citizens in American political processes (Han, 2009). According to the Task Force on Inequality and American Democracy (2004), the advantaged "roar with a clarity and consistency that policymakers readily hear and routinely follow," while "citizens with lower or moderate incomes speak with a whisper that is lost on the ears of inattentive government officials" (p. 1).

The civic empowerment gap between historically privileged and historically marginalized young people is exacerbated by the inequity of access to civic engagement opportunities during K-12 schooling. High-quality opportunities for action are rare in schools serving lower income students (Levinson & Levine, 2013), and research demonstrates that racially diverse classrooms often have relatively low levels of political discussion, including about current events (Campbell, 2007). Lower income students and students of color are also less likely to attend college, a space which would offer additional opportunities to learn and practice the habits of citizenship (Godsay et al., 2012).

Analysis of data from the 2010 National Assessment of Educational Progress (NAEP) suggests that both class and race are related to a lower likelihood of scoring "proficient" on the NAEP assessment (CIRCLE, 2013), and that White students and students from higher socioeconomic backgrounds reported engaging more frequently in instances of pedagogical practices that encourage and support action, such as debates and simulations (Kawashima-Ginsberg, 2013). Researchers found that parental education level and eligibility for free or reduced lunch programs, which are both indicators of a family's socioeconomic status, were highly predictive of exposure to a high-quality civics education (Kawashima-Ginsberg, 2013). The lack of opportunity is particularly problematic as some research suggests that high-quality civic education may provide significant benefits to some of the least-advantaged students, including children of color, children from low-income families, and girls (CIRCLE, 2013; Torney-Purta & Wilkenfeld, 2009).

INTEGRATING THE *C3 FRAMEWORK* AND PARTICIPATORY LITERACY

Within the field of social studies, the *College, Career, and Civic Life (C3) Framework* (NCSS, 2013) has brought renewed attention to engaging students in inquiry-based instruction that results in students taking informed action. The *C3 Framework* centers around an inquiry arc – an instructional design that supports students as they develop capacities for analyzing, knowing, explaining, and arguing about interdisciplinary challenges in the social world in which we live (NCSS, 2013). An outline of this instructional support, called the Inquiry Design Model (IDM) blueprint, is appended to this chapter (Appendix 1).

Research has demonstrated that engaging in disciplined inquiry provides students the opportunity to learn more deeply and in a more sustained manner (Saye, 2017). In addition to learning content knowledge and critical thinking skills, student engagement in inquiry provides participatory experiences for students, with real world opportunities to bring about change. Similarly, Barton and Levstik (2004) noted the importance of inquiry in the social studies discipline in particular, as students learn the aptitudes and knowledge necessary for democratic life. Perhaps most fruitful for engaging students in civic action is to first engage students through collaborative inquiry processes in the social studies (Thacker, Lee, & Friedman, 2017), which may help establish the habits necessary for continued engagement in civic life.

The inquiry design model (IDM) therefore provides a structure for teachers to scaffold student work throughout the *C3 Framework*, beginning with a compelling question and moving through a series of supporting questions. Each supporting question includes formative assessment tasks focused on analyzing primary and secondary sources. Here, teachers can engage students in exploring digital content focused on critical social studies issues using heuristics or guides to support their analysis of primary and secondary sources. The structure of the inquiry design model helps students develop the skills and content knowledge to complete the summative assessment and translate those conclusions into action, and the framework is intended for use for all students between kindergarten and grade twelve – an acknowledgement that inquiry, participatory literacy, and informed civic action do not need to be reserved for only the brightest or eldest students. Indicator bands help identify and guide student growth within and among grade levels.

The inquiry arc is comprised of four dimensions, which align with and mutually support each other -- Dimension 1, "Developing questions and planning inquiries"; Dimension 2, "Applying disciplinary concepts and tools;" Dimension 3, "Evaluating sources and using evidence;" and Dimension 4, "Communicating conclusions and taking informed action." From a civics perspective, this framework not only provides a structure to scaffold for inquiry, but also explicitly supports civic learning. According to Croddy and Levine (2014), the inquiry arc "anticipates the concepts and tools necessary for informed, skilled, and engaged participation in civic life" (Croddy & Levine, 2014, p. 262). C3 inquiries culminate in summative performance tasks in which students communicate conclusions and take informed action, completing the cycle of inquiry, reflection, and action that drives democratic civic and political processes.

Dimension 4: Communicating Conclusions and Taking Informed Action

According to the authors of the *C3 Framework,* social studies requires that "students use disciplinary knowledge, skills, and perspectives to inquire about problems involved in public issues; take constructive, independent, and collaborative action; reflect on their actions; and create and sustain groups" (NCSS, 2013, p. 62). These aims align with the characteristics and purposes of participatory literacy when applied to digital contexts or include digital tools. For example, Dimension 4 of the *C3 Framework* requires that students are able to apply "a range of deliberative and democratic strategies and procedures" to make decisions and take action "in their classrooms, schools, and out-of-school civic contexts" (see D4.3, NCSS, 2013, p. 62). Here, experiential learning becomes an essential element of social studies, and through taking action young people learn to be citizens by working with others who are also learning to be, act, and think like citizens (Levinson & Levine, 2013). These collaborative efforts may also support students in considering what it means to be a citizen, and who or what has made those decisions about inclusion and eligibility in the past.

Despite the importance of taking informed action, and the need for students to learn about citizenship by actually *doing* citizenship, Dimension 4 remains the most ignored and inconsistently implemented step of the *C3 Framework* (Kumler & Vosburg-Bluem, 2014). Teachers often report feeling overwhelmed by the realities of implementing a plan to take informed action (Thacker, Lee, & Friedman, 2017). Teachers find Dimension 4 to be the most intimidating component of the inquiry arc framework, and cite time constraints, fear of parental and community pushback, and lack of knowledge about how to get started as major factors that either prevent them from implementing Dimension 4 or significantly slow their process of doing so (Swan, Lee, & Grant, 2018).

Taking Informed Action With Participatory Literacies

Participatory technologies provide exciting new opportunities for students to engage in informed civic action both inside and outside of the K-12 social studies classroom and may help teachers overcome some of these factors currently hindering the full implementation of the *C3 Framework.* Whereas traditional approaches to teaching and learning often center the teacher as the gatekeeper of knowledge, where knowledge is scarce and held only by experts (Huang & Behara, 2007), the prevalence and proliferation of participatory technologies in this new information age have served to blur these lines of teacher and learner. It is much easier for students and teachers alike to be both consumers and producers of information and knowledge, challenging traditional ideas about who or what serves as an authority on knowledge (Farkas, 2012), and opening up online civic spaces or "participatory online communities of practice" (Nagle, 2018, p. 87).

Teachers can integrate participatory technologies like social media and Web 2.0 technologies into K-12 social studies classrooms to connect students with the world beyond school. While much of the research regarding civic engagement refers specifically to action opportunities in government- or civics-focused high school courses, the *C3 Framework* provides support for teachers in grades as young as kindergarten and in four major disciplines of social studies, including history, geography, and economics in addition to civics. Leveraging participatory technologies in these spaces has the potential to create more engaging learning environments and empower students with a greater sense of autonomy (McLoughlin & Lee, 2008). Collectively, these affordances may help to address traditional issues of accessibility and relevance frequently cited within the field of social studies (e.g., Banks, 2007; Choi et al., 2011; Ladson-Billings, 1994; Ross, 2014; Schug, Todd, & Beery, 1984). Students may also begin to discern for themselves the blurring of the line between teacher and student, perhaps developing the understanding that knowledge is fluid and changes over time, and thus teaching and learning are lifelong processes (Farkas, 2012).

Whereas previously it may have been difficult for teachers to engage students in taking civic action within the classroom, participatory technologies offer students unprecedented access to online civic networks. Through the thoughtful integration of information technologies and carefully scaffolded inquiry-based learning activities, teachers can support students in developing participatory literacy in addition to content knowledge using the Inquiry Design Model (IDM). For example, in order to complete each major part of the C3 inquiry – answering compelling questions through summative performance tasks, addressing supporting questions through source analysis and formative performance tasks, and taking informed action – students must demonstrate "creativity, reasoning, focus, critical thinking, and capacity to collaborate" associated with participatory literacy (IGI, 2019, n.p.). At the same time, students could "contribute to blogs, wikis, social networking and sharing sites, virtual worlds, and gaming environments" (IGI, 2019, n.p.) as part of the project work produced over the course of the C3 inquiry. Table 1 provides an overview of potential connections between the major learning activities that make up the C3 IDM, social studies disciplinary skills/concepts, and relevant participatory literacy skills. For each learning activity, the authors provide an example task for students to complete that integrates social studies learning and participatory literacy. Perhaps participatory literacy aligns with the *C3 Framework* because both frameworks espouse a commitment to democratizing learning spaces.

Participatory Technologies as Democratizing Agents

Participatory technologies promise the potential for increasingly democratic civic spaces and deeper engagement among and between citizens, suggesting that developing students' participatory literacies may help reduce barriers to civic participation. Once a person has accessed the Internet and is online, data suggest that barriers to participation in any particular group or site are often low. For example, a 2009 Civic Health Index (CHI) survey conducted by the National Conference on Citizenship revealed that civic uses of social networking sites were common across income and educational groups; low-income youth and youth without college experience were nearly as likely to use social networking sites for civic purposes as youth who had higher income levels or collegiate experience (National Conference on Citizenship, 2009). More recent data suggest a promising trend that differences in political engagement online across income levels are more moderate than they are for in-person political engagement;

Table 1. Connecting the C3 framework with participatory literacy

Major learning activities of C3 IDM	Social studies disciplinary skills/ concepts	Relevant participatory literacy skills	Learning examples
Summative performance task	Creating a disciplinary-appropriate argument	Creativity Reasoning Critical thinking	Students post arguments to blogs, wikis or other social networking sites.
Formative performance task	Analyzing/synthesizing primary and secondary sources	Reasoning Critical thinking Collaboration	Students analyze digital history or other multimodal social science texts or data available through digital collections or archives and create a multimedia product.
Taking informed action	Address a discipline specific issue relevant to the world beyond school	Creativity Reasoning Critical Thinking Collaboration	Students create a website, game or virtual tour to raise awareness and inform the general public or other students about a persistent public issue.

however, educational differences continue to persist across all groups (Smith, 2013). Studying access itself and reporting on the Youth and Participatory Politics Survey, Joseph Kahne and Ellen Middaugh (2012) found that Internet access "varies only a fraction" across the four racial groups included in the study - Black, Latino, Asian-American, and non-Hispanic White youth - and that access was above 94% for each group (p. 54).

Beyond the ease of access, participatory technologies provide opportunities to democratize civic participation by helping students develop the skills and abilities that are necessary for full and effective civic engagement in democratic society where people of different backgrounds and perspectives must learn to live and work together. Participatory technologies are critical for our K-12 youth because while young people are often excluded from major, more formal, political institutions, social media spaces provide greater opportunity for youth leadership and more significant roles in consuming, circulating, and producing civic and political content (CIRCLE, 2013). This may also be true for youth from traditionally marginalized communities; recent research suggests that participation in social media can empower Latino youth as information leaders and activists in immigrant communities (McDevitt & Butler, 2011). In a time of increasing residential and school segregation (see for example Frankenberg, 2013; Ladson-Billings & Tate, 1995; Orfield & Frankenberg, 2014), participatory media also provide opportunities for young people of diverse backgrounds and experiences to interact in ways that they may not otherwise be able to. The Internet can be an important tool for helping increase social capital for African Americans, Latino/as, and individuals without a college education, as these groups are more likely than Whites, Asians, and college graduates to use the Internet to attempt to broaden their social networks (Gonzales, 2017). Douglas Kellner and Jeff Share (2007) note that media and information community technology can be tools for empowerment "when people who are most often marginalized or misrepresented in the mainstream media receive the opportunity to use these tools to tell their stories and express their concerns" (p. 62).

Perhaps one reason young people are increasingly drawn to social media to engage civically is due to their increased autonomy and independence from traditional gatekeepers of news and information in these spaces. Unlike with traditional news sources, or the social studies textbooks that students read in school, social media provide the opportunity for youth to help create or co-create narratives about news and information, augmenting their influence on the flow of information. Social media provides a place for the conversation and interaction among youth and their peers to continue, long after the event has ended in real-time (Kahne & Middaugh, 2012).

Digital media provides ample opportunities for students to dig deeply into critical social issues. However, students need support to identify credible information, synthesize that information, and draw meaning from it. While today's youth are more frequent users of web technology tools for leisure and entertainment, they are not inherently able to discern what information on the web is credible and what is not (Cohen, Kahne, Bowyer, Middaugh, & Rogowski, 2012; Kahne & Bowyer, 2017). Media literacy is an essential component of any social studies inquiry process, particularly with the increasing prevalence of misleading, exaggerated, and false stories in today's political and social sectors. Beyond basic considerations of truth, myth, and exaggeration, students should also be prompted to explore issues of power and identity within the media messages that they examine. Media continues to be an increasingly dominant force in identity construction, aided by the increasing use of and dependence on media by today's K-12 student population; however, media messages continue to not only be "devoid of cultural clues about how to form genuine, interdependent relationships with people from diverse backgrounds" (Carducci & Rhoads, 2005, p. 5) but also often serve to reinforce the dynamics of power and expressions of status quo found in the larger society (Kellner & Share, 2007).

The increasing ease of cross-border communication and the prevalence of new forms of media also provides expanding opportunities for students to make local-global connections and develop understandings of global social issues (Grossman, 2017). Today's youth, more so than their predecessors, are citizens of a globalized world environment, and schools have the ability to "constructively harness" the potential of new media to prepare them for global citizenship (Grossman, 2017, p. 544).

Of course, despite promising data such as those analyzed by Kahne and Middaugh (2012), access to the Internet does remain unequal. The United States continues to experience a digital divide, with access more difficult for Black and Hispanic students and students living in low-income communities and rural areas (Anderson & Perrin, 2018; Perrin, 2017), and this remains a critical component in the discussion of the democratizing potential of the Internet. These considerations are crucial for teachers, who must ensure their explorations of participatory spaces are accessible for all students.

PARTICIPATORY LITERACY IN PRACTICE

There are a variety of websites geared towards teens that focus on critical social issues that provide students with information, resources, and an online community surrounding both broader and more specific projects and topics. See, for example, TakingITglobal (https://www.tigweb.org/), which seeks to engage and connect youth around the world by empowering them to understand and act on local and global challenges in pursuit of a more inclusive, peaceful, and sustainable world. Similarly, the International Education and Resource Network (iEARN, see https://us.iearn.org/) was started in 1988 to support an international community of K-12 educators and youth to collaborate and learn together on projects that are aligned with the United Nations' Sustainable Development Goals (SDGs). Research also suggests the potential of participatory digital media for fostering students' global awareness and understanding, crucial for today's increasingly globalized citizen. Milson and Earle's (2007) case study of ninth grade geography students revealed that students who participated in world geography classes using Internet-based global information system (GIS) gained "enhanced cultural awareness and empathy for the complexity of the problems facing African peoples and countries" (Grossman, 2017, p. 545). These examples and resources suggest the possibilities for collaboration and communication that exist for students taking action on social issues affecting their local, national, and/or global communities.

A focus on improving student participatory literacy could also be leveraged to augment students' decision-making processes in taking action. Digitally-mediated communication allows learners not just to consume digital information, but to also contribute to digital spaces both within and beyond the classroom walls. Teachers could consider many different uses of digital communication in this manner. For example, students can turn a more critical eye toward their preferred social networks, using their social media channels to gather sources, evaluate the reliability and accuracy of those sources, and/or to critically monitor the spread of misinformation, fake news, and exaggerated claims.

Students can also use these participatory digital spaces to synthesize the information and sources they gather to present them to a larger audience. For example, teachers could consider collaborative and organizational tools like Padlet to encourage analysis and synthesis. Finally, teachers may also consider the use of student-created blogs and microblogs, such as Twitter, as potential means by which students can contribute to both the classroom conversation and the broader civic arena. Given young people's widespread use of social media networking sites, such as Twitter, both to communicate and share news and information, intentioned and purposeful use of these social networking sites may be an effective and efficient way for students to take informed action on authentic civic issues.

Sample inquiry blueprints, housed on the C3 teachers resource hub (see www.c3teachers.org), illuminate the possibilities for integrating participatory literacy development and inquiry-driven social studies instruction using the *C3 Framework*. For example, a sample inquiry for middle schoolers related to *Uncle Tom's Cabin* and slavery poses the compelling question of whether words can lead to war (see Appendix 2). As a conclusion to an inquiry process in which students utilize a variety of primary sources and formative assessments to analyze Harriet Beecher Stowe's *Uncle Tom's Cabin*, seventh graders can identify a contemporary human rights issue, create a list of possible ways to address the issue using words (e.g., letters, editorials, videos, protests, social media), and then choose and implement one of these options (C3 Teachers, n.d.-b; see the full blueprint in Appendix 2). In contrast to a traditional multiple choice test or even an in-class essay, the incorporation of participatory technologies here, such as social media, videos, and digital texts, provides opportunities for students to engage with both historical and contemporary issues and produce meaningful and authentic work in order to convey their solutions, resolutions, and further questions.

In a related inquiry for high school students, students develop an informed and critical perspective on the United States Constitution as it was written at the conclusion of the 1787 Constitutional Convention in order to respond to the compelling question of whether the Constitution established a just government (see Appendix 3). Following a similar process of document-based analysis and formative assessment, students bring their inquiries into the present by researching efforts made since 1787 to make the Constitution more just via the amendment process and evaluate the ways in which unsuccessful amendments could have contributed to a more just Constitution. Students can engage with participatory technologies throughout this process and also as they take action by selecting a proposed amendment that they believe will make the Constitution more just and contacting an organization or individual promoting that amendment to inquire about ways to advocate and participate. Again, students are thus able to transition their learning beyond the four walls of their social studies classrooms into the authentic world in which policy debates and civic processes happen every day (C3 Teachers, n.d.-a; see the full blueprint in Appendix 3). Each of these planned inquiries provides students with a structured and scaffolded framework for critically approaching historical and contemporary questions of democracy and justice and integrating participatory literacy skills can amplify the depth and breadth of students' learning.

It should be noted that new media and participatory technologies are not transformative in and of themselves; they must be integrated and developed in an intentional and structured manner. Teachers must incorporate specific instruction in utilizing and engaging with the different digital media themselves; while today's K-12 students are often assumed to be "digital natives" (Wineburg et al., 2016, p. 4) who have grown up using technology, students enter classrooms with vastly different competencies and expectations in regards to using technology as an academic and/or civic tool (Farkas, 2012). Students must continue to develop new literacies as their participation and engagement in increasingly digitally mediated cultures evolves and deepens.

CONCLUSION

The authors argue for the need to engage students in taking informed action in order to support their development as engaged and critical citizens, and particularly in light of the civic education gap. The existence and maintenance of a vibrant and successful democracy depends on a deeply engaged and active citizenry, and thus inequitable access to and development of opportunities for youth to engage in authentic civic action is problematic for our democracy. Despite the inconsistency in taking action, this final element of the *C3 Framework* is critical and necessary: its placement as the last step in the process is intended to ensure that students have worked towards a purposeful, informed, and reflective experience of taking action (Kumler & Vosburg-Bluem, 2014) before the cyclical process begins anew. Integrating action into social studies courses may also serve to increase student engagement and interest in the curriculum, helping students to see the connections between content and their everyday lives. Students often feel detached from social studies courses, where they find the content and traditional pedagogies like lectures and working out of textbooks to be irrelevant or boring; this feeling is often more significant for immigrant students and students of color, who find little relevance in social studies curricula that overemphasizes the achievements of white men and often misrepresent or ignore the contributions of their own families and cultures (see for example Banks, 2007; Choi et al., 2011; Godsay et al., 2012; Ladson-Billings, 1994). Given the increasingly ubiquitous role of digital technologies in our students' lives, participatory literacies provide an intriguing opportunity for students to engage in civic action and ensure greater potential for future civic engagement.

Ultimately the aim for all education is to help students analyze, understand, engage with, and positively contribute to the world beyond school. This chapter suggests that the *C3 Framework*, with its emphasis on taking informed action, can provide a structure for explicitly supporting students' participatory literacy. In this context, web-based media becomes both the content and tool for students to analyze critical issues, develop arguments, take action, and share their findings. "Taking informed action provides students opportunities to adapt and apply their work in the disciplines that constitute the social studies in order to develop the skills and dispositions necessary for an active civic life" (NCSS, 2013, p. 59). Digital media and content circumscribe active civic life, and today's educators must help students develop the necessary participatory literacy skills to navigate this new context.

REFERENCES

C3 Teachers. (n.d.a). High school Constitution inquiry: Did the Constitution establish a just government? *C3 Teachers*. Retrieved from http://www.c3teachers.org/wp-content/uploads/2015/08/NewYork_11_Constitution.pdf

C3 Teachers. (n.d.b). New York state social studies resource toolkit: 7th grade *Uncle Tom's Cabin* inquiry. *C3 Teachers*. Retrieved from http://www.c3teachers.org/wp-content/uploads/2015/06/NewYork_7_UncleTomsCabin.pdf

Anderson, M., & Perrin, A. (2018, October 26). Nearly one-in-five teens can't always finish their homework because of the digital divide. *Pew Research Center*. Retrieved from http://www.pewresearch.org/fact tank/2018/10/26/nearly-one-in-five-teens-cant-always-finish-their-homework-because-of-the-digital-divide/

Banks, J. A. (2007). *Educating citizens in a multicultural society* (2nd ed.). New York, NY: Teachers College Press.

Barton, K. C., & Levstik, L. S. (2004). *Teaching history for the common good*. Mahwah, NJ: Lawrence Erlbaum. doi:10.4324/9781410610508

Campbell, D. E. (2007). Sticking together: Classroom diversity and civic education. *American Politics Research*, *35*(1), 51–78. doi:10.1177/1532673X06294503

Carducci, R., & Rhoads, R. A. (2005). Of minds and media: Teaching critical citizenship to the plugged-in generation. *About Campus: Enriching the Student Learning Experience*, *10*(5), 2–9. doi:10.1002/abc.142

Center for Information & Research on Civic Learning and Engagement (CIRCLE). (2013). *All together now: Collaboration and innovation for youth engagement: The report of the commission on youth voting and civic knowledge*. Medford, MA: CIRCLE. Retrieved from https://civicyouth.org/wp-content/uploads/2013/09/CIRCLE-youthvoting-individualPages.pdf

Choi, Y., Lim, J. H., & An, S. (2011). Marginalized students' uneasy learning: Korean immigrant students' experiences of learning social studies. *Social Studies Research & Practice*, *6*, 1–17.

Cohen, C. J., Kahne, J., Bowyer, B., Middaugh, E., & Rogowski, J. (2012). *Participatory politics: new media and youth political action*. Oakland, CA: Youth and Participatory Politics Research Network. Retrieved from http://ypp.dmlcentral.net/sites/all/files/publications/YPP_Survey_Report_FULL.pdf

Croddy, M., & Levine, P. (2014). The C3 Framework: A powerful tool for preparing future generations for informed and engaged civic life. *Social Education*, *78*(6), 282–285.

Farkas, M. G. (2012). Participatory technologies, pedagogy 2.0 and information literacy. *Library Hi Tech*, *30*(1), 82–94. doi:10.1108/07378831211213229

Frankenberg, E. (2013). The role of residential segregation in contemporary school segregation. *Education and Urban Society*, *45*(5), 548–570. doi:10.1177/0013124513486288

Godsay, S., Kawashima-Ginsberg, K., Kiesa, A., & Levine, P. (2012). *"That's not democracy." How out-of-school youth engage in civic life & what stands in their way*. Medford, MA: CIRCLE. Retrieved from https://civicyouth.org/wp-content/uploads/2012/08/CIRCLE_ThatsNotDemocracy_WebFinal.pdf

Gonzales, A. L. (2017). Disadvantaged minorities' use of the internet to expand their social networks. *Communication Research, 44*(4), 467–486. doi:10.1177/0093650214565925

Grossman, D. L. (2017). Global education. In M. M. Manfra & C. M. Bolick (Eds.), *The Wiley handbook of social studies research* (pp. 518–568). Malden, MA: John Wiley & Sons, Inc. doi:10.1002/9781118768747.ch23

Han, H. (2009). *Moved to action: Motivation, participation, and inequality in American politics*. Stanford, CA: Stanford University Press.

Huang, C. D., & Behara, R. S. (2007). Outcome-driven experiential learning with Web 2.0. *Journal of Information Systems Education, 18*(3), 329–336.

IGI. (2019). *What is participatory literacy*. IGI Global. Retrieved from https://www.igi-global.com/dictionary/participatory-literacy/52242

Kahne, J., & Bowyer, B. (2017). Educating for democracy in a partisan age: Confronting the challenges of motivated reasoning and misinformation. *American Educational Research Journal, 54*(1), 3–34. doi:10.3102/0002831216679817

Kahne, J., & Middaugh, E. (2012). Digital media shapes youth participation in politics. *Phi Delta Kappan, 94*(3), 52–56. doi:10.1177/003172171209400312

Kawashima-Ginsberg, K. (2013). *Do discussion, debate, and simulations boost NAEP civics performance?* Medford, MA: CIRCLE. Retrieved from https://civicyouth.org/wp-content/uploads/2013/04/CIRCLE_NAEPBechtelFactSheetApril30.final_.pdf

Kellner, D., & Share, J. (2007). Critical media literacy is not an option. *Learning Inquiry, 1*(1), 59–69. doi:10.100711519-007-0004-2

Kumler, L. M., & Vosburg-Bluem, B. (2014). Climate change in the social studies classroom: A "why" and "how to" guide using the C3 Framework. *Social Education, 78*(5), 225–229.

Ladson-Billings, G. (1994). *The dreamkeepers: Successful teachers of African American children*. San Francisco, CA: Jossey-Bass.

Ladson-Billings, G., & Tate, W. F. (1995). Toward a critical race theory of education. *Teachers College Record, 97*(1), 47.

Levinson, M. (2010). The civic empowerment gap: Defining the problem and locating solutions. In L. Sherrod, J. Torney-Purta, & C. A. Flanagan (Eds.), *Handbook of research on civic engagement* (pp. 331–361). Hoboken, NJ: John Wiley & Sons. doi:10.1002/9780470767603.ch13

Levinson, M. (2012). *No citizen left behind*. Cambridge, MA: Harvard University Press. doi:10.4159/harvard.9780674065291

Levinson, M., & Levine, P. (2013). Taking informed action to engage students in civic life. *Social Education, 77*(6), 339–341.

McDevitt, M., & Butler, M. (2011). Latino youth as information leaders: Implications for family interaction and civic engagement in immigrant communities. *InterActions: UCLA Journal of Education and Information Studies, 7*(2), Article 2.

McLoughlin, C., & Lee, M. J. W. (2008). The three p's of pedagogy for the networked society: Personalization, participation, and productivity. *International Journal on Teaching and Learning in Higher Education, 20*(1), 10–27.

Milson, A. J., & Earle, B. D. (2007). Internet-based GIS in an inductive learning environment: A case-study of ninth grade geography students. *The Journal of Geography, 106*(6), 227–237. doi:10.1080/00221340701851274

Nagle, J. (2018). Twitter, cyber-violence, and the need for a critical social media literacy in teacher education: A review of the literature. *Teaching and Teacher Education, 76*, 86–94. doi:10.1016/j.tate.2018.08.014

National Conference on Citizenship. (2009). *America's civic health index 2009: Civic health in hard times.* Washington, DC: Author.

National Council for the Social Studies (NCSS). (1994). *Expectations of excellence: Curriculum standards for social studies.* Washington, DC: NCSS.

National Council for the Social Studies (NCSS). (2013). *The College, Career, and Civic Life (C3) Framework for social studies state standards: Guidance for enhancing the rigor of K-12 civics, economics, geography, and history.* Silver Spring, MD: NCSS.

Orfield, G., & Frankenberg, E. (2014). Increasingly segregated and unequal schools as courts reverse policy. *Educational Administration Quarterly, 50*(5), 718–734. doi:10.1177/0013161X14548942

Parker, W. C. (2003). *Teaching democracy: Unity and diversity in public life.* New York, NY: Teachers College Press.

Perrin, A. (2017, May 19). Digital gap between rural and nonrural America persists. *Pew Research Center.* Retrieved from http://www.pewresearch.org/fact-tank/2017/05/19/digital-gap-between-rural-and-nonrural-america-persists/

Ross, E. W. (2014). *Social studies curriculum: Purposes, problems, and possibilities* (4th ed.). Albany, NY: SUNY Press.

Saye, J. W. (2017). Disciplined inquiry in social studies classrooms. In M. M. Manfra & C. M. Bolick (Eds.), *The Wiley handbook of social studies research* (pp. 336–359). Malden, MA: John Wiley & Sons, Inc. doi:10.1002/9781118768747.ch15

Schlozman, K. L., Verba, S., & Brady, H. E. (2012). *The unheavenly chorus: Unequal political voice and the broken promise of American democracy.* Princeton, NJ: Princeton University Press.

Schug, M., Todd, R., & Beery, R. (1984). Why kids don't like social studies. *Social Education, 47*(5), 382–387.

Smith, A. (2013, April 25). Civic engagement in the digital age. *Pew Research Center*. Retrieved from http://www.pewinternet.org/2013/04/25/civic-engagement-in-the-digital-age/

Swalwell, K. (2015). Mind the civic empowerment gap: Economically elite students and critical civic education. *Curriculum Inquiry*, *45*(5), 491–512. doi:10.1080/03626784.2015.1095624

Swan, K., Lee, J., & Grant, S. G. (2018). Inquiry design model: Building inquiries in social studies. Silver Spring, MD: National Council for the Social Studies and C3 Teachers.

Task Force on Inequality and American Democracy. (2004). *American democracy in an age of rising inequality*. Washington, DC: American Political Science Association. Retrieved from https://www.apsanet.org/portals/54/Files/Task%20Force%20Reports/taskforcereport.pdf

Thacker, E. S., Lee, J. K., & Friedman, A. M. (2017). Teaching with the C3 Framework: Surveying teachers' beliefs and practices. *Journal of Social Studies Research*, *41*(2), 89–100. doi:10.1016/j.jssr.2016.08.001

Torney-Purta, J., & Wilkenfeld, B. S. (2009). *Paths to 21st century competencies through civic education classrooms: An analysis of survey results from ninth-graders*. Washington, DC: Campaign for the Civic Mission of Schools and American Bar Association Division for Public Education.

Wineburg, S., McGrew, S., Breakstone, J., & Ortega, T. (2016, November 22). *Evaluating information: The cornerstone of civic online reasoning*. Stanford, CA: Stanford History Education Group.

Wohlwend, K. E. (2017). Who gets to play? Access, popular media and participatory literacies. *Early Years Journal of International Research and Development*, *37*(1), 62–76. doi:10.1080/09575146.2016.1219699

Youniss, J. (2012). How to enrich civic education and sustain democracy. In D. E. Campbell, M. Levinson, & F. M. Hess (Eds.), *Making civics count: Citizenship education for a new generation* (pp. 115–133). Cambridge, MA: Harvard Education Press.

KEY TERMS AND DEFINITIONS

C3 Framework: Inquiry-based framework for social studies instruction, based around an inquiry design model (IDM) and intended to be used in concert with individual state social studies standards.

Civic Engagement: Individual or group action in the local, national, and/or global community that is intended to make some difference in political and/or civic processes.

Informed Action: A means of civic engagement in which individuals or groups of people take some kind of action to address a social or political question, following a process of inquiry, analysis, reflection, and decision-making.

Inquiry: Pedagogical approach and approach to learning that is based upon student investigation of broad, compelling, questions. This approach is closely tied to the purposes and goals of social studies education.

Media Literacy: Ability to locate, evaluate, analyze, and draw conclusions from media sources, including the ability to discern bias, truth, and accuracy. Also includes ability to critically evaluate media messages for connotations of power and identity.

Participatory Technologies: Web-based and/or technological tools that allow individuals the ability to actively engage with and produce knowledge; in contrast with passive tools that might allow individuals only to consume but not create or produce knowledge themselves.

Social Studies: Collectively refers to the many branches of study that deal with how people live and work together, including but not limited to history, economics, geography, psychology, and civics. In the elementary and middle grades in the United States, "social studies" is taught as one discipline; high schools often structure social studies courses as subjects by the individual branches (e.g., geography).

APPENDIX 1

Table 2. Inquiry design model

<table>
<tr><th colspan="4">Inquiry Design Model (IDM) Blueprint™</th></tr>
<tr><td>Compelling Question</td><td colspan="3"></td></tr>
<tr><td>Standards and Practices</td><td colspan="3"></td></tr>
<tr><td>Staging the Question</td><td colspan="3"></td></tr>
<tr><td colspan="2">Supporting Question 1</td><td>Supporting Question 2</td><td>Supporting Question 3</td></tr>
<tr><td colspan="2"></td><td></td><td></td></tr>
<tr><td colspan="2">Formative Performance Task</td><td>Formative Performance Task</td><td>Formative Performance Task</td></tr>
<tr><td colspan="2"></td><td></td><td></td></tr>
<tr><td colspan="2">Featured Sources</td><td>Featured Sources</td><td>Featured Sources</td></tr>
<tr><td colspan="2"></td><td></td><td></td></tr>
<tr><td rowspan="2">Summative Performance Task</td><td>Argument</td><td colspan="2"></td></tr>
<tr><td>Extension</td><td colspan="2"></td></tr>
<tr><td>Taking Informed Action</td><td colspan="3"></td></tr>
</table>

(Source: C3 Teachers)

APPENDIX 2

Figure 1.
(Source: C3 Teachers)

NEW YORK STATE SOCIAL STUDIES RESOURCE TOOLKIT

7th Grade *Uncle Tom's Cabin* Inquiry

Can Words Lead to War?	
New York State Social Studies Framework Key Ideas & Practices	7.7 REFORM MOVEMENTS: Social, political, and economic inequalities sparked various reform movements and resistance efforts. Influenced by the Second Great Awakening, New York State played a key role in major reform efforts. Gathering, Using, and Interpreting Evidence · Chronological Reasoning and Causation · Comparison and Contextualization
Staging the Question	Consider the power of words and examine a video of students using words to try to bring about positive change.

Supporting Question 1	Supporting Question 2	Supporting Question 3	Supporting Question 4
How did Harriet Beecher Stowe describe slavery in *Uncle Tom's Cabin*?	What led Harriet Beecher Stowe to write *Uncle Tom's Cabin*?	How did people in the North and South react to *Uncle Tom's Cabin*?	How did *Uncle Tom's Cabin* affect abolitionism?
Formative Performance Task	**Formative Performance Task**	**Formative Performance Task**	**Formative Performance Task**
Write a summary of the plot of *Uncle Tom's Cabin* that includes main ideas and supporting details from Stowe's description of slavery in the book.	List four quotes in the sources that point to Stowe's motivation and write a paragraph explaining her motivation.	Make a T-chart comparing viewpoints expressed in newspaper reviews of *Uncle Tom's Cabin* and make a claim about the differences.	Participate in a structured discussion regarding the impact *Uncle Tom's Cabin* had on abolitionism.
Featured Source	**Featured Source**	**Featured Source**	**Featured Source**
Source A: Summary of *Uncle Tom's Cabin* **Source B:** Excerpts from *Uncle Tom's Cabin* **Source C:** Illustrations from *Uncle Tom's Cabin*	**Source A:** Harriet Beecher Stowe's concluding remarks to *Uncle Tom's Cabin*. **Source B:** Letter from Harriet Beecher Stowe to Lord Thomas Denman	**Source A:** Review of *Uncle Tom's Cabin* published in the *Boston Morning Post* **Source B:** Review of *Uncle Tom's Cabin* published in the *Southern Press Review*	**Source A:** Excerpt from Charles Sumner's Senate speech **Source B:** Article by John Ball Jr. published in *The Liberator* **Source C:** Sales of *Uncle Tom's Cabin*, 1851–1853

Summative Performance Task	ARGUMENT Can words lead to war? Construct an argument (e.g., detailed outline, poster, essay) that discusses the impact of *Uncle Tom's Cabin* using specific claims and relevant evidence from historical sources, while acknowledging competing views.
	EXTENSION Create an educational video of the argument that responds to the compelling question "Can words lead to war?"
Taking Informed Action	UNDERSTAND Identify and describe a human rights issue that needs to be addressed (e.g., child labor, trafficking, or poverty). ASSESS Create a list of possible actions that involve words. This may include letters, editorials, social media, videos, and protests. ACT Choose one of the options and implement it as an individual, small group, or class project.

C3 TEACHERS™ idm INQUIRY DESIGN MODEL™

 2

APPENDIX 3

Figure 2.
(Source: C3 Teachers)

High School Constitution Inquiry

Did the Constitution Establish a Just Government?

Framework for Teaching American Slavery	Summary Objective 7: Demonstrate the ways that the Constitution provided direct and indirect protection to slavery and imbued enslavers and the slave states with increased political power.
Staging the Question	Read the preamble to the Constitution and discuss how a government could achieve the goals it establishes.

Supporting Question 1	Supporting Question 2	Supporting Question 3	Supporting Question 4
Why did the framers of the United States Constitution feel a new document was necessary?	How did the Constitution structure the government?	How did the framers protect slavery in the Constitution?	How democratic was the 1787 Constitution?
Formative Performance Task	**Formative Performance Task**	**Formative Performance Task**	**Formative Performance Task**
Generate a list of concerns that led to the creation of a new government through the Constitution.	Create a graphic organizer that illustrates the branches of the federal government and their functions.	Write a paragraph using evidence to explain how the framers protected slavery in the Constitution.	Develop a claim supported by evidence that explains the degree to which the 1787 Constitution is a democratic document.
Featured Sources	**Featured Sources**	**Featured Sources**	**Featured Sources**
Source A: Letter to James Duane from Alexander Hamilton, Excerpt (1780). **Source B:** Letter to James Warren from George Washington, Excerpt (1785). **Source C:** Letter to Thomas Jefferson from John Jay (1786).	**Source A:** Selections from the Constitution (Art. 1, Sec. 7-9; Art. 2, Sec. 2-3; Art. 3, Sec. 2) (1787). **Source B:** *The Federalist No. 51* by James Madison or Alexander Hamilton, Excerpt (1788).	**Source A:** Selections from the Constitution (Art. 1, Sec. 2, Clause 3; Art. 1, Sec. 9, Clause 1; Art. 4, Sec.2, Clause 3) (1787). **Source B:** *Notes of Debates in the Federal Convention of 1787* by James Madison, Excerpt. **Source C:** Speech by Benjamin Franklin, Excerpt (1787).	**Source A:** Selections from the Constitution (Art. 1, Sec. 2; Art. 2, Sec. 1-2; Art. 4, Sec. 4; Art. 5; Art. 6) (1787). **Source B:** *Notes of Debates in the Federal Convention of 1787* by James Madison, Excerpt. **Source C:** *The Federalist No. 43* by James Madison, Excerpt (1788).

Summative Performance Task	ARGUMENT Did the Constitution establish a just government? Construct an argument (e.g., detailed outline, poster or essay) that addresses the compelling question using specific claims and relevant evidence from historical sources while acknowledging competing views.
	EXTENSION Examine political cartoons developed during the ratification debates and create your own political cartoons that praise or deride the justness of the proposed Constitution.
Taking Informed Action	UNDERSTAND Research efforts to use the amendment process to make the Constitution more just. ASSESS Evaluate the extent to which a proposed or unratified amendment (e.g., the Equal Rights Amendment) could have contributed to a more just Constitution. ACT Select a proposed amendment that would make the Constitution more just and contact an individual or organization promoting that amendment to find out ways to advocate for it.

C3 TEACHERS™ idm INQUIRY DESIGN MODEL™

2

Chapter 4
The Truth We Can't Afford to Ignore:
Popular Culture, Media Influence, and the Role of Public School

Danielle Ligocki
Oakland University, USA

Martha Ann Wilkins
Lewis University, USA

ABSTRACT

Popular media has become a central aspect of life for many individuals. With that exposure to media comes imagery that contains messages both covert and overt that are readily consumed by the viewers. Adolescents are especially influenced by these images because of their frequency and use of media. This study addresses the ways in which middle school students interpret and internalize stereotypical imagery found in popular culture, specifically reality television, and examines the role of the teacher and greater school community in helping students to identify and mediate stereotypical images. Through participatory literacy strategies, classrooms everywhere can become an educative, critical, thoughtful space for both students and teacher.

INTRODUCTION

The influences of popular culture and media in American society are undeniable; their power permeates every aspect of our existence, including the lives of our nation's youth. In a 2015 study conducted by the nonprofit organization, Common Sense Media, youth ages 8-13 spent an average of six hours a day engaged with various forms of media, while teenagers on average spent up to nine hours each day (Marshall & Sensoy, 2016, p. 1-2). The level of influence that is possible is astounding and has been magnified by new technological advances that allow popular cultural tropes to be disseminated and reproduced instantaneously across various forms of media. Many of these images and ideas perpetuate

DOI: 10.4018/978-1-7998-0000-2.ch004

age-old stereotypes, particularly those that are harmful to women and people of color. As these ideas infiltrate the academic landscape, 21st century educators are challenged with not only being aware of these ideologies, but also with helping students learn to negotiate and mediate these images in their own lives. In order to stay relevant and critically conscious, schools and teachers are now tasked with becoming fluent in this new form of digital currency. Through pedagogical practices such as the teaching of critical media literacy and explicit critical thinking instruction, public schools can position themselves as conduits towards social change. Armed with the knowledge that media is an unrelenting force in the lives of youth, teachers can work to counteract this pedagogue with a series of critical and practical strategies that may help to mediate the imagery that young people are interacting with on a daily basis.

This chapter addresses the ways in which middle school students interpret and internalize stereotypical imagery found in popular culture, specifically reality television, and examines the role of the teacher and greater school community in helping students to identify and mediate stereotypical images. Through participatory literacy strategies, classrooms everywhere can become an educative, critical, and thoughtful space for both students and teacher.

THEORETICAL FRAMEWORK

In order to analyze the ways in which the participants of this study viewed, interacted with, and consequently internalized the stereotypical images and messages found in various reality television programs, social cognitive theory was used. Social cognitive theory (Bandura, 1986, 1994, 2001) is a research lens used to explain the effects that television and other forms of mass media have on the perceptions of its viewers. According to this theory, individuals create cognitive symbols and meaning from images situated in environmental events (Bandura, 1994, 2001), which is why it is imperative to examine individual's thoughts and perceptions of reality television and other 'constructed' media images. This study sought to use social cognitive theory as a means of understanding the ways in which participants were making meaning and assigning meaning from images in popular culture, specifically those found within reality television programs.

A central tenant of social cognitive theory is the role of modeling. Models can be formed for individuals through interpersonal observations or from media sources; these models can then act as a guide for governing one's own behaviors and attitudes (Bandura, 1986, 1994, 2001, Williams, 2008). These models are external observations created from images that influence the individual's actions and beliefs. This means that through consumption of various media images, a viewer's own behaviors and attitudes can adapt to reflect more closely those that have served as models. Bandura furthers this notion by positing that some viewers even go on to imitate said behaviors through what he refers to as 'social prompting' (Bandura, 1986, 1994, 2001) Thus, it is important to understand the frequency and types of models that young people are exposed to as indicators of how they might internalize these messages. "People have the potential to and will behave altruistically if given examples and models to follow" (Williams, 2008). However, it is important to note that the influence of media imagery does not influence individuals in isolation.

Although individuals have self-agency (Bandura, 2001), interactions with media imagery commonly act as a form of observational learning (Bushman & Huesmann, 2006) which is what social cognitive theory seeks to understand. When an individual views the images and messages that they see through popular media, those images connect to an already-established personal schema (Bushman & Huesmann,

2006, Fiske, 2017). "Neuroscientists and cognitive psychologists posit that the human mind acts as an associative network in which ideas are partially activated, or primed, by stimuli that they are associated with. The activation produced by an observed stimulus spreads in the network and moves even remotely related concepts closer to the threshold of influence" (Bushman & Huesmann, 2006). Therefore, it can be understood that the consumption of images must happen either in high frequency or in conjunction with other images in order to have the greatest impact.

Social cognitive theory has been commonly used in educational research as a means to underscore the ways in which children and adults are influenced by the consumption of violent media (Bandura, 2006, Bushman & Huesmann, 2006, Crick & Dodge, 1994, Josephson & Proulx, 2008). In these studies, social cognitive theory asserts that individuals can view their interactions with media as learning environments (Bushman & Huesmann, 2006, Josephson & Proulx, 2008). Our study takes a similar position to suggest that participants are interacting with and learning from their experiences with different forms of media and in doing so are informed about other groups of people and the underlying and often stereotypical messages that media presents. It was important to identify media as a learning environment considering the amount of time in which adolescents interact with media. This amount of daily contact suggests that individuals could potentially learn from their experiences with media.

CRITICAL MEDIA LITERACY

When working with young people in classrooms, a critical frame of reference is not impossible to attain. Unfortunately, although popular in Great Britain, Canada, and Australia, (Kellner and Share, 2007) explicit instruction in critical media literacy in schools in the United States is not a standard practice. Schools in the United States have the tendency to approach literacy from an English Language Arts perspective, working to address the basics of reading and writing and eventually getting to some higher order thinking skills. This notion of literacy instruction completely ignores the role that not only media, but also texts of all varieties play in the lives of young people in schools. While there are small pockets of amazing teachers doing work to educate their students in media literacy, the reality is that critical media literacy is still on the fringes of education in America's schools.

Kellner and Share (2005, 2007) point out that when there is media literacy instruction happening in schools, the critical piece is left out. They argue that media literacy often takes three simplistic approaches: the protectionist approach, the media arts education approach, and the media literacy movement. Each of these approaches has their flaws and ignore the need for critical questioning when it comes to media instruction. In the protectionist approach, educators work to keep their students in a bubble, by protecting them from "the dangers of media manipulation and addiction" (Kellner and Share, 2007). When using the media arts education approach, educators help students see the beauty and aesthetics of media and the arts, while encouraging them to create their own forms of media. Finally, with the media literacy movement, educators work to bring different forms of popular culture into their classrooms, with the focus being on helping students to access, analyze, evaluate and communicate. While each of these approaches may seem to have their own redeeming qualities, the fact is that none of these approaches works to bring the much-needed critical angle to the work. As Kellner and Share remind their readers,

The critical component of media literacy must transform literacy education into an exploration of the role of language and communication to define relationships of power and domination because below the surface of that iceberg lies deeply embedded ideological notions of white supremacy, capitalist patriarchy, classism, homophobia, and other oppressive myths. (p. 62, 2007)

From this definition, one can see that educators and public schools have a long way to go in terms of how media literacy is addressed with students everywhere. However, while schools in the United States wait for this approach to media literacy to enter the classroom, students continue to suffer from a lack of education in this area. This lack of education in the digital-age can have very real consequences for students, and these consequences were evident in the research that was conducted with pre-teens and teenagers that contributed to this chapter.

METHODS AND METHODOLOGY

This study was conducted as a qualitative case study. This approach, along with Phil Carspecken's (1996) methods of data analysis and interpretation aided our exploration of social issues and human phenomena. When working with young people and seeking to have critical, honest dialogue, conducting a qualitative case study allowed a method of working with participants that enabled data and evidence to be collected which offered insight in a way that a quantitative approach would not. The data was gathered through semi-structured interviews (see Appendix) during focus groups and one-on-one meetings. In order to facilitate discussions that would uncover participants' perceptions and understandings, interviews were conducted in a semi-structured manner. This process allowed the researcher to probe participants with follow-up questions and requests for clarification. This research strategy allowed for intimate, authentic, fluid, and complex conversations between the researcher and participants. While conversational in tone, this research method helped frame interviews that were neither too casual nor too rigid or uncomfortable for participants (Edwards & Holland, 2013, Weiss, 1994). This strategy was used to facilitate discussion that would allow the participants to be as reflective as possible on their experiences with media and the ways in which they were and may have been influenced by its messages and imagery. Moreover, the semi-structured interview method facilitated the use of social cognitive theory as a tool of analysis. By allowing participants to answer questions that were expressive of their own feelings, beliefs, behaviors, and interactions with their environments, (Bandura, 1996) they were ultimately allowed to tell their own narratives about the ways in which media can be perceived and interpreted in their lives. Additionally, after the four focus group meetings, the researcher was able to tailor specific follow-up questions to each participant, based on their remarks during the group discussions. Once all of the focus groups and one-on-one interviews were complete, the data was transcribed. The researchers then coded and analyzed the participants' responses.

Participants were chosen based on their interest in reality television and their willingness to participate. As researchers, we felt as though young people would be more willing to be honest and thoughtful with someone they already had a relationship of trust with, so participants were members of one of the researcher's algebra classes. Seven participants were chosen, after receiving the proper child assent and parent consent forms. These seven participants ranged in age from 12 to 14. Four students identified as male, while three identified as female. Of the male participants, two were Caucasian and two were Mexican. Of the female participants, two were African American and one was Caucasian. All of the participants had been classmates for years, which helped build a feeling of trust and comfort during the focus groups.

During data analysis, the researchers focused on the first two tenets of social cognitive theory, the model of causation and the idea of symbolizing capability (Bandura, 1996). These aspects address respectfully the ways in which "people are both producers and products of their environment" (p.5513) and the ways in which they symbolize the experiences of others as guides for their reasoning and actions (p.5514). These tenets provided the theoretical lens by which participants' responses were analyzed. Both of these facets undergird the idea that although society influences media imagery, it is also actively influencing its consumers.

LITERATURE REVIEW

The Rise of Reality Television Within Popular Culture

In spite of a 7900% increase in the number of reality television shows on air from 2000 to 2010 (Ocasio, 2010), there are some television critics, educators, academics, parents, and young people who still choose to dismiss media and electronic texts as harmless entertainment. However, there are others who realize the direct and indirect impact these texts have on the lives, thinking, and well-being of young people as international citizens. Media sources such as the *Washington Post*, the *San Francisco Chronicle*, and the *New York Post* have all contributed to the dialogue that reality television has turned different forms of cruelty into entertainment. Authors such as Laurie Ouellette (2009), Susan Murray (2009), and Jennifer Pozner (2010) have written about the potentially negative effects that reality television may be having on viewers. Still, the impact that these shows have on young people continues to remain relatively unstudied.

When reality television first started to gain attention and popularity, it was often dismissed as a passing fad. However, when the website Reality Blurred indicates that over 750 reality shows aired in the year 2015, it should become clear that reality television is not, in fact, a passing fad at all. While MTV's *The Real World* is often viewed as the first reality show to air and the one that paved the way for the state that we currently occupy as it relates to the overabundance of reality television shows on air, that is not entirely true. *An American Family*, which documented the daily lives of five members of the Loud family, debuted in 1973 and was the first episodic reality show, airing over 300 hours of footage over 12 episodes (Galanis, 2013). In addition, even before *An American Family*, viewers were treated to *Candid Camera*, which first aired in 1948. Interestingly, at the time *Candid Camera* was on the air, it was viewed as progressive and as an interesting experiment in sociology, which is a far cry from how most viewers and critics think about reality television today. Even though *Candid Camera* aired sporadically for decades, it was never in a weekly or episodic format, like the reality television shows occupying network programming today.

While one can see that reality shows existed for many years before MTV got involved, it was the launch of *The Real World* that caused people to sit up and take notice and brought into existence the overwhelming number of reality shows that are on-air today. Spin-offs of *The Real World*, including *Road Rules* and *The Challenge* developed quickly and it is from here that content, premise or thought ceased to matter. We argue that with the rise of these types of shows, the types that seem to showcase the worst of human behavior, came the infiltration of harmful stereotypical images that are so prevalent today.

The Perpetuation of Stereotypes Found on Reality Television

Jennifer Pozner -- a media critic, journalist, activist and founder of the education and advocacy organization Women in Media & News -- has studied reality television for years. In her book, *Reality Bites Back: The Troubling Truth about Guilty Pleasure TV*, Pozner explains the stereotypes of females that are often enacted on reality television. These are the same stereotypes that have been present in media since 1800s Minstrel Theater, early 1900s radio and the sitcoms of the 1950s. Pozner mentions that the primary narratives for women of color on reality television shows are "Jezebels, Mammies, and Sapphires, "spicy" Latinas and "exotic" (or passive) Asians" (Pozner, 2010, p. 194). Because of this continued portrayal, the pervasive cultural understanding of women becomes negatively impacted and intertwined with these images. The same can be said for White women on reality television, who are often portrayed as dumb and inept, gold diggers or untrustworthy. Worse than this, the portrayal of young African American men in reality television, just like in mainstream media, is horrifying. These men are portrayed as thugs, gangbangers, jobless, and as negative role models. Portrayals such as these only further the existing hegemonic messages about Black men in America. All of these images then begin to become a part of the dominant discourse and work as a constant cultural reminder regarding the value and ability of women and people of color.

Pozner's explanation of these over-the-top stereotypes perpetuated in the media bring to light how often this type of toxic imagery is placed in front of viewers. While many viewers would like to think they are aware of the ways in which reality television shows operate, that they are not 'real life' depictions or 'unscripted' illustrations of a person's daily life, the fact remains that having these harmful roles played out over and over again on countless types of television shows is not healthy for constructing an unbiased view of other people. Pozner quotes the work of Sut Jhally and Justin M. Lewis at length at the opening of her book, in order to give readers context regarding why these stereotypes are so harmful.

The whole process of watching television [has] social significance. Television provides us with pictures of the world, of our world, and the knowledge that most of these pictures are fictional does not immunize us from believing in them. The beliefs we form become part of the context within which we understand who we are. To understand prime-time television, then, is to understand an important part of the way we view the world and ourselves. (Jhally & Lewis, as cited in Pozner)

What Jhally and Lewis are trying to make clear here is the concept that -- even though viewers might know that what they are seeing on reality television is not, in fact, indicative of real life -- that does not necessarily lighten the impact that these images and productions have on one's way of thinking. Additionally, parents and educators need to think even deeper about this concept, as much of this research and understanding is based on work with adults, who are generally aware of the role that editing and production play in reality television shows. If enlightened adults are aware of the falsehoods behind this imagery, yet still affected by it, what might be happening to the young people who are engaging with these shows, who might not be fully aware of the behind-the-scenes work in these productions? What might be happening to young people interacting with these shows, who do not have a critical frame of reference through which they can think about these issues?

VOICES OF YOUNG PEOPLE

When working with the young participants in this study, it became clear that the imagery present in the media, and specifically in reality television, was a big part of their world and their thinking. During these interviews, students shared their thoughts and feelings, frustrations, opinions, and had honest dialogue not only about the reality television shows they engaged with, but also about what kind of impact these shows had on them as individuals. Some of the most poignant comments are as follows.

Stereotypes

"So I'm like, why do they automatically assume they're like these stereotypes? I don't understand, like, you should come to my house, because my house is very clean. And my father's in it. I only have two siblings. My mother is not a crack head."

Jasmine, 14-years-old

This came from Jasmine, an African American young woman who was speaking out in terms of stereotypes that upset her. She was one of the most vocal participants and became visibly emotional at times during our discussions. When discussing the imagery specifically around the African American community, she worked to push back against the dominant discourse, as seen in her statement above. What was interesting about working with Jasmine was that, even though she was aware of – and upset by – the ways in which Black women were portrayed in reality television shows, she felt no need to stop watching her shows of choice. The reality shows that Jasmine watched regularly were those that were full of physical and verbal altercations and that often worked to oversexualize the female participants. These shows are shocking for adults to watch, so one can only imagine how Jasmine felt watching it. Even more troubling is that, while Jasmine articulated her thoughts on stereotypes well, this study was one of the first chances that she had to process what she was seeing, which is a true disservice to Jasmine and her education.

Impact of Reality Television

"I think girls are trying to be the people they see on T.V."

Malaysia, 12-years-old

Malaysia made this comment in our focus group interviews and did not receive a great deal of disagreement from her peers. Interestingly, Malaysia, an African American young woman from a single-parent household was the participant most connected to reality television, letting the group know that reality television functioned as a 'big sister' to her, since her mother was much older than her and she did not have any siblings. Malaysia also made it clear to the group that she would really like to participate in a reality television show one day. While Malaysia remarked on how others may want to be like the girls they see on reality television, she also let us know that some of these shows had taught her how to interact in social settings and how to approach dating. For Malaysia, the negative imagery inherent in reality television did not seem to upset her, as she often described women she viewed as 'ghetto', while describing herself as 'ghetto' as well. Malaysia also shared how much she enjoyed all of the drama that is present on the shows that she chose to watch.

"I mean, if you see someone on T.V., you think they're like better than you, or popular, or you should be like them. Like they're a role model because they're on T.V."

John, 14-years-old

John, a White young man from a low-income family made it clear repeatedly that people on television -- even those who were only on reality television -- are worthy of time and attention. While he initially said that he did not engage with many reality television programs, he spoke fondly of shows like "Big Brother" and "Survivor", making personal connections to some of the characters and describing himself as being similar to one in particular. John watched reality television with his mom and he often talked about the allure of the prize money involved in competition-style shows. For John, part of the reason for looking up to the people on television was for the money that he assumed they had.

"Our generation is, you know, kind of gone a little bit, and whenever they see something on T.V., they say oh, my God, that's how it must be in real life."

Marty, 13-years-old

This statement from Marty was an interesting one, as Marty was a participant who often had to 'sneak' his reality television choices around the watchful eye of his mother. Because of this, the shows that he engaged with were not critically discussed, since it was not common knowledge that he was watching shows like "Jackass" and "Wife Swap". While Marty did acknowledge watching with his dad and older brother for laughs, it appeared as though he kind of threw up his hands and just took what he was seeing at face value. For Marty, the pain, danger, humiliation and emotional anguish that was often present in the shows that he watched were all left unquestioned.

Drama

"Because who would like to see a show that's like, actual reality? We just want to see fights and stuff like that."

Jake, 13-years-old

Jake, a White male who was extremely vocal during all of the focus group meetings, shared this idea with the group early on in our discussions, and much of the group agreed with him. From the start of our work together, Jake appeared to have a basic understanding of the roles that producers play in how certain circumstances and characters are framed on reality television shows, but he also believed that some shows were more realistic than others. However, he makes clear here that the level of reality in reality television shows doesn't even matter, as young viewers don't want to engage with shows that feel like real life.

This notion of drama carried throughout all of our discussions together. Interestingly, while six of the seven participants mentioned that they tune into reality television shows strictly for the level of drama, one participant shared that the drama that underscores most interactions on reality television shows was the reason that he does not choose to watch a great deal of reality television. The notion of drama was brought up in every focus group meeting, where the participants mentioned issues of alcohol abuse, physical fights, sexual situations, over-the-top interactions between cast mates and just a general display of nonsensical behavior. While this may not sound particularly appealing to some readers, these are the traits of shows that enticed young people to watch; and yet, these are the exact issues that we are not talking about in classrooms.

DISCUSSION

During this study, young participants often discussed the stereotypes that they saw on the reality shows they watched, and some had strong feelings regarding what they saw. Throughout the coding and analysis of transcripts, it became clear that reality television shows were acting to inform these young people and act as a pedagogue, which is in alignment with the ideas presented in social cognitive theory. Pedagogy is widely understood by Merriam Webster's definition: "the function or work of a teacher." While the word "teacher" is used here, that teacher does not have to be, and often is not, a human being standing in front of a classroom. Instead, different parts of our world act as pedagogical forces, and in this case, reality television is one of them. Anna McCarthy (2009) explains the pedagogy of reality television by noting that these shows often invite viewers to juxtapose drama and real life, and this act of comparing and contrasting can lead viewers to an understanding of the world around them. Notice that we do not say "better understanding," as it is not clear that reality television is offering a better understanding of anything.

Reality Television as a Pedagogue

The problem with reality television acting as a pedagogue is that over time elements of deception have been added into the mix. McCarthy paralleled the work of social scientists and reality television producers in the 1950s and 1960s and described it in the following way:

> These men [producers] shared a sense of theatricality, simulation, and dissimulation as necessary tools for understanding the complex dimensions of human behavior in modern society. Each saw techniques of deception as components of empirical investigation, and each articulated a working model of realist representation as the foundation for such investigations.
>
> (McCarthy, 2009, p. 33)

This illustrates that the need to make "real life" more exciting was clear and present in reality television from its inception. If this is true, then shows that are being touted as "real" and that are working to educate viewers on an endless number of topics, including the behavior of women and people of color, are educating viewers under false pretenses. This is problematic when thinking about pre-teen and teenaged viewers who may be unknowingly relying on these shows for a great deal of information about culture, people who may be different from them, locations that they have never been to, or even something as simple as how to act in a social setting. It should be clear then that the implications of reality television for young viewers might be far more serious than initially thought.

When we think about this power of reality television as a pedagogue, we see it reflected in the ways that the participants discussed the imagery and stereotypes that were most prevalent. The concept that stands out the most is the idea of being 'ghetto'. This word was brought up many times throughout the focus groups and individual interviews. When Malaysia worked to define what ghetto means, her peers agreed with her. There was no question about her definition as she was describing ghetto as someone who is loud, chomps their gum, wears their hair a certain way and basically has no social or cultural capital. All of the young people around the table appeared to agree regarding this definition and nobody suggested that maybe characters were framed in this way or maybe they were playing a role that producers asked them to play. Instead, when characters (or even people outside of a reality show) were identified as 'ghetto', this label was left unquestioned and the person was then deemed as 'less than' by those who had applied the label. Being called 'ghetto' was the equivalent of a put down, which is interesting to think about when Malaysia told the group that she is ghetto, she knows it, and she is okay with it.

Reality Television and Race

In contrast to this, however, was the pushback against what it means to be Black in society. As mentioned above, Jasmine in particular was troubled by the stereotypical imagery of Black families on television and she worked to explain to both the researcher and her peers that the tightly held stereotype of what it means to be Black was so far from her own experience. In addition to Jasmine's vocalization of her feelings regarding Black stereotypes, there was also mention during the focus groups that ". . . they feed the stereotypes so that people believe the stereotype even more". While who 'they' are was not clearly defined, there seemed to be an emerging critical awareness that the ways in which characters are portrayed on reality television shows may not be authentic representations of that person as an individual, or of the larger group as a whole. This tiptoe into the waters of critical questioning gives a glimpse into the thinking we could help facilitate in our young people, if only we worked to bring critical media literacy and participatory literacy strategies into the classroom on a regular basis.

Critical Media Literacy and Participatory Literacy in the Classroom: Strategies for the Classroom

When viewing education through the lens of critical media literacy, there are six important conceptual understandings that anchor the work. Jeff Share, Douglas Kellner and Steven Funk (2016) collaborated on a framework that outlines what critical media literacy involves, its conceptual understandings, and the types of questions that can and should be answered as a means to address these concepts. This framework explains that in order for students to be educated in the field of critical media literacy, they must have understandings of social constructivism, language, audience and positionality, politics of representation, production, and finally, social and environmental issues. These concepts can be explored with students by asking questions such as: Who are the people who helped make this text? How was this text constructed and delivered? How could this text be understood differently? What values or points of view might be missing from this text? Why was this text created? And whom does this text advantage or disadvantage? We would argue that these types of questions and interactions with all forms of media can be implemented in classrooms that house students of all ages.

When thinking about participatory literacy practices for P-12 students, the practices involved in critical media literacy can act as a springboard for a seemingly endless number of activities. Once students have been instructed in what critical media literacy is, why this approach to media and texts is important and how having these critical thinking/viewing skills is imperative to their ability to become a well-informed member of a critical democracy, the types of classroom activities that can follow (and still fall in line with standards and curriculum expectations) are endless. For example, in math, students can go online and view statistics as they relate to homelessness, joblessness, how the government spends their money, and how schools are funded. They can work to find the same statistics on different sites and try to make sense of why they are not presented in the same way. In social studies, they can deconstruct the telling of history through a variety of textbooks and work to question why not all presentations are the same. After this, they can create their own text that explains a historical event from a different point of view. Science is another class that lends itself well to critical media literacy skills. One example would be to look at the ways in which issues of climate change are reported. What do the headlines say? Who wrote them? How does one article or multi-media presentation juxtapose with another? Why do you think this is? After examining multiple sources and thinking about these questions, students could then create their own visual or video presentation in regards to climate change, backed by evidence and centering their own voices.

Finally, English language arts is an obvious choice when thinking about participatory literacy practices. Because a big part of critical media literacy is centered on creation of new media, students can interact with classic texts and then work to disrupt them and provide a new retelling. Students can also use digital formats to discover new versions of classic stories and then work to merge the old and the new as an educative tool for younger peers. Deconstructing advertisements is another creative participatory literacy strategy that can easily be implemented into the English language arts classroom. Students can examine popular advertisements to look at the mechanisms employed by marketers. They can also view advertisements without sound to see if they are even able to determine what the commercial is trying to sell. These are just a few examples from core subjects in P-12 settings, but all examples are realistic, relevant, and will meet the demands of standards and curriculum, all while educating students in the area of critical media literacy.

Even though educational standards must be an area of focus in today's standardized-test driven society, these do not need to act as a negative force when it comes to scaring teachers away from participatory literacy strategies in their classrooms. NAMLE, the National Association for Media Literacy Education, has a fantastic resource that documents the ways in which the goals of media literacy education can work to support the Common Core State Standards (namle.net). This document provides five clear connections for educators, along with discussion questions to help guide the work in the classroom. While we argue that this work still falls short of truly engaging in *critical* media literacy practices, it is a solid starting point and a helpful tool for educators. In addition to the work of NAMLE, The Global Critical Media Literacy Project (gcml.org), which is supported by ACME, Project Censored, and Sacred Heart University, hosts an incredible website that takes the work of critical media literacy and makes it tangible for classroom teachers. This work has been created and curated by classroom teachers and the website even shares work samples. For educators struggling with how to implement these practices in their classrooms without having it feel overwhelming, this website can be hugely beneficial.

Critical media literacy and participatory literacy practices do not need to feel like an 'add-on' in the classroom, nor do they need to be a scary prospect for teachers, or one that pushes against state standards. There are a growing number of helpful resources available that help illustrate how this work can be done, as well as frameworks available that help guide how to structure these approaches, what types of questions should be guiding the work, and how this relates to the experiences and knowledge of students in all grade levels.

CONCLUSION

As aforementioned, popular culture and media influence are factors that are ever-present in American society and youth culture. Youth are engaging with media in ways that were never before possible and at higher frequencies (Marshall & Sensoy, 2016), which is exactly why practices of critical media literacy and participatory literacy need to be implemented in every classroom. This study, like other emerging research queries on topics of media influence and youth, only begins to investigate and question the effects of media within our 21st century context, more specifically the ways in which media acts as a vehicle to perpetuate negative or stereotypical messages and ideologies. By analyzing the participants' comments throughout the interview process and through the lens of social cognitive theory, we posit that media influence is a palpable factor within our society and believe that there is a need, especially at the school level, for more work to be done to provide youth with the tools necessary to mediate hegemonic ideas and notions that are presented throughout popular media.

Because of the pervasiveness of these ideas and images, the educational community at large cannot ignore the need to equip youth with the skills necessary to question, challenge, and critique popular culture. Schools and classroom teachers particularly find themselves situated in an important position to facilitate many of these skills. Explicit instruction in areas like critical media literacy is vital to the development of critical thinkers and socially responsible members of society. Critical media literacy "expands the notion of literacy to include different forms of mass communication and popular culture as well as deepens the potential of education to critically analyze relationships between media and audiences, information and power" (Kellner & Share, 2007, p. 4). Scholars like Douglas Keller describe this teaching as critical inquiry "that addresses issues of class, race, gender, sexuality, and power and also promotes the production of alternative counterhegemonic media" (Kellner & Share, 2007, p. 62). Kellner's frequent co-author, Jeff Share, has done amazing work with both pre-service teachers and practicing teachers in the area of critical media literacy, working to ensure that they enter their classrooms with the ability to educate their students in the area of critical media literacy. This type of work is hugely important, yet we continue to see a lack of critical media literacy curriculum in schools in the United States.

Through the exploration of topics like critical media literacy, schools and teachers can help to be change agents in the lives of youth who have been or are currently marginalized by stereotypical images. In education, we often say that we need to meet our students where they are. The truth that can longer be ignored is that today's youth are deeply embedded in all forms of texts, technology, and media, with reality television still holding strong as one choice of entertainment. If we are truly to meet our students where they are and help them to not only resist stereotypical imagery but also develop strong critical questioning skills, we must understand the ways in which media imagery impacts young people and then work with them to push back against these impacts.

REFERENCES

Bandura, A. (1986). *Social foundations of thought and action: A social cognitive theory*. Englewood Cliffs, NJ: Prentice-Hall.

Bandura, A. (1994). Social cognitive theory of mass communication. *Media Psychology*, *3*(3), 265–299. doi:10.1207/S1532785XMEP0303_03

Bandura, A. (2001). Social cognitive theory: An agentic perspective. *Annual Review of Clinical Psychology*, *52*(1), 1–26. doi:10.1146/annurev.psych.52.1.1 PMID:11148297

Bushman, B. J., & Huesmann, L. R. (2006). Short-term and Long-term Effects of Violent Media on Aggression in Children and Adults. *Archives of Pediatrics & Adolescent Medicine*, *160*(4), 348. doi:10.1001/archpedi.160.4.348 PMID:16585478

Carspecken, F. P. (2013). *Critical Ethnography in Educational Research*. Abingdon, UK: Routledge.

Crick, N. R., & Dodge, K. A. (1994). A review and reformulation of social information- processing mechanisms in children's social adjustment. *Psychological Bulletin*, *115*(1), 74–101. doi:10.1037/0033-2909.115.1.74

Fiske, S. T. (2017). *Social cognition*. Reading, MA: Sage Publications.

Galanis, P. (2013, June 16). The mother of all 'Housewives'. *New York Times*. Retrieved from http://www.nytimes.com/2013/06/16/fashion/the-mother-of-all-housewives.html

Grabe, S., Ward, L. M., & Hyde, J. S. (2008). The role of the media in body image concerns among women: A meta-analysis of experimental and correlational studies. *Psychological Bulletin*, *134*(3), 460–476. doi:10.1037/0033-2909.134.3.460 PMID:18444705

Josephson, W. L., & Proulx, J. B. (2008). Violence in Young Adolescents' Relationships: A Path Model. *Journal of Interpersonal Violence*, *23*(2), 189–208. doi:10.1177/0886260507309340 PMID:18162636

Kellner, D., & Share, J. (2005). Toward critical media literacy: Core concepts, debates, organizations and policy. In Discourse: Studies in the cultural politics of education (Vol. 26, No. 3, pp. 369–386). The University of Queensland, Australia: Routledge.

Kellner, D., & Share, J. (2007). Critical media literacy is not an option. *Learning Inquiry*, *1*(1), 59–69. doi:10.100711519-007-0004-2

Kellner, D., & Share, J. (2009). Critical media literacy, democracy, and the reconstruction of education. In D. Macedo & S. Steinberg (Eds.), *Media literacy: A reader*. New York: Peter Lang.

Lenhart, A. (2015, April 9). *Teens, social media & technology overview 2015*. Pew Research Center. Retrieved from http://www.pewinternet.org/2015/04/09/teens-social-media- technology-2015/

Marshall, E., & Sensoy, Ö. (2016). *Rethinking popular culture and media*. Milwaukee, WI: Rethinking Schools.

McCarthy, A. (2009). "Stanley Milgram, Allen Funt and Me": Postwar social science and the "first wave" of reality TV. In S. Murray & L. Ouellette (Eds.), *Reality TV: Remaking television culture*. New York: New York University Press.

Merriam-Webster's collegiate dictionary. (2003). (11th ed.). Springfield, MA: Merriam-Webster Incorporated.

Murray, S., & Ouellette, L. (Eds.). (2009). *Reality TV: Remaking television culture*. New York, NY: New York University Press.

National association for media literacy education. (n.d.). Retrieved from https://namle.net/

Nielsen. (2005). *Nielsen 2005 Report on Television*. New York: Nielsen Media Research.

Nielsen. (2011, September 21). *10 years of primetime: The rise of reality and sports programming.* Retrieved from http://www.nielsen.com/us/en/insights/news/2011/10- years-of-primetime-the-rise-of-reality-and-sports-programming.html

Ocasio, A. (2014, December 18). Reality TV by the numbers. *ScreenRant.* Retrieved from http://screen-rant.com/reality-tv-statistics-infographic-aco-149257/

Ouellette, L. (2010). Reality TV gives back: On the civic functions of reality entertainment. *The Journal of Popular Film and Television, 38*(2), 67–72. doi:10.1080/01956051.2010.483347

Pew Research Center. (2012). *Teens fact sheet.* Retrieved from http://www.pewinternet.org/fact- sheets/teens-fact-sheet/

Pozner, J. (2010). *Reality bites back: The troubling truth about guilty pleasure TV.* Berkeley, CA: Seal Press.

Share, J., Funk, S., & Kellner, D. (2016, Nov 5). *Critical media literacy framework.* Retrieved from https://www.academia.edu/29786076/Critical_Media_Literacy_Framework_updated_No v._5_2016_

The Common Sense Census: Media Use by Tweens and Teens. (2015). Retrieved December 1, 2018, from https://www.commonsensemedia.org/sites/default/files/uploads/research/census_research report.pdf

The global critical media literacy project. (n.d.). Retrieved from gcml.org

KEY TERMS AND DEFINITIONS

Critical Media Literacy: An approach to literacy instruction that not only examines a variety of texts (including digital texts) but also encourages students to question issues of power, voice, representation, and equity.

Hegemony: Ideas commonly accepted as truth, with very little question or critique.

Pedagogy: Something that serves as the function of a teacher or the work of teaching.

Reality Television: Popular programming on network and cable television that purports to present the real lives of people in an unscripted way.

Social Cognitive Theory: A research lens used to explain the effects that different forms of imagery have on the perceptions of individuals. According to this theory, individuals create cognitive symbols and meaning from images situated in environmental events.

APPENDIX

Interview Protocol

Protocol for Individual Interviews

1. Can you tell me your full name and how old you are?
2. How would you describe your family background?
3. How would you describe how much time you spend watching television?
4. What are your favorite types of shows to watch?
5. Why do you watch those particular shows?
6. What do you enjoy the most about the shows that you watch? The least?
7. Do you feel like you relate to any of the shows that you watch?
8. Out of your favorite shows, are there any particular characters that you identity with? Why or why not?
9. Do you watch reality television shows?
10. What do you think of those shows?
11. How would you describe the characters on reality television?
12. Do you feel that people on reality television are portraying their real lives? Why or why not?
13. Has there ever been a television show that you watched that changed your perspective or point of view on someone or something?
14. Do your friends watch the same types of television shows that you do? If not, what do they like to watch?
15. Do you talk much with your friends about the shows that you watch?
16. Do you feel that you and your friends have anything in common with the shows that you watch? What about the characters on the shows?
17. We've talked a lot in the past about popular culture and how it affects teenagers. What are your thoughts on that? Specifically, how reality television affects teenagers?
18. Do you have any final comments that you would like to add?

Protocol for Focus Groups

1. Can you each start by telling everyone your name and age?
2. Can you start by describing why you think we are here?
3. How would you describe how much time you spend watching television?
4. What are your favorite types of shows to watch?
5. Why do you watch those particular shows?
6. What do you enjoy the most about the shows that you watch? The least?
7. Do you feel like you relate to any of the shows that you watch?
8. Out of your favorite shows, are there any particular characters that you identity with? Why or why not?
9. Do you watch reality television shows?

10. What do you think of those shows?
11. How would you describe the characters on reality television?
12. Do you feel that people on reality television are portraying their real lives? Why or why not?
13. Has there ever been a television show that you watched that changed your perspective or point of view on someone or something?
14. Do your friends watch the same types of television shows that you do? If not, what do they like to watch?
15. Do you talk much with your friends about the shows that you watch?
16. Do you feel that you and your friends have anything in common with the shows that you watch? What about the characters on the shows?
17. We've talked a lot in the past about popular culture and how it affects teenagers. What are your thoughts on that? Specifically, how reality television affects teenagers?
18. Do you have any final comments that you would like to add?

Section 2

Participatory Literacy Practices in Community Contexts

Chapter 5
Place-Based Learning and Participatory Literacies:
Building Multimodal Narratives for Change

Sharon Peck
State University of New York at Geneseo, USA

Tracy A. Cretelle
University of Rochester, USA

ABSTRACT

Participatory literacies are central to developing instruction that makes curriculum real, relevant, and alive to students. This chapter focuses on how to integrate participatory practices and place-based narratives into instruction in order to engage students in reading, writing, and taking action in their school communities. The chapter looks at ways that teachers have incorporated multimodal narratives and multiliteracies to engage students in both using and producing products through written, oral, and digital modes. Guided by theoretical views of participatory literacies, place, community-based pedagogies, and multimodal narratives, the chapter explores ways to engage students in creating multimodal content to represent their learning as well as take action within the school and wider community.

INTRODUCTION

Our students' voices matter. Their voices matter in our schools, our communities, and beyond. As teachers, we want our students to discover their own voices. We want them to know the power of their voices. We want them to know the power of others' voices, and we want them to know the power of their collective voices. Most important, we want to help them discover how their voices might impact our world and to be empowered to use their voices to speak out for equity and justice. (NCTE, 2018)

In an age of accountability and assessment, how can teachers and students engage in authentic experiences that not only validate individual experiences but also amplify their voices to be powerful agents of change? Steeped in a tradition of multiliteracies and experiential learning, we present strategies for

DOI: 10.4018/978-1-7998-0000-2.ch005

teachers to frame curriculum as real, relevant, and alive to students (Wohlwend, 2017). This chapter focuses on how to integrate participatory practices with place-based pedagogy in order to engage students in reading, writing, and taking action in their school communities. This work is guided by theoretical views of place and community-based pedagogies, participatory literacies, and multimodal narratives, but structured in a manner that is easy to implement such as, place-based writing, storytelling, wikis, and VR platforms. These formats can support student understanding of community, and transform acts of reading and writing into powerful modes of communication and invitations for community involvement and change. Most importantly, this work demonstrates ways to empower learners as agents of change.

Many school structures make it difficult for educators to utilize curriculum based on participatory practices. At times it would seem that current educational practices have students preparing for some arbitrary future instead of applying it to the life they currently live. However, in order for learning to stick, a student must be engaged in the material in the classroom and be able to find connections between that material and his/her world.

Based on the experiences of urban teachers immersed in creating participatory place-based pedagogy, we present ways to engage students in creating multimodal content to represent their learning and engage in social action within the school and wider community.

THEORETICAL PERSPECTIVES

Bringing together place-based instruction, participatory literacies, and multimodal narratives provide a powerful space for students to authentically act on their literate knowledge within curriculum which is relevant and directly connected to their lives. When teachers incorporate local connections into their curriculum, "...students find more interest, because it's not something that happened a long time ago or far away or in a theoretical sense. But it's happening… [it] has relevance to the environment today" (Mills, 2016, p.48).

PLACE-BASED PEDAGOGY

This work is informed by place and community-based pedagogy which holds the potential to transform the space and place of learning, through intersections of place, community, and local knowledge (Sobol & Smith, 2015, Cresswell 2004). Focusing curriculum within school communities provides a means for students to become more deeply connected to the community, and to find and strengthen their own voices. Place-based instruction is characterized by four tenets (Smith, & Sobel, 2014):

1. Teachers act as co-learners and brokers of community resources,
2. local phenomena guide curriculum,
3. students act as creators of knowledge rather than consumers,
4. students' questions, concerns, engagement, and agency become central to the curriculum.

The impact can be observed as co-ownership of curriculum and learning activities that strive to bring down the walls between school and community. This leads students to become invested in curricular goals, and boundaries between their school lives and home lives begin to disappear (Demarest, 2017). This is especially pronounced when making connections includes bringing community members from outside of school into the classroom. Content, including knowledge gained experientially as part of one's home economy, education, literacies, culture, and religion, becomes relevant to students. This work honors the individual identities of all the students as they collaborate together to explore their school community.

For example, students might be engaged in inquiry that initiates exploration of a variety of places within the community. Collecting photos and artifacts along with accompanying historical information that provides context for its inclusion in the exploration leads the student back to the classroom in order to create a representation of their learning. Students' relation to place is foundational to place-based education because the process establishes students' personal and community identity as each member discovers commonalities that they share. This builds student interest and investment in the curriculum. Exploration as a community of learners develops both shared and individual interests as they co-construct foundational knowledge and work on culminating projects together (Rogoff, 2008).

Taking on this place-based stance can provide experiences for teachers to re-see the resources within their school communities and use local phenomena to guide curriculum. It also requires teachers to shift from teaching a set curriculum to engaging students in co-creating knowledge together. In this way, student questions, concerns, engagement, and agency become central to the curriculum. The role of the teacher shifts, from the purveyor of knowledge to co-learner and broker of community resources. When the connection between school and communities are strengthened, students are engaged in the community and the community within the classroom (Demarest, 2017).

When students and teachers become re-acquainted with the resources in their own school communities and bring this inquiry into the curriculum, the focus shifts from enacting curriculum to co-creating knowledge together. As teacher and students share in the learning, the excitement of weaving experiences together to create a shared narrative creates a community bond that celebrates community assets as opposed to its deficits or weaknesses for all those within the group (Ghiso & Low, 2013; Gillespie, 2010; Knobel & Lankshear, 2014; Peck, 2015; Rogoff, 1994). As a result, students begin to re-see both the school and neighborhood communities. Most importantly, students can see alternate ways to position themselves within their community, their school and their future (Demarest, 2017).

PARTICIPATORY LITERACY

Place-based instruction is strengthened through participatory practices. Participatory literacy is often defined as ways of interpreting, making, sharing, and belonging in increasingly globally and digitally mediated cultures across multiple media platforms (Wohlwend, 2017). Through creating multimodal narratives students are able to embody, own, and transform curriculum in order to make it relevant to their own interests (Jewett, 2008). This work is especially fitting for urban settings which have higher populations of diverse students and English Language Learners, who often feel marginalized by the curriculum (Ghiso & Low, 2013; Gillespie, 2010; Mills, 2016; Peck, 2015).

Conventional literacies, the basics of literacy--reading, writing, speaking and listening--all skills one needs in order to engage in participatory literacies. They support foundational skills required for independent learning, exploring individual interests, and for thinking more deeply about the subject matter at hand. Developing proficiency in conventional literacies support one's growing understanding of the nuances of language, semiotics associated with tone of voice and messages embedded in all forms of language, and is also necessary when reading books with complex characters, detailed settings, and twisty plots (Knobel & Lankshear, 2014).

Instruction of conventional literacy skills is often designed to support individual achievement and requires individual assessment, however participatory practices can support similar goals through high-interest learning activities that require collaboration with fellow students. Collaborative and participatory learning activities facilitate learning that sticks. One example of this is Google classroom or Google docs. This technology allows for the co-creation of almost anything, and even primary level students can participate in writing in Google docs with a peer. Students become energized and inspired by one another's ideas and before they know it, they've written a lengthy, imaginative story that they can't wait to share with their peers (Bruns, 2008).

Participatory learning practices promote a sense of belonging through identity formation (Caraballo, 2018). This is a result of teachers who are able to tap into the students' feelings of pride and competence as part of the buy-in of learning in the context of relevance and purpose. As students invest more and more of their emotions, time and effort, they self-direct their inquiries while creating their mark. Demarest (2017) suggests that "Involvement in the community offers young people a chance to test themselves in new roles… creating for themselves a vision of a personal future (p.14)."

MULTIMODALITY

Pahl and Roswell (2010) put forth a theory of artifactual literacies which links literacy, multimodality and the material together by recognizing the role of artifacts in the narratives of students' lives and inviting those into the classroom. Using artifacts in the literacy curriculum creates opportunities for students to bring their home cultures into school. As students share personal stories through artifacts, they and their teachers connect, share, see, and learn to value each other. It can also lead to understanding alternative perspectives, awareness of systems of belief, and questioning assumptions and biases (Dejaynes, 2018). It can be very empowering for teachers to see the ways in which students become motivated by the possibilities, begin to see their own place within the community, and most importantly, see the impact of their voices.

"Multimodality can afford, not just a new way to make meaning, but a different kind of meaning" (Cope & Kalantis, 2009, p. 166). Enacting participatory literacies fit well with the purposes of place-based instruction; and supporting students in creating multimodal products opens up possibilities for sharing knowledge beyond the classroom.

A student who wants to review multiple books from the same author can read, capture quotes from favorite parts of the text, use digital Post-its to insert their personal responses and solicit their friends' reactions by sharing through a texting app, creating a Powerpoint presentation, even by creating a video-clip to discuss features of the author's work that they find interesting. Throughout the process, the student is moving through a cycle of reading, processing, writing, responding and producing new texts that are the products of transformed knowledge. One's ability to use each of these digital tools constitutes aptitude or progress toward having mastered a particular literacy associated with the production value of the digital tool.

Engaging students in creating multimodal narratives of their learning gives students experiences with 21st-century literacies (Morrell, 2012). To be successful students must be able to read and create a range of paper-based and online texts (newspapers, pamphlets, websites, books, Kindle, and so on), participate in and create virtual settings (classrooms, Second Life, Facebook, Elluminate, blogs, wikis) that use interactive and dynamic Web 2.0 tools, and critically analyze multimodal texts that integrate visual, musical, dramatic, digital, and new literacies to meet standards (Hutchison, & Colwell, 2014, Beach, & O'Brien, 2014; Beach, Hull, & O'Brien, 2011). These virtual platforms and online experiences provide ways to collaborate and better come to know and understand one's place in the community. Integration of multimodal literacies encourages us to re-conceptualize and re-envision what constitutes literacy (Leu, Kinzer, Coiro, Castek, & Henry, 2017; Hutchison,& Colwell, 2014; Caraballo, 2018).

Multimodal literacies have the potential to represent varied narratives, thus broadening the knowledge valued in schools and nurturing mutual edification in increasingly diverse classrooms (Ghiso & Low, 2013). So, to include the narratives and identities of more of our students in the classroom, we need to understand, expand and take seriously the modes and genres through which they may choose to make sense of and communicate their experiences. It is important that we encourage such exploration and creation with narrative modes and genres far beyond the early years when stories that bend time and space and explore magical ways of knowing are much more readily accepted. It is "in the process of 'doing' literacy [that] students learn 'what counts as literacy'" (Unsworth, 2001, p. 246).

Ultimately, the power of integrating place-based pedagogy, participatory literacies and multimodality open up many ways to engage students and teachers to co-create curriculum and to take action within their school community. Sobel (2005) argues that place-based education increases student achievement and " ...helps students develop stronger ties to their community, enhances appreciation for the natural world, and creates a heightened commitment to serving as active contributing citizens" (p.7).

Engaging students in an inquiry about place provides connection and purpose as students investigate their own school community. During exploration, sharing the work, teaching each other about our skills and interests outside of school, encourages student engagement and agency. Along the way, opportunities to partner with local landmarks, businesses, educational programs, and families brings the community into the classroom. And using digital modes can be a very effective way for students to create products demonstrating their findings, and to take action in the wider community.

DESIGNING RELEVANT CURRICULUM

So how does one design relevant curriculum? The origins of our work began with a partnership offering ongoing professional development program offered to teachers in a large urban district serving diverse students of poverty. Throughout a six-year professional development collegial circle, teachers chose to study both literacy pedagogies and to investigate the literacies and funds of knowledge evident in their school communities (Moll, 2014). The focus stemmed from two guiding questions: How do we best support urban students to become independent readers and writers? And how do we make learning relevant and related to our students? Most teachers felt that an obstruction or barrier to student learning was a lack of background knowledge and vocabulary. Rather than a deficit view, teachers moved to a social justice perspective and use an exploration of racism and poverty as a starting point for teachers to notice and question their own perceptions of urban students' lives.

Over the course of six years, teachers explored the neighborhoods and surrounding communities of their students. Part of the exploration involved taking a critical look at themselves as they analyzed their biases and stereotypes in order to promote a positive view of students and their families. In addition to developing culturally responsive, participatory teaching practices, teachers wanted to improve relationships with all students, parents and community members. Through exploration and participation teachers shifted from holding a deficit view to working to bring the cultural practices students engage in at home into schools. Their investigations also led them to realize the ways in which their curriculum didn't represent their student population. Teachers moved to integrate relevant texts, based not only on the representation of diverse students and ethnicities, but to represent the urban environments where their students live and study. This led them in search of the many resources available within the city limits and in the region.

They explored the following methods of place-based pedagogy and construction of multimodal narratives. They started with curriculum, then moved into integrating participatory literacies, adding more and more as they witnessed the impact on their students. Students became more engaged, were more involved in school, and were motivated to curate and share their learning in a variety of settings.

To develop a curriculum focusing on the school community, teachers worked together to explore their own identities, their own school communities, to determine resources existing within the school community that they may or may not have known about, determined the needs of the community, and the possible partners they might work with. Throughout the creation of the local curriculum, they considered ways in which student-created texts could generate change within the school and community.

They did not abandon curricular goals and state standards. Rather, they looked for the role of community within the curriculum and asked challenging questions to explore the ways in which the curriculum included relevant texts, information, and skills. What they noticed was an incongruence of the curriculum with their student population. They did not see texts and materials that represented their school community. With these outcomes and goals in mind, they began to explore the local resources, asking:

- What are the texts that are privileged in my school? Do they represent my students and school community?
- What are the types of literacy valued in my school? Does it represent the ways in which literacy is used in the community?
- What are the community norms and literacy rituals that families engage in after school?
- Explore students' understandings of the school community. Have they visited local sites? Are they aware of them?
- Look at the possibilities of cultural studies that your school community affords- be it cultural, historical, environmental, geographical, creative, collaborative or civic or a combination of all of the above.
- Consider the critical needs of the community. Do citizens have access to what they need? What are the key issues facing citizens?
- Brainstorm the possibilities- start by thinking big and then review to start at a realistic place.
- Think about ways of making connections in the community to invite into school and ways to get beyond school walls to lead students to make those connections.
- How can students take ownership of the curriculum? What could students do to support the local community? How could their investigation be shared in the community? What types of texts could students produce for school and community use?

As teachers looked at the texts that were prioritized in their curriculum they searched for relevant texts that represented, if not their own community, similar urban settings. They realized first how few texts they had access to. Then they realized that while they found many good titles, they didn't find enough. This led them to devise more projects that would result in classroom "texts."

Exploring participatory literacies led them to realize many ways for students to both showcase their learning and give back to the community at the same time. This might include developing performative texts such as podcasting, digital videos, blogging, and VR mapping. Teachers explored projects that they could use to augment the curriculum, and products that students could collaboratively create to demonstrate and share their learning in the community. Using technology to create multimodal texts made it easier to share their work within the school and beyond.

Next teachers began developing local inquiries using the following framework from Demarest (2017) as a guide:

- Personal connections are the foundation of all learning: How can I better relate school to my students' life experiences?
- Local Investigations Deepen Student Understanding: How can I help students better understand how this big idea works in the real world?
- Local Investigations Build Holistic Understandings of Places: How can I help students better understand this place?
- Local Investigations Build Opportunity for Civic Engagement: How can I help students better understand themselves and their possible futures?

After exploring the potential of participatory literacies, we would now add:

- Participatory literacies are strengthened when students create multimodal narratives. How can I engage students in producing multimodal narratives for a change?

Teachers researched, explored, visited, and interacted with their school community to devise inquiries to engage students in re-envisioning the community around them and their place in it. Some started small, integrating activities into their current curriculum, others developed full units centered around key issues and needs facing their communities. Each of them drew on multimodal literacies and strove to share work beyond classroom walls.

The next section highlights ways in which multimodal literacy can be used to present and share student learning. In particular, writing about identity and place through multimodal narratives. Students created maps of their homes, schools, and communities on paper and using online map recording tools such as My Maps and Thinglink. Teachers and students explored school neighborhoods through projects such as Neighborhood Prints and neighborhood walks. They represented learning through multimodal and digital means using the essence of poetry to help students hone in on identity and place, through I am Poems to participating in slam poetry. Other examples include creating collaborative artifacts like photographs, picture books, and alphabet books, maps and virtual reality maps, digital video, curricular investigations, wikis, digital stories, blogs, and podcasts.

IDENTITY AND COMMUNITY EXPLORATION

There are many ways to embed place-based learning, multimodal literacies, and participatory literacies into the curriculum that provide ways for students to move from performing learned reading skills to applying literacy skills in a context mediated by technology (Belshaw, 2012). Also, digitally literate students are able to make meaning as a social practice and use their literacy knowledge at a meta-level as they mediate digital technologies (Belshaw, 2012).

In addition to applying literacy skills, many literacy activities serve as a means for understanding both identity and community, including collecting artifacts, images, and texts from the students and the community. Students can explore multiple modes of sharing their learning from exploring, naming, and discussing the contents of student backpacks, neighborhood walks to identify artifacts significant in the community, and creative noticing such as the ideas offered in Keri Smith's *How to Be an Explorer of the World: Portable Life Museum (2008).* These activities foster observation and wonder and make the practice of noticing active and engaging. They also engage students in using literacy in meaningful and relevant ways as they take on the role of co-creating curriculum and sharing their learning.

Artifact Sharing

Inviting out of school artifacts into the classroom can be very informative (Pahl & Roswell, 2010) and can lead students to questions their own biases (Dejaynes, 2018). For instance, A third-grade teacher began a unit on immigration by asking students to bring in an item that represented their family. This sharing led to the identification of cultures in the community. Students became interested in finding out how so many different cultures found their way to their own community. They invited family members into the school and interviewed them about their immigration stories. They shared their learning by pairing images of culture with the immigrant's stories. Other teachers used student artifacts to inspire writing as they compared their objects to their friends'.

Neighborhood Prints

With the goal of understanding where students come from we asked teachers to engage in a neighborhood prints project, and then to enact them with their students. Students were provided with disposable cameras and used their photos to create narratives of their own community. Participants are asked to take a walk through their neighborhood with a digital camera. They should look for and take photos of:

- Something meaningful to you in your neighborhood.
- Something in your neighborhood which you are proud of.
- Something in your neighborhood which you like.
- Something in your neighborhood which you don't like.
- Your house.
- Your family.
- A neighbor.
- Something that characterizes your neighborhood.

Teachers then used their findings to reflect on how their own views of their neighborhoods contrasted or meshed with the neighborhood impressions of their students. It was interesting to explore the places and rationales for images of what they didn't like in their own neighborhood. Students used their projects to explore community needs and possible routes of action. For instance, one student was very upset by an abandoned home in his neighborhood where teens would often go to use drugs. He wrote a letter to the police department, who in turn invited him to ride around the area to note such places for the police. It led to a stronger police presence in the neighborhood, and a student who saw the value of his own observations (Peck, 2015).

Word and Image Collages

Students can delve into their own identity by creating collages of images and words that represent their homeland and home communities. These collages engage students in evaluating the imagery that represents their homelands and provides a space for students to present an authentic conception of their country, rather than a romanticized one. They can even focus just on the vocabulary of their community through Wordle (Higdon, Reyerson, McFadden & Mummey, 2011). For example, one TESOL teacher engaged her students in creating large collages using civic related concepts such as "democracy", "citizenship", and "cultural practices". The students located images of what they felt was central to their culture from magazines and resources found online. As each concept was explored, students generated accompanying texts that outlined essential elements of the concept being explored. Their academic discourse included interdisciplinary language needed to compare cultures and to document supplemental resources from multiple genres. Therefore, not only did students learn vocabulary, they developed additional layers of understanding of each concept as they leveraged functional language needed to explore the topic.

Poems and Prose

Many English teachers make use of poem frames, such as those offered by Christianson (2009) to unpack identity. "I am From Poem or I was Raised By" formats allow students space to think about their origins and what makes them unique, without being overly focused on the poetic form. One outcome of these poems is the dialogue that ensues when students note similarities and differences between their experiences and their peers. It can bring students together and provides an opportunity for empathy.

Using poetry can be a low-risk way to engage students in writing about place and identity. Poetry is short, with evocative vocabulary to portray deep meanings. It helps students connect with their senses and their emotions, making interaction with content more memorable. Engaging students in creating poems about themselves can be risky, but asking them all to do it reduces the risk, and as they share and create common understandings which strengthen feelings of belonging and community.

Asking students to consider their own identities leads to many questions. How is identity formed? How are we shaped by the place we live, our peers, our families? The bond between place and identity leads students to see place as more than geographical. Do our identities change depending on where we are? Can we be from a place that isn't a geographical location, but a community, such as family, congregation or team? The I Am poem leads students to go beyond the familiar aspects—such as ethnicity, gender, and age—to place as geographical and more, such as experiences, relationships, hopes, and interests. "Where I'm from" poems can clarify elements of identity, as well as build peer relationships to foster a cohesive, empathetic learning community.

Poems need not be limited to students, but it can be very revealing to engage parents and community members in writing poetry about place and identity. Look for poems that are emotionally charged, that include a description, provide room for reacting to or presenting content, and is easily replicable. One framework that can be particularly helpful in bringing out the key essences of place is the poem frame, 'Some people say…'. This can be a powerful way to look at stereotypes and real experiences to present both sides. For instance, the following poem was written by an urban teacher:

People say that inner-city parents are lazy and not caring.

But I witnessed loving, caring, and wet parents who walked blocks in a windy rainstorm to conference with their child's teacher.

People say that inner-city parents are selfish.

But I see parents that give up vacation days to help on a field study.

People say that inner-city parents don't value education.

But I see parents helping with homework, picking kids up after Extended Day, working on PTA, and seeing hundreds of parents crowding our halls on exhibition nights.

People say that inner-city parents are all on welfare.

But I collaborate with musicians, authors, educators, and business professionals.

Inner-city parents are like all other parents; they want the best for their children.

Part of the power of these poems is the community that is created when they are shared publicly. This may be in class at an author celebration, or with the whole class at a local coffee house, or even to be donated to local museums to be put on display. Teachers in our cohort engaged students in using poetry to explore identity and community. The poems were presented to families at a school achievement night. Even kindergarten students were able to connect with their identity through *I am From Poems.* One classroom created poems about animal welfare and protection that were then put on display at the local Zoo.

Alphabet Books

Adopting the structure of children's books can be an easy way to get more texts into the curriculum. Teachers can create books or engage students in authoring using Google slides or iBook author. Books can focus on places, artifacts, and even text found in the community. Alphabet books are most effective when each page has only one or two identifiable objects or places, objects with several names should be avoided, and the common sounds of the letters, rather than blends, digraphs, and silent letters should be used (Criscoe, 1988). While it would be ideal for students and teachers to use only photographs that they have taken, this can provide an authentic space for teaching about copyright regulations as students search for images online. It also allows for keen decision making to decide what should be included, and it requires a thoughtful inclusion of the alphabet. One teacher solved the dilemma of not having a place for the letter Y by putting a mirror on the page, stating "the most important part of this community is "Y"ou!" An added benefit of creating alphabet books to demonstrate what was learned in an inquiry is that it adds texts to the classroom and teaches visual literacy (Pantaleo, 2015).

Maps

Engaging students in creating maps of their neighborhood or school community can be an interesting way to note the meaning that students assign to places they frequent. Maps reflect our relationship to ourselves, to one another and to the environment. We each see our community differently, have different connections to place, and have a distinct way of seeing and being in the world. Mapping as a pedagogical and planning tool has the potential to conceptualize, make, and use images of place. Engaging students in creating maps, individually, and in community mapping, can help make clear the stories and geographies embedded in our views of place. Community mapping focuses on what people value and what they envision for the future (Dunsmore, Ordoñez-Jasis, & Herrera, 2013). Encouraging students and community members to create simple mental maps can be quite useful to share stories and ideas.

Teachers asked students to draw a map of their neighborhoods after reading the picture book, *Me on The Map* (Sweeney, 1996). Students tend to include the places that hold meaning for them, even if they are not in the immediate vicinity of their home. Students can map all kinds of resources in their communities, places to play, access to nature, whatever relates to their inquiry. And they can create maps of their school community to see the ways in which different constituents; students, teachers, and administrators see their own community (Gillespie, 2010).

Maps can tell stories effectively and with so many accessible apps. For instance, using *My Maps* or *Esri Story Maps* students can curate their own stories of place. *MyMaps* is a web-based free app that allows users to create and layer their own maps on top of existing maps. Users can add, edit and store information including place-markers, lines, shapes, text, photos, and video, on top of the regular Google Maps at any zoom level. Users can develop maps collaboratively and then easily share the maps by sharing a link to their creation. My Maps is also easy to learn and is applicable even in elementary classrooms (Elliot, 2009).

Through such apps students can present place, conflicts, and patterns as they develop visual literacy, cartographic and technical skills. It is easily adaptable for project-based learning tasks for a class, for groups or for individuals. Esri Story Maps allows students to use existing maps and data to their presentation.

Podcasts

Podcasts are engaging ways to encourage students in performing literacy. It takes a microphone, computer (Mac or PC), and speakers, staples in most classrooms. To create a podcast, users can go to different websites that allow them to record, publish, and even send their podcasts for free by email. Much like the "*What's in a name?*" (Bevington, 2018) podcast put out by Georgia public radio, teachers engaged students in exploring the origins of street and place names in their school community. Students reached out to local historians, explored historical maps, and learned about key players in the development of their school communities. Students then produced short podcasts to share their learning, posting the podcasts on the school website, and sharing it with local history teachers.

Blogs

Creating a blog allows students to share personal interests, write creatively, teach others a skill and use digital, multimodal methods of representing their personal preferences (Colwell & Hutchison, 2015). Participating in community writing is accessible and motivating for students to see their published work instantly while receiving real feedback and interactions from friends, families, school and sometimes the larger community.

In urban communities with high populations of culturally diverse students, blogs offer a medium to teach one another through their culture. One teacher spent a year helping her students investigate their cultures through sharing food, invitations to various cultures like dance recitals with traditional clothing and music and visiting multiple cultural organizations around the city.

Students responded positively to sharing. For instance, over the course of the year, one Nepali student and one Somali student, who had spent earlier years at odds, became friends after sharing their refugee experiences with one another. As students learned from each other, they wrote poetry, creative nonfiction, and uploaded photographs and digital recordings of their milestone events. Only invitees could edit the blog, so the blog was kept secured by teacher access only. There are many safe methods for blogging online.

Digital Storytelling

Digital video is easy to produce, and video and still images can be curated along with music and captions (Brenner, 2014). Digital storytelling asks students to become creative storytellers through the traditional processes of selecting a topic, conducting some research, writing a script, and developing an interesting story. This material is then combined with various types of multimedia, including computer-based graphics, recorded audio, computer-generated text, video clips, and music so that it can be played on a computer, uploaded on a web site, or burned to a DVD. Composing with digital video to create digital stories, requires students to examine how to produce, distribute, invent, explore, persuade, and create impact with texts written for specific audiences (Ohler, 2013).

In our cohort, teachers were asked to develop video introductions to their school communities. Teachers grappled with how to introduce their communities, what iconic places defined their communities, and which images could convey meaning effectively. They shared their outcomes with their peers and their own school communities while considering ways to make this work accessible to their students. From driving along the highways to montages of key landmarks, and interviews with locals. Some chose to narrate their videos, others chose meaningful music.

Many teachers in our cohort explored photo story applications with their students. Using digital cameras, teachers took photos of students and then compiled the stories on the applications, with students narrating the text. These "texts" were shared with family and community members. One kindergarten teacher engaged her students in a photo story called, *Can You Say Peace?* Students taught viewers to say peace in a variety of languages and drawing pictures for a collage. The unit culminated with, "Peace begins with us."

Digital Presentations

Students can share their findings with a larger community beyond school walls by creating a web space or web presentation through Slides or Prezi. They can create wiki's to present the information gleaned about the community. These wikis can be interactive and even used to gather data as students can pose questions for community members to respond to. The range of possibilities from blogs to My Maps and even VR spaces to engage students in 360-degree views of their community. Students can use Aurasma to enhance bulletin boards and static representations of their learning, making it even more enticing for viewers to engage with their findings.

Virtual Reality Apps

Using virtual reality can be very motivating for students and adds layers of meaning to representations. Teachers we worked with explored the apps Aurasma and Thinglink. In Aurasma, users can overlay any video or image on top of anything that a tablet, cell phone, or any other mobile device can scan with its camera. Using Aurasma is very much like using a QR code reader. In order to activate the overlayed image or video, the object will be scanned using the Aurasma app. So, when students aim the app at an image, it brings them to a web space, image, text or video. A student might have a photograph of a local monument, that when the Aurasma app is aimed at it, brings the user to an interview with the mayor and the sculptor of the statue. These applications can be advantageous, engaging, and also challenge students in providing multiple ways to represent place (Akcayir & Ackcayir, 2017). Thinglink is a similar platform to My Maps. Students are able to pin text, images or video on 360-degree video images. The images are very compelling for students and can be an effective way to note key aspects of a particular landmark or cultural resource. It lends itself well to having students give virtual tours of their community.

Interactive Projects

The possibilities for participatory literacies about place seem boundless. Teachers have engaged students in building little free libraries, hosting a run for health after studying childhood obesity rates, and pairing with adult literacy agencies to provide relevant curriculum and strategies for adult literacy tutoring. Students have toured local homeless shelters and raised money to support them. Some teachers engaged in creating tabletop games based on their school community and then put the games into the school library for circulation. Teachers gathered to create a collection of services available to families in the wider community. Once you pair the interests and needs of the community with your goals and the interests of your students, it becomes easier to see the possibilities for participatory literacies in your instruction.

PARTICIPATORY OUTCOMES

Standardized curriculum 'eclipses the importance of local knowledge' (Sanchez, 2011, p. 332). In fact, formal education policy discounts place and views it as a contributing factor to negative consequences for marginalized communities (Smith & Sobol, 2010). However, incorporating place-based pedagogies with participatory literacies provides new ways to see the local. Employing these methods goes beyond the dimensions of participatory literacies, to creating new spaces and new ways for students to identify and position themselves within the larger community. Some theorists find it hard to make a distinction between place-based instruction and critical literacies (Gruenwald, 2008; Comber, 2011). As students delve into creating narratives through 'their own' modes, they can decide if they want to take up the story or confront it.

Curriculum becomes local, real, meaningful and relevant. And, the purpose of education becomes clear for both students and teachers. As students engage in consuming and creating texts and collaborating in the classroom and online they are able to focus on social justice initiatives. Teachers and students become part of the process of understanding and shaping communities.

In enacting this work, teachers were surprised by the ways in which investigating the local through the eyes of their students led them to revise their understandings of their own students and their school communities. Most of the teachers did not live within the urban district, rather in surrounding suburbs. They came to have more nuanced understandings of the school community and began to see the affordances that the community holds. This shift provided agency as teachers learned more ways to support the high needs of their students, and teachers developed practices that they have continued to hone. Teachers talk about the Neighborhood Prints project as one they engage in each year. This simple practice let teachers see their students' neighborhoods from a different perspective. And it led them to collaborate with students to address the areas of concern or high needs that students identified. Teachers changed the way they think about curriculum and now welcome devising more ways to bring in participatory literacies, to partner with local resources and partners, and to ensure that curriculum is active and engaging rather than passive and static.

Teachers engaged in expeditions wherein small groups they spent a day exploring a section of the city to learn about the neighborhoods. A parent provided the tour, and they ate in parents' homes, discovered resources, libraries, and even a farm within the city. They were touched to be welcomed by parents and were eager to share their findings together. Teachers were given the task of learning about the resources available in each neighborhood. They visited the neighborhood, guided by a parent leader, and met with officials there, had lunch in a parent's home, and toured the area.

Teachers were very moved by the experience. They came together at the end of the day and created a "data wall" to share what they learned. From this, they came away with goals of wanting to improve their communication with parents, wanting to learn more about community resources, and wanting to find more ways to involve communities in their everyday instruction.

Later, teachers visited a larger homeless shelter, eating dinner with some residents there. They were surprised to hear a resident talk about the impact that teachers made on him. They also left with deeper understandings of poverty and privilege.

Teachers learned a lot about their students along the way. Teachers stopped making assumptions about student awareness of their own community and region. When playing a skinned version of the game Monopoly based on our city, students revealed that they did not know many of the key influencers of their city. They had not visited many cultural landmarks, nor realized that some of the things they use daily originated right in their city.

Teachers also learned of the myriad of local factors that impacted student and family ability to be active in the expectations of the school activities. For instance, when teachers in a school, whose students come from across the city, rather than the local neighborhood, learned that transportation was the main reason that families didn't attend conferences, they arranged for taxi services for families. These 'aha' moments led teachers to delve more deeply into the access that students had to community services, afterschool care, green space and play areas. Teachers then set to work compiling brochures and a website for families listing the services in their neighborhoods.

Exploration of possibilities and creation of a wide variety of texts pushed teachers and students to revise their understandings of their own spaces and place. Multimodal texts demonstrated how place and community-based pedagogy support student motivation and agency and builds ownership in the curriculum. "When people work together and solve problems, they generate a new vision of schools and community (Demarest, 2017, p18)." Bringing together participatory literacies, multimodal narratives and place leads students to see education as more valuable. It is this shift that teachers were most excited about. They were able to witness students taking a sincere interest in their own communities and recognizing the role they themselves had in shaping that community.

In his treatise of advice *For White People Who Teach in the Hood*, Christopher Emdin (2016), urges teachers to leave their schools and get to know their students as three-dimensional people outside the classroom. He implores teacher to get to know their communities as places that are not bereft of advantages but filled with strength and possibilities. Shedding the deficit view is empowering for teachers and students. Emdin calls for teachers to value the unique realities of minority children by incorporating their culture into classroom instruction. Place-based pedagogies do just that, and further, they often place students' culture in the center of their work.

For our urban teachers, Jensen's (2016), work on supporting students of poverty reminds us that academic success must be culturally acceptable among students, that is, socially acceptable to publicly engage in. The social nature of this collaborative work lends itself to making such learning a priority among the students. He agrees that students need to be engaged, to see the relevance of the curriculum. He urges educators to make connections to students' worlds in ways that help them see a viable reason to play the academic game.

The possibilities for making curriculum engaging and relevant to learners through place-based pedagogy and participatory literacies are unlimited. The outcomes for students, teachers, and communities center around belonging. Students find their place in their community. Teachers better understand their students and the school community. And both impact the community through participating and creating narratives of change.

FUTURE POSSIBILITIES

Engaging teachers in developing a place-based curriculum with participatory literacies is a good starting point. Further research could employ a more critical investigation of the curriculum to evaluate how students and community are represented, and how student identity and culture is treated within the curriculum and school community. Other conceptions of the impact of place on learning should be considered. Work could address Sanchez's (2011) notion of placemaking, to further explore the ways in which our experiences in a place or in a community affirm and construct our conception of place and contribute to our cultural imagination.

Future research could take up the question of keeping place-based pedagogies critical through staying grounded in thoughtful understandings of identity, community, and place. McKerny, Smith, and Down (2011) suggest the following questions to take on a more critical stance:

- What are the best features of our community? What could be done to make it a better place for all?

- What do monuments and public architecture tell us about the heritage that is most highly valued in this community? What groups are under-represented or rendered invisible?
- What might we do to ensure a more inclusive and accurate record of community heritage in our school and community?
- What is the quality of our local environment – the air, water, soil, native flora and fauna? What might we do to conserve our environment and resources to achieve a more sustainable future?
- To what extent does our school model as well as promote good environmental practices?
- What are the social, economic and cultural assets of our community? How fairly are they distributed? What can we do to work for a more just community?
- Who gets to make the decisions in our community? Whose voices are largely unheard? What might we do to achieve a more democratic society?

Teachers we met with were delving into this work with students who were taking their energy to the streets to bring about change in their own communities. Students have the potential to bring key ideas to light and to challenge the dominant narratives in ways that others may not.

New technologies are emerging daily which have the potential to transform the curriculum. These technologies can change the way students see, act within, and represent their understandings of place. Teachers are increasingly asking students to become producers of knowledge rather than consumers (Bruns, 2008). Students are more engaged in designing, creating and presenting their learning through new technologies. The possibilities for engaging in participatory literacies to transform are also growing. As teens continue to become activists and make use of social media, they pave the way for students to see the value of their voices.

CONCLUSION

It can be challenging for educators to design instruction that facilitates collaborative learning activities based on curricular standards using a pre-packaged curriculum, but it's not impossible. Using participatory literacies as a means of motivating students to take ownership of learning in school, the community and online with place-based pedagogy and culturally relevant instruction allow educators to bring agency and engagement into the classroom.

For teachers, the act of drawing on the local to design curriculum has affected their practice and helped to generate a sense of efficacy, inspiring confidence and a renewed commitment to teaching. This confidence to share the power of creating knowledge with their students led teachers to be open to students' ideas and suggestions for ways to share their learning, and ways to make the curriculum more relevant to student interests. By offering choices, welcoming cultural knowledge and online formats for sharing, teachers learned to tap into students' motivation. It is this transformation of curriculum, of the role of teacher, of the agency of the student, that makes this work so rich.

REFERENCES

Akçayır, M., & Akçayır, G. (2017). Advantages and challenges associated with augmented reality for education: A systematic review of the literature. *Educational Research Review*, *20*, 1–11. doi:10.1016/j.edurev.2016.11.002

Beach, R., Hull, G., & O'Brien, D. (2011). Transforming English language arts in a Web 2.0 world. Handbook of research on teaching the English language arts.

Beach, R., & O'Brien, D. (2014). *Using apps for learning across the curriculum: A literacy-based framework and guide*. Routledge. doi:10.4324/9781315769127

Belshaw, D. (2012, July 12). On the important differences between literacies, skills and competencies [Web log post]. Retrieved from http://www.dougbelshaw.com/blog/2012/07/12/on-the-importantdifferences-between-literacies-skills-and-competencies/

Bevington, R. (Producer) (2018). *What's in a name?* [audio podcast]. Retrieved from https://www.npr.org/podcasts/

Brenner, K. (2014). Digital Stories: A 21st-Century Communication Tool for the English Language Classroom. In *English Teaching Forum* (Vol. 52, No. 1, pp. 22-29). US Department of State. Bureau of Educational and Cultural Affairs, Office of English Language Programs.

Bruns, A. (2008). *Blogs, Wikipedia, second life, and beyond: From production to produsage*. New York: Lang.

Caraballo, L. (2018). Multiple literacies as culturally sustaining pedagogy in English language arts. In *An Authentic English Language Arts Curriculum* (pp. 172–199). Routledge. doi:10.4324/9781351167161-6

Coiro, J., Knobel, M., Lankshear, C., & Leu, D. J. (Eds.). (2014). *Handbook of research on new literacies*. Routledge. doi:10.4324/9781410618894

Colwell, J., & Hutchison, A. C. (2015). Supporting teachers in integrating digital technology into language arts instruction to promote literacy. *Journal of Digital Learning in Teacher Education*, *31*(2), 56–63. doi:10.1080/21532974.2014.991813

Comber, B. (2011). Making space for place-making pedagogies: Stretching normative mandated literacy curriculum. *Contemporary Issues in Early Childhood*, *12*(4), 343–348. doi:10.2304/ciec.2011.12.4.343

Cope, B., & Kalantzis, M. (2009). "Multiliteracies": New literacies, new learning. *Pedagogies*, *4*(3), 164–195. doi:10.1080/15544800903076044

Cresswell, T. (2004). *Place: A short introduction*. Oxford, UK: Blackwell Publishing.

Criscoe, B. L. (1988). A pleasant reminder: There is an established criteria for writing alphabet books. *Reading Horizons*, *28*(4), 2.

Dejaynes, T. (2018). "What makes me who I am?": Using artifacts as cosmopolitan invitations. *English Journal*, *108*(2), 48–54. Retrieved from https://proxy.geneseo.edu/login?url=https://proxy.geneseo.edu:5742/docview/2155618863?accountid=11072

Demarest, A. B. (2014). *Place-based curriculum design: Exceeding standards through local investigations*. Routledge. doi:10.4324/9781315795195

Doering, A., Beach, R., & O'Brien, D. (2007). Infusing multimodal tools and digital literacies into an English education program. *English Education*, *40*(1), 41–60.

Dunsmore, K., Ordoñez-Jasis, R., & Herrera, G. (2013). Welcoming their worlds: Rethinking literacy instruction through community mapping. *Language Arts*, *90*(5), 327–338.

Elliot, R. (2009). Using Google my maps for classroom projects. *TESL-EJ*, *12*(4), 1–14.

Emdin, C. (2016). *For White folks who teach in the hood... and the rest of y'all too: Reality pedagogy and urban education*. Beacon Press.

Esri Story Maps - Harness the Power of Maps to Tell Your Story. (n.d.). Retrieved October 25, 2018, from https://storymaps.arcgis.com/en/

Gee, J. P. (2017). Identity and diversity in today's world. *Multicultural Education Review*, *9*(2), 83–92. doi:10.1080/2005615X.2017.1312216

Ghiso, M. P., & Low, D. E. (2013). Students using multimodal literacies to surface micro-narratives of United States immigration. *Literacy*, *47*(1), 26–34. doi:10.1111/j.1741-4369.2012.00678.x

Gillespie, C. A. (2010). How Culture Constructs our Sense of Neighborhood: Mental Maps and Children's Perceptions of Place. *The Journal of Geography*, *109*(1), 18–29. doi:10.1080/00221340903459447

Google. (n.d.). Google MyMaps mapping application. Retrieved from https://www.google.com/maps/about/mymaps/

Gruenewald, D. A. (2008). The best of both worlds: A critical pedagogy of place. *Environmental Education Research*, *14*(3), 308-324.

Higdon, J., Reyerson, K., McFadden, C., & Mummey, K. (2011). Twitter, Wordle, and ChimeIn as student response pedagogies. *EDUCAUSE Quarterly*, *34*(1).

HP. (n.d.). *Aurasma App now called HP Reveal*. Retrieved from https://www.aurasma.com/

Hutchison, A. C., & Colwell, J. (2014). The potential of digital technologies to support literacy instruction relevant to the common core state standards. *Journal of Adolescent & Adult Literacy*, *58*(2), 147–156. doi:10.1002/jaal.335

Jensen, E. (2009). *Teaching with poverty in mind: What being poor does to kids' brains and what schools can do about it*. ASCD.

Jewett, C. (2008). Multimodality and Literacy in School Classrooms. *Review of Research in Education*, *32*(1), 241–267. doi:10.3102/0091732X07310586

Knobel, M., & Lankshear, C. (2014). Studying new literacies. *Journal of Adolescent & Adult Literacy*, *58*(2), 97–101. doi:10.1002/jaal.314

Leu, D. J., Kinzer, C. K., Coiro, J., Castek, J., & Henry, L. A. (2017). New literacies: A dual-level theory of the changing nature of literacy, instruction, and assessment. *Journal of Education*, *197*(2), 1–18. doi:10.1177/002205741719700202

McInerney, P., Smyth, J., & Down, B. (2011). 'Coming to a place near you? 'The politics and possibilities of a critical pedagogy of place-based education. *Asia-Pacific Journal of Teacher Education*, *39*(1), 3–16. doi:10.1080/1359866X.2010.540894

Miller, S. M. (2007). English teacher learning for new times: Digital video composing as multimodal literacy practice. *English Education*, *40*(1), 61–83.

Mills, K. A. (2015). *Literacy theories for the digital age: Social, critical, multimodal, spatial, material and sensory lenses*. Multilingual Matters. doi:10.21832/9781783094639

Moll, L. (2014). *L.S.Vygotsky and education*. New York: Routledge.

Morrell, E. (2012). 21st-century literacies, critical media pedagogies, and language arts. *The Reading Teacher*, *66*(4), 300–302. doi:10.1002/TRTR.01125

National Council of Teachers of English. (2018). *Conference Proceedings, Raising Student Voice: 2018 NCTE Annual Convention*. Houston, TX: NCTE.

Ohler, J. B. (2013). *Digital storytelling in the classroom: New media pathways to literacy, learning, and creativity*. Corwin Press. doi:10.4135/9781452277479

Pantaleo, S. (2015). Language, Literacy and Visual Texts. *English in Education*, *49*(2), 113–129. doi:10.1111/eie.12053

Peck, S. M. (2015). Extending school communities through university–school partnerships. In University Partnerships for Community and School System Development (Innovations in Higher Education Teaching and Learning, Volume 5). Emerald Group Publishing Limited.

Rogoff, B. (1994). Developing understanding of the idea of communities of learners. *Mind, Culture, and Activity*, *1*(4), 209–229.

Rogoff, B. (2008). Observing sociocultural activity on three planes: Participatory appropriation, guided participation, and apprenticeship. *Pedagogy and practice: Culture and identities*, 58-74.

Sánchez, L. (2011). Building on young children's cultural histories through placemaking in the classroom. *Contemporary Issues in Early Childhood*, *12*(4), 332–342. doi:10.2304/ciec.2011.12.4.332

Shulsky, D. D., Baker, S. F., Chvala, T., & Willis, J. M. (2017). Cultivating layered literacies: Developing the global child to become tomorrow's global citizen. *International Journal of Development Education and Global Learning*, *9*(1), 49–63. doi:10.18546/IJDEGL.9.1.05

Smith, G. A., & Sobel, D. (2014). *Place-and community-based education in schools*. Routledge. doi:10.4324/9780203858530

Smith, K. (2008). *How to be an explorer of the world: portable life museum*. Penguin.

Thinglink. (n.d.). *Thinglink App*. Retrieved from https://www.thinglink.com/

Unsworth, L. (2001). *Teaching multiliteracies across the curriculum*. Buckingham, UK: Open University Press.

Windschitl, M. (2002). Framing constructivism in practice as the negotiation of dilemmas: An analysis of the conceptual, pedagogical, cultural, and political challenges facing teachers. *Review of Educational Research*, *72*(2), 131–175. doi:10.3102/00346543072002131

Wohlwend, K. (2017). Chasing Literacies Across Action Texts and Augmented Realities: E-Books, Animated Apps, and Pokémon Go. In *The Case of the iPad* (pp. 49–66). Singapore: Springer. doi:10.1007/978-981-10-4364-2_4

ADDITIONAL READING

Arizona Geographic Alliance. (2002). *Geoliteracy*. K-8 lessons that integrate the social studies standards with reading and writing standards. Retrieved from http://geoalliance.asu.edu/azga_site/node/3

Comber, B. (2011). Making space for place-making pedagogies: Stretching normative mandated literacy curriculum. *Contemporary Issues in Early Childhood*, *12*(4), 343–348. doi:10.2304/ciec.2011.12.4.343

Comber, B. (2015). *Literacy, place, and pedagogies of possibility*. Routledge. doi:10.4324/9781315735658

Cope, B., & Kalantzis, M. (2009). "Multiliteracies": New literacies, new learning. *Pedagogies*, *4*(3), 164–195. doi:10.1080/15544800903076044

Dejaynes, T. (2018). "What makes me who I am?": Using artifacts as cosmopolitan invitations. *English Journal*, *108*(2), 48–54. Retrieved from https://proxy.geneseo.edu/login?url=https://proxy.geneseo.edu:5742/docview/2155618863?accountid=11072

Demarest, A. B. (2014). *Place-based curriculum design: Exceeding standards through local investigations*. Routledge. doi:10.4324/9781315795195

Gruenewald, D. A., & Smith, G. A. (Eds.). (2008). *Place-based Education in the Global Age: local diversity*. New York: Lawrence Erlbaum.

McInerney, P., Smyth, J., & Down, B. (2011). 'Coming to a place near you?' The politics and possibilities of a critical pedagogy of place-based education. *Asia-Pacific Journal of Teacher Education*, *39*(1), 3–16. doi:10.1080/1359866X.2010.540894

Sánchez, L. (2011). Building on young children's cultural histories through placemaking in the classroom. *Contemporary Issues in Early Childhood*, *12*(4), 332–342. doi:10.2304/ciec.2011.12.4.332

Smith, G. A., & Sobel, D. (2014). *Place-and community-based education in schools*. Routledge. doi:10.4324/9780203858530

KEY TERMS AND DEFINITIONS

Artifactual Literacies: A theory of recognizing the role of artifacts in the narratives of students' lives and inviting those into the classroom.

Community: A physical or representational space whereby members engage in activities based on shared interests.

Critical Pedagogy: A teaching approach which attempts to help students question and challenge domination, and the beliefs and practices that contribute to the oppression of others through an imbalance of power.

Culturally Relevant Instruction: A theory that informs instructional practice focusing on academic achievement, cultural competence and sociopolitical consciousness.

Multiple Literacies: A broader view of literacy, also referred to as "new literacies" or "multiliteracies." These multiliteracies include linguistic, visual, audio, spatial, and gestural ways of meaning-making.

Participatory Literacies: An approach to learning, texts are used as part of a mix of that includes magazine articles, student-generated materials, hypermedia productions, visuals, which students use, create, and collaborate on for larger audiences.

Place-Based Instruction: An immersive learning experience that places students in local heritage, cultures, landscapes, opportunities and experiences, and incorporates this study across the curriculum, often resulting in social change.

Placemaking: This refers to the ways in which our experiences lead us to our conceptions of a place.

Chapter 6
Exploring Cultural Responsiveness in Literacy Tutoring:
"I Never Thought About How Different Our Cultures Would Be"

Dana L. Skelley
University of Alabama in Huntsville, USA

Margie L. Stevens
Greenville Health Systems, USA

Rebecca S. Anderson
The University of Memphis, USA

ABSTRACT

Embracing a culturally responsive teaching pedagogy in classrooms is one means for addressing literacy inequities with students of color. Afterschool literacy tutoring is another means of addressing these inequities, but little is known about implementing culturally responsive teaching in afterschool environments. This qualitative case study explored how cultural differences impacted an urban elementary afterschool literacy tutoring program. Grounded in participatory literacy theory, the authors conclude that it is normal for cultural differences to occur and cause disruptions during tutoring; however, culturally responsive teaching can mitigate these interruptions through developing caring relationships, creating a safe learning environment, implementing a participatory student-centered curriculum using online resources, and critiquing social inequalities. The discussion offers seven principles of culturally responsive teaching to use in literacy instructional environments.

DOI: 10.4018/978-1-7998-0000-2.ch006

INTRODUCTION

Literacy learning is not equitable for all learners (Banks & Banks, 1995; Zirkel, 2008). For example, the National Center for Education Statistics (2019) revealed 79% American Indian, 44% Asian/Pacific Islander, 80% African American, 77% Hispanic, and 53% White fourth-grade students scored below proficiency in reading on the 2017 National Assessment for Educational Progress test. As evidenced, culturally diverse learners are struggling disproportionally with literacy. Two effective approaches for addressing this issue are afterschool literacy tutoring (Burns, Senesac, & Symington, 2003; Vadasy, Sanders, Peyton, & Jenkins, 2002) and culturally responsive teaching in the classroom (Delpit, 1995; Gay, 2010; Ladson-Billings, 1994, 1995). However, little is known about using culturally responsive teaching specifically in afterschool tutoring. Addressing this need, this year-long qualitative case study explored how cultural differences between college tutors and elementary-aged students of color impacted an afterschool literacy tutoring program. Research questions included: (a) How do tutors experience culturally mismatched events? (b) How do children experience culturally mismatched events? (c) How are culturally mismatched events mitigated?

BACKGROUND

An essential lens used to frame this study is the concept of participatory literacy. Jurmo (1993) discussed that participatory literacy includes key characteristics such as learners engaging actively in their learning, exerting control and responsibility, and working as a team all while facilitators operate as a guide and resource to the learners. Consequentially, power is shared "equally among learners and staff" (Fingeret & Jurmo, 1989, p. 1). Ideally, the learner functions at a level of participation manifesting great control, responsibility, and reward from the activity instead of merely being physically present in the program (Jurmo, 1993). The application of this framework in an instructional environment can therefore bring efficacy to learning, promote identity development, and be a catalyst for social change (Campbell, 1996; Deluca, 2018; Jurmo, 1993; Yang, 2010).

In Tierney's (2018) work with cross-cultural meaning making, he discussed the idea that participatory literacy can "promote approaches that are cooperative, collaborative, and contrastive but respectful and reciprocal" (p. 413). To complement the cooperative nature of participatory literacy, the framework of culturally responsive teaching was also chosen since it can address issues of social injustice and ways of acknowledging all learners' backgrounds (Banks & Banks, 1995; Gutiérrez & Jurow, 2016). In this vein, culturally responsive teaching was embraced to illuminate ways teachers incorporated the learner's culture into the teaching process (Aronson & Laughter, 2016; Lee, 1992; Lewis, Enciso, & Moje, 2007; Lipman, 1995). Frequently interchanged with the term culturally relevant pedagogy (Ladson-Billings, 1994), this paper uses the term culturally responsive teaching which Gay (2010) defines as: "using the cultural knowledge, prior experiences, frames of references, and performance styles of ethnically diverse students to make learning encounters more relevant to and effective for [students]" (p.31).

Culturally responsive teaching aims to narrow the academic achievement gap between culturally diverse students and their White counterparts by building on "what students bring to school" (Cochran-Smith, 2004, p. 69). Research has supported this technique of celebrating learners' various backgrounds (Howard, 2001) and although not inclusive, the following lists some of the culturally responsive teaching components Gay (2002) recommends: (a) acquiring a knowledge base about ethnic and cultural diversity;

(b) developing a culturally relevant curriculum; (c) demonstrating cultural caring and building a learning community; (d) understanding cross-cultural communications; and (e) providing cultural congruity in classroom instruction. Teachers using this pedagogy can connect education and social justice to empower students and inspire them to maintain their cultural integrity (Bassey, 2016; Howard, 2001; Ladson-Billings, 1995).

It is important to note, however, that teachers experience challenges with this pedagogy such as: (a) understanding relevant teaching methods, (b) lacking teaching experience with students of color, (c) misunderstanding how to relate to students of color or connect to their families, and (d) being reluctant to address culturally sensitive issues in the classroom (Gay, 2013; Kea, Campbell-Whatley, & Richards, 2006). Also, ideas first promoted through culturally responsive teaching have been challenged and expanded through the theory of culturally sustaining pedagogy, a framework advocating for pedagogy that "perpetuate(s) and foster(s) linguistic, literate, and cultural pluralism as part of the democratic project of schooling" (Paris, 2012, p. 93).

Tutoring

In recent years, the availability of programs providing academic tutoring during afterschool hours has grown tremendously (Zimmer, Hamilton, & Christina, 2010). Tutors have an advantage over classroom teachers by being able to customize instruction to the individual needs of students (Chin, Rabow, & Estrada, 2011; Elbaum, Vaughn, Tejero Hughes, & Watson Moody, 2000). With this individualized instruction, tutoring is recognized as an effective tool in improving literacy skills when it complements classroom teaching (Burns, Senesac, & Symington, 2003; Vadasy, Sanders, Peyton, & Jenkins, 2002). A meta-analysis also confirmed that tutoring conducted by adult, non-professional tutors is an effective intervention that enables tutees to improve academically (Ritter, Barnett, Denny, & Albin, 2009).

Although the effectiveness of individual tutoring is widely accepted, there is no clear agreement related to the qualifications of tutors (Allor & McCathren, 2004, Shanahan, 1998). Volunteer tutors are often college students, parents, and community members. Though there is no definitive indicator of which of these groups make the most successful tutors, Elbaum, et al. (2000) found that children who made the greatest gains were tutored by college students. Regardless of a tutor's background, researchers agree that it is crucial for all volunteers to receive special training and be supervised by a reading specialist or certified teacher (Pullen, Lane, & Monaghan, 2004; Wasik, 1998; Woolley & Hay, 2007); yet, the most effective content and amount of training has yet to be identified (Ritter, et al., 2009).

Method

This qualitative case study (Yin, 2009) is part of a year-long inquiry that explored the implementation of a university literacy center's afterschool tutoring program (Skelley, Stevens, & Anderson, 2016; Stevens, Skelley, & Anderson, 2016). The afterschool program was located in a large urban district PK-5 public school serving students who identified as 84% African American, 13% Hispanic, and 3% White. School enrollment was 1,153 with over 150 students enrolled in the school-wide afterschool program and 76% receiving free or reduced lunch. Afterschool services began at 3:15 PM and ended at 6:00 PM.

Program Details

Tutors for the program were undergraduate students from a local university who participated in nine hours of tutor training, co-created lesson plans, and tutored two children for one and a half hours weekly for 10 weeks. A university instructor supervised all sessions and tutors participated in class-wide debrief discussion directly after tutoring to share issues, concerns, and what was going well in their sessions. During tutor training, iPads, children's books, art supplies, and a sample semi-structured lesson plan were distributed while tutors participated in instructor-modeled sessions, developed their own lesson plans for sessions, and practiced implementing these plans. Lesson plans included process writing, mini-lessons, connections to literature, and reflection activities. Training for the second semester also included direct instruction on culturally responsive teaching where tutors read articles, watched videos, and enacted scenarios to foster awareness and sensitivity to the diversity in their tutoring environment. Tutors were also provided a handout with guidelines on promoting cultural competence which they referenced throughout the semester.

The overall program objective was for each tutoring group to write and illustrate an e-book about their city that would be published and donated to children at the local cancer hospital. During weekly sessions, children and tutors produced a page and illustration about their city on the following topics: downtown, restaurants, sports, museums, outdoor locations, music, famous people, and the zoo. Children used iPads to research and create the e-book using the *Book Creator* app. They read children's books connected to the weekly writing themes and received a free take-home book. Tutors also used the iPads as a means to communicate student work to parents via postings on the program blog and to share their e-books during an end of the semester parent celebration. When the books were printed, each tutor and child received a copy along with children in the hospital.

Participants

Tutors were students at a large urban university enrolled in either an honors or education program and registered in a three-credit hour elective course titled *Literacy Tutoring.* During first semester, seven undergraduate females were enrolled in the program: one Asian American and six White. All were enrolled in the honors program and two were also education majors. During second semester, nine honors students and one education major enrolled: six females and four males. One male was Hispanic while three were White; one female was Multiracial and five were White.

Child participants were already enrolled in the school-wide afterschool program and were not receiving special education services. School administrators recruited and accepted these second and third grade children on a first-come basis with the only criteria for enrollment being parent permission to participate. 14 children participated during fall semester and, along with seven additional students, during spring semester. All 21 children were African American with seven males and 14 females.

The instructor during fall semester was a literacy doctoral graduate assistant. The spring semester instructor was a professor and director of the literacy center. A doctoral student in educational research worked as a non-participant researcher throughout the year and all three worked together to analyze and report findings. To protect anonymity, pseudonyms are used.

Data Collection

The same data were collected fall and spring semesters. Tutor data included background questionnaires, end of semester semi-structured individual interviews, weekly teaching reflections which contained seven questions and were submitted online to instructors per class requirements, and 30-minute group debriefing discussions which occurred immediately after each tutoring session. Data collected from the children included intake forms, end of semester focus group interviews, and participant observer field notes. Interviews were conducted with eight of the children for approximately 45 minutes with a focus on their perceptions and experiences in the tutoring program. Data were also collected from weekly instructor reflection journals. All interviews were audio taped and transcribed. Debriefing between the researchers followed each data collection.

DATA ANALYSIS

Data were analyzed using a thematic analysis (Braun & Clarke, 2006). In Vivo and Descriptive Codes were developed during the initial coding procedures (Saldaña, 2009) which included: rapport, trust, care and respect, racial differences, social economic status, honor child's culture, technology, struggles with racial topics, power structures, privilege, and social inequalities. During second cycle coding, Pattern Coding was utilized to organize the corpus of data and attribute meaning to the categories as themes emerged (Saldaña, 2009). These themes were analyzed through the lenses of participatory literacy theory and culturally responsive teaching. With this thematic analysis, five major variables regarding cultural differences in the tutoring program emerged and are discussed below. Triangulation of the findings (Lincoln & Guba, 1985) occurred throughout the analysis process by using multiple data sources to corroborate findings and the researchers meeting weekly.

FINDINGS

According to the data, there were five variables of cultural differences that impacted the afterschool literacy tutoring program: (a) diverse social classes and cultural backgrounds between tutors and children created misunderstandings, (b) culturally sensitive topics disrupted the flow of tutoring, (c) student-centered strategies bridged cultural mismatches and expanded cultural understandings, (d) participants established caring and respectful relationships, and (e) children recognized and critiqued social inequalities.

Diverse Social Classes and Cultural Backgrounds between Tutors and Children Created Misunderstandings

Throughout the program there was evidence that differences in social classes existed between tutors and children. Initially tutors did not understand this or the privileges that their social class afforded them, as this tutor stated:

I never thought about how different our [tutor and children] cultures would be. I was adopted. My parents are White, but I am mixed-race so I thought that we would be more alike. I probably looked a lot like the two little girls that I was tutoring, but I realized we have totally different socioeconomic backgrounds and that obviously makes a big difference.

Also stated in field notes, "Tutors were in disbelief that students had not visited the local zoo, parks, or museums as these community spaces were a typical part of the tutor's childhood."

It was also found through participatory discussions that children held false assumptions about their tutors. This was evidenced in field notes that stated:

Tonight writing about local restaurants, a tutor asked her child if she liked eating [Gary's] Fried Chicken. The child quickly responded, 'What do you know about chicken? White people don't eat chicken!' The tutor looked at the child in disbelief and stated, 'Of course I like chicken. White people do eat chicken!'

Cultural differences led to misunderstandings between tutors and children and were found to occur during all sessions.

In sum, tutors who were in a higher social economic class failed to see the privilege that their social class afforded them. Additionally, there were cultural differences between tutors and children that weren't initially recognized or understood, but subsequently occurred throughout the program. This led to misunderstandings and false assumptions by both tutors and children.

Culturally Sensitive Topics Disrupted the Flow of Tutoring

It was found that culturally sensitive topics impacted the tutoring process for both tutors and children. Tutors were uncomfortable with topics such as race or the American Civil Rights Movement, and the flow and participatory nature of lessons were interrupted, as field notes captured after tutors read the book *Martin's Big Words* (2001):

When segregation and the assassination of Dr. Martin Luther King, Jr. were discussed, some tutors quit making eye contact with the children, expedited the lesson without allowing time for the children to ask questions, or struggled to regroup and continue.

Another instance occurred when a child illustrating his story on museums drew a picture of Ku Klux Klansmen with KKK written on their robes. When asked why he chose that as his illustration he stated, "Because those are the men that hate us [Black people]." The tutor, shocked at both the image and response, later sought advice from the class instructor during tutor debriefing stating:

My student decided to draw a picture of the KKK for his picture on the Civil Rights Museum page. I know the KKK was an important part of the Civil Rights Movement, but I don't want my name in a book that has a picture of the KKK to give to children at a hospital. I think we could make another picture that wouldn't be so, you know, offensive.

Field notes indicate the program director responded, "Maybe ask him to put himself in the shoes of the children at the hospital. Would they enjoy the illustration?" Field notes also cite the tutor made the advised suggestion to the child who affably decided to replace his illustration with a drawing of people picketing for civil rights. Although, the power differential between the tutor and child may have played a part in the child's change in the illustration, it is worth noting that the child retained the same theme of protest and white-dominate power as his illustration indicated a large number of Black people holding protest signs and a few blue people holding protest signs. He explained, "The blue people [stick figures in his illustration] are the White people because not all White people hate us [Black people]."

While tutors experienced discomfort and confusion with culturally sensitive topics, it was found that during these instances children often enthusiastically took over the lesson, reversing roles and exhibiting positive responses as would be encouraged in participatory settings. As field notes documented, "Children were eager to discuss Dr. Martin Luther King, Jr. and were knowledgeable about the topic. The children became very animated and spoke louder than the tutor during this lesson." In another example, children were quick to demonstrate their pride in the musical heritage that was celebrated in their home. In a session where music was the focus, the tutor named different artists as the children sat quietly looking puzzled. However, when the tutor mentioned Aretha Franklin, both children immediately stood up and started dancing as one said, "We sing 'Respect' all the time at my house with my momma and sister." The tutor encouraged the children to sing and link the song to the session's writing.

In sum, when racial topics arose, tutors were sometimes uncomfortable and unclear about how to proceed, disrupting the participatory nature of the sessions. However, on many occasions children took over the sessions with enthusiasm and expertise which contributed to the participatory goals of shared power and the creation of shared knowledge as children had the opportunity to share their social identity in Black culture with their tutors.

Student-Centered Strategies Bridged Cultural Mismatches and Expanded Cultural Understandings

When culturally mismatched events occurred, tutors used four student-centered strategies to bridge gaps in learning. First, tutors used iPads to build background knowledge by quickly turning to the Internet when they realized children had not visited or experienced topics and locations related to that day's session. Child questions and participation guided these activities. One tutor reflected, "They were asking so many questions! …so it was fun for them to look it up on the iPad. I think it was also beneficial for them retaining the information." The children, however, were not the only ones who needed the Internet to learn new information. For example, during a tutoring session featuring favorite local restaurants, some tutors were not familiar with their children's choices. Observational field notes indicate:

During a session where favorite local restaurants were the theme, some of the children were seen giving blank stares at the tutors when the tutors named local restaurants. In one instance, the child had never heard of a named restaurant even though it had been featured on a national food television show. The tutor used the iPad to show the child the restaurant and even found video segments of the restaurant being featured on the cooking show. The child appeared to enjoy the fact that a restaurant in their hometown was featured on television but was otherwise unimpressed with the restaurant. The tutor then asked the child, "So what restaurant do you like eating at?" The child's eyes brightened and he quickly stated the name of a restaurant that was within a mile from the school. The tutor quickly used the iPad to search the Internet for the restaurant. The child became very excited when he saw the photo of his favorite restaurant exclaiming, "That's it! Now find the nachos with chili. That's what daddy and me get when we go there!" The tutor found the photo of the menu item and the child decided to use that photo as a template for illustrating his favorite local restaurant and food for the book.

As illustrated, the iPads were a student-centered tool that made learning meaningful, real, and participatory, and they provided a quick and motivating means to research missing knowledge during sessions giving students the control of guiding discovery.

Second, tutors broadened cultural understandings when children expressed false assumptions toward cultures other than their own by speaking in honest, nonthreatening ways about race as evidenced in field notes:

During a session where Elvis Presley was being discussed, the children did not recognize his name; however, when the tutor played some of his music, the children quickly started singing along. After the children wrote their story, they requested the tutor find photos of him to help with their illustrations. When one of the children saw Elvis's photo, she immediately appeared shocked and stated to her White tutor, 'Elvis is White? I hate White people!' The other child quickly replied, 'Anna! You can't say that to them [White people]!' The tutor said, 'We shouldn't hate anyone.' The child looked at the tutor as if she just realized she was speaking to a White person and said, 'But I love you Miss Laurie!' The tutor hugged the child and the session continued.

In another tutoring group a child asked, "Why did Elvis like Black people and sing Black people music?" The Hispanic-American tutor explained his response in an interview:

I said, man, culture changes. The only people who were imposing that type of segregation were the upper-middle class and rich. It wasn't poor people. ...it's an attempt to make one group of people think that they are better than another.... Elvis understood that. That's why he hung around speakeasies and... promoted African-American music.

These instances illustrate how through collaboration, the children were expressing their thoughts and questions about race while tutors were expanding their understandings, answering their queries, and at the same time honoring the child's culture in thoughtful ways.

Third, allowing children to write about their personal experiences was a student-centered strategy that allowed for shared power during the tutoring experience and helped bridge cultural mismatches by making learning relevant. It was observed children valued the book project because it was linked to their home life and community and became an outlet for their voice. Children were actively engaged throughout all sessions with these field notes capturing a child's excitement about incorporating her personal cultural experiences in the book, "I'm drawing chicken like grandmamma makes because nobody's food is as good as hers." When explaining an illustration, another child stated, "My picture is nachos because me and daddy always get them when we go to the baseball games. And we get that chili on them too, but momma don't like it." These examples of children including special family experiences in their writing allowed them to celebrate their culture.

Finally, the participatory activity of creating books to be donated to a children's hospital provided an authentic audience, increasing children's commitment and motivation to complete the project with culturally accurate and engaging content. In an interview, one tutor expressed:

When I signed up for this class I thought the tutoring would just be helping the kids with homework and that's alright, but when our instructor explained that we were going to be creating a real book and donating it to the children of the hospital, I became very excited about the class. I think the books came out great! I never dreamed the books would end up so cool, but I'm really proud of our book.

Another tutor added, "The kids were so excited about being authors. I was too. It made us work harder because we wanted our book to be impressive. I mean, since when does a kid get to be an author of a book?" Similarly, children were proud of their work as one voiced, "When I'm an author, I'm going to be famous and people will ask me for my autograph."

It's important to note, that according to the tutors, learning how to implement these four student-centered strategies occurred during training and debriefing sessions. Tutors also credited the collaboration with their peers and social interactions with instructors for supporting and sustaining them throughout the program, as this tutor articulated:

At first, I was overwhelmed by everything we were taught in the training, but it really helped me be prepared to be a good tutor. The training you provided on culture made me think of situations that might occur that I had not thought up. It also made me think about how I see myself and others.... Being able to talk to other tutors after tutoring was also helpful. You know, we were able to share our experiences.

During another interview one tutor concurred, "I would not have known where to begin without the training. ...I never thought about how different our cultures would be."

In sum, tutors utilized four student-centered strategies to create a participatory learning environment that concurrently bridged cultural mismatches during their tutoring sessions: using iPads to bridge knowledge gaps, broadening cultural understandings from children's false assumptions, having students write about personal experiences, and expecting accurate and engaging content for an authentic audience. Training and ongoing support helped tutors grow in their understandings about cultural differences and how best to implement these strategies. Evolving relationships with their children also assisted in these areas as explained in the next finding.

Participants Established Caring and Respectful Relationships

Polite, kind relationships cultivated between tutors and children occurred almost immediately. Although each made false assumptions about the other, their caring feelings toward each other sustained them through misunderstandings. Both children and tutors were observed sharing personal information with the other as their friendships grew. These bonds formed quickly, as evident in week three field notes:

The child entered the tutoring space, saw her tutor, and ran across the room to her. The child had a big smile on her face and excitedly said to her tutor, 'I'm going to be a big sister! My momma's pregnant! And we get the baby this summer!' The tutor whom appeared equally excited hugged the child and said, 'You are going to be a great big sister!'

Children also shared life events that were not so pleasant as this child shared regarding a personal family matter:

'I love my dad and I want to stay with him, but I can't because he don't have a house so we only get to go out on Sundays.' The tutor responded, 'I'm sorry, sweetie. That must be hard.' The child responded, 'It makes me sad, but daddy said he is going to get a house soon and I could stay with him then.' The tutor hugged the child and softly said, 'I hope so, sweetie. It will all work out.'

Children were not the only ones to share personal life events. As these field notes indicated, when a child asked the tutor how he was doing the tutor stated:

I'm a little stressed out and tired. [Tutor laughs nervously.] Midterm exams are coming and I have been working long hours at the cupcake shop so I guess I will be spending this weekend working on homework and studying. What are you doing this weekend?

Over time, tutors and children did get to know one another, gained insights, and grew in their understandings of each other. As one tutor verbalized:

I learned so much about the kids' life because they wanted to put it in the book. They would share good stories about their life, like how they sing and dance with their momma when they are doing the dishes, and not so good stories like how they missed their dad because he didn't live with them or that he was looking for a job. I really became attached to them and I think they became attached to me. It's funny, sometimes I would find myself thinking about them [the children] on the weekend. I learned a lot about their culture and them and I think they learned about me too."

This growing knowledge about the children's culture prompted tutors to help the children integrate their background knowledge and experiences to meet the expectations of the project. In this finding, children were encouraged to talk about their personal connections to the lessons and were given an opportunity for their voices to be heard. In this way, tutors demonstrated their commitment to participatory learning, the caring relationships they developed, and the respect they had for the children's culture.

In sum, tutors and children built relationships of trust and respect that allowed tutors to become facilitators of knowledge versus dispensers. The relationships were a pivotal component for children's motivation and engagement. The bonds helped children know that although tutors expected them to successfully write and illustrate a book, they had their best interest at heart, giving them a voice to honor their background.

Children Recognized and Critiqued Social Inequalities

According to the data, when culturally sensitive topics arose during tutoring sessions, a space opened for children to recognize and critique historical events that were culturally significant to them. Field notes reported a conversation between a tutor and child:

Child: Man, that's messed up [referring to segregation]! Tutor: Yes, it is. I don't know why there was so much hate for Black people. Child: But it ain't like that today, but some White people still don't like Black people. Like that guy who killed Trayvon Martin. Tutor: That's true, but because of people like Martin Luther King, we're learning to get along better. Maybe one day. Child interrupts and says: He said use your words not your fist; love not hate. But why did they have to kill him [Dr. Martin Luther King, Jr]? I think he was nice. Tutor: He did seem like a really nice person. But he didn't die in vain; he taught us all to stand-up for our rights and for other people's rights. Child: That's why people protested and won. Tutor: Yep.

Children did not resist talking about culturally sensitive issues. Rather they were eager to critique topics such as a sanitation strike and having separate water fountains. By linking prior knowledge and situating themselves in these experiences, children identified how they would address these inequalities in today's world. For example, one child stated, "I think I like Rosa Parks best! She wasn't having none of that bullying. I would be like her if that happened to me." At times, children reflected on what their responses would have been had they been part of injustices of the past.

In sum, as children and tutors acknowledged social inequalities of the past, they became cognizant of the social injustices of today. These connections helped children recognize that strategies for social justice from the past were still applicable today.

CONCLUSION AND RECOMMENDATIONS

In conclusion, social class and cultural differences existed between tutors and children in this afterschool tutoring program. These differences were frequently not recognized by tutors, thereby creating misunderstandings and false assumptions between tutors and children. These cultural differences occurred throughout the program, were centered around culturally sensitive topics, led to tutoring disruptions, and often were the catalyst for tutors attempting to speed through lesson content or children taking the lead during sessions. These occurrences were mitigated by culturally responsive teaching, specifically implementing a participatory, student-centered curriculum using online resources, developing caring relationships, and critiquing social inequalities. The salient conclusion in this study is the apparent cycle, outlined in Figure 1, which illustrates how social and cultural differences during tutoring sessions cause disruptions but are mitigated through culturally responsive teaching. Yet, it should be noted the cycle is fluid, meaning new cultural differences will regularly occur during teaching, which in turn trigger the cycle to start again.

RECOMMENDATIONS

From the findings of this study and the literature cited below, we offer seven principles of culturally responsive teaching for tutors, K-12 teachers, and literacy university teacher educators. Although our setting involved tutors in an afterschool program, our hope is educators in other settings can also find them helpful.

Figure 1. The cycle of cultural differences in afterschool tutoring. This figure illustrates how existing cultural differences cause disruptions but can be allayed through culturally responsive teaching. However, new cultural differences will occur, starting the cycle again.

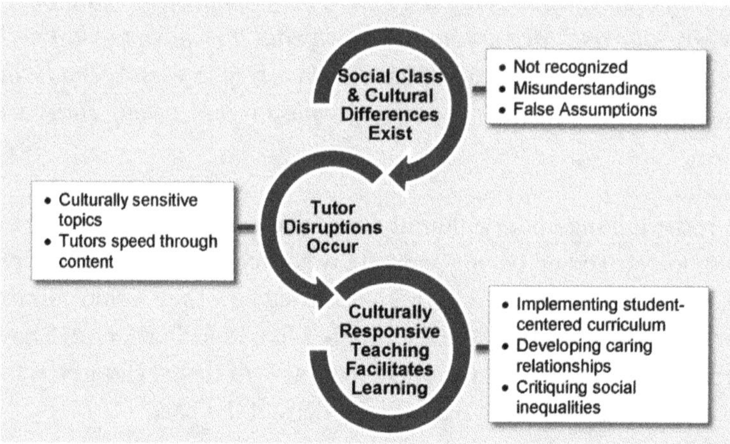

Make It Personal

Educators and students need a shared understanding of each other's beliefs, values, and cultural experiences. This is ideally accomplished through the recruitment of more teachers of color, a dire need in the field of education. But, the more personal we make instruction, the less misunderstandings will occur. Also, adapting differentiated instruction allows the lesson to be tailored to the needs of the child. Creating a curriculum that allows students to incorporate their culture creates pride and excitement about learning. Strategies to implement include getting-to-know-you activities and modeling instruction with relatable stories, games, and information about oneself. Other examples could include encouraging students' participation by sharing information about their home's culture, such as the ways food or entertainment are enjoyed with the family, sharing multicultural literature, and researching other cultures. Incorporating and honoring students' cultures in the lesson will allow them to maintain their "cultural integrity" (Ladson-Billings, 1994, p. 160). While, consistent with Gay (2010), an established relationship between students and educators further engages students and motivates them to succeed.

Be Open-Minded

It is normal for misunderstandings related to cultural differences to occur in a classroom setting, making it necessary to be open-minded about different ways of being. Instead of being shocked, scared, or possibly shutting down because of false assumptions, educators can approach misunderstandings as an opportunity to learn more about another culture while honoring students' social identities. A myriad of learning possibilities can be created with participatory literacy and allowing students to express their viewpoints and perspectives allows them to become active participants in their education (Campbell, 1996; Nieto, 1996). As Gay (2002) suggests, educators need to acquire knowledge of their learners varying ethnic, cultural backgrounds, and become culturally competent. Cultural competence requires the educator to adopt the skills necessary to effectively teach students who come from different cultural backgrounds (Howard, 2010). These skills include accepting and respecting different cultural backgrounds that exist in a diverse society while not viewing them in a hierarchical manner. Educators must also acknowledge culture is a dynamic force, constantly changing, making the adoption of cultural competence skills an ongoing process (Paris & Alim, 2014). This process requires individuals remain reflective about their beliefs, behaviors, and dispositions, while also recognizing how all value their personal culture equally (Howard, 2010).

Implement Digital Tools

The use of digital tools provides opportunities to incorporate students' culture into learning while challenging them to incorporate information about other cultures (Ellison & Solomon, 2018; Ladson-Billings, 1995; Villegas, 1991). Educational sessions need lessons that integrate technology such as blogs, iPads, and the Internet for communicating, researching, building background knowledge, and motivating students to succeed. Digital tools can offer marginalized students a medium of expression, and giving learners the power to choose their writing topic follows participatory literacy tenets by providing the student the opportunity for a personal, authentic, valued voice in the literacy activity (Barrett & Cocq, 2019; Campbell, 1996; Gibson & Smith, 2018). The use of technology allows for immediate discovery of information in multimodal forms and creates an ideal means for bridging cultural gaps in knowledge. This aligns with Ladson-Billings (1995) statement that digital tools help link curriculum to the 21st century learner and addresses the prevailing disconnect between school learning and the real-world needs of students, particularly students of color.

Create a Caring and Safe Environment

Establishing caring relationships between educators and students is essential for creating a safe learning environment. These environments make it easier for students to engage, take risks with their learning, and demonstrate pride and motivation to succeed. Educators can establish bonds and equitable relationships with students through respectful actions toward them and their cultures, promoting honest discussions, and creating a collaborative learning environment (Jurmo, 1993; Tierney, 2018). Ladson-Billings (1994) indicates effective teachers provide a space of "psychological safety" and allow the student to feel "comfortable and supported" (p.73). As trust is developed, students and educators will each thrive. However, in order for this trust to be developed, educators will need to develop a racial awareness. Racial awareness recognizes and acknowledges how the historical, social, political, and economic consequences of being a member of a racially marginalized group in the United States shapes students' worldviews and how they see themselves racially (Howard, 2010; Tatum 2007). Racial awareness also entails an understanding of how whiteness influences culture and practices in the United States (Sleeter, 1996). Racial awareness further requires that educators be mindful of the role that racism plays (Howard, 2010). Educators need to be prepared to listen to students talk about their racialized experiences in order to better understand and respond to the student. Otherwise, the unprepared educator may withdraw from the conversation and appear to adopt a "colorblindness" mentality, the idea that race does not matter, which may translate to the student that the educator is racist or does not care about them (Howard, 2010). Becoming racially aware requires educators to ask themselves the following questions, "Who am I racially? What do I believe about other racial groups?" and "Does who I am and what I believe about race have ramifications for students I teach?" (Howard, 2010, p. 122). Furthermore, racial awareness may also be difficult as it will require White educators to acknowledge their own racial privilege.

Communicate to Create Understanding

When working with students from diverse backgrounds, sensitive issues can arise and effective communication must include thoughtfulness and empathy. Educators should expect mismatches and avoid taking them personally. It is also important for educators to be prepared to discuss any misunderstandings that arise. In instances of cultural mismatches, educators can roleplay with students to take another's perspective and help them develop empathy for others. When appropriate, educators can exchange personal stories related to sensitive issues, and literature can be used as a catalyst for discussions on sensitive topics. Understanding cross-cultural communications is imperative for educators to gain insight into students' behavior (Gay, 2002; Sheets, 1996; Tierney, 2018). These participatory communications help learners build understanding and empathy while broadening their worldview (Aronson & Laughter, 2016; Prior, 2006).

Evaluate Concepts of Power

In a participatory literacy environment, power is shared between the child and the educator (Campbell, 1996; Fingeret & Jurmo, 1989). Educators should consider their beliefs and actions regarding their role in the learning environment and evaluate any preconceived notions of power they may bring to the setting. The sharing of power also nurtures the collaborative and cooperative nature of the participatory literacy event. When developing a participatory literacy activity, the educator should consider: How can the child help develop the curricular event? What participatory role will the child play in the creation of the culminating literacy project? How can I ensure the child's identity and authentic voice are being honored throughout the process? Ideally, the activity should be a mutual learning and growth activity for both the educator and child so that "the teacher is no longer merely the-one-who-teaches, but one who is himself taught in dialogue with the students" (Friere, 1970/2005, p. 80). Obtaining this requires a release of power from the educator so that shared power allows agency and a voice to all.

Develop Sociopolitical Consciousness

When students engage in curriculum that confronts issues and inequities situated in their local community, they develop awareness of social injustices as connected to a democratic society. Friere (1970/2005) discusses the need for educators to collaborate with learners to develop a "critical consciousness" in order to work on "the problems of human beings in their relations with the world" (p. 79). Educators can incorporate participatory projects that include sociopolitical topics that lead to social change related to the students' cultural heritage. Also, educators can provide a climate that invites open and honest conversations about historical and current events. Ladson-Billings (1995) also stresses the importance of providing opportunities for "students to recognize, understand, and critique current and social inequalities" (p. 476). She further indicates teachers must first be aware of sociopolitical issues that exist.

FUTURE RESEARCH DIRECTIONS

This study provides insights into substantive issues surrounding how to structure participatory literacy practices for P-12 classrooms in the digital age and generates questions for further research: (a) How can tutors and teachers be trained to use digital literacy in culturally responsive teaching? (b) How does culturally responsive teaching impact literacy achievement? (c) How does culturally responsive teaching impact children's writing identities? (d) When and how should digital literacy be used to create cultural competency? (e) How do parents respond to their children engaging in digital literacies through culturally responsive teaching methods? As scholars address these questions, it is our hope that educators will become more culturally competent, possess a strong racial awareness, and be able to confidently mediate any cultural misunderstandings—the children's or their own.

ACKNOWLEDGMENT

This research received no specific grant from any funding agency in the public, commercial, or not-for-profit sectors.

Support for this research was provided by The University of Memphis Center for Literacy Research and Practice, College of Education, Department of Instruction and Curriculum Leadership, School Library Information Specialist Program, and ICL Literacy Program. Support was also provided by Shelby County Books from Birth, St. Jude Children's Research Hospital, Dr. Gene Whittington, and CMYK Printing.

REFERENCES

Allor, J., & McCathren, R. (2004). The efficacy of an early literacy tutoring program implemented by college students. *Learning Disabilities Research & Practice*, *19*(2), 116–129. doi:10.1111/j.1540-5826.2004.00095.x

Aronson, B., & Laughter, J. (2016). The theory and practice of culturally relevant education: A synthesis of research across content areas. *Review of Educational Research*, *86*(1), 163–206. doi:10.3102/0034654315582066

Banks, C. A. M., & Banks, J. A. (1995). Equity pedagogy: An essential component of multicultural education. *Theory into Practice*, *34*(3), 152–158. doi:10.1080/00405849509543674

Barrett, J., & Cocq, C. (2019). Indigenous storytelling and language learning: Digital media as a vehicle for cultural transmission and language acquisition. In C. Cocq & K. P. H. Sullivan (Eds.), *Perspectives on Indigenous Writing and Literacies* (pp. 89–111). Leiden, The Netherlands: Brill Publishing; doi:10.1163/9789004298507_006

Bassey, M. O. (2016). Culturally responsive teaching: Implications for educational justice. *Education in Science*, *6*(4), 1–6. doi:10.3390/educsci6040035

Braun, V., & Clarke, V. (2006). Using thematic analysis in psychology. *Qualitative Research in Psychology*, *3*(2), 77–101. doi:10.1191/1478088706qp063oa

Burns, M. K., Senesac, B. V., & Symington, T. (2003). The effectiveness of the hosts program in improving the reading achievement of children at-risk for reading failure. *Reading Research and Instruction, 43*(2), 87–103. doi:10.1080/19388070409558406

Campbell, P. (1996). Participatory literary practices: Exploring social identity and relations. *Adult Basic Education, 6*(3), 127.

Chin, T., Rabow, J., & Estrada, J. (2011). *Tutoring matters: Everything you always wanted to know about how to tutor*. Philadelphia: Temple University Press.

Cochran-Smith, M. (2004). *Walking the road: Race, diversity, and social justice in teacher education*. New York, NY: Teachers College Press.

Delpit, L. (1995). *Other people's children: Cultural conflict in the classroom*. New York, NY: The New Press.

Deluca, K. (2018). Shared passions, shared compositions: Online fandom communities and affinity groups as sites for public writing pedagogy. *Computers and Composition, 47*, 75–92. doi:10.1016/j.compcom.2017.12.003

Elbaum, B., Vaughn, S., Tejero Hughes, M., & Watson Moody, S. (2000). How effective are one-to-one tutoring programs in reading for elementary students at risk for reading failure? A meta-analysis of the intervention research. *Journal of Educational Psychology, 92*(4), 605–619. doi:10.1037/0022-0663.92.4.605

Ellison, T. L., & Solomon, M. (2018). Digital play as purposeful and productive literacies in African American boys. *The Reading Teacher, 71*(4), 495–500. doi:10.1002/trtr.1657

Fingeret, A., & Jurmo, P. (1989). *Participatory literacy education*. San Francisco: Jossey-Bass.

Friere, P. (2005). *Pedagogy of the oppressed* (M. B. Ramos, Trans.). New York, NY: Continuum International Publishing. (Original work published 1970)

Gay, G. (2002). Preparing for culturally responsive teaching. *Journal of Teacher Education, 53*(2), 106–116. doi:10.1177/0022487102053002003

Gay, G. (2010). *Culturally responsive teaching: Theory, research, and practice* (2nd ed.). New York, NY: Teachers College Press.

Gay, G. (2013). Teaching to and through cultural diversity. *Curriculum Inquiry, 43*(1), 48–70. doi:10.1111/curi.12002

Gibson, P., & Smith, S. (2018). Digital literacies: Preparing pupils and students for their information journey in the twenty-first century. *Information and Learning Science, 119*(12), 733–742.

Gutiérrez, K. D., & Jurow, A. S. (2016). Social design experiments: Toward equity by design. *Journal of the Learning Sciences, 25*(4), 565–598. doi:10.1080/10508406.2016.1204548

Howard, T. C. (2001). Telling their side of the story: African-American students' perceptions of culturally relevant teaching. *The Urban Review, 33*(2), 131–149. doi:10.1023/A:1010393224120

Howard, T. C. (2010). *Why race and culture matter in schools: Closing the achievement gap in America's classrooms*. New York: Teachers College Press.

Jurmo, P. (1993). Participatory literacy education: An update. Columbus, OH: The Ohio State University. Retrieved from the ERIC database. (ED 354298)

Kea, C., Campbell-Whatley, G., & Richards, H. (2006). *Becoming culturally responsive educators: Rethinking teacher education pedagogy*. National Center for Culturally Responsive Educational Systems. Retrieved from: http://www.champaignschools.org/sites/default/files/Teacher_Ed_Brief.pdf

Ladson-Billings, G. (1994). *The dreamkeepers: Successful teachers of African American children* (1st ed.). San Francisco, CA: Jossey-Bass Publishing Co.

Ladson-Billings, G. (1995). Toward a theory of culturally relevant pedagogy. *American Educational Research Journal, 32*(3), 465–491. doi:10.3102/00028312032003465

Lee, C. D. (1992). Literacy, cultural diversity, and instruction. *Education and Urban Society, 24*(2), 279–291. doi:10.1177/0013124592024002008

Lewis, C., Enciso, P., & Moje, E. (Eds.). (2007). *Reframing sociocultural research on literacy: Identity, agency and power*. Mahwah, NJ: Lawrence Erlbaum Associates.

Lincoln, Y. S., & Guba, E. G. (1985). *Naturalistic inquiry* (Vol. 75). Newberry Park, CA: Sage Publications.

Lipman, P. (1995). Bringing out the best in them: The contribution of culturally relevant teachers to education reform. *Theory into Practice, 34*(3), 202–208. doi:10.1080/00405849509543680

National Center for Education Statistics. (2019). *The nation's report card 2017: Reading grade 4*. Retrieved from https://www.nationsreportcard.gov/reading_2017/nation/achievement?grade=4

Nieto, S. (1996). *Affirming diversity: The sociopolitical context of multicultural education* (2nd ed.). White Plains, NY: Longman.

Paris, D. (2012). Culturally sustaining pedagogy: A needed change in stance, terminology, and practice. *Educational Researcher, 41*(3), 93–97. doi:10.3102/0013189X12441244

Paris, D., & Alim, H. S. (2014). What are we seeking to sustain through culturally sustaining pedagogy? A loving critique forward. *Harvard Educational Review, 84*(1), 85–100. doi:10.17763/haer.84.1.982l873k2ht16m77

Prior, P. (2006). A sociocultural theory of writing. In C. A. MacArthur, S. Graham, & J. Fitzgerald (Eds.), *Handbook of writing research* (pp. 54–66). New York, NY: Guilford Press.

Pullen, P. C., Lane, H. B., & Monaghan, M. C. (2004). Effects of a volunteer tutoring model on the early literacy development of struggling first grade students. *Reading Research and Instruction, 43*(4), 21–40. doi:10.1080/19388070409558415

Rappaport, D. (2001). *Martin's big words: The life of Dr. Martin Luther King, Jr.* New York, NY: Hyperion Books for Children.

Ritter, G. W., Barnett, J. H., Denny, G. S., & Albin, G. R. (2009). The effectiveness of volunteer tutoring programs for elementary and middle school students: A meta-analysis. *Review of Educational Research*, *79*(1), 3–38. doi:10.3102/0034654308325690

Saldaña, J. (2009). *An introduction to codes and coding. The coding manual for qualitative researchers.* Thousand Oaks, CA: Sage Publications.

Shanahan, T. (1998). On the effectiveness and limitations of tutoring in reading. *Review of Research in Education*, *23*, 217–234.

Sheets, R. H. (1996). Urban classroom conflict: Student-teacher perception: Ethnic integrity, solidarity, and resistance. *The Urban Review*, *28*(2), 165–183. doi:10.1007/BF02354383

Skelley, D. L., Stevens, M. L., & Anderson, R. S. (2016, November). *A university literacy center moving to offsite afterschool tutoring: Perceptions of tutors, children, and parents.* Roundtable discussion presented at the 2016 Association of Literacy Educators and Researchers Conference, Myrtle Beach, SC.

Stevens, M. L., Skelley, D. L., & Anderson, R. S. (2016, December). *Exploring cultural responsiveness in afterschool literacy tutoring: "White people don't eat chicken!"* Roundtable discussion presented at the 66th Annual Conference Literacy Research Association, Nashville, TN.

Tatum, B. D. (2007). *Can we talk about race?: And other conversations in an era of school resegregation.* Beacon Press.

Tierney, R. J. (2018). Toward a model of global meaning making. *Journal of Literacy Research*, *50*(4), 397–422. doi:10.1177/1086296X18803134

Vadasy, P. F., Sanders, E. A., Peyton, J. A., & Jenkins, J. R. (2002). Timing and intensity of tutoring: A closer look at the conditions for effective early literacy tutoring. *Learning Disabilities Research & Practice*, *17*(4), 227–241. doi:10.1111/1540-5826.00048

Villegas, A. M. (1991). *Culturally responsive pedagogy for the 1990s and beyond. Trends and issues paper No. 6.* Washington, DC: ERIC Clearinghouse on Teacher Education.

Wasik, B. A. (1998). Volunteer tutoring programs in reading: A review. *Reading Research Quarterly*, *33*(3), 266–291. doi:10.1598/RRQ.33.3.2

Woolley, G., & Hay, I. (2007). Reading intervention: The benefits of using trained tutors. *Australian Journal of Language and Literacy*, *30*(1), 9–20.

Yang, A. (2010). Engaging participatory literacy through science zines. *The American Biology Teacher*, *72*(9), 573–577. doi:10.1525/abt.2010.72.9.10

Yin, R. K. (2009). *Case study research: Design and methods* (4th ed.). Thousand Oaks, CA: Sage Publications.

Zimmer, R., Hamilton, L., & Christina, R. (2010). After-school tutoring in the context of No Child Left Behind: Effectiveness of two programs in the Pittsburgh Public Schools. *Economics of Education Review*, 2918–2928. doi:10.1016/j.econedurev.2009.02.005

Zirkel, S. (2008). The influence of multicultural educational practices on student outcomes and intergroup relations. *Teachers College Record, 110*(6), 1147–1181.

ADDITIONAL READING

Frederick, R., Donnor, J. K., & Hatley, L. (2009). Culturally responsive applications of computer technologies in education: Examples of best practice. *Educational Technology, 49*(6), 9–13.

Ladson-Billings, G. (1998). Just what is critical race theory and what's it doing in a nice field like education? *International Journal of Qualitative Studies in Education: QSE, 11*(1), 7–24. doi:10.1080/095183998236863

Lewis, C., Enciso, P., & Moje, E. (2007). *Identity, agency and power: Reframing sociocultural research on literacy*. Mahwah, NJ: Lawrence Erlbaum Associates.

May, S., & Sleeter, C. E. (Eds.). (2010). *Critical multiculturalism: Theory and praxis*. New York, NY: Routledge. doi:10.4324/9780203858059

Price-Dennis, D., Holmes, K. A., & Smith, E. (2015). Exploring digital literacy practices in an inclusive classroom. *The Reading Teacher, 69*(2), 195–205. doi:10.1002/trtr.1398

Price-Dennis, D., Wiebe, M. T., & Fowler-Amato, M. (2014). Learning to develop a culturally relevant approach to 21st century writing instruction. *Teaching/Writing. The Journal of Writing Teacher Education, 3*(2).

Rogoff, B. (1994). Developing understanding of the idea of communities of learners. *Mind, Culture, and Activity, 1*(4), 209–229.

Sleeter, C. E. (2001). Preparing teachers for culturally diverse schools research and the overwhelming presence of whiteness. *Journal of Teacher Education, 52*(2), 94–106. doi:10.1177/0022487101052002002

Villegas, A. M., & Lucas, T. (2002). Preparing culturally responsive teachers: Rethinking the curriculum. *Journal of Teacher Education, 53*(1), 20–32. doi:10.1177/0022487102053001003

Wasik, B. A., & Slavin, R. E. (1993). Preventing early reading failure with one-to-one tutoring: A review of five programs. *Reading Research Quarterly*, 179–200.

KEY TERMS AND DEFINITIONS

Cultural Competence: Valuing and respecting diversity, becoming culturally self-aware, and understanding the dynamics of cultural interactions.

Cultural Differences: Differences that can appear when people of different ethnic, religious, socioeconomic, or geographical backgrounds interact.

Cultural Mismatches: The confusion or misunderstandings that can occur due to cultural differences manifesting in ways of living, speaking, and being.

Culturally Responsive Teaching: A method of instructional pedagogy that encompasses sensitivity to and acknowledgement of cultural differences among learners.

Digital Literacies: Literacies which require digital platforms in order to transfer meanings; a means of learning and communicating online.

Digital Tools: Digital or computerized tools that allow for meaning-making with digital literacies such as cell phones, tablets, laptop computers, e-readers, etc.

Racial Awareness: Recognizing and acknowledging the historical, social, political, and economic consequences of being a member of a racially marginalized group.

Sociopolitical Consciousness: A personal awareness of the social, cultural, and political privileges and freedoms not available for some races, genders, ethnicities, and sexual orientations.

Student-Centered Strategies: Instructional techniques that allow students to take the lead in the learning environment.

Chapter 7
"I Would Like Other People to See His Stories Because He Was Woke!": Literacies Across Difference in the Digital Dialogue Project

Julie Rust
Millsaps College, USA

Sarah Alford Ballard
Murrah High School, USA

ABSTRACT

This chapter explores the varied participatory practices that were triggered during the Spring 2016 iteration of the Digital Dialogue Project (DDP), an initiative that connected different age groups in distinct subject-area classes within contrasting schools embedded inside divergent communities. During the project, youth (from 3rd grade to 12th grade) engaged in three phases: (1) producing multimodal products connected to curricular goals, (2) virtually sharing/viewing/commenting on the digital product with small groups of 3-5 youth from different schools, and (3) meeting face to face at a culminating field trip to engage in collaborative theater exercises to dramatically embody the groups' digital stories. Authors provide concrete examples of the kinds of participation that the DDP evoked as well as key pedagogical commitments to literacies that were central to designing and implementing the project. Throughout the chapter, real talk for practicing teachers is provided in order to offer guidance for those interested in imagining similar participatory projects for youth.

DOI: 10.4018/978-1-7998-0000-2.ch007

INTRODUCTION

Participatory literacies, socially embedded interaction and production as a means of moving, being, and impacting the world, have been slow to infiltrate formal, in-school spaces (Rheingold, 2008; Jenkins et al., 2009). Much of this has to do with the fact that standardized curricula rarely leave room for the wandering, improvisatory, sometimes unruly dimensions of digital meaning making across youth. Yet, it is just in these spaces that democracy resides (Rheingold, 2008). We argue that, in order to prepare youth to participate in a civic society, they must first be given plenty of scaffolded opportunities to make meaning within smaller, safer publics: their teacher, classmates, youth in their community (Rheingold, 2008). In this chapter, we follow the ripples of one such designed, scaffolded mini-public in order to uncover the possibilities that might manifest when space is carved out during the school day for digital production, virtual sharing of these digital products, and embodied representations of these digital stories.

BACKGROUND

The entrance of technology into K-12 classroom spaces have opened up a range of opportunities for teachers and youth interested in multimodal meaning making. By enabling the weaving together of music, image, voice, layout, video, and text, such composition practices enable a host of semiotic potential for communicating a message to a wider array of audiences (Kress, 2009; Jewitt, 2009; Hull & Nelson, 2005). It is becoming common practice for teachers to engage youth in slideshow design to demonstrate research findings (e.g. Sewell & Denton, 2011); assign book trailers in place of book reports (e.g. Dalton & Grisham, 2013); and imagine podcast production as a means to demonstrate learning beyond traditional essays (e.g. Goodson & Skillen, 2010). Without a doubt, the entrance of new media into contemporary society has ushered forth the need for, not merely familiarity with new technologies, but a new literacies *ethos* (Lankshear & Knobel, 2007), one that readily accepts the ever changing, multiplicity of tools for meaning making that call for dispositions and practices "central to full civic, economic, and personal participation in a world economy" (Leu et al., 2014, p. 14). Multiliteracies (NLG, 1996) have thus replaced the more stagnant view of a monomodal conceptualization of literacy as merely decoding and encoding print (Cope & Kalantzis, 2000).

In this chapter, we expand on the burgeoning work in the field of multiliteracies to explore the varied participatory practices that were triggered during the Spring 2016 iteration of the Digital Dialogue Project (DDP), an initiative that connected different age groups in distinct subject-area classes within contrasting schools embedded inside divergent communities. During the project, youth (from 3rd grade to 12th grade) engaged in three phases: (1) producing multimodal products connected to curricular goals, (2) virtually sharing/viewing/commenting on the digital product with small groups of 3-5 youth from different schools, and (3) meeting face to face at a culminating field trip to engage in collaborative theater exercises to dramatically embody the groups' digital stories.

In past work (Rust & Ballard, 2016), we highlighted an earlier iteration of the Digital Dialogue Project in Spring 2015, zooming in on Sarah's high school seniors and their experiences moving their stories from page to screen to body. In this work, we broaden our gaze to share how various schools, content areas, and grade levels collaborated in this project to create participatory opportunities. In addition, we utilize a transliteracies lens (Stornaiuolo et al., 2017) to theorize how participatory literacies moved from page to screen to bodies: from individual multimodal design, to virtual small group sharing, and finally to face-to-face dramatic collaboration. We argue that participatory and transliteracies offer far more comprehensive frameworks than new literacies because they resist an exclusionary obsession with the types of materials, tools, and even dispositions with which youth are making meaning. Instead, they lend a focus on what varied engagements with materials and tools for sensemaking in K-12 *produce* for and with(in) particular youth: sometimes equity but also sometimes inequity; often mobility but also often immobility; at times vivid participation, but also other times paralysis.

This chapter will provide a snapshot of a creatively engaging participatory project for classroom teachers of all levels struggling to balance teaching core objectives and preparing students for high stakes testing while still capturing students' imagination and triggering true inquiry and academic curiosity. By examining the array of participation that arose from the entanglements of bodies, technologies, schools, communities, and materials, we paint a more variegated picture of participatory literacies to better inform teacher educators, preservice teachers, and practicing teachers invested in these kinds of multimodal opportunities for youth. We begin this chapter by providing concrete examples of the kinds of participation that the DDP evoked throughout each stage for the various participating youth. We then move on to unpack key conceptual commitments that undergirded the design and implementation of the Digital Dialogue Project in hopes that they might inform others interested in such work. Throughout, we interject perspectives from Sarah, a co-author of this chapter and practicing teacher that was central in both iterations of the project. Her "Teacher Talk" sections afford practitioners tips, observations, and resources/ideas to inspire their own participatory projects for youth.

THE DIGITAL DIALOGUE PROJECT

Julie, an education professor and coauthor of this piece, initially designed the DDP as a way to bring together youth to dialogue across a range of differences (age, socioeconomic, race, etc.); Table 1 below gives a brief summary of the diverse contexts of the five teacher and around eighty student participants, representing various age groups, socio-economic and racial lines, and even classroom subject areas.

In this first section, we unveil the three participatory phases of the DDP, sharing concrete examples of what was produced at each stage for practitioners interested in adapting our framework for their contexts. Figure 1 below provides a brief overview of the three phases that Julie co-planned and co-initiated with five classroom teachers (including Sarah) located in the same metropolitan area of the Deep South. Each phase is described in depth in the subsections below: multimodal composition; virtual sharing, viewing, and commenting; and the culminating field trip.

Phase 1: Multimodal Composition

During this phase, youth designed a variety of multimodal projects that were (1) linked to their teachers' curricular goals and (2) included wide parameters for personal expression, creativity, modality, and topic. We mention curricular goals first, not because they take precedence over youth's choice, but because we remain staunchly aware that the current accountability-driven climate of K-12 schooling often shapes the reality of teacher priorities and decision making (Luke & Woods, 2009). Despite the often negative trickle down effects of such measures, we conceptualize K-12 teachers as professionals who often expertly juggle *both* the prescribed demands they receive and their own personal-professional beliefs about what experiences youth will benefit from. The inclusion of youths' personal choice/expression to

Table 1. Participating schools in the Digital Dialogue Project (DDP)

School	Class	Context Data
St. Francis Episcopal Lower School	3rd Grade Technology	*Independent School *Located in urban center *71.5% White; 13.5% Black; 8.1% Asian; 6.1% Multiracial *Yearly tuition: $17,130
Scholar Prep Charter	5th Grade History	*Charter School *Located in urban center *>95% Black; <5% White, Hispanic *>95% Free/Reduced Lunch
St. Francis Episcopal Middle School	6th Grade Technology	*Independent School *Located in suburb *71.5% White; 13.5% Black; 8.1% Asian; 6.1% Multiracial *Yearly tuition: $17,130
Clark High School	8th grade English	*Public school *Located in rural county *79% White; 21% Black; .3% Hispanic *52% Free/Reduced Lunch
Smith High School	12th Grade AP English	*Public School *Located in urban center *97% Black; 2%White; 1% Hispanic *100% Free/Reduced Lunch

enhance their engagement and potential for communicating was heavily influenced by writing workshop theorists (Atwell, 1998; Calkins, 2006; Kittle, 2008; Hicks, 2009).

This phase was centered within the classroom and led by the classroom teachers, and although students knew they would be sharing their products with 3-5 youth from different schools, the composition process was personally and individually situated. Students began with processes such as traditional writing on paper, storyboarding, outlining, deconstructing mentor texts, etc. They then moved to digitally compose in a variety of means and modes. The brief examples from the five classroom participants below are shared so that readers might get a sense of the scope and diversity of ways that youth might digitally compose in concert with curricular objectives. We invite readers to think creatively about what blend of assignment prompt, platforms, and scaffolds might best meet their own contextualized curricular goals.

Figure 1. 3 Phases of the Digital Dialogue Project (DDP)

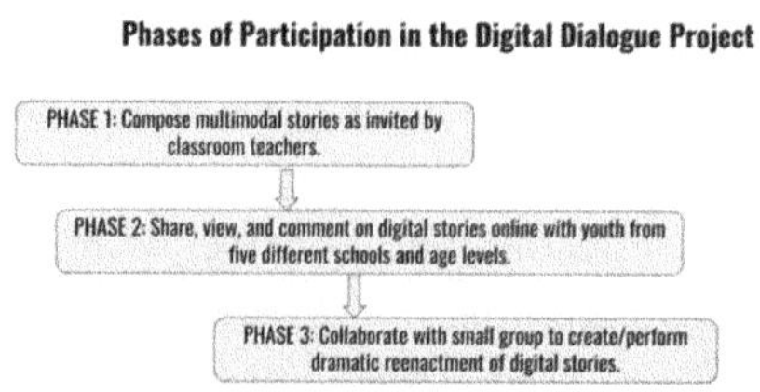

Technology, Third Grade, Private School

This particular assignment was the result of the intersection of two different sets of curricular goals: the third grade classroom teachers sought to provide youth experience writing imagery-filled personal narratives while the technology teacher sought to provide youth experience with building block coding skills, as afforded by a platform called Scratch (https://scratch.mit.edu/). As a result, a multi-step project was designed by the team of teachers: (1) Youth wrote first person narratives using imagery to depict their favorite places. (2) Youth recorded an audio voiceover of the narratives. (3) Youth coded an accompanying digital story using Scratch and layered the audio on top of the visual. Tools most commonly employed in Scratch include choosing background photos and central images to represent self. Students also coded in speech bubbles and particular objects to appear at particular moments.

Figure 2 below features a screenshot from one sample digital story, which was accompanied by the following voiceover, performed by the author:

My room is as messy as a junkyard, but it is still grand. The pointy Legos scrape my feet. They feel like needles. The bed feels like the down of a goose and I plop onto it. The room smells like the candy canes I keep in here. A marbles rolls and sounds like someone barely tapping a gong. I remember when I first went into my room when it was painted. I didn't like it at all. My mom didn't like my complaints either. We got into a big argument but finally she won. I had to deal with the color of my room. I learned a lesson: you can't beat a parent in an argument.

History, Fifth Grade, Charter School

During a Civil Rights Unit based in the mid-20th century US context, the fifth grade history teacher who joined the DDP assigned a series of readings: current events articles about civil rights abuses. Her aim was multifaceted: to increase students' reading comprehension of current events articles as well as

Figure 2. Third grader's multimodal narrative "my favorite place"

to discover connections/overlap between inequities decades ago and inequity today. First, youth were asked to choose a current article in the popular media related to civil rights and then summarize its contents using a graphic organizer. They then composed a vlog or slideshow with voiceover that connected the contemporary subject of their article (e.g. persecution of Muslim women wearing headscarves) to civil rights battles that took place among African Americans in the US in the mid-20th century. The transcript below features the audio in one representative fifth grader's multimodal composition in which he compares the treatment of Muslim women with headscarves to the violent treatment of black men by police during the Watts Riots in 1965. Note that in his voiceover he also nods to the fact that unfair interactions between authorities and African-Americans are not merely an issue in our history, but are a reality in our current landscape.

. . . The response you are about to hear from me is about inequality today. In the article "Identified by Head Scarves: Muslim Women Being Confronted across the US," Muslim women are being treated unequally because they are being harassed based on the way they are dressed which represents the Muslim religion. This harassing problem results in a bullying problem . . . This issue relates to the Civil Rights Movement because it relates to the issue between the police and the black teenagers. The issue between the police and the black teenagers is all about the way they look. I chose this article because it relates to the same issue that is going on now between police and black teenagers.

Technology, Sixth Grade, Private School

This project was initiated by the middle school technology teacher because of his interest in giving youth experience working with the art of audio composition and editing platforms. Youth first spent guided time deconstructing mentor NPR stories and podcasts to get a sense of the elements of the genre: use of ambient noise during interviews, music, and editing were highlighted. Students were then asked to choose a theme they were interested in exploring and conducted interviews and created podcasts themed around investigatory reporting of some locally-situated school area of interest (e.g. food in the cafeteria, balancing academics with athletics, etc.) The transcript below is drawn from one podcast that investigated how it feels to be a sixth grade teacher in the morning.

*Hi, I'm *Sonya and I'm interviewing the sixth grade teachers. I want to know what it feels like to be a sixth grade teacher in the morning. Let's see what they say. . .*

*(Sonya's voice): Hi, Ms. *Taylor I'm Sonya. Now tell me, when you arrive at school in the morning, how are you feeling?*

*(Teacher's voice): Well, *Sonya I'm glad you asked that question. You know, most mornings I get to school I'm literally sort of washing around because I'm not necessarily the best morning person, but as I'm driving up I'm thinking, "What do I need to be planning for today? . . . I want to be sure to have plenty of fun and challenging activities and oh my goodness, is our copier working?"*

English, Eighth Grade, Rural Public High School

In this assignment, an eighth grade English teacher aimed to provide students the opportunity to interpret a novel through multiple modes and also reflect on their artistic choices in a written artist's statement. As a result, students were given class time to paint their favorite scenes of *Lord of the Flies* while listening to the movie soundtrack. They then typed up an artist's statement explaining the choices that they made while painting. Finally, they uploaded a slideshow with an introductory "all about me" slide, an introduction to the novel, and a snapshot of their painting with an accompanying voiceover that featured the introductions and audio of a composed artist's statement. (For an example, see Figure 3 and 4.)

(Voiceover accompanying slide in Figure 3 above): Hi. Before I share with you my project, and I want to share a little more about me. . . I'm in love with music so I'm in both of the show choirs the school has to offer. . . Something else that I'm quite passionate about is writing and reading. In my free time I tend to write all the time, whether that be a short story or a story with 12 pages and quickly gaining . . . yeah I'm kind of a nerd, but even though I'm not the most outgoing person, I still like seeing new people and making new friends . . . I'm super excited to be able to take part in this really cool project with you.

Figure 3. Introductory slide for 8th grader's digital artist's statement

Figure 4. 8th grader painting inspired by Lord of the Flies

Figure 5. One 12th grader's personal college essay transformed into iMovie

(Voiceover accompanying slide in Figure 4 above): This piece of artwork depicts the sickness that was shown in the boys. This drawing shows the evil and, the dark desires, and the animalistic nature brought out in the boys during their stay on the island through the most obvious example: Jack. The pain on Jack's face is the mask he hid behind when he committed his most vicious of acts. The blood dripping from the corners of his mouth is to symbolize his thirst and lust for blood and death. The smile on his face shows that he enjoys the destruction of his cause. The fangs are used to signify the animalistic urges that took over the boys. The fire around them is to represent the devastation on the island. One could see this piece in two ways. You could see it in a very literal sense, but you could also see the figurative aspects that if offers.

English, Twelfth Grade, Urban Public High School

In this assignment, Sarah aimed for AP Literature and Composition students to continue working on narrative writing, having composed a college essay earlier in the year. Students considered the story they told in their college essay, and were given the freedom to use that story as the catalyst for their project or tell another personal story that they believe to be integral in their own identity. The students transformed their personal narratives into digital stories, which had to incorporate their voice, visual imagery and music. The students were given freedom to choose whatever platform with which they felt most comfortable to produce their digital story, but most used iMovie. They published their finished digital stories to Voicethread and were able to share their stories with their class, their teacher, and their DDP assigned groups. Figure 5 below features one snapshot of one such story, entitled "The Girl Who Wears Skirts."

*My name is *Catherine. If you didn't know my name, you'd probably identify me as the girl who wears the skirts all the time. For many of you who don't know, wearing skirts is a part of my church's doctrine. If you'd like me to explain why, I'd probably say "I don't know" or come up with an explanation that may or may not make sense. . . . if you've had a conversation with me for longer than 20 minutes I have no doubt in my mind you've asked me these questions: "Do you wear skirts to bed?" I would answer,*

"No." "You don't own a single pair of pants?" "Nope- not even khakis." "Can you wear like shorts?" "Uh- not outside of my home." "Are you a Mormon?" "What's a Mormon?" I'd ask out of pure ignorance. "What's that religion?" "Will you wear skirts when you're older?" "I don't know." I've often wondered how it felt wearing pants and so many times I've felt the desire to. But over the years in my maturity, I've noticed that wearing skirts makes me stand out in the crowd. It makes me different. It's more than just my doctrine. Wearing skirts is ultimately who I am.

Looking across all of the examples in this section, it is clear that although this initial composition phase was participatory and active, it did not ask youth to collaborate in any sustained way. Instead, youth were focused on fulfilling the individual assignment that their teacher had planned to meet a specified objective. Yet it is also just as clear that these multimodal assignment held space for youth's own personal exploration. For instance, the third grader author was successful in practicing the descriptive language objectives his teacher held as central, particularly in the form of similes and imagery. At the same time he was given the space to describe his room: a place he clearly loves. The fifth grader featured exercised some important reading and summarizing muscles on his way to produce his slideshow/voiceover, but the connections he made paved the way for something deeper and more personally resonant: an understanding of the ways that inequity echoes from era to era, sometimes taking on different shapes, but never fully dissolving. The sixth grader above learned how to write an audio story script and record/edit, but she also chose a topic that intrigued her and pushed her to have honest conversations with a variety of her teachers in order to determine just how it felt to experience their daily lived reality. In the eighth grade English class, youth benefitted from transposing their comprehension of a novel into a work of art and then were pushed to articulate their artistic choices into words on the page. However, they also enjoyed autonomy in what to paint and how to paint, and many of them spent a surprising amount of time in their introductory slide collage to serve as their first impression in Phase 2. Finally, the twelfth grade students gained experience translating their more formal narrative college essays into digital stories that younger students could view and in doing so, were given room to explore deeply rooted aspects of self, such as the interplay between religiously-derived expectations about dress and personal identity.

TEACHER TALK: Many of the students initially found the personal freedom in their digital composition to be intimidating and sometimes paralyzing, being used to most assignment's very rigid and precise instructions and guidelines. However, the teachers believed that for the students to have personal buy-in, they needed to work through that gray area and find their voice within each project. When I first started branching out into assigning projects for my students that were a bit messier and less structured, I often found that my students helped shape the assignment as we progressed from stage to stage. As a teacher, you have to let go of some control for this to work. Making a plan for what objectives you need to address in each phase will help you feel grounded, but be flexible and make room for discoveries.

Phase 2: Virtual Sharing, Viewing, Commenting

Phase 2 was orchestrated by Julie, and involved placing one student from each participating school into heterogeneous groups on Voicethread. Although this was logistically time consuming, we found it well worth the hassle; carving out authentic audiences for student work beyond just the teacher is so key in enhancing engagement and the diversity of feedback they might then receive (Duke et al., 2006; Magnifico, 2010; Curwood et al., 2013). The students were not matched based on topics or relatability, but were simply divided into the groups to provide contact with youth from different schools and age groups producing a variety of products. For example, one single group of five included the authors of five different stories to view and comment on: a third grader's story entitled "My Favorite Place", a fifth grader's v-log named "The Struggle to Become a First Class Citizen" a sixth grader's podcast about uniforms, an eighth grader's artistic representation of a novel, and a twelfth grader's iMovie entitled "Race for Life."

Each teacher in the DDP requested that students take time to explore the different projects in their group and provide peer feedback. The Voicethread platform enabled a wide variety of modes of feedback: audio comment, video comment, and text comment. The vast majority of youth used the text-based comment feature. Because in the first iteration of the DDP teachers noticed that students often offered short, surface-level feedback, teachers spent time this round explicitly encouraging "substantive feedback," defined as feedback that made connections, specifically pointed out what was well done, or offered constructive critique. This phase, then, (1) opened up opportunities for youth to see what other students at different schools had been working on, (2) gave them practice offering thoughtful responses to other authors' stories, (3) enabled youth to receive positive affirmation of their work from peers, and (4) aided in youth taking the first step in building a relationship with the other students in their group.

The comments on the Voicethread projects range in maturity and analysis, often (but not always) correlated to the age of the group member. Figures 6-8 reveal the range of sophistication with which youth commented by highlighting the various responses a fifth grader's v-log about civil rights abuses evoked from his group members: a third grader (Figure 6), an eighth grader (Figure 7), and a senior (Figure 8).

Figure 6. Representative comment from third grade youth during phase 2

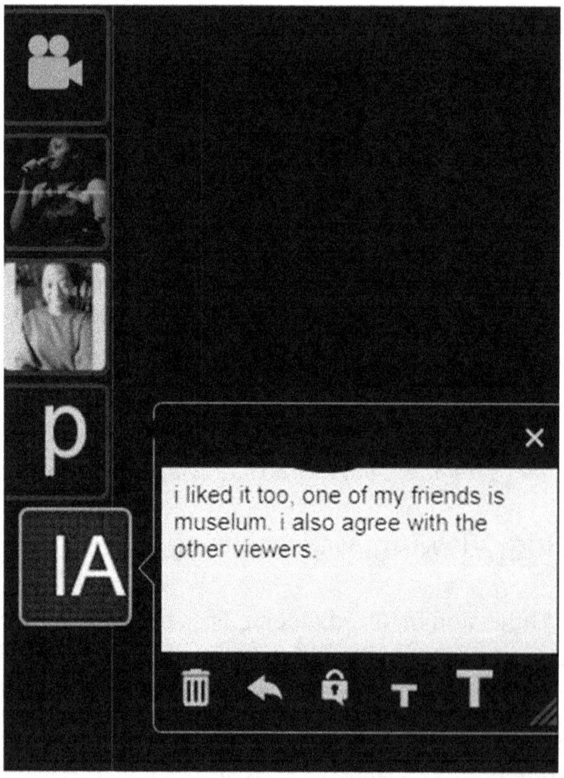

Figure 7. Representative comment from eighth grade youth during phase 2

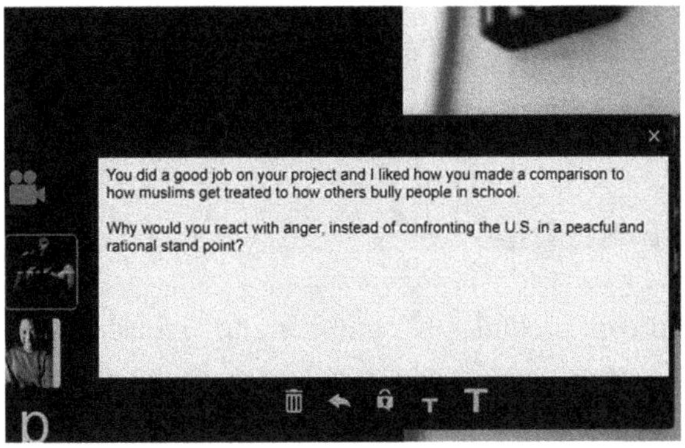

Some of the group members took on more constructive criticism in their feedback. In Group 5, for instance this commenter offered suggestions for improvement:

Great job on your Voicethread! I enjoyed your topic. However, I could barely hear you even though I had my volume turned all the way up. So just try to speak a little louder if you can, if you can't it's fine:) But overall great job.

Many of the participants had a personal reaction to their group member's project, especially the ones that were more personal. In the same group, Group 5, one student said about a project titled "The Struggle with My Best Friend": "I loved how you told me about you(r) relationship with your family and how you worked really hard on this. You did a great jo(b). PS. this video made me cry." Because youth were able to choose to leave either a written or voice/video comment, not only were the different youth reading peer reaction to the different projects, but they could also hear the voices of many of the students they had yet to meet.

TEACHER TALK: Assigning a project that is reliant on technology can be a barrier, especially in a school that lacks funding for technology and has a student population that may not have access to internet at home. However, our student's reality is based upon being tech savvy and resourceful; therefore, it is imperative that teachers provide opportunities for participatory projects. Do not be afraid to ask

Figure 8. Representative comment from twelfth grade youth during phase 2

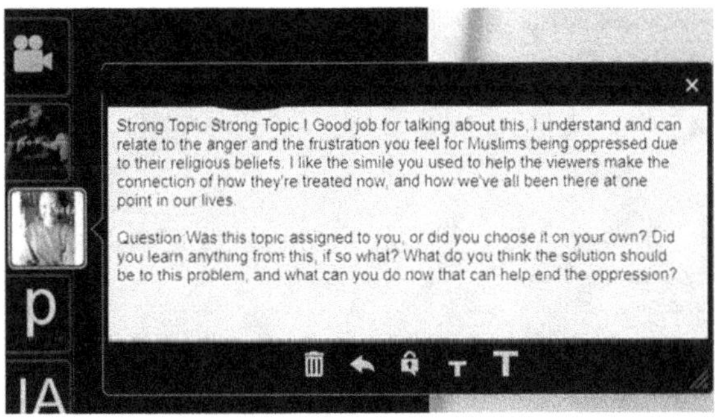

students to help you think through how to make the project work. Can you borrow a set of laptops from the library or can students use their phones? Teachers must also build time into their day to allow their student's access to the technology needed to complete the assignment. Although we used Voicethread to facilitate sharing and commenting, there are also free platforms that facilitate similar types of functions such as FlipGrid or perhaps private Youtube channels.

Phase 3: Culminating Field Trip

During the culminating field trip, around 80 youth from all five separate schools made their way to Julie's college campus. The participating teachers and Julie designed the gathering to finally enable a face-to-face meeting of the heterogeneous groups of 4-5 that had already dialogued virtually on Voicethread during Phase 2. Around ten preservice teachers aided to help organize, chaperone, and lead the event. Youth walked in and began engaging in a series of warm up theater games and were then directed to sit in a circle with their small group. After a brief introduction and quickshare of the various purposes behind each school's set of multimodal compositions, the small groups engaged in a few more theater games and icebreaker activities. At that point, the main project of the day was introduced: small groups were given 30 minutes to work together to create a performance of some kind that integrated a key line from all 3-5 represented digital stories in their group. The goals in this creative challenge were for youth in each group (which together represented a diverse set of ages, socioeconomic, racial, and other backgrounds) to (1) practice collaborating across difference (2) find areas in which their stories overlapped, revealing a semblance of common ground (3) transpose their digital stories to a new form entirely: embodied dramatic performance. Figure 9 is a shot of the room when groups were hard at work: while most groups chose to stay seated in their small circles, several moved to the side of the room so they could stand up and practice blocking/poses.

After the work time expired, each group took a turn sharing their performance. Performances varied in form: from more traditional skits, to tableaus/poses with key lines, to a collaboratively authored and performed poem. For example, one group used the frame of a family dinner table scene to meld together the key lines/themes from their digital stories. It begins with the mother role asking "how was your day today?" Youth around the table recall reading *Lord of the Flies* in English class (an allusion to the 8th grader's digital story), making steps toward repairing a relationship with a family member (an allusion to the 12th grader's iMovie), bullying at the school (pointing toward the third grader's digital story), and witnessing an act of intolerance at the shopping market (drawing from the 5th grader's slideshow about

Figure 9. Small group Digital Dialogue Project dramatic collaboration

inequity). They end by stating the "moral of the skit," a theme that ties across the varied digital stories represented: "you should treat everyone fairly and how you'd like to be treated."

Skits were the most popular form of performance, and the majority of them took place in school contexts. One was designed drawing on the game show genre using "Would You Rather" to tie together various key lines. Others leaped from setting to setting to encapsulate the various contexts that defined each digital story (e.g. from school to a desert island to someone's bedroom). Another was designed as a text or social media conversation from youth to youth, and it utilized hashtags in a humorous way that successfully produced laughter in the audience.

Another type of performance that was utilized several times was having each individual youth state the key line from the digital story and then having the whole group pose in a moving or still tableau. Figure 10 below depicts one such performance, and the impact of stating and embodying each key line next to each other was viscerally powerful in shedding light on the connections between their diverse set of projects.

Finally, one particularly effective group chose to not merely put their key lines in close proximity, but to write them into a poem with the shared theme (and title) of "Coping." They did so using a method that the senior had learned at a creative writing camp: the snake poem. They then performed the poem, each reading their key line that showed up in their digital story and passing the microphone down to the next group member. The entire audience was captivated as they spoke their simple but personal truths:

Coping

(12th grader): How similar do the three of us look to you?

We're all white, we're all young, yet we're all a bit different too.

(3rd grader): We all need personal space when we're mad or angry.

(8th grader): Dealing with different things depends on how your day is going, what you're going through, or how stressed you are,

(12th grader): All of these contribute to our different reactions,

Figure 10. Tableau performance during phase 3

Our mechanisms shift as we lift up our lives to the light and examine our days with spite or with might.

(3rd grader): When I am sad or mad I go into my closet so I can have time to myself.

(8th grader): When I am dealing with something I don't want the world to know about I go into my room and hide away.

(12th grader): When I have a bad day or a bad run of luck with the month I run and I write until my limbs fall off. We all cope . . . a bit differently. We all look . . . a bit similarly. But the important thing we want you to take away is we are all pretty healthy.

After the performances, the whole group had a brief, whole-group conversation facilitated by Julie about "how it went" and "what they liked" about other group's skits. They then voted for their favorites in several categories: most funny, best integration of key lines, best teamwork, and most polished. Pizza, cookies, and lemonade were served, and although some youth reverted back to their friend groups from their school, several of the DDP groups stayed together during the free lunchtime. Winners were announced and students loaded the buses to head back to their respective schools.

TEACHER TALK: Field trips can be a total nightmare to plan; however, if given the chance, they are the most participatory of the stages. When students can build on the relationships they have formed online, the online experience transcends an assignment to become a lasting part of their matriculation. When planning a field trip that brings the heterogeneous groups together, think about what space is going to allow room for movement and collaboration and what activities will help bridge the awkward initial meeting.

WHAT WAS SO PARTICIPATORY ABOUT THE DIGITAL DIALOGUE PROEJCT?

Now that each phase of the project has been introduced in applied terms, we zoom out in the subsections below to conceptually describe how participatory (Rowsell & Wohlwend, 2016) and transliteracies (Stornaiuolo et al., 2017) frameworks were taken up pedagogically to inform the design and implementation of the Digital Dialogue Project. These interweaving frameworks informed our vision of the possibilities of meaning making across school contexts. Transliteracies and participatory literacies triggered a series of commitments and beliefs about literacies, highlighted in the subsections below, which drove the planning and practical enactment of the project. We share the literacy tenants below (literacies as socio-identity practices; literacies as agentic, emergent, playful production; literacies move fluidly; and literacies as (re)producing (in)equity) in hopes that they might serve as helpful foundational commitments for others in the field initiating similar collaborative meaning making experiences.

Literacies as Socio-Identity Practices

At its center, the Digital Dialogue Project (DDP) was designed to foreground the socially-embedded nature of meaning making. Participatory literacies (PL) emphasize the move from perceiving literacy as decontextualized skills (e.g. spelling, grammar, decoding/encoding print text) to thinking about literacy as a myriad of socio-identity practices that involve a multitude of forms of active meaning-making (Rowsell & Wohlwend, 2016; Rheingold, 2008). PL thus decenter the importance of isolated literacy skills (e.g. decoding/encoding words on paper) and instead foreground the social underpinnings that motivate meaning making to begin with. In the case of designing the DDP, the central shape of the project involved connecting youth of different ages, races, socio-economic statuses, and experiences to create, share, and collaboratively embody multimodal compositions. The hopes were that, as a result of these partnerships across difference, literacies would be "co-constructed in conversation or in the midst of play others" (Rowsell & Wohlend, 2016, p. 197). Rheingold (2008) writes:

Participatory culture shifts the focus of literacy training from individual expression onto community involvement: the new literacies are almost all social skills which have to do with collaboration and networking. These skills build on the foundation of traditional literacy, research skills, technical skills, and critical analysis skills which should have been part of the school curriculum all along. (p. 99)

If the DDP had been designed to stop after the first phase, when youth produced a multimodal composition and turned it in to their teacher, it would not have been fully participatory. The built-in opportunity in Phase 2 to share stories with small groups of 3-5 students (one from each school), however, created a mini-social-milieu for youth to engage with, one that shifted the exercise away from mere "individual expression" and into "community involvement." It is important to note that the DDP didn't immerse youth into the community at large; instead, they were put in a carefully controlled partnership with a set of four other schools. However, we believe, with Rheingold (2008), that "social scaffolding" is essential "for any interventions involving self-expression" (p. 99). First, youth shared their products with their immediate, familiar peers and teacher. Then, they shared them with four youth of different age groups and school contexts. Cultivating an audience for student work should be a key concern for those of us invested in participatory literacy since, after all, "it isn't 'voice' if nobody seems to be listening" (Rheingold, 2008, p. 99).

Clear elements of participatory culture (Jenkins et al., 2009) lurked throughout each phase of the DDP: *expressions* (the production of new creative forms through digital composition and dramatic performance), *affiliations* (fostered through the small groups on Voicethread that later met to collaborate), *circulations* (sharing and commenting on each others' stories), and *collaborative problem solving* (working together on the day of the field trip to create embodied performances) (Jenkins et al., 2009). Rowsell & Wohlwend (2016) write about participatory culture as "connected" in this way:

A participatory culture is a culture with relatively low barriers to artistic expression and civic engagement, strong support for creating and sharing one's creations, and some type of informal mentorship whereby what is known by the most experienced members is passed along to novices. A participatory culture is one in which members believe their contributions matter and feel a degree of social connection with one another (at the least, they care what other people think about what they have created). (p. 200)

In the DDP, students of varied skill levels contributed a wide range of digital products, such as investigatory podcasts, watercolor renderings of scenes from a recently read novel, and transformations of written personal narratives into iMovies. As a result, there were relatively "low barriers" to artistic expression. During the second and third phases of the project, mentorship flowed freely and came in the form of comments made on Voicethread as well as during the co-construction of performances: often from older youth to younger youth. Throughout the process, the assumption was that youth would care more because of the social practices so integral to the DDP.

Making space for social practices can be messy, dangerous, and unpredictable. Yet, "democracy lives precisely within the unruly peer-to-peer relationships, networks, and norms that young people seek to develop for themselves" (Rheingold, 2008, p. 102). In fact:

Youth need publics- networked or physical- before they can engage in any form of political life. Politics start first with the school, with your friends...then they grow to being about civics. Pushing the other way won't work. You need to start with the dramas that make sense to you" (boyd, p. 22; as cited in Rhiengold, 2008, p 103).

In this way, we built the DDP to provide more than just opportunities to build relationships and practice the complex art of self-positioning with new people; we designed it in hopes of giving youth opportunities to give voice and volume to cultivate their growing sense of self as civically engaged citizen, the subject of the next section.

TEACHER TALK: Because many of our schools are not diverse- either racially, socio-economically, or culturally- it is our job to purposefully provide opportunities for our students to interact with diverse peers and to move literacy out of the textbook. Literacy in the classroom often gets regulated to what the students score on a certain benchmark with a particular objective. But we know that is not true literacy. When I am thinking through a new project that seems a little out of the confines of traditional literacy, I like to ground the project with a piece of literature. It may help you in planning your own digital dialogue project to pick a powerful anchor text as a starting point, as well. The text provides the teacher and students a more familiar platform from which to transcend as the project pushes them into making personal meaning. The text is a way into the project that the whole class can use as a collective resource. With my advanced students I usually chose a text based on HOW the writer manipulates language for purpose, but with younger students the text could be based on theme or subject matter.

Literacies as Agentic, Emergent, Playful Production

Another key consideration that shaped the design of the DDP was the importance of making room for youth agency through choice-driven, emergent playful production. A participatory literacy framework compels an appreciation of the creation of content (Rowsell & Wohlwend, 2016), play (Jenkins et al., 2009), and performance (Jenkins et al., 2009). More important than the creation of a perfect product is the understanding of the "layered literacies" that youth move through as they engage with "various modalities and practices" in order to "[assert] agency" (Rowsell & Wohlwend, 2016, p. 199). These broader and more agentic conceptualizations of literacies make space for recognizing the messiness of meaning-making as it surfaces in "moment-to-moment" and "improvised engagements" (Rowsell & Wohlwend, 2016, p. 198). In this way, the DDP was designed as an antidote to the prescribed, standardized, test driven curricula that so often currently mark K-12 school experiences today. Smith et al.(2018) explain:

A transliteracies approach to teaching and learning focuses one's attention toward these emergent, unplanned, and contingent dimensions of meaning making. Such an approach calls for educators to bracket their preconceived ideas of how a student will come to learn a concept, and instead follow the ways literacies emerge in activity. (p. 22)

In other words, the DDP was not "backwards designed" from College and Career Readiness Standards (CCRS) or AP Test Preparation Guides. Instead, it sought to open up ways for youth to produce and then connect in both structured and spontaneous ways across the course of the semester. Nevertheless, as is often the case in truly engaging, authentic meaning making, youth ended up practicing on demonstrating mastery of a host of CCRS Standards along the way.

During every phase of the DDP, youth choice remained central. In the first phase, youth were assigned a particular curricularly-aligned prompt, but they were also given a good deal of latitude in specific content and form. For instance, eighth graders painted a scene from *The Lord of the Flies,* but they were able to choose the scene, the style of painting (from abstract to realistic), and they constructed their own artist's statement to defend and articulate their artistic visions. Emergence and improvisation were central to this phase; for instance, a student may accidentally smear the paint and then be forced to reconceptualize the entire layout of the piece. As youth moved into the second phase (sharing/commenting on Voicethread with group members from different schools), they had the responsibility to produce feedback for their peers but could choose which form best suited their needs for expression (audio comments, video comments, or simply text comments.) In the third phase, youth had to collaboratively produce an embodied performance for the group of 80 or so students. They could choose any kind of performance, and group choices ranged from snake poems to tableaus, to game show skits and more. There was a good deal of play among group members, and much improvisation as youth had a limited time to prepare their performances.

Rheingold (2008) sees this play with various media as a powerful complement to"interest in civic engagement". He asks: "Might teachers enlist these young people's enthusiasm for using digital media in the service of civic engagement? I propose one way to do this: help students communicate in their public voices about issues they care about" (Rheingold, 2008, p. 97). Indeed, several teachers in the DDP assigned initial multimodal products that made space for issues of citizenship. For instance, fifth graders at the charter school were asked by their history teacher to create a video essay comparing/contrasting any civil rights issue today with a civil rights issue in the past. Sixth graders at the private school created podcasts revolving around school issues and interviews with stakeholders (e.g. "should we be required to wear uniforms?" and "what do teachers really think about us?"). These prompts paved the way for youth to become "active creators as well as consumers of culture" (Rheingold, 2008, p. 97).

TEACHER TALK: What we found in this project is that when given the space, most students will go deeper than the assignment initially calls for. The students want to perform well on the test that they are told determines their graduation and the school's rankings. So, teachers cannot just ignore these expectations. Equally, most of students will want to know how they will be graded for this project. Along with anchoring participatory projects with a strong mentor text, providing a rubric will ease their minds and allow them more freedom for creativity. If you have administrators who want to see a direct link between core objectives and the project, the rubric is a good place to soothe any concerns.

Literacies Move Fluidly Across Places, Spaces, Bodies, Technologies, Platforms

Despite the tendency to bifurcate in-school/out-of-school, digital/face-to-face, and academic/social literacy practices, we built our project on the assumption that meaning making flows freely across places, spaces, times, technologies, and platforms (Dovchin & Pennycook, 2017; Buck, 2012; Leander & McKin, 2003). Literacies, then, can be described as "nested" within a wide variety of contexts and semiotic systems (Rowsell & Wohlwend, 2016, p. 198).Julie's initial conception of three separate phases of the Digital Dialogue Project directly stemmed from a desire to make space for a flow across a variety of spaces, platforms, and times: first youth created multimodal digital stories, then they shared and commented on each other's in small groups, and finally they collaboratively remixed their stories into an embodied performance when they met face to face. Each phase, then, ushered forth particular spacetimes and platforms, including everything from home spaces, school spaces, iMovie, Voicethread, the college campus, and the use of embodied performative practices as meaning making. In past work, we call the way youth's stories traveled from page to screen to bodies "traversing literacies" (Rust & Ballard, 2016). This *networked* nature of literacies enables meaning to travel from text and speech to home and school to image and sound and bodies (Rheingold, 2008; Jenkins et al., 2008). This "ability to follow the flow of stories and information across multiple modalities" is referred to by Jenkins et al. (2009) as "transmedia navigation."

In the first phase the DDP asked youth to navigate the many modes and platforms inherent in digital composition practices within and outside of physical classroom spaces. (For example, seniors began with a college narrative essay they had written. They then worked to translate the essay on a page into an iMovie. In order to do so, they often spent time browsing through personal photographs on their phones to use in their movies while sitting in the school library. When the library computers didn't work, they retreated back to their iPhones and most did an iMovie creation, editing on their small personal devices.) In the second phase, when youth were asked to view each other's multimodal stories on Voicethread, they "met" new peers from different schools through screens and digitized means. When youth traveled to the college campus for a field trip, they were asked to work collaboratively face-to-face to create embodied performances in which they took a key line from each of the 3-5 digital stories produced by group members to combine all five stories into a single performance. In this way, the DDP was designed to engage youth in *remixing* group members' media content into dramatic performance (Jenkins et al., 2009). In sum, the DDP facilitated the flow of stories across modes, space, platform, and time, but it also facilitated the merging and reshaping of these very stories through dialogue with other stories and other selves.

TEACHER TALK:Transmedia navigation can happen with your students in so many different ways. You can reach out to neighboring schools in your community. Or, if that feels too daunting or not applicable, reach out to different grades and/or subject matter. What an interesting way to break down social barriers in your school to have students "meeting" each other online and then joining together for a culminating community experience. Teachers, we must scaffold the flow of literacy outside the classroom and into more spaces, which allows our students freedom and a chance to see the power in their expression.

Literacies as (Re)producing (In)equity

The DDP was centrally designed with the understanding that access, experiences, and resources vary widely based on perceived skill-levels, socioeconomic status, and age of youth (Rheingold, 2008, Jenkins et al., 2009). As a result, four very different schools representing quite divergent communities in the metro area were invited to participate, in hopes that this experience would prove to be equalizing and in the belief that we as humans grow the most when we are asked to collaborate with those that have different backgrounds than us. In fact, Jenkins et al. (2009) writes that one key new media literacy skills necessitated to move across participatory cultures is "negotiation", "the ability to travel across diverse communities, discerning and respecting multiple perspectives, and grasping and following alternative norms" (Jenkins et al., 2009). The third phase of the DDP most vividly reached for these lofty aims, as youth worked together in teams of 3-5 youth of different ages and backgrounds to creatively embody a performance that illustrated the common ground that exists between all of us as humans.

Still, it is almost impossible to overemphasize the diversity of challenges that participants in the DDP faced. The inherently collaborative nature of the DDP at times paralyzed, rather than mobilized youth in various ways: imagined audience at times inhibited free personal composition, unestablished relationships with the students from different schools placed resulted in discomfort and misunderstanding, and the diversity of ages, socioeconomic statuses, dis/abilities, and races represented had the potential to unearth monolithic assumptions about "the other" (Rust, 2019). Nevertheless, the majority of reflective interviews after the fact revealed that the DDP helped youth transcend preconceived boundaries, such as this twelfth grader who recounted her surprise after viewing a fifth grader's compelling and socially conscious vlog about racial inequality:

I would like other people to see his stories because he was WOKE. . . I feel like a lot of times teachers for younger kids want to shelter them and keep them from what's going on so when they get to higher grades . . . In middle school you are hit with everything . . . It's good to start breaking them in: "this is what happening, you can get through this, let's talk about this." It allows them to expose their opinions ...This is just getting them out there to say what they think about real world issues.

Despite these positive accounts, more practical challenges surfaced. Youth/teachers at schools with larger populations of traditionally disenfranchised groups faced greater difficulties in the open-ended, technology-centric phases of the project. After all, such communities are often thrust into test preparation, more mandated or standardized curricula, and face fewer resources, training, or technical support (Rheingold, 2008). As a result, "accountability and innovation are often locked into a zero sum game" (p. 99). Because of this, we found it important to provide extra support, through a small grant of funds and additional teacher support, for schools that faced additional obstacles to the DDP. We believed, like Rheingold (2008), that

Arguing for the place of participatory media literacy in the curriculum is not a peripheral debate, but is part of one of the defining conflicts of our time, a power struggle that involves political, economic, technological, as well as educational dimensions. Participatory media literacy is an active response to the as-yet-unsettled battles over political and economic power in the emerging mediasphere, and to the possibility that today's young people could have a say in shaping part of the world they will live in—or might be locked out of that possibility. The struggle for participatory media literacy in schools must be seen in the context of these broader societal conflicts. (Rheingold, 2008, p. 100)

These broader social conflicts don't merely result in fewer participatory opportunities for some youth during the school day, they also result in inhibited mobility when participatory opportunities present themselves, such as during the DDP. As has been explored elsewhere (Rust, 2019), just because social opportunities have been set up in a collaborative pedagogical situation does not mean that all participants flow with the same degree of freedom within these social spaces. Recent (re)imaginings of transliteracies have pushed teachers/researchers to move beyond just thinking about literacies traversing platforms, but to "consider the connections and intersections that arise as people, ideas, and objects move and interact" (Smith et al., 2018, pp 21-22). This critical lens enables us, as pedagogical designers, to not merely take into account "the multiplicity and diversity of people and communicative forms" but also to "[pay] close attention to how those people and things move and interact in various relationships" (Smith et al., 2018, p. 21). Interestingly, the more global, connected, and participatory meaning-making becomes the more opportunities there are for barriers to impede the flow of meaning making for some. In other words, "even as some people and things move freely, others are restricted, constrained, or immobilized" (Smith et al., 2018, p. 22).

A transliteracies approach to meaning making involves a critical examination of whose voices, movements, and practices are curtailed and how that curtailment is tied to historical and systemic forms of marginalization. This involves pressing beyond necessary yet insufficient discussions of technological access to consider how technologies are being used, by whom, and in what ways. (p. 22)

These questions are resonant with Jenkins et al. (2009) concerns about the participation gap, "the unequal access to the opportunities, experiences, skills, and knowledge that will prepare youth for full participation in the world of tomorrow" (p. 3) In fact, Jenkins et al. (2009) introduce multiple terms that suggest the need for those with an eye toward equity to enact more policy/pedagogic interventions: the participation gap (unequal access to opportunities and skills), the transparency problem (challenges to see how various sources mediate our vision of the world), and the ethic challenge (breakdown of traditional forms of socialization to prepare youth to engage with communities) (p. 3). The DDP was designed to intervene most particularly with the participation gap by giving youth opportunities to design multimodal compositions and share these virtually. It was also designed to interrupt the ethics challenge by giving youth the opportunity to meet and collaborate with those from different communities. Both aspects of the DDP were designed to enhance what Jenkins et al. (2009) call new media literacies: "a set of cultural competencies and social skills that young people need in the new media landscape" (Jenkins et al., 2009, p. 4).

This focus on equity in the design and implementation of the DDP helped us as researchers, teachers, and youth confront differences in resources, interactions, collaborations, and larger time scales and contexts across the school participants. Throughout the various phases, we found ourselves continuously asking ourselves how different youth would experience each phase of the project, how they would position themselves with the other members of their groups, and how we as a teacher and researcher could create moments for meaning to flow equitably across difference. In a sense, it was this commitment to equity that initially provoked the initial vision of the DDP. We felt keenly that youth at all five schools had different pathways and trajectories, with varied degrees of mobility to share their stories. The idea to open up various timespaces, platforms, and modes for making meaning was birthed in hopes of equalizing the playing field for youth at schools that often didn't make room for these practices. At the same time, however, we recognize that the DDP, as a pedagogical intervention, was far from universally successful in meeting this utopian aim. While the DDP sought to increase mobility among all of the youth participants, it also inadvertently and simultaneously initiated flows that served to "(re)produce, exacerbate, and/or challenge social inequities" (Stornaiuolo et al., 2017, p. 17).

TEACHER TALK Because I teach in a school with limited technology and a large focus on testing, I had to constantly rethink how I was going to make time and space for this project. My school is very supportive of providing opportunities for our students to learn, but as a Title 1 public school, we are heavily tied to test scores in order to improve our "school grade." Almost all resources goes toward that goal. Parts of this transliteracy project were more successful than others, and that is okay. Some of the schools had an easier time with classroom flexibility, technological resources, and field trip funding. However, driving all the teachers was the desire to close the participation gap and the realization that equity won't happen organically; educators must be diligent and purposeful in designing a transliteracy project.

CONCLUSION

In this chapter, we first outlined how we designed and enacted three phases of the Digital Dialogue Project: multimodal composition, sharing and commenting with youth online, and embodied dramatic collaboration. We included specific cases throughout each phase in order to generate ideas of the range of ways teacher-practitioners invited youth into meaning-making with others, as well as to highlight the compelling diversity of the ways that youth might choose to take up these invitations. We then illuminated some key beliefs, bolstered by participatory and transliteracy frameworks, that might serve as a guideposts for those interested in designing similar opportunities for youth: literacies as socio-identity practices; literacies as agentic/emergent production; literacies as moving fluidly across spaces, places, bodies, and platforms; and literacies as (re)producing (in)equity.

Whereas participatory literacies are most commonly thought about in relation to informal, out-of-school spaces, this chapter offers one snapshot of the kinds of projects that teachers can initiate in collaboration with partners in close geographical proximity. A beautiful array of participatory practices surfaced when we made space for students to tell their stories and create a product that was authentic, sometimes raw, other times refined, but ultimately real. However, just the process of digital composition was not enough. It was in sharing their stories that youth digitally moved outside of their classrooms to interact with diverse audiences, far more vital preparation for existing in our global world than any standardized test. In addition, this chapter posits that, while the majority of scholarship on participatory literacies foregrounds digital tools, participatory literacies travel fluidly across paper, screens, bodies, and a myriad of other meaning-making platforms. Finally, although autonomous and ideological theories of literacy are often pitted against each other as incompatible (Rowsell & Wohlend, 2016), this collaboration suggested that when youth are engaged in socially-rich opportunities for contextualized meaning making, basic literacy skills are simultaneously enhanced. We hope this chapter will serve as generative fuel for others who are entering the field of teaching as well as those teachers that continually seek to open up the range of ways that youth can make meaning for themselves/with others.

REFERENCES

Atwell, N. (1998). *In the middle: New understandings about writing, reading, and learning*. Portsmouth, NH: Boynton/Cook Publishers, Inc.

Buck, A. (2012). Examining digital literacy practices on social network sites. *Research in the Teaching of English, 47*(1), 9–38.

Calkins, L., Martinelli, M., Kesler, T., Gillette, C., Cruz, M. C., McEvoy, M. & Collins, K. (2006). *Units of study for teaching writing, grades 3-5* (Vol. 4). FirstHand.

Cope, B., & Kalantzis, M. (Eds.). (2000). *Multiliteracies: Literacy learning and the design of social futures*. New York: Psychology Press.

Curwood, J. S., Magnifico, A. M., & Lammers, J. C. (2013). Writing in the wild: Writers' motivation in fan-based affinity spaces. *Journal of Adolescent & Adult Literacy, 56*(8), 677–685. doi:10.1002/JAAL.192

Dalton, B., & Grisham, D. L. (2013). Love that book: Multimodal response to literature. *The Reading Teacher, 67*(3), 220–225. doi:10.1002/TRTR.1206

Dovchin, S., & Pennycook, A. (2017). Digital metroliteracies. In K. A. Mills, A. Stornaiuolo, A. Smith, & J. Z. Pandya (Eds.), *Handbook of writing, literacies, and education in digital cultures* (pp. 211–222). New York, NY: Routledge.

Duke, N. K., Purcell-Gates, V., Hall, L. A., & Tower, C. (2006). Authentic literacy activities for developing comprehension and writing. *The Reading Teacher, 60*(4), 344–355. doi:10.1598/RT.60.4.4

Goodson, L. A., & Skillen, M. (2010). Small-town perspectives, big-time motivation: Composing and producing place-based podcasts. *English Journal, 100*(1), 53–57.

Hicks, T. (2009). *The digital writing workshop*. Portsmouth, NH: Heinemann.

Hull, G. A., & Nelson, M. E. (2005). Locating the semiotic power of multimodality. *Written Communication, 22*(2), 224–261. doi:10.1177/0741088304274170

Jenkins, H., Purushotma, R., Weigel, M., Clinton, K., & Robison, A. J. (2009). *Confronting the challenges of participatory culture: Media education for the 21st century*. Cambridge, MA: MIT Press. doi:10.7551/mitpress/8435.001.0001

Jewitt, C. (Ed.), *The Routledge Handbook of Multimodal Analysis*. New York: Routledge.

Kittle, P. (2008). *Write beside them. Risk, voice, and clarity in high school writing*. Portsmouth, NH: Heinemann.

Kress, G. (2009). *Multimodality: A social semiotic approach to contemporary communication*. London: Routledge. doi:10.4324/9780203970034

Lankshear, C., & Knobel, M. (2007). Sampling "the new" in new literacies. In A new literacies sampler (vol. 29, pp. 1-24). New York: Peter Lang.

Leander, K. M., & McKim, K. K. (2003). Tracing the everyday sittings' of adolescents on the internet: A strategic adaptation of ethnography across online and offline spaces. *Education Communication and Information*, *3*(2), 211–240. doi:10.1080/14636310303140

Luke, A., & Woods, A. (2009). Policy and adolescent literacy. In Christenbury, L.; Bomer, R.; Magnifico, A. M. (2010). Writing for whom? Cognition, motivation, and a writer's audience. *Educational Psychologist*, *45*(3), 167–184.

Rheingold, H. (2008). Using participatory media and public voice to encourage civic Engagement. In W. L. Bennet (Ed.), *Civic life online: Learning how digital media can engage youth* (pp. 97–118). Cambridge, MA: The MIT Press.

Rowsell, J., & Wohlwend, K. (2016). Free play or tight spaces? Mapping participatory literacies in apps. *The Reading Teacher*, *70*(2), 197–205. doi:10.1002/trtr.1490

Rust, J. (2019). Immobilizing Literacies: Collisions of Difference During the Digital Dialogue Project. In D. Pyles, R. Rish, & J. Warner (Eds.), *Negotiating Place and Space through Digital Literacies*. Information Age Publishing.

Rust, J., & Ballard, S. (2016). I Am/You See: Traversing literacies from page to screen to body. *English Journal*, *105*(5), 61–67.

Sewell, W. C., & Denton, S. (2011). Multimodal literacies in the secondary English classroom. *English Journal*, *100*(5), 61–65.

Smith, A., Stornaiuolo, A., & Phillips, N. C. (2018). Multiplicities in motion: A turn to transliteracies. *Theory into Practice*, *57*(1), 20–28. doi:10.1080/00405841.2017.1390334

Stornaiuolo, A., Smith, A., & Phillips, N. C. (2017). Developing a transliteracies framework for a connected world. *Journal of Literacy Research*, *49*(1), 68–91. doi:10.1177/1086296X16683419

ADDITIONAL READING

Ahmed, S. (2018). *Being the Change: Lessons and Strategies to Teach Social Comprehension*. Portsmouth, NH: Heinneman.

Boldt, G., Lewis, C., & Leander, K. M. (2015). Moving, feeling, desiring, teaching. *Research in the Teaching of English*, *49*(4), 430–441.

Dockter, J., Haug, D., & Lewis, C. (2010). Redefining rigor: Critical engagement, digital media, and the new English/language arts. *Journal of Adolescent & Adult Literacy*, *53*(5), 418–420. doi:10.1598/JAAL.53.5.7

Doerr-Stevens, C. (2017). Embracing the Messiness of Research: Documentary Video Composing as Embodied, Critical Media Literacy. *English Journal*, *106*(3), 56–62.

Ehret, C., & Hollett, T. (2014). Embodied composition in real virtualities: Adolescents' literacy practices and felt experiences moving with digital, mobile devices in school. *Research in the Teaching of English, 48*(4), 428–452.

Perry, M., & Medina, C. (2011). Embodiment and performance in pedagogy research: Investigating the possibility of the body in curriculum experience. *Journal of Curriculum Theorizing, 27*(3), 62–75.

Vasudevan, L., Schultz, K., & Bateman, J. (2010). Rethinking composing in a digital age: Authoring literate identities through multimodal storytelling. *Written Communication, 27*(4), 442–468. doi:10.1177/0741088310378217

Weltsek, G., & Koontz, N. P. (2018). Subversive Literacy: Arts-Based Learning for Social Justice, Equity, and Student Agency. *English Journal, 107*(6), 61–68.

KEY TERMS AND DEFINITIONS

Dialogue Across Difference: The ability to both listen and communicate with others that have had any kind of different life experiences (e.g., different age, gender, socioeconmic status, sexual identity, race, ability, etc.).

Digital Dialogue Project (DDP): A semester-long project that partnered youth across age groups and school settings to virtually share and comment on multimodal compositions and then perform their stories together during a culminating field trip.

Embodied Literacies: Meaning-making that is made visible by using the body, often during any kind of dramatic performance.

Literacy Toward Equity: Providing meaning-making opportunities that recognize and account for systemic and personal obstacles that individuals and groups face in order to promote a more just society.

Multiliteracies: A new literacies paradigm that broadens the understanding of literacy (decoding print on page) to a more varied set of practices involving a range of tools, platforms, and purposes.

Multimodal Composition: Any form of composition or design (e.g., the creation of a podcast, movie, or website) that incorporates more than one mode (e.g., text, image, audio).

Participation Gap: The notion that not all meaning makers have equal access to the most generative forms of digital technologies, platforms, mentors, and experiences.

Participatory Literacies: An understanding of literacies that highlights the active, social, ideological underpinnings of meaning-making over independent, isolated skills.

Socio-Identity Literacy Practices: Meaning-making practices that foreground self-expression and social affiliation/communication.

Transliteracies: A frame that accounts for the (im)mobility of meaning making that flows across time, spaces, technologies, and modes.

Section 3

Participatory Literacy Practices in Teacher Preparation

Chapter 8
Preparing 21st Century Teachers:
Supporting Digital Literacy and Technology Integration in P6 Classrooms

Salika A. Lawrence
CUNY Medgar Evers College, USA

Rupam Saran
CUNY Medgar Evers College, USA

Tabora Johnson
CUNY Medgar Evers College, USA

Margareth Lafontant
CUNY Medgar Evers College, USA

ABSTRACT

When teachers use technology and digital tools for academic purposes, they are more apt to introduce it to their K-12 students. This chapter describes methods used by teacher educators to incorporate technology into their courses to help candidates meet professional standards, and methods used by teacher candidates to incorporate technology into their teaching to help P6 students meet technology and 21st century standards. Teacher preparation programs should introduce candidates to different technologies and software programs, provide opportunities for candidates to use the tools, and guide candidates as they develop learning resources in the field using the technology. Three factors impacted candidates' use of technology: their perceptions about their capabilities as users of technology in academic contexts, their experiences using technology, and their access to resources such as digital devices and software. Although some pitfalls occurred with program-wide technology integration, the study offers strategies for addressing these obstacles.

DOI: 10.4018/978-1-7998-0000-2.ch008

INTRODUCTION

Disconnect between campus courses and school-based experiences pose a challenge for teacher education programs around the country (Zeichner, 2010). Field experiences are authentic opportunities for candidates to apply their knowledge, but school settings are complex (Zeichner, 2010). While working in the field, pre-service teacher candidates can find it challenging to identify ways to enact their knowledge about teaching practices acquired during their program. In the ongoing quest to strengthen "the connections between what our student teachers do in their school and community placements and the rest of their teacher education program" (Zeichner, 2010, p. 90), we used case study methods to examine how our teacher education program prepares pre-service teacher candidates for 21st-century classrooms. The aims were to document how the program provides candidates with opportunities to use digital tools and technologies and explore the extent to which these practices transfer to P-6 classrooms.

Given the global call for science, technology, engineering, and math (STEM) education, teacher preparation programs have a critical role to play in preparing teachers to integrate technology in the classroom (McCulloch, Hollebrands, Lee, Harrison, & Mutlu, 2018). We examined how our teacher education program (a) educates candidates on using technology as a tool within the content area through an integrated experience (Brenner & Brill, 2016); (b) enables candidates to create their own technologies through authentic projects and learning experiences; and (c) allows candidates opportunities to work collaboratively with cooperating teachers in technology-rich contexts. Our program-level efforts for technology integration include interdisciplinary and integrated curriculum projects using science, technology, research, arts, engineering, and math (STREAM) (Lawrence, Donnantuono, Mitchell, & Johnson, 2018). More specifically, we collaborated with a library media specialist in a local school to help pre-service teacher candidates examine how children's literacy can be used to springboard students into engaging, critical thinking, and problem-solving experiences to foster STEM literacy (Lawrence, Donnantuono, Mitchell, & Johnson, 2018). Although candidates have reported they receive support in their teacher education programs to hone their skills and use technology (Brenner & Brill, 2016), our research shows few can transfer the strategies to the field.

This chapter describes the ways teacher educators integrated technology into their courses, strategies used to support teacher candidates' use of technology, and how candidates used technology in P-6 classrooms. First, we provide background information on preparing teachers for twenty-first century classrooms by identifying outcomes and expectations of professional standards. Next, we use examples from teacher education courses to discuss pedagogical strategies using technology. Then, we examine whether candidates in the teacher education program effectively used tech-based strategies while working in the field with P-6 students. The chapter concludes with recommendations and implications for improving technology integration in P-6 contexts by supporting pre-service teacher candidates' technology skills. The questions framing our work were:

1. How are candidates prepared to work with technology and digital tools?
2. How are candidates using digital tools during field placements in P–6 classrooms?
3. What are the pitfalls and benefits of using technology for teaching and learning?

BACKGROUND: TECHNOLOGY INTEGRATION IN P-6 CLASSROOMS

Preparing Twenty-First Century Teachers

Today, teachers are expected to employ different technology in the classroom. Standards from the Association for Childhood Education International Elementary Education (ACEI) note that initial teacher candidates should adapt the curriculum and instruction by using technology resources; candidates should know how to use appropriate technology so their students can use the technology tools. These expectations parallel standards from the International Society for Technology in Education (ISTE) (2016), which calls for teachers, students, and administrators to use technology for teaching and learning. Current expectations and standards provide teachers with a framework to guide technology integration in elementary classrooms. With a rapidly changing technological landscape, there has been an increase in the way technology is used for teaching and learning. In the context of curriculum and content delivery, ACEI standards identify expectations that clearly state all content area teachers must use various resources, including technology and numerous information resources in both print and electronic form to benefit their students. For example, teaching through digital or visual presentations, assessments, and assigned learning tasks for students can focus on personal development. These in-class uses of technology and various software can help scaffold learners in the classroom and help to streamline complex aspects of teaching.

The Council for the Accreditation of Educator Preparation (CAEP) (2015) also requires that teacher preparation programs use various indicators and appropriate technology-based applications in all clinical placement settings. The International Society for Technology in Education (ISTE) (2019) calls upon educators to improve their practice by exploring ways in which they can leverage technology to improve student learning and support student achievement. Furthermore, the Council for Exceptional Children (CEC) (2015) requires teacher candidates to use technology to design appropriate adaptations for all individuals with special learning needs and exceptionalities. In keeping with the pattern of other accreditation organizations, the National Association for the Education of Young Children (NAEYC) (2009) expects teacher preparation programs to teach candidates how to use technology appropriately and effectively when working with young children. Therefore, it is important that teacher candidates understand how to enhance their instruction with technology; and for them to become proficient in their use of developmentally appropriate technology that helps students become capable technology users through communication, problem solving, and collaborative and self-directed learning. Teachers should be strategic about the types of digital tools and technology resources used to support students' academic development, while ensuring that their practice is developmentally appropriate.

Technologically Literate Teachers

Teacher preparation programs engage in intentional curriculum planning and mapping to identify courses and information and communications technology (ICT) experiences for candidates (Starcic, Cotic, Solomonides, & Volk, 2016). Hong, Lawrence, Mongillo, and Dunnantuono (2015) reported that incorporating iPads into the teacher preparation program as an instructional tool can help prospective literacy specialists explore how tablets can be used to support the literacy development of struggling readers. Candidates in the literacy program worked with K-12 students in the university-based reading clinic to evaluate students' reading skills, identify individualized reading and vocabulary activities for individualized reinforcement, and scaffold students during small group instruction (Hong, Lawrence, Mongillo, & Dunnantuono, 2015). Although many teacher candidates today may have competency using technology and digital tools including computer software and interactive white board (Jamil, Majoka, & Sahibzada, 2018), they need to use and consider the educational applications of these devices. Providing opportunities to examine and use digital tools while enrolled in the teacher preparation program allow candidates to explore and practice using the devices under the supervision and with support from teacher educators. Candidates can use the devices as instructional tools while learning about methods and approaches in their course.

Integrating ICT, multimodal design, and use of digital tools is critical because teachers need to be prepared to support the multiple literacy needs of 21st-century learners in educational contexts. Research shows that pre-service teachers underestimate the digital literacy skills of students (Mourlam, Strouse, Newland, & Lin, 2019). In a study of preschool students' technology skills, pre-service teachers found that most preschoolers between 3 and 5 years old can complete assigned tasks using an iPad without teacher support: unlock and open the iPad, adjust the volume, draw, take a picture, record and playback a video, play a learning app and game (Mourlam, Strouse, Newland, & Lin, 2019). The disconnect between pre-service teachers' perceptions of preschoolers' technology skills and the preschoolers' demonstrated iPad skills suggests that teachers need to adjust their expectations for students; with lower expectations teachers are likely to limit rigorous and enrichment experiences for students.

The research also suggests teachers should be more proficient using a wide range of digital devices and be able to adjust the curriculum to better support the technology literacy and development of students' skills in these areas. With coaching and support pre-service and in-service teachers can design integrated curriculum that considers ways to use children's literature and technology to support students' STEM literacy (DeJarnette, 2018; Lawrence, Donnantuono, Mitchell, Johnson, 2018).

Our study looks at the pedagogical competencies of candidates when using digital tools introduced during our preparation program. We were curious whether a gap existed between university-based courses and candidates' field experiences (Zeichner, 2010) in planning and implementing lessons when they worked onsite in urban schools. Field work or service learning is a way to bridge the gap between theory and practice (Jia, Jung, & Ottenbreit-Leftwich, 2018). Providing real-world experiences allow candidates to solve authentic problems as they arise. This enables candidates to consider what they might encounter in the classroom: students' technology skills, access to digital tools and technology, time constraints, and their ability to apply technology tools introduced during their teacher education courses (Jia, Jung, & Ottenbreit-Leftwich, 2018). Given the challenges faced in urban and rural classrooms namely underfunding (Ginwright, 2004; Haberman, 1996; Siwatu, 2011; Weiner, 2000) and oft outdated technology, preservice teachers who know how to use and can bring innovative technology into these classrooms may increase student technological exposure.

Technology in Real Classrooms

The Partnership for Twenty-First Century Learning (2016) states that to succeed in work, life, and citizenship today, students need to demonstrate skills such as critical thinking, communication, collaboration, and creativity, as well as information, media, and technology skills. Therefore, use of technology has moved beyond passive interactions such as watching videos and movies to using interactive devices such as computers, tablets, games for educational purposes (Mourlam, Strouse, Newland, & Lin, 2018). Many teachers have reported the benefit of using interactive technologies in K–12 classrooms. Recent survey research shows that 75 percent of classroom teachers believe technology benefits students by addressing students' individualized learning styles, reinforcing key concepts and vocabulary through online apps and activities, and facilitating access to resources and information that expands learning beyond the curriculum (Edudemic Staff, 2014). The research suggests that using digital tools, including those previously used for social purposes, and bringing these resources into academic spaces helps to support students' academic literacy development in such areas as vocabulary, reading comprehension, and writing. Technology also helps teachers differentiate to address the multi-layered literacy needs and varied learning styles encountered in the classroom. Since 2012 there has been a 20% increase in the use of digital tools such as tablets and e-readers; today, one-third of classroom teachers use these devices (Edudemic Staff, 2014). With the rapid increase of digital tools available in the classroom today, teachers need specific pedagogical strategies to prepare to use these resources in everyday practice.

For candidates to feel capable using technology, they must build efficacy with digital tools. They can gain experience by planning and designing lessons for students in real classrooms. These tasks will enable them to reflect on the strategies used—identifying strengths and areas for improvement. Ladson-Billings (2013) describes the digital divide that happens when educators are out of touch with their students. She calls for us to use more imaginative and creative means to teach and reach our students. This is the case for candidates, who must be able to use the latest technology seamlessly in their classrooms to ensure that they are not out of touch with their students.

To address challenges such as those posed by limited time in the curriculum or access to software, teachers have engaged in mindful and intentional planning to design and implement technology into the curriculum. Some problem-solving can highlight potential pitfalls when using specific instructional approaches that incorporate technology. This can help candidates reflect and consider approaches for their lesson plans – tenets inherent in professional development driven by action research (Thoma, Hutchison, Johnson, Johnson, & Stromer, 2017). For instance, candidates can consider ways to use technology tools within the content area and limitations of using those tools in real classrooms, prior to teaching the lesson. Completing action research in the field can help candidates explore what worked and what did not when implementing their approach.

Teachers in rural and urban contexts have similar experiences, two of which are diverse populations who bring a range of cultural and educational histories and limited access to resources. A survey of 24 early-career teachers shows other barriers that impact technology integration include amount of content, time to create technology-based lessons, and limited software accessible in the school (Brenner & Brill, 2016). Research shows that although teacher candidates have "positive intentions to integrate technology within their lesson to facilitate student-centered learning" (Sadaf, Newby, & Ertmer, 2016, p. 39) they are unable to transfer those good intentions into student teaching because of barriers such as the cooperating teacher's attitude towards technology and access to technology (Sadaf, Newby, & Ertmer, 2016). Most often access to limited resources are encountered in urban, high needs schools and rural schools. Leonard, Mitchell, Barnes-Johnson, Unertl, Outka-Hill, Robinson, & Hester-Croff (2018) used culturally responsive teaching to examine how rural elementary and middle school teachers used game design and robotics to increase STEM practices, computer science interest,, and knowledge of students. Although teachers in the study had prior knowledge of technology and robotics, participating in professional development to learn how to use the digital tools in their everyday teaching helps to increase application of technology and students' ability to use technology in classrooms to learn about such topics as coding. Research shows (1) teachers' attitudes and perceptions of themselves and their students' competencies with technology informs their use of technology for STEM learning; and (2) teachers were able to facilitate opportunities for students to use technology to express their culture and identity through game-design (Leonard, Mitchell, Barnes-Johnson, Unertl, Outka-Hill, Robinson, & Hester-Croff, 2018). Teachers' use of technology is also driven by time constraints, instructional goals, and access – whether devices are available, compatible, and easy to use (McCulloch, Hollebrands, Lee, Harrison, & Mutlu, 2018).

SOLUTIONS AND RECOMMENDATIONS

Methods

Our institution, City University of New York-Medgar Evers College, is part of the largest urban, public college system within the United States. The School of Education at Medgar Evers College (MEC), currently has three initial licensure programs: Early Childhood Special Education, Childhood Education, and Childhood Special Education. While enrolled in their methods and Clinical Practice (student teaching) course, candidates simultaneously complete field work in partnering local schools. In order to scaffold and ensure that candidates meet professional standards and state certification requirements, the field experiences vary by the number of hours and tasks required, grade level, subject areas, and population based on certification requirements (special education, general education, integrated co-teaching (ICT), etc.).

The program has a diverse student population with teacher candidates who have a broad array of background knowledge and skills with technology and teaching. Most of the candidates enrolled in the programs are nontraditional, first-generation students (mostly immigrant women) who are seeking a bachelor's degree. The nontraditional students in our context are individuals who return to college after a gap of 5–20 years, between the range of 30–55 or over. Some of them are stay-at-home mothers returning to college after 10-15 years. Most of these candidates have limited knowledge and experiences with technology and have expressed a fear of technology. Additionally, some have not had exposure to online library databases to engage in research-based activities such as conducting searches for peer reviewed academic journals.

In terms of preparing candidates to teach in 21st-century classrooms, many of our nontraditional students do not demonstrate basic proficiency skills with technology (keyboarding skills, knowledge of hardware and software, etc.). In addition, many of these candidates express apprehension towards the required computer-based state certification exams because they lack basic typing and other technological skills. This group has also received less exposure to technology in their own education, and are not well versed in using educational apps, games and cloud-based technology in the classroom. They are however, excited to learn and implement their new knowledge when these skills are explicitly taught, modelled, and practiced in their teacher education courses.

Additionally, we have noticed that "millennials" who have access to a plethora of technology, may not know how to use digital tools for academic purposes. Although more proficient than nontraditional students described above, younger students have basic knowledge of technology and digital tools and software, but do not often use technology to support their learning – conducting research using academic databases, evaluating print and nonprint sources during the selection process when constructing an argument. Some of these candidates have no teaching experience.

We also have another group of younger pre-service teacher candidates who bring varying experiences working in schools: some have worked in schools as paraprofessionals or school aides. A few candidates bring teaching experiences acquired outside of the country and are enrolled in our program to obtain licensure in New York. Working with local school partners, candidates complete field assignments such as classroom observations, one-on-one tutoring, small group tutoring, and student teaching. Most of the students attending partnering schools (over 85%) are African American and Latinx, more than 70% receive free and reduced lunch, and students speak a range of languages including Spanish, Bengali, Haitian Creole, and Urdu.

Rather than just using a stand-alone technology course in the teacher preparation program – a widely used approach in teacher preparation (Jia, Jung, & Ottenbreit-Leftwich, 2018), we provide teacher candidates with opportunities to use technology and digital tools throughout the program. As they progress through their teacher preparation curriculum, candidates use various digital tools in their courses including assistive technologies for use with exceptional learners, iPads and online tools such as Kahoot, Quizlet, Blackboard, ECHO360 and Plicker to learn how these resources can be used to support teaching and learning. Candidates also use apps such as Remind to communicate with each other and their course instructor, a tool which gives them an opportunity to at times receive real time feedback and/or responses.

One program-wide tool used by all candidates is an electronic portfolio (ePortfolio), which is introduced to candidates when they take the stand-alone course, "Computers in Education." Pre-service candidates take this foundational course during the second year of their teacher preparation program. The course focuses on using technology to develop basic competencies (Edwards & Burnham, 2009) such as communication, critical thinking and analytical reasoning, leadership and professionalism, along with a sense of community and interpersonal relationships. We use ePortfolios rather than paper portfolios because ePortfolios are easy to develop, maintain, share, store and replicate. Another goal for using the ePortfolio in this foundation course was to improve candidates' learning and engagement in the classroom by creating an inclusive and conducive environment and by developing a sense of belongingness, creativity, reflective practices, ownership, and connectedness for students. Following Yancey's (2009) ideas on reflection and reflective artifacts, candidates used their ePortfolios to design multilayered assignments, specifically reflective essays. The development of ePortfolio follows a five step model of identifying the objective and context of the digital portfolio, to collect and select artifacts that have specific learning objective, to reflect on their learning trajectory and process, to present their showcase artifacts, and to assess and evaluate the learning process that includes development of skills and competencies (Yancey 2009). The formative use of ePortfolio enable faculty to examine and capture evidence of preservice teachers' learning and practice, guide personal inquiry, and inform teaching decisions regarding active student engagement with video evidence, and self- motivated plans for improvement.

The ePortfolio facilitates creation of an organized and reflective environment that is built upon a process of scaffolding for students to document their learning and professional development. Scaffolding occurs as faculty construct multi-layered assignments and learning experiences. Assignments allow students to build their background knowledge of different technology tools, which are modeled by faculty. Then candidates apply this knowledge while working with peers in class, reflecting and problem-solving application in P-6 contexts. Next candidates design, use, and reflect upon their use of the technology tools in the field with P-6 students. Using a step-by-step process helps candidates achieve success as they reflect on their growth. Part of the reflective experience is embedded in construction of the ePortfolio. Brandes and Boskic (2008) noted how ePortfolio enables students to create a site map that guide their audience through the ePortfolio with an explanation of how it was constructed and organized, and how artifacts were selected and interrelated and how they produced an artifact with scaffolding techniques applied by their instructor. The process of constructing an ePortfolio, which includes organizing and reorganizing artifacts, reflecting on learning, receiving feedback, and revising assignments helps students to become deeply engaged in the learning process.

Since 2011, we have used Digication for ePortfolios. Now we are transitioning to a new cloud based system—Chalk and Wire. Integrating Digication, and now Chalk and Wire into the teacher preparation program helps candidates learn how to use computers as an instructional tool by creating a virtual learning community where they feel comfortable sharing their lived-world and life-stories with peers and faculty as they address the program's learning and competency objectives. As candidates progress through the program, they store their performance on each assignment as examples of each core competency in the showcase component of ePortfolio. Candidates could also add other relevant experiences from outside of the classroom. For example, if they studied abroad, taught in schools within or outside the United States, or had special talents or expertise, these details can be added to their ePortfolio. The digital documentation of their work provides quality information that candidates can use to examine their own growth and progress over time and enrich their learning experiences. Given the longitudinal nature of the portfolio, we hypothesized that the reflections would become richer and more complex as candidates advanced in their academic programs. To evaluate the effectiveness of using the program, a multi-pronged ePortfolio strategy was used to evaluate candidates' performance: identifying and tracking development; documenting knowledge, skills, potentials, and abilities; educational and instructional planning; assessing growth and learning; and monitoring performance (Eynon, 2009).

Data for this study comes from an evaluation of the methods, curriculum, research, and theory courses in the teacher preparation programs at MEC. Sources included course syllabi, presentation lectures, instructors' field notes and reflections, field supervisors' observation reports and rubric scores, completed action research papers (reports) documenting evidence of planning, instruction, and assessment in English language arts/literacy and math), and reports collected during Clinical Practice (student teaching). Data also included course-level assignments requested from faculty that provide evidence of preparing pre-service teachers to use technology such as research papers, projects, reflective papers, and field-based assignments. For example, candidates conduct research and prepare a paper on the kinds of digital software and electronic tools available for children with exceptional needs.

To examine the quality of candidates' performance in the field, we focused on scores from comprehensive field assessment rubrics. Field supervisors and cooperating teachers use the rubric to evaluate candidates' planning, implementation, and reflection during student teaching. The rubric is aligned to the initial preparation professional standards. For example, one element on the rubric for Childhood Special and Childhood candidates, which addresses ACEI standard 3.5 and ISTE standard 2, asks candidates to use various media and technological tools to enhance student learning - a direct call for educators to enable students to positively contribute to and responsibly participate in the digital world. All rubrics in the three teacher preparation programs use a four-point scale to assess candidates' performance in the use of technology. The levels range from unsatisfactory (lowest level where candidates do not show evidence of meeting the standards), emerging, target, and exemplary (highest level). At the Exemplary level of the rubric candidates are expected to "create lessons that integrate technology for teaching, (i.e., PowerPoint presentations and interactive video programs). They engage children in using a variety of media and technology learning tools, like WebQuests, Skype, and creating videos in response to assignments, that both enrich and enhance children's engagement in learning and acquisition of content knowledge." At the Target level, "candidates create effective and creative PowerPoint presentations for their lessons. They use some innovative technology – computer cameras and webcams – when available to enhance children's learning." The Emerging level "candidates' lessons use basic communication tools – overhead projectors, tape recorders – to aid in their teaching." We collected the rubric scores from field observations of 54 candidates conducted from Fall 2014 to Spring 2017 (n=216 observations).

Qualitative data were analyzed using the constant comparative method to recursively revisit the data. This iterative process led to patterns that identified common practices across all cases as well as differences between the contexts (Cortazzi, 1993). Content analysis of candidates' work samples helped to characterize and document the nature of their use of technology in college courses and when working in the field. During analysis, notations were made to capture significant departures from the trends found across contexts. The initial stages of data analysis generated a range of emerging themes including teacher educators' use of technology, candidates' use of technology, application of technology in the field, using varied technology tools, discipline-specific uses of technology, and benefits and challenges of using technology. These themes were grouped into similar categories and subsequently used as codes to reexamine the data. Then illustrative examples were extrapolated and used to document the findings. To triangulate findings, we used field supervisors' observation reports and rubric scores for candidates' performance in the field.

Results

Candidates Develop a Technology-Literate Identity by Using Digital Tools

Our teacher preparation program has been using print portfolios as an integral part of the accreditation and graduation processes. Historically, print portfolios are a collection of student self-assessments in the form of reflective essays about their learning. In general, candidates viewed print portfolios as a cumbersome task that has "no practical use." One candidate expressed, "Portfolios are good for collecting dust." As we shifted to ePortfolio, candidates were more engaged in creating the artifact as well as reflecting on the process.

In Fall 2014, 26 candidates completed an ePortfolio; 23% (6 out of 26) of them were acquiring English as a new language. For example, Valerie (all names are pseudonyms), emailed the following note to the professor: "I feel I cannot go on… I have three children and my husband is not with me. I work full time… I will drop out; my English is not good. I cannot do technology assignments. I am no good in technology." At first, Valerie did not want to share her projects and personal narrative with her classmates on the assumption that they would ridicule her because of her limited English proficiency, lack of technology competencies, and culture. However, as the semester progressed, she became very engaged in the writing process and creating assignments to post on her ePortfolio. Through scaffolding such as the peer editing process, she used help from peers to construct her ePortfolio.

For one ePortfolio assignment, "All About Me," candidates created a welcome message and a narrative, which they shared with the class. Candidates were given specific instructions to organize their ePortfolio with a Table of Contents to identify resources and materials they would potentially use when seeking employment, such as a resume and artifacts from their courses (Figure 1).

Several pre-service candidates shared Valerie's fears of a class that emphasizes the use of technology in instructional design. Technology played a role in her technology identity development, namely the constant process of revision, reflection, and evaluation of self-progress required to submit entries for the ePortfolio. Many students learned from each other and shared that peer mentoring and the technological support of their classmates boosted their morale and technology skills. The ePortfolio assignment required that candidates use the tool to share their own stories while exploring the digital platform as a resource.

Figure 1. Two examples of "All About Me" table of contents

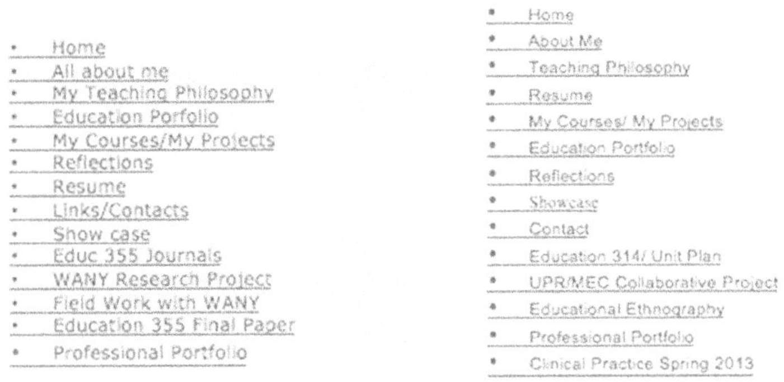

Like Valerie, Sasha developed a sense of belongingness. Initially, Sasha did not feel she belonged in a course that integrated technology. She confided to her professor, "I do not fit in this class… I am at this college for two years and I always feel out of place because of my age and my culture." The group work and peer editing that focused on the process of reviewing, projecting, and revising (Yancey, 2009) enabled Sasha to develop connections and create a resource network. At the end of the semester Sasha wrote, "I will not fail the course. I am not out of place anymore. I am walking with [progressing] everybody." Slowly, Sasha began to participate more in class without concern for her English language barrier. In her teaching philosophy she wrote, "A teacher should respect all children and teach children to treat their peers respectfully… everybody should be proud of their culture and family. In a sympathetic classroom environment, students learn and want to do better. I like my ePortfolio. I can help children to make one."

Roberta's initial "All About Me" essay contained only four lines. However, using the writing process and a workshop environment in the course, she benefited from peer editing, and many attempts to revise the essay. By the end of the semester she stepped into a leadership role to assist peers in making their ePortfolio. She announced, "I will do something in technology… I like it… I learned it." She later became the ePortfolio Tech Mentor for candidates in the education program. Analysis of the candidates' work revealed that they

- Constructed creative PowerPoint presentations for their lessons;
- Used digital tools such as computer cameras, video, and audio clips to enhance their ePortfolio;
- Developed WebQuests, which were used as learning objects for students in the field; and
- Included various artifacts and multimodal texts to convey their personal stories through photographs of themselves, maps of their native country hyperlinked to their ePortfolio with pictures, as well as pictures of their school placements in local schools.

Candidates expressed that the ePortfolio activities and projects were meaningful learning experiences. These included *Website Research Paper, Assistive Technology Paper, WebQuest, ePortfolio, and Technology Resource Guide for Parents*. In general, by the end of the semester most of the candidates reported that they developed and improved their technology and were comfortable with the ePortfolio. Most of the nontraditional candidates approached the instructor for extra time outside the class to get hints on making their ePortfolios. Many students learned from each other and shared that peer mentoring and the technological support of their classmates boosted their morale and technology skills.

Throughout the teacher preparation program, other projects provide candidates with opportunities to hone their skills creating digital presentations using PowerPoint. One project is embedded in the course "Introduction to Early Childhood Special Education" class, taught in the fall. Most of the candidates from that class go on to take "Assessment in Early Childhood" in the spring with the same professor. Employing this looping strategy to scaffold candidates allows them to further build on the prior knowledge and content introduced in the fall, then expand upon their previously acquired skills in technology.

To help candidates to meet professional standards that measure their ability to use technology to summarize and effectively communicate ideas, the first project asks candidates to use PowerPoint to create a memoir of a young child. Candidates read one memoir from a selection of over 24 such books on families that have had to raise a child with a disability (see Appendix). Then they create a PowerPoint to teach about both typical and atypical child development and its impact on the family, school and community. These areas have long been recognized as being a particularly powerful and effective learning activity for teacher candidates (Boyatzis, 1992; Hollander, 2001). This genre allows candidates to get a bird's eye view of the life of the developing child with a disability (e.g., autism, Down's Syndrome, fetal alcohol syndrome) and the many basic and nuanced factors that impact on the lives of these children and families.

At the onset of this project, candidates receive step-by-step instruction and support to create compelling PowerPoint presentations; utilizing minimal words, but selecting key pictures, videos, and/or sounds instead to convey ideas. Working in groups of five or six, candidates create a learning object they can share with peers to summarize the course content. The instructor provides specific requirements for assembling the PowerPoint. All slides are ordered as shown on Table 1.

For example, one group of teacher candidates read the book, *The Boy Who Loved Windows* by Patricia Stacey and subsequently created a project entitled "The Power of Appropriate Early Intervention and Support" (Figure 2). To develop the PowerPoint, candidates used images, texts, and graphics. The multimodal product they created was subsequently used as a study guide for peers.

Working collaboratively, candidates synthesized information, closely examined discipline-specific vocabulary gleaned from reading and discussing the book, and determined important information to share with peers. In summary, candidates used PowerPoint to develop a learning object for peers that provides alternate access to the course content.

Table 1. Order to PowerPoint slides on learning disabilities

Slide #1: *Cover Slid-e* Title, Representative Picture of the Book, and Names of Group Members
Slide #2: Setting and Introduction to the Book
Slide #3: Main Character (the developing child with a disability)
Slide #4: Other Main Characters
Slide #5: The Family Finds Out & Reacts
Slide #6: The World Finds Out
Slide #7: History of Services
Slide #8: Rewriting the Service History: How would it be different for this child and / or family today?
Slide #9: IFSP Goals for 4 months, 2½ years old, and IEP Goals for 6 years old
Slide #10: Professionals Have the Potential to Do Both Good and Bad
Slide #11: Summarize the presentation from beginning to end
Slide #12: Lessons Learned & Conclusions

Figure 2. Sample slides from PowerPoint presentation on learning disabilities

In the second semester, when candidates transitioned to the "Assessment in Early Childhood" course, they were assigned a semester-long project. The project required that they videotape their play-based assessment activities with children. The candidates analyze the video with their instructor and later assess the video on their own as they prepare group papers and PowerPoint presentations. Through the video analysis, candidates produce detailed observations of the children as opposed to merely offering vague, general comments (Rosaen, Lundeberg, Cooper, Fritzen, & Terpstra, 2008). At this stage of the teacher preparation programs, the assignments place emphasis on more structured, academic uses of technology. Candidates used their video to document their practices. Creating the videos—another form of digital text—enabled candidates to use it as a resource. When preparing their PowerPoint, they cited evidence from the video to support their assertions. The video analysis serves a self-assessment where candidates can reflect on their practice. As shows in Figure 3, candidates learned ways to use technology for designing instructional aids and digital learning objects as alternative sources for content. Using PowerPoint facilitated opportunity for candidates to produce their own text- content that can be used to foster learning by others. For this PowerPoint assignment, students summarize their evaluation of a child they assessed who is between the ages of birth to 2 years old. Require slides are named in Table 2, immediately followed by a complete sample of such a PowerPoint that was conducted on a 2-year-old girl.

Teacher Educators Introduce and Use Technology Tools

As candidates progressed through the program, their use of technology focused on discipline-specific strategies and application in P-6 classrooms. "Teaching Reading I" and "Teaching Reading II" are a

Table 2. Order of slides for PowerPoint on assessment

Slide #1: Background
Slide #2: Health History: Prenatal to Present
Slide #3: First Impressions of the Child
Slide #4: Results of Developmental Screening Test: Center for Disease Control (CDC)
Slide #5: Results of Play-Based Assessment: Developmental Assessment of Young Children (DAYC)
Slide #6: Video Clips of Child
Slide #7: Summary
Slide #8: Clinical Opinion of Child & Family
Slide #9 Recommendations

Figure 3. Sample slides from PowerPoint presentation on assessment

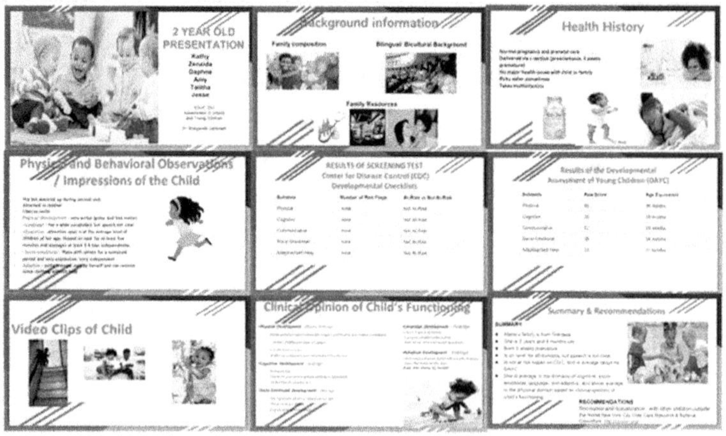

two-semester sequence taken by candidates before they enter Clinical Practice. Candidates also have the option to take "Teaching Social Studies." These methods courses introduce candidates to instructional strategies for supporting students' academic literacy development and content knowledge in English language arts and social studies. During the 2016–2017 academic year, one faculty member taught all three courses and designed an action research project to engage candidates with informational texts, specifically primary source, by integrating technology. Prior to implementing the new technology-based experiences, the instructor observed that although candidates engaged in class activities, they participated in only a limited way when asked to discuss and reflect on texts. When candidates were assigned multiple texts to read, there was little evidence of problem-solving or synthesizing information across texts. As an intervention strategy, the instructor integrated technology to increase student-to-student collaboration, as well as problem-solving, and problem-posing when responding to texts.

Given the college's initiative to increase technology across courses this instructor selected ECHO360, an online platform for discussion and real-time teacher-student interaction. The instructor, who was introduced to ECHO360 during faculty training offered during the summer, was already using Blackboard to supplement the face-to-face course: disseminate information, conduct assessments, and periodically facilitate online discussions. The goal of the action research study was to explore how ECHO360 can help to better facilitate interactions with texts. Table 3 shows the various approaches used during the action research project.

Although the instructor and candidates were proficient in using Blackboard, the instructor explored various ways to integrate the technology. Using a six-week action research project, the instructor problem-solved technology integration. In this context, because Blackboard was already embedded in the course, ECHO360 appeared to have minimal value-added impact on fostering student engagement. Most of the candidates were resistant to using the new software for online discussions. Some asked, "why can't we use Blackboard?" Others pointed out that the user platform "looks weird" on their mobile device. The candidates' comments at the end of the semester indicated they perceived the technology as "disruptive" to the flow of the class. Because the course already engaged candidates in small group discussions, investigations, and collaborative learning experiences using Blackboard, the candidates preferred using the new technology as an outside-of-class resource to increase their interactions with informational texts. Ultimately, candidates used ECHO360 outside of class to interact with multimodal texts, videos,

Table 3. Instructional approaches and reactions to using ECHO360 in methods courses

Session	Context	Field Notes on Practices	Instructors' Reflection/ Action Plan
1	Computer Lab	• Candidates asked lots of questions about technology • A lot of time spent setting up the online access • Frequent pauses impacted the flow of the class • Discussion prompts were designed as in-class activities • Candidates expressed they did not like session, specifically using the discussion feature in class	• Use discussion feature outside of class
2	Classroom	• Candidates used their personal devices to access the platform (laptop, mobile phones, tablets) • WiFi was problematic • Some candidates expressed they did not want to use their data plan • The whole class worked together to complete all activities using the classroom projector and console	• Include more whole class activities into PowerPoint using ECHO360 to make lectures more interactive and less teacher-directed • Deploy activities via ECHO360 for completion outside of class • Use a flipped-classroom model
3 & 4	Classroom	• Technology issues prevented candidates from accessing the platform • Candidates used their own devices to view the site	
5	Outside of Class	• Candidates assigned an activity, which required analysis of informational texts, primary sources, and videos. Then answered questions and shared a brief reflection via ECHO360 • Low participation rate (13%)	• Although only a few students completed the task, the quality of their work was really good. • Use this process again but earlier in the course.
6	Classroom	• Printed out the ECHO 360 slides and activities for in-class task	• All students participated actively but this is similar to previous experiences in the course, which did not include technology.

and primary sources. This approach facilitated candidates' high-quality responses to texts because they were able to draw upon more resources for their written reflections and online discussions. Other digital tools introduced and modeled in the course were better received by the candidates. For example, the instructor used Flicker and Kahoot in class for formative assessment of course readings. In addition, after initial trepidation, candidates videotaped themselves teaching a small group in a guided reading lesson and uploaded the video clip to their ePortfolio on Digication. Their written reflections indicate that they appreciated the opportunity to watch the video, self-assess, and identify areas for improvement.

Reflection Helps to Problem-Solve Solutions

As candidates work in the field, they discover how technology has been integral to their own classroom learning experience and affects their work as teachers. As mentioned above, candidates used video recording devices at different points in the program: recording a play-based assessment as well as videotaping a small group, a guided reading lesson, and several lessons in a unit plan for edTPA – a performance-based teacher certification exams in the state. During Clinical Practice (student teaching), candidates must become acutely familiar with videotaping and laws around using technology in classrooms with minors. Candidates learn how to record, edit, and transfer videos from one device to another. More importantly, these recordings serve as one tool they use to reflect upon and articulate their decision-making when teaching. After watching themselves, candidates learn how to self-assess their teaching and student learning to make modifications in their methods.

During Clinical Practice, candidates complete a year-long action research project. Some candidates incorporate a technology-based intervention to examine its impact on P–6 students' academic achievement. One candidate, Ahmed, posed this research question, "*How do culturally responsive visual representations of math concepts affect the engagement of a 1st grade student working independently?*" He wanted to engage students and increase their math performance using digital tools. When he first inquired about the technology at his field site, he found that the school lacked SMART Boards and other in-class computer devices. To address this issue, he bought a portable 19-inch tablet that he carried to his clinical practice placement to conduct his technology-based research by using images on a tablet to present math problems. His research revealed that students' time spent on task increased almost 40% when using culturally responsive visual representations. The candidate characterized culturally responsive visual representations as *"models that portray the math concept, or... graphic organizers that allows students to personally incorporate images that represent their culture assets. Ex: A comic-strip of Grandma asking for help."* In his final paper, he noted, "*Computer technology and the internet have allowed children to be a part of cultural experiences without physically being in a setting.*" His research is significant because a) his work had a direct, positive impact on P-6 students, and b) he gained valuable skills in learning how to use technology to enhance his teaching and student learning.

Another candidate, Robin, used web-based manipulatives to examine how students process mathematical concepts.

- Pictorial and interactive representation of base blocks
- Interactive graphic organizers
- Stimulation and concept tutorial:
  - math critical thinking
  - stimulated word problems
- Computer-manipulated images

When she began her research, Robin found that her cooperating teacher did not utilize the school's technology. In contrast, when she used *"the base-ten blocks manipulative* [via technology] *the following week the teachers used it."* As a pre-service teacher she was able to impact her cooperating teacher's practice. In contrast to a more traditional narrative about cooperating teachers mentoring their candidates, we found that Robin, who is more comfortable using technology in the classroom mentored a tenured classroom teacher on how to use web-based manipulatives.

In her action research report, Robin reflected on the dichotomy between her practice and that of her cooperating teacher. She stated:

...the teachers were not enthusiastic about [technology]. Therefore, I had to interact with the students during web-based manipulative... The teachers did not know what to do. It was easy to implement the manipulative. Students were comfortable, they [asked] questions... They were curious. After observation, survey, and my interaction with the students, it was evident that students' learning can be constructed but students construct their own understanding through scaffold instruction, prompting, repeated instruction. It was also evident that teachers' limited interaction with web-based manipulatives were not encouraged and those that they students utilize were not aligned with mathematics instructions.

Robin ends by expressing the lack of social constructivism in the classroom. Her reminder is timely as we think of how we can incorporate more 21st-century learning in classrooms and remain relevant in a world where technology changes more swiftly and is ubiquitous.

The examples above are representative samples of how candidates performed in the field, and the impact they had on P-6 students and cooperating teachers. As previously noted, field supervisors used a four-point rubric to evaluate candidates' use of technology. Rubric scores present a snapshot of one perspective of candidates' performance during the time faculty strategically focused on technology integration in their teacher preparation courses. Rubric scores also show how candidates' performance on using technology fluctuated throughout the semester though there was overall improvement over the last two years. Most candidates (48%) received a Competent level rating and 37% received Emerging level rating when using technology in the field. Only 15% of all candidates over the two years received Exemplary level rating. Although we cannot conclusively show a one-to-one correlation for the factors impacting these outcomes, this data suggests that during the time faculty increased focus on using technology in their teacher preparation courses, candidates in the field also increased their use of technology while working in urban schools. We found that 70% of the classroom observations show the SMARTBoard in the classrooms were turned off. In 50% of the observations and field reports, candidates indicated that the SMARTBoard in their assigned classroom was not working or had not been set up.

At the end of the evaluation rubric, field supervisors can provide candidates with qualitative feedback on their performance. During our analysis, we categorized the various comments and notations to characterize the observed practices. We sorted the field notes into effective and ineffective examples of candidates' performance. Examples of effective use of technology use in the field during student teaching includes:

- using audio equipment;
- using chart paper to display visuals/images;
- using technology such as video clips to engage students before teaching mini lessons to help activate students' prior knowledge about the topic; and
- integrating technology to provide students with alternative access to the content.

One field supervisor provided a candidate with the following feedback: "You used technology effectively—stopping intermittently to check for understanding and clarify elements of the video." Another candidate's report stated "the SmartBoard [sic] was used to differentiate and engage students with visuals during the mini lesson, which fostered a more effective use of the technology beyond just projecting slides." An ineffective use of technology was using PowerPoint to project the lesson objectives and standards, but not referring to these items in any way during the lesson.

Several candidates reported similar site-based challenges that limit interactive use of technology. One candidate, Melissa, stated that although her cooperating teacher had a SMARTBoard, it was never used. She stated "when I brought in technology students were more engaged....everytime [sic] I did a lesson students [knew] I would use technology and they listened right away." Esther talked about the ways in which she influenced her cooperating teacher's practice by incorporating technology into her lessons. She said, "I brought in technology because the [cooperating] teacher didn't want to use it but the students want to work with [me] rather than the teacher [when using technology]." Robin describes being placed in a class that was well equipped with technology that was not used or was underused. Her example is telling, as we see where even in an optimal situation for our field sites, there are technologies that are not being used as interactive tools. She provides some details when she adds:

This is a well-equipped technology-based classroom, meaning there are iPads available for each child to use. The setup of the classroom is quite different from traditional classrooms, meaning there is a smart board rather than a chalkboard. In addition, there is a large collection of manipulative materials in the math section that was still in their packaging. I was the first to open some of the manipulatives to incorporate with my lessons.

Similarly, Rhonda reported that her cooperating teacher did not use any form of manipulatives and was apprehensive about using technology. She reported, "My cooperating teachers declare 'I don't know much about computers.' They check their emails, print worksheet activities, and type in the site for students' activity programs." We see that the cooperating teacher's interaction with technology in the classroom revolves around emails; most of the teachers in this school did not use technology as a teaching tool with their students.

FUTURE RESEARCH DIRECTIONS

This study has implications for preparing teacher education candidates for 21st-century classrooms. Teacher preparation is a unique field because educators work with candidates so they can build efficacy to teach a wide variety of subjects to a range of diverse learners. Therefore, the candidates can develop and hone broad skill sets to prepare them to work in today's classrooms. Candidates need to use digital tools for their own learning so that they can demonstrate uses of digital tools in their own teaching. This means teacher educators need to be strategic about the type of experiences that will better prepare candidates. While engaging in these experiences, candidates need to simultaneously reflect on what they are learning and doing and consider ways to use their knowledge to impact learning in P–6 classrooms. Reflecting on experiences and making connections through reflection is a skill acquired over time, and candidates need frequent and multiple opportunities to reflect on their practice.

When teacher preparation programs engage in intentional curriculum planning and mapping it can foster course- and field-related opportunities for candidates to use ICT in authentic ways (Starcic, Cotic, Solomonides, & Volk, 2016). Integrating ICT and multimodal design is critical because teachers need to be prepared to support the multiple literacy needs of 21st-century learners in educational contexts. In addition, teachers need to be prepared to use the latest technologies in their classrooms, so they can connect with and engage students who are often more technologically advanced than their teachers. Particularly in urban settings, we leave students behind their peers when they are unable to use technology in viable ways. It is another form of marginalization when we exclude the use of technology in urban classrooms. Teacher educators and teacher candidates can increase their knowledge of what 21st-century students need when we find effective ways to use technology to enhance student learning.

CONCLUSION

Like King and Allen's (2018) work in rural education, we found that embedding technology tools into the teacher education courses, introduced candidates to a range of digital tools and technologies they can use to support teaching and learning in the discipline. These included using videos, Blackboard and ECHO360 for online discussions and blogging, PowerPoint, and various applications. Faculty used digital tools in classrooms for lectures and to facilitate discussions and analysis of practices. A gradual release approach (Lapp & Fisher, 2010), provided candidates with structured learning experiences using technology prior to their independent application of the technology in the field. When a technology strategy was modeled, candidates worked independently or with peers to create a learning experience using the technique. As candidates progressed through the program, they used technology for different purposes, specifically practices within their discipline, and then candidates were expected to use technology in the field for teaching and learning.

Despite the on-campus exposure to different digital tools, while completing field work in local schools, candidates' use of technology to engage students and teach their content was inconsistent. During their fieldwork in urban classrooms, candidates had to plan and find innovative ways to design their own technology-based lessons and activities. Candidates used technology to develop digital instructional materials and learning experiences for students. However, some candidates did not always have immediate access to reliable internet, digital tools, or software to facilitate technology integration while working with students. Many candidates sought outside resources to move beyond what was being done in field-based classrooms and made effective use of the available technology. For example, several pre-service candidates, primarily within the millennial age group, conducted action research to examine use of virtual manipulatives and in some instances taught their cooperating teachers how to use these technologies. Some disconnect did exist between the frequency of using technology tools and the kinds of technologies used in the field. There were no examples of online discussion forums and innovative software such as those used in the teacher preparation courses. Future inquiries can include follow up research with in-service teachers to explore the impact on classroom practice long after the pre-service teachers left their field placements. This will help document whether the in-service teachers continued using various digital tools with their students.

In terms of specific instructional strategies with technology, the ePortfolio appeared to improve student engagement and to motivate candidates who were on the verge of dropping out of college. Through explicit instruction and peer-to-peer scaffolding, reflective, integrative pedagogy and creating an inclusive climate for all students, the ePortfolio helped the candidates merge what they have learned through traditional instruction and assignments with their lived experiences. The candidates learned to use various media and technological tools to enhance and enrich their own learning. Although the ePortfolio is a developmental learning process for candidates, it promotes integrative learning. Our findings indicate that when new software or digital tools were introduced in teacher education courses, candidates did not initially perceive the benefits of using these tools. However, over time they grew to appreciate the technology and produce high quality work using the digital resources. Candidates overcame challenges posed by their perceptions of using technology, to demonstrate tremendous growth and efficacy in their technology literacy. Candidates learned new technologies, and they learned how to use these tools to create learning devices to teach others. The candidates gained new skills that they would be able to take into their own classrooms.

Teacher preparation is a unique and complex context because educators work with candidates so they can build efficacy to teach a wide variety of subjects to a range of diverse learners. Therefore, the candidates need to develop and hone broad skill sets to prepare them to work in today's classrooms. Candidates need to use digital tools for their own learning so that they can demonstrate uses of digital tools in their own teaching. When preparing teacher education candidates for 21st-century classrooms, teacher educators need to be strategic to better prepare candidates. While engaging in these experiences, candidates need to simultaneously reflect on what they are learning and doing and consider ways to use their knowledge to impact learning in P–6 classrooms. Because reflecting on experiences and making connections through reflection is a skill acquired over time, candidates need frequent and multiple opportunities to reflect on their practice. In order to connect to students who are often more technologically advanced than their teachers, we must ensure that we prepare teachers who can use the latest technology in their classrooms. Particularly in urban settings, we leave students behind their peers when they are unable to use technology in viable ways. It is another form of marginalization when we exclude the use of technology in urban classrooms. Teacher educators and teacher candidates can increase their knowledge of what 21st-century students need when we find effective ways to use technology to enhance student learning.

REFERENCES

Association for Childhood Education International (ACEI). (2007). *Elementary education standards and supporting explanation.* Retrieved from http://caepnet.org/~/media/Files/caep/program-review/aceielementarystandardssupportingexplana.pdf?la=en

Boyatzis, C. J. (1992). Let the caged bird sing: Using literature to teach developmental psychology. *Teaching of Psychology, 1*(4), 221–222. doi:10.120715328023top1904_5

Brandes, G. M., & Boskic, N. (2008). Eportfolios: From description to analysis. *International Review of Research in Open and Distance Learning, 9*(7), 1–17.

Brenner, A. M., & Brill, J. M. (2016). Investigating practices in teacher education that promote and inhibit technology integration transfer in early career teachers. *TechTrends, 60*(2), 136–144. doi:10.100711528-016-0025-8

Chan, E., Narcisee, N., & Moreno, C. (2015). *Medgar Evers College Snapshot, Academic Year 2014–2015.* Medgar Evers College: Office of Institutional Research and Assessment.

Council for Exceptional Children. (2015). *What every special educator must know.* Arlington, VA: Author.

Council for the Accreditation of Educator Preparation. (2015). *Standard 2: Clinical partnerships and practice.* Retrieved from http://caepnet.org/standards/standard-2

DeJarnette, N. K. (2018). Early childhood steam: Reflections from a year of steam initiatives implemented in a high-needs primary school. *Education, 139*(2), 96–110.

Edwards, T., & Burnham, C. (2009). The promise of ePortfolios for institutional assessment. In D. Cambridge, B. Cambridge, & K. Yancey (Eds.), *Electronic portfolios 2.0: Emergent research on implementation and impact.* Stylus Publishing, LLC.

Eynon, B. (2009). Making connection: Laguardia Eportfolio. In D. Cambridge, B. Cambridge, & K. Yancey (Eds.), *Electronic portfolios 2.0: Emergent research on implementation and impact.* Stylus Publishing, LLC.

Ginwright, S. (2004). *Black in school: Afro-centric reform, urban youth, and the promise of hip-hop culture*. New York, NY: Teachers College Press.

Haberman, M. (1996). Selecting and preparing culturally competent teachers for urban schools. In J. Sikula (Ed.), *Handbook for research on teacher education* (2nd ed.; pp. 747–760). New York: Macmillan.

Hollander, S. (2001). Taking it personally: The role of memoir in teacher education. *Electronic Journal for Inclusive Education, 1*(5). Retrieved 7/3/17 from http://corescholar.libraries.wright.edu/cgi/viewcontent.cgi?article=1034&context=ejie

Hong, C. E., Lawrence, S. A., Mongillo, G., & Donnantuono, M. (2015). Using iPads to support K-12 struggling readers: A case study of iPad implementation in a university-based reading clinic. In H. An, S. Alon, & D. Fuentes (Eds.), *Tablets in K-12 Education: Integrated Experiences and Implications* (pp. 296–309). Hershey, PA: IGI Global. doi:10.4018/978-1-4666-6300-8.ch017

International Society for Technology in Education. (2019). *ISTE Standards for educators.* Retrieved from https://www.iste.org/standards/for-educators

Jamil, S., Majoka, M. I., & Sahibzada, H. E. (2018). Investigation of information and communication technology (ICTs) related resources and prospective teachers' competencies in ICTs at university level. *FWU Journal of Social Sciences, 12*(2), 99–111.

Jia, X., Jung, J., & Ottenbreit-Leftwich, A. (2018). Learning technology integration from a service-learning project: Connecting preservice teachers to real-world problems. *Journal of Experiential Education, 41*(3), 261–276. doi:10.1177/1053825917738269

King, L., Hinterland, K., Dragan, K. L., Driver, C. R., Harris, T. G., Gwynn, R. C., ... Bassett, M. T. (2015a). Community Health Profiles 2015, Brooklyn District 8. *Crown Heights and Prospect Heights, 32*(59), 1–16.

King, L. H., & Allen, A. E. (2018). Beyond preservice special educators: Embedding assistive technology content throughout a teacher education program of study. *Rural Special Education Quarterly, 37*(4), 228–234. doi:10.1177/8756870518773474

Lapp, D., & Fisher, D. (2010). Critical literacy: Examining the juxtaposition of issue, author, and self. *Multicultural Perspectives, 12*(3), 156–160. doi:10.1080/15210960.2010.504494

Lawrence, S. A., Donnantuono, M., Mitchell, R., & Johnson, T. (2018, December). The STREAM framework: Integrating literacy, research, and content across disciplines. *Literacy Today, 36*(3), 28–30.

Leonard, J., Mitchell, M., Barnes-Johnson, J., Unertl, A., Outka-Hill, J., Robinson, R., & Hester-Croff, C. (2018). Preparing teachers to engage rural students in computational thinking through robotics, game design, and culturally responsive teaching. *Journal of Teacher Education, 69*(4), 386–407. doi:10.1177/0022487117732317

McCulloch, A. W., Hollebrands, K., Lee, H., Harrison, T., & Mutlu, A. (2018). Factors that influence secondary mathematics teachers' integration of technology in mathematics lessons. *Computers & Education, 123*, 26–40. doi:10.1016/j.compedu.2018.04.008

Mourlam, D. J., Strouse, G. A., Newland, L. A., & Lin, H. (2019). Can they do it? A comparison of teacher candidates' beliefs and preschoolers' actual skills with digital technology and media. *Computers & Education, 129*, 82–91. doi:10.1016/j.compedu.2018.10.016

National Association for the Education of Young Children. (2009). *NAEYC Standards for early childhood professional preparation: Position statement.* Retrieved from https://www.naeyc.org/sites/default/files/globally-shared/downloads/PDFs/resources/position-statements/2009%20Professional%20Prep%20stdsRevised%204_12.pdf

Rosaen, C. L., Lundeberg, M., Cooper, M., Fritzen, A., & Terpstra, M. (2008). Noticing: How does investigation of video records change how teachers reflect on their experiences? *Journal of Teacher Education, 59*(4), 347–360. doi:10.1177/0022487108322128

Sadaf, A., Newby, T. J., & Ertmer, P. A. (2016). An investigation of the factors that influence preservice teachers' intentions and integration of Web 2.0 tools. *Education Technology Research Development, 64*, 37–64. doi:10.100711423-015-9410-9

Siwatu, K. O. (2011). Preservice teachers' sense of preparedness and self-efficacy to teach in America's urban and suburban schools: Does context matter? *Teaching and Teacher Education, 27*(2), 357–365. doi:10.1016/j.tate.2010.09.004

Starcic, A. I., Cotic, M., Solomonides, I., & Volk, M. (2016). Engaging preservice primary and preprimary school teachers in digital storytelling for the teaching and learning of mathematics. *British Journal of Educational Technology, 47*(1), 29–50. doi:10.1111/bjet.12253

Strudler, N., & Wetzel, K. (2005). The diffusion of electronic ePortfolio in teacher education: Issues of initiation and implementation. *Journal of Research on Technology in Education, 337*(4), 411–433. doi:10.1080/15391523.2005.10782446

Thoma, J., Hutchison, A., Johnson, D., Johnson, K., & Stromer, E. (2017). Planning for technology integration in a professional learning community. *The Reading Teacher, 71*(2), 167–175. doi:10.1002/trtr.1604

Yancey, K. B. (2009). Reflection and electronic portfolio. In D. Cambridge, B. Cambridge, & K. Yancey (Eds.), *Electronic portfolios 2.0: Emergent research on implementation and impact.* Stylus Publishing, LLC.

Zeichner, K. (2010). Rethinking the connections between campus courses and field experiences in college- and university-based teacher education. *Journal of Teacher Education, 61*(1–2), 89–99. doi:10.1177/0022487109347671

ADDITIONAL READING

Chen, R., & Liu, I. (2013). Research on the effectiveness of information technology in reducing the rural-urban knowledge divide. *Computers & Education, 63*, 437–445. doi:10.1016/j.compedu.2013.01.002

Choy, D., Wong, A. F. L., & Ping, G. (2009). Student teachers' intentions and actions on integration technology into their classrooms during student teaching: A Singapore study. *Research on Technology in Education, 42*(2), 175–195. doi:10.1080/15391523.2009.10782546

Farjon, D., Smits, A., & Voogt, J. (2019). Technology integration of pre-service teachers explained by attitudes and beliefs, competency, access, and experience. *Computers & Education, 130*, 81–93. doi:10.1016/j.compedu.2018.11.010

Nelson, M. J., Voithoder, R., & Cheng, S. (2019). Mediating factors that influence the technology integration practices of teacher educators. *Computers & Education, 128*, 330–334. doi:10.1016/j.compedu.2018.09.023

Ottenbreit-Leftwich, A., Liao, J. Y., Sadik, O., & Ertmer, P. (2018). Evolution of teachers' technology integration knowledge, beliefs, and practices: How can we support beginning teachers' use of technology? *Journal of Research on Technology in Education, 50*(4), 282–304. doi:10.1080/15391523.2018.1487350

KEY TERMS AND DEFINITIONS

Digital Tools: Electronic devices that may or may not be portable including computers, laptops, tablets, clickers, SMARTboard, projectors, etc.

E-Portfolio: A digital platform used to collect and organize electronic materials and information.

Pre-Service Teacher Candidates: Prospective teachers seeking initial teaching certification and licensure.

Technology Integration: Embedded technology or digital tools that are seamlessly incorporated into coursework and curriculum to enhance teaching and learning experiences.

Technology Software: Software include applications (apps) used to accomplish various tasks with digital tools such as word processing or presentation (e.g., PowerPoint).

APPENDIX 1

Table 4. List of approved memoirs of families raising a child with a disability used to design digital learning objects

ADHD, Learning Disabilities, & Mental Retardation *Boy Without Instructions: Surviving the Learning Curve of Raising a Child with ADHD* by Penny Williams *The Child Who Never Grew* by Pearl S. Buck *Retarded Isn't Stupid, Mom* by Sandra Kaufman
Multiple Handicapped (MH) / Medical/ Neurological *This Lovely Life* by Vicki Forman (MH) *Broken Chord* by M. Dorris (Fetal Alcohol Syndrome) *Fragile Innocence: A father's Memoir of His Daughter's Courageous Journey* by J. Reston *Dana's Legacy: From Heartbreak to Healing: Strengthening Families with Disabilities* by Gayle Slate
Blindness / Deafness *No Excuses: Growing Up Deaf and Achieving My Super Bowl Dreams* by Derrick Coleman & Marcus Brotherton *Planet of the Blind* by S. Kuusisto *The Story of My Life* by Helen Keller
Autistic Spectrum Disorder / Giftedness A *Different Kind of Boy: A Father's Memoir About Raising a Gifted Child with Autism* by Dan Mont *The Boy Who Loved Windows: Opening the Heart and Minds of a Child Threatened with Autism* by Patricia Stacy *Carly's Voice* by Arthur Fleishman *Raising Blaze* by Debra Ginsberg
Genetic *Choosing Naia: A Family's Journey* by Mitchell Zuckoff *Expecting Adam: A True Story of Birth, Rebirth, and Everyday Magic* by Martha Beck *Spelling Love with an X: A Mother, a Son, and the Gene that Binds Them* by Clare Dunsford *Schuyler's Monster: A Father's Journey with his Wordless Daughter* by Robert Rummel-Hudson
Emotional *January First: A Child's Descent into Madness and Her Father's Struggle to Save Her* by Michael Schofield *Nowhere Near Normal* by Tracy Foust *A Child Called It* by Dave Pelzar *Three Little Words* by Ashley Rhodes-Courter

Chapter 9
Can Everyone Code?
Preparing Teachers to Teach Computer Languages as a Literacy

Laquana Cooke
West Chester University of Pennsylvania, USA

Jordan Schugar
West Chester University of Pennsylvania, USA

Heather Schugar
West Chester University of Pennsylvania, USA

Chris Penny
West Chester University of Pennsylvania, USA

Hayley Bruning
West Chester University of Pennsylvania, USA

ABSTRACT

The learn-to-code movement is no longer just supported in computer science classrooms; instead, coding instruction has proliferated widely throughout the kindergarten through 12th-grade levels. Yet, educators are just beginning to understand the complexities with teaching students to code. In this research, the authors posit that coding is a language that can be taught through a literacy-based lens. In this chapter, the authors share findings from a study that examined pre-service teachers' aptitudes, interests, and background knowledge for teaching Swift to elementary school students. In addition, the authors explain how teachers were able to transfer what they learned about coding in Swift Playgrounds to a similar task on a different platform. The chapter ends with examples of how primary-grade teachers employed aspects of literacy instruction to teach basic coding using a variety of applications and tools.

DOI: 10.4018/978-1-7998-0000-2.ch009

INTRODUCTION

Unbeknownst to many, the screw - an early simple machine, is the unheralded catalyst for modern day literacy. Johannes Gutenberg, when it came time to design the printing press, naturally looked towards other screw press machines for inspiration. As printers could now affordably produce more books, thus providing more of the general population access to texts, the transmission of language and culture commenced at a furious pace throughout Europe. Currently, the field of education is experiencing another renaissance of sorts, with the proliferation of mobile devices spurring a new generation of learners to use technology, and the required coding involved, for creative problem solving. Mobility, then, lies at the heart of these new, participatory literacies in which technology users fluidly engage and navigate various media platforms as producers of content rather than mere consumers.

In the media, messages about the importance of coding as an essential literacy are abundant, where the general message is that everyone should learn to code in order to be fully literate participants in our future society (Dimeo, 2017). Annette Vee (2017) argued that coding "is a socially situated, symbolic system that enables new kinds of expressions as well as the scaling up of preexisting forms of communication" (p. 3). As such, we as a global population are in the midst of "scaling up" this communication; one only has to look at how younger generations converse with each other. Each day, technology users recognize and employ programming terms and algorithms as they refine their search parameters and script their music playlist by organizing, *liking*, and developing classes of information.

The intentional ways software developers (e.g., MIT's Scratch and App Inventor) and educators are making programming— formerly an exclusively computer science laden term—more accessible to the general population are contributing to the cultural shifts in how and where programming is taught. For example, the mere utterances of "coding" signify this shift. However, in order to make coding truly accessible to the general population through contemporary and effective teaching practices, it is important for us to first consider what factors are associated with the ease with which pre-service teachers learn to code and what types of preparation pre-service teachers receive in order to provide quality coding instruction.

BACKGROUND

On September 12, 1962, then President John F. Kennedy stated while speaking to about 35,000 people at Rice University, "We set sail on this new sea because there is new knowledge to be gained and new rights to be won, and they must be won for the progress of all people" (n.p). While the propaganda associated with this speech has been debated widely, undoubtedly these words helped spawn an entire generation of engineers, scientists, mathematicians and computer scientists in the global pursuit to put humans on the moon. The impact of this agenda dynamically changed our way of life and the tendrils of this movement generated massive changes in education, pop culture, sciences, literature, economics, business and manufacturing. Creativity blossomed, science and technology boomed, and soon a whole generation of problem-solvers were able to send multiple individuals to the moon and back with computing power lower than what is contained in a modern-day smartphone.

We may be in the midst of another technological renaissance similar to the one described above; today's movement spurred the private sector's space race of both Elon Musk and Richard Branson's mission to send "ordinary" people into orbit as well as the U.S. government's desire to send humans to Mars (Obama, 2010). As such, science, technology, engineering, art, and mathematics, collectively coined

STEAM, drives both funding and test scores in schools. At the heart of this movement is the learn-to-code initiative led by organizations like Code.org and Codeacademy.com which have been promoting coding in our schools through the Hour of Code (https://hourofcode.com/) initiative. Technology giants such as Google and Microsoft have also been pushing and encouraging more learning about coding for the younger generations. Apple, too, has been heavily involved in coding through their "Everyone Can Create" initiative that takes coding, creative problem solving, and computational thinking to another level. Tim Cook (RTL Z, 2016), Apple CEO, argued at Startup Fest Europe that coding should be a "second language" taught to all children. Cook went as far to say, "I think we're doing our kids a disservice if we're not teaching them [to code]" (n.p.). Former House Majority leader Eric Cantor (2013) echoed these same sentiments through Twitter, "Becoming literate in code is as essential to being literate in language and math. #hourofcode" (n.p.).

These initiatives do not represent the birth of makers and coders, for educators cannot ignore the social and cultural moves in everyday practices. For instance, the shifts from mass media to social media indicate the blurred lines between consumption and production. Nowadays, youth are remixing, modding (i.e., modifying), and creating their own applications, software, and video games. The emergence of what Henry Jenkins and his colleagues (2009) critically explored as the participatory culture warrants a more formal recognition and discussion. A participatory culture "is a culture with relatively low barriers to artistic expression and civic engagement, strong support for creating and sharing one's creations, and some type of informal mentorship whereby what is known by the most experienced is passed along to novices" (Jenkins, 2009, p. xi). While the ways one participates within this digital and global culture (Wohlwend, 2017) involve new skills/competencies (e.g., appropriation, networking, and negotiation) (Jenkins, et al., 2009, p. 4), new forms of exclusions emerge as well. For instance, what if one does not possess the new (necessary) literacies to effectively contribute to this new global-digital landscape? What if one is not attuned to the new ethical standards that are socially required in these highly interactive spaces? These "participation gaps" invert the democratic ethos of these participatory spaces, where the lack of these newly required critical skills and ethical standards can marginalize, diminish, and exclude others. Thus, the initiatives described above (e.g., CS4All, hour of code), inherently suggest a necessity for all to be able to not only participate in the global economy, but to simply be able to participate in the social and cultural spaces they encounter. Here the authors argue that coding—a type of practice—and computational thinking—an algorithmic, problem-solving mind frame—afford this type of participation.

Learning to Code as a Participatory Literacy

Learning to code may not be as inherently easy as some experts make it out to be, and teaching coding as a participatory literacy may be even more difficult. In the study described below where pre-service teachers used mobile technologies exclusively, some of the challenges may lie in teachers' perceptions of how mobile pedagogies and app integrations occur in classroom spaces (Domingo & Gargante, 2016). Baran (2014) noted that "research on mobile learning and teacher education technology has mostly investigated teachers learning about mobile technologies rather than learning with them" (p. 30). The layers of complexity associated with teaching coding, and even teaching teachers to teach coding as a participatory literacy, are challenging but not insurmountable.

As discussed earlier, the cultural shifts and the tools needed to learn how to teach coding are already available and in motion. The intersectionality of coding and programming connotes a cultural shift in the new demands of living, working, and learning in the 21st Century (See Tuomi, et al., 2018). For instance, *programming* is historically situated within the computer science discipline indicating communication between humans and machines. Programming languages that are closest to the computer hardware (numerical machine language), are *assembly* languages that are relegated to the linguistic demands of the machine (in terms of having to correspond directly to machine instructions). However, with the emergence of compilers (translators of human-specific input into machine language), system programming languages, such as C and C++, have moved to the background (literally) in order to efficiently support scripting languages, such as Python and JavaScript (Ousterhout, 1998).

Of course, there is a long history of these innovations and translations, but such brief mentioning is to preface similar moves and trends occurring in literacy-based research. The intersection of scripting languages and the "influx of newly self-taught technophiles" has opened the gateway for *coding*—the "playful and non-intimidating description of programming for beginners" (Prottsman, 2015, para. 6). Thus, while computer science-based education has focused on the universality of *machine* language, the shift to coding has privileged *human* language, opening the door for a literacy-based approach to learning to code (See Yadav, et al., 2015). For the sake of this chapter, literacy is defined as "the ability to read, write, speak and listen, and use numeracy and technology…to express and understand ideas and opinions, to make decisions…to achieve their goals, and to participate fully in their community and in wider society" (Literacy Advance of Houston, 2019, n.p.). Rather than stifling these trends for the sake of privileging the sacrality of programming (the formal and skillful assemblages of languages), App developers and educators are fostering informal participatory literacy through object-oriented scripting interfaces (e.g., Scratch) and initiatives (e.g., Hour of Code).

Understanding How Computational Thinking and Doing Informs Participatory Literacy

As previously discussed, participatory literacies (e.g., networking and appropriation) require a shift in both practice and mindset. Appropriating and remixing digital media calls for a problem-solving knowledge framework that internalizes and externalizes computer-based communication skills. That framework is computational thinking. The ambiguity of computational thinking can be attributed to its popularity and malleability in various fields: in art, computational thinking—i.e., iterative design and algorithmic problem solving—is used in visual programming environments to create computer-generated art such as, video games, animations, and other interactive projects (Knochel & Patton, 2015, p. 27); and in other STEM-related spaces, computational thinking (i.e., modeling and simulation) is used to compile and parse big data into visualizations for economic, social and cultural phenomenological analyses and predictions (Manovich, 2011) Since its inception by the late Seymour Papert, computational thinking is a term to point us to the constructionist paradigm of learning and to acknowledge the type of learning that is fostered by the social and cultural spaces. In his seminal text *Mindstorms: Children, Computers, and Powerful Ideas*, Papert (2000) laid the groundwork for paradigmatic shifts of computational thinking, introducing *mathetic cultures* (e.g., domains of knowledge) and microworlds (i.e., LOGO) as meta and material frameworks learners can develop and transfer new knowledge within and/or through. Furthermore, he dispels common technological deterministic myths of computers in classrooms by emphasizing the learner *as* the epistemologist and giving weight to the material culture:

In my experience, the fact that I ask myself to "think like a computer" does not close off other epistemologies. It simply opens new ways for approaching thinking. The cultural assimilation of the computer presence will give rise to a computer literacy. This phrase is often taken as meaning knowing how to program, or knowing about the varied uses made of computers. But true computer literacy is not just knowing how to make use of computers and computational ideas. It is knowing when it is appropriate to do so. (p. 155)

Since then, computational thinking has been largely defined by those who continue to functionalize its ethos in various fields, such as robotics, physics, games development, fields of education and educational psychology, and even art. These efforts and advocacies of computational thinking have been useful in building relevant instructional approaches, thereby further legitimizing why everyone should develop this computational mindset, especially teacher educators.

Over 10 years after Papert's conceptualization of computational thinking, computer scientist researcher and professor Jeannette Wing (2006) suggested it as a skill useful to not only computer scientists, but a skill anyone can use. Currently, coding activity has been the result of this latest push for computational thinking. In addition, K-12 and Higher Education researchers and teachers are looking to programming to foster this type of thinking. Here, we are seeing a rather different paradigm emerging in which coding (and programming) and computational thinking are dialogic, developing into a form of experiential learning. For example, Brennan and Resnick (2012) observed, in regards to their research on Scratch (a program that enables people to create interactive stories and simulations), that "computational thinking helps [the authors] think about learning with Scratch, and, in turn, [they] believe that programming with Scratch provides a context and set of opportunities for contributing to the active conversations about computational thinking" (p. 2). Learners are brought closer to the understanding of object and code by coding video games and animations; they employ and enact computational thinking concepts (e.g., *parallelism*, *loops*, and *conditionals*) and practices (*iteration*, *debugging*, and *abstraction*; Brennan and Resnick, 2012). Such activities in practice are significant here where it creates a constructionist environment that gives students agency over their learning trajectories (Papert, 2000, p. 138).

Students need computational thinking to code, which enable them to become better coders. In the same vein, students need to participate in coding practices in order to become better computational thinkers. With this idea in mind, the authors suggest taking a step back and asking what this recursive process means for pedagogical instruction. Thus, computational thinking needs to be part of the focus when teaching of coding. Resnick and his colleagues (2009) used the term "digital fluency" when referring to the technological abilities of young people today; they argue that in order for them to get the most out of their modern-day resources, they "need to learn some type of programming" in order to "[expand] the range of what [they] can create" and "what [they] can learn" (p. 62). Computational thinking and doing requires a level of agentic learning, whereas some classroom spaces are still riding the wave of a behaviorist approach to coding. For example, often coding curricula relies on learning a specific strategy, such as writing a loop, through repetition to solve basic game-like problems. Alternatively, computational literacy is more apt to develop if coders have a true purpose for learning to code and are motivated and take ownership over their own learning. Thus, instead of learning to code for the sake of coding, learners can show agency in using code to solve real-life problems.

A learning environment that is conducive to this type of interactive practice requires a participatory space. The heart of computational thinking requires a Papertian (1980) constructionist approach centered on coding, and so rather than the teacher serving as a depositor of computational knowledge, they should approach computational thinking through a lens where knowledge is constructed through social and material interactions. Thus, if teachers obtain computational skills and competencies through experiential learning, they can continue to develop and foster sociocultural learning spaces for students who are coding and honing their computational literacy. Saeli and her colleagues (2011) laid out the consequences of the disconnects between the teachers having computational thinking and their teaching of programming, a disjuncture between the knowledge of content and the knowledge of the pedagogy. Students' inabilities to solve programming problems are largely a result of their inabilities to communicate with machines. Pedagogical emphases are placed on syntax and basic commands and not on the application towards addressing a larger problem within a constructionist paradigm. To circumvent these issues, instructors can create coding (i.e., playful and non-intimidating context-specific-language-based) scenarios for students to solve many problems that are "chosen independently from any programming language," (e.g., writing recipes, giving instructions, and creating interactive interfaces) (p. 81). Furthermore, instructors should serve as facilitators of knowledge, rather than authoritarians of learning, so that students can have agency in "analyzing their intuitions and connecting them to the designated tasks" (Ibid.).

What is needed for coding literacy pedagogy, then, is an understanding of how the research in computational thinking transfers to real world problems and solutions. In fact, at the heart of our study design was a transfer activity that asked pre-service teachers to apply what they learned in one learning environment to another. As English professors with interdisciplinary backgrounds, much of what the authors know about transfer emanates from observations of first-year writing curriculum; hence, for the purposes of this paper, the authors focus on what the literature says about the transfer of literacy-related skills and how the specific methods teachers implement can apply when learning how to teach coding in the classroom. Perkins and Salomon (1992) noted that transfer happens "when learning in one context or with one set of materials impacts on performance in another context or with other related materials" (p. 3). Thus, while a student displays ordinary learning when applying grammar skills on an English test, these skills must be applied beyond the original context in order to be considered transfer. Particularly in reference to college writing, Robertson, Taczak, and Yancey (2012) viewed transfer "as a dynamic activity through which students, like all composers, actively make use of prior knowledge as they respond to new writing tasks" (para. 1). For transfer to successfully exist, students must draw from knowledge of the past, reworking prior knowledge in the face of new tasks, and create new practices for themselves through trial and error (Robertson, et al., 2014).

Transfer terminology helps in understanding the varying processes and results of transfer within numerous contexts. The contrast between positive and negative transfer demonstrates that the impacts from learning in one context are not always beneficial in another (Perkins & Salomon, 1992). An example of a difficulty that arises with transfer stems from the problematic distinction between high school and college writing. Robertson and her colleagues (2014) found that students primarily read imaginative literature in high school and nonfiction in college. Through questionnaires and interviews, they found many students defining writing as a form of expressing oneself, rather than "a vehicle for dialogue with a reader or an opportunity to make knowledge, both of which are common conceptions in college writing environments" (Robertson, et al, 2014, n.p.). Similarly, Sommers and Saltz (2004) noted that students new to college "have difficulty synthesizing sources to see the 'big picture'" of a given topic (p. 133); many freshmen writing students simultaneously experience the *push* of college writing conventions and the *pull* of their familiar high school models of writing (p. 133). This combined obstacle compares to the obstacles students face when learning to code for the first time; the unfamiliarity prevents them from immediate expertise, and so students may initially draw on previous knowledge, but hesitate to integrate old practices with new methods. Teachers in both fields must assist students in transferring their knowledge outside of the classroom.

The authors compare writing code to literacy exercises because they believe teachers can present these exercises in analogous ways. While transfer sometimes occurs organically, teachers often must implement mechanisms to make transfer occur more effectively. Perkins and Salomon (1992) listed two possible methods: hugging and bridging. Hugging, an exploitation of "reflexive transfer," allows students to actively practice or perform a trial run before the official performance of a given task. Bridging uses abstractions in order to encourage metacognition and appropriate planning. One teacher assigns his class to a trial exam before the actual exam, enabling them to "'hug' the target performance," while another teacher asks her class to develop an exam strategy in preparation for the real test, using bridging to "[exploit] the high road to transfer" (Salomon, 1992, p. 8). In addition, teachers might take a more direct approach by asking their students to "participate in creating a knowledge" that will fill in the strategical, educational gaps that formed between high school and college (Robertson et al., 2014). Teachers can provide the methods of bridging, hugging, and initiating through verbal discussions with their students about transfer strategies when teaching coding in the classroom.

Teaching Coding as a Literacy

Traditionally, coding practices have been taught within computer science courses, and although the word "language" is used to describe various codes that coders can use to write for various purposes, rarely do researchers apply the findings from the substantial body of literature in literacy to their recommendations for coding instruction. The authors hold the belief that coding languages can be taught in terms of reading and writing literacies, with particular focus on helping students apply the decoding, vocabulary, and comprehension strategies they already use to read and write in spoken language. For instance, in the Swift language, coders need to be able to decode that a "brace" ({}) signifies a closure, or a way to capture a "self-contained block of functionality" in a way that can "capture and store references to any constants or variables from the context in which they are defined" (Apple Developer, 2017, n.p.). Likewise, to read and write code, coders must have a basic vocabulary of important terms such as function and loop. Finally, in order to become literate in code, coders will need to be able to put together the symbols and letters in a way that makes meaning for the machine, and ultimately, other humans-as-users. The main difference between STEM-based coding curriculums versus literacy-based coding curriculums is the intended outcome. STEM-based programs inherently train students for jobs in particular fields (e.g., software development and/or computer/cyber security) while literacy-based coding focuses on giving access to all people to have the skills and language to fully participate in a democratic society.

When teaching coding, teachers may find it useful to organize their instruction within the framework of explicit instruction or use elements of vocabulary instruction to help students learn and apply coding languages. Literacy instructors have long touted explicit instruction as a way to organize and scaffold new cognitive strategies (Dole, Nokes, & Drits, 2009), as gradually releasing students' responsibility for employing new strategies allows for time understand *why* a strategy is applicable, *when* a strategy should be used, and *how* a strategy can be implemented. With the game-based nature of many learn-to-code curricula, it becomes increasingly important for teachers to scaffold their instruction so that students truly understand the why, when, and how for applying coding strategies to new contexts outside of the coding platform they are initially using to learn. In addition, a literacy approach to coding values the language students will need to use to effectively communicate about coding. For instance, instead of listing a bunch of actions they took to complete a task, "I *moved forward twice* and then *picked up a gem*" students who have received literacy-based vocabulary instruction as part of their coding instruction would be expected to use the language of coding to discuss their actions, "I noticed that there was a *pattern* to the actions that I needed to take, so I created a *loop* so that I only needed to write out the code for the list of actions once." Thus, a benefit of the literacy-based approach is that it gives students a vocabulary to talk about and apply coding strategies in a way that makes sense beyond the specific task at hand.

A STUDY OF PRE-SERVICE TEACHERS' READINESS TO TEACH CODING

This study followed 77 pre-service teachers at a Mid-Atlantic university as they learned to code in Swift using Apple's Swift Playground app across four 300-level educational technology classes.

The researchers invited pre-service teachers in these classes to participate in this study of pre-service teachers' readiness to teach coding and the ease of which they learned the very basics of the Swift coding language. In order to assess how prepared these pre-service teachers were to teach coding, the participants completed two surveys – one survey to capture their background knowledge of computer languages and programming, and another survey to gather information about their interests and comfort with technology, coding, music, and art. In addition, the authors gathered data on the pre-service teachers' SAT scores as a measure of verbal, mathematics, and writing aptitude. Although SAT scores have bounds for what they say about pre-service teachers' verbal, mathematics, and writing skills, these scores served as a consistent metric for all 77 participants in this study. Yet, the authors faced similar limitations with other options of measuring aptitude such as college course grades or aptitude tests delivered for the purpose of this study, so the authors decided to use the SAT as a formal, recognized test of literacy and mathematical skills.

After completing the surveys, the pre-service teachers were introduced to the Swift Playgrounds app and completed a whole class activity to acclimate them with the purposes of using coding language to give directions for completing a task. Independently over the course of a week, pre-service teachers completed Units 1 through 3 of Swift Playgrounds Swift Playgrounds is an app that Apple designed in order to teach basic concepts that learners will need to code in Apple's signature programming language, Swift. Units 1 through 3 provide an extremely basic introduction to the coding concepts of commands, functions, and loops. Upon completing Units 1 through 3, learners will have the most basic of skills needed to learn more advanced coding skills (See https://www.apple.com/swift/playgrounds/ for examples of the types of tasks that the pre-service teachers completed). Each unit has the learner program actions for a character named Byte to help him navigate a maze by turning left and right, moving forward, collecting objects, and triggering switches. At the end of the week, pre-service teachers completed the end of Unit Task assessment that is provided within Swift Playgrounds. The authors were also interested in whether pre-service teachers could transfer what they had learned outside of the app, so pre-service teachers also completed a coding task that was similar to the end of unit assessment provided by Swift Playgrounds, but completed outside of the app. The transfer task was visually similar to the types of tasks that pre-service teachers completed in Swift Playgrounds, however, the maze was provided in paper form, and students typed the code into a blank document on their iPad.

To evaluate the preservice teachers' code, the authors used a features checklist to qualitatively examine pre-service teachers' code in order to look for elements such as functions and loops. Then, this qualitative data was quantified into numerical data (0 for no use, 1 for incorrect use, and 2 for correct use). Using linear discriminant analysis (Tatsuoka & Lohnes, 1998), a technique closely related to ANOVA, the authors were able to use these variables to predict whether participants would be successful or unsuccessful on a coding task. Linear discriminant analysis was used to model the differences between pre-service teachers who were successful in completing a coding task and those that were not because the dependent variable was categorical and the independent variables were both categorical and continuous.

Research Questions

This study sought to examine how pre-service teachers learn basic programming skills they will need to effectively implement elementary-appropriate, coding curriculum like Hour of Code into their kindergarten through fourth-grade classrooms. The authors posit that implementation of coding curriculum in today's classrooms may be more valuable if teachers approach the teaching of coding language as a literacy. However, in order to do so, teachers themselves will need to learn the vocabulary and syntax of the language(s) they will be teaching.

The research questions guiding this study were:

1. How are pre-service teachers' verbal, math, and writing aptitudes associated with their success in learning to code?
2. How are pre-service teachers' background knowledge about coding associated with their success in learning to code?
3. How are pre-service teachers' interests and attitudes about coding associated with their success in learning to code?
4. How are pre-service teachers' experiences with art and music associated with their success in learning to code?
5. Are pre-service teachers able to transfer what they learn in Swift Playgrounds to an independent coding task outside of the app?

Coding's connection to STEM is widely known, as the elements of science, technology, engineering and mathematics are all integral to the processes of computer programming. However, more recently, researchers have begun to explore the role of literacy skills (e.g., reading and writing) in computer programming. For instance, Vee (2017) explained how "programming is the act and practice of writing code that tells a computer what to do" (p. 19). As a coder, one must be able to write and read source code, or the "code that programmers' type" which "often contains words that might be recognizable to speakers of English" (Vee, 2017, p.19). This source code is then translated into language that the computer can read and act upon, but that humans are unlikely to be able to decipher (Vee, 2017, p.19). Given perspectives such as Vee's that are beginning to examine coding outside of the context of STEM, our first research question sought to understand the intersectionality of mathematics and literacy in pre-service teachers' abilities to code.

Research Question 2 examined the role of participants' background knowledge about coding. Since the majority of our pre-service teachers will be expected to teach coding to some extent in the field, the authors wanted to determine how much background knowledge they had about coding, as familiarity with the concepts of coding would likely be associated with their success with the coding tasks.

The goal of Research Question 3 was to better understand the role that interest played in participants' success with the coding tasks. The premise of this question was based in Knezek and Christensen's (2016) Will, Skill, Tool Model which found that teachers' will (motivation and interest) and skill (abil-

Table 1. Summary statistics for variables used in the discriminant analyses (N=77)

Summary statistics for variables used in the discriminant analyses (N = 77)

Variable	n	Mean	Std. Deviation	Minimum	Maximum
SAT Verbal	72	532.9	74	330	740
SAT Math	72	536.7	75	360	700
SAT Writing	71	547.2	67	400	720
Uses Functions Task	68	.544	.888	0	2
Uses Loops Task	68	.985	.999	0	2
Task Success	69	.739	.455	0	1
Uses Functions Transfer	69	.551	.777	0	2
Uses Loops Transfer	69	.623	.709	0	2
Transfer Success	69	.455	1.14	0	1
Comfort with iPad	77	4.36	.76	1	5
Interest in Coding	67	3.13	1.20	1	5
Comfort Teach Coding	77	4.36	.76	1	5
Plays Instrument	67	1.61	.78	1	5
Participates in Art Activities	67	2.81	1.31	1	5
Background Survey Score	74	8.27	1.97	0	13

ity) along with their access to technological tools and their teaching style predicted teachers' likelihood of integrating technology into their classrooms.

In Research Question 4, the authors explored how students' music and art inclinations were connected to their success on the coding tasks, as there is evidence that people with musical and artistic inclinations have skills that situate them to be strong coders. For instance, musicians have skills that enable them to recognize patterns in code (Hughes, 2017) as well visualize and recognize the significance of each action in the whole program instead of taking a line-by-line approach to coding (Melymuka, 1998). Based on what others have found as the importance of musicians' abilities to use their visual abilities to code, the authors decided to also survey our participants to see if artistic inclinations were associated with their introductory coding abilities.

Finally, Research Question 5 examined how participants transferred the coding skills they learned in Swift Playgrounds to a task outside of the app. Overall, apps are highly unregulated and users' abilities to transfer skills learned and practiced in an app to other settings can vary greatly. Thus, the authors wanted to assess whether the skills learned in the game-based Swift Playgrounds would transfer to a task outside of the app.

Results

In using a discriminant linear analysis, the authors were able to model the differences between pre-service teachers who were successful in the completion of a coding task within Swift Playgrounds and those that were not. This statistical method tests the hypothesis that the two groups have equal means based on the dependent variable values. In addition, the authors can use discriminant analysis to establish which variables are the best predictors of pre-service teachers' abilities to successfully complete a coding task. Table 1 summarized the descriptive statistics for the variables used in this study.

Verbal, Mathematics, and Writing Abilities

The authors found that pre-service teachers' verbal and mathematics aptitudes as measured by the SAT were statistically significantly associated with their abilities to demonstrate basic coding knowledge (See Table 2).

Pre-service teachers' teachers' coding abilities were associated with their verbal SAT scores (p = .002), mathematics SAT scores (p = .000), and writing SAT scores (p=.009). Higher scores in the verbal, mathematics, and writing sections of the SAT were associated with better success in learning to code in Swift using the Swift Playgrounds app.

Transferability of Coding Skills

Although 77% of pre-service teachers were able to complete an end of unit assessment within the Swift Playgrounds environment, some of them took roundabout ways to solve the puzzle. For instance, Units 1, 2, and 3 in Swift Playgrounds focused on the basics of coding in Swift, including how to write functions and loops. 54% of pre-service teachers used functions in their code, and 100% of those that used functions were able to complete the task successfully. Pre-service teachers' use of functions was statistically significantly associated with their ability to complete the initial coding task (p=.035).

Since functions are a named set of commands that make codes more efficient, pre-service teachers who utilized functions may have been less likely to make mistakes in their code. For instance, pre-service teachers were given a code for how to turn left in the game, but they were not given a code to turn right. Therefore, each time they needed to go right, they needed 3 left turns – unless they created a function to streamline the code. For example, pre-service teachers could create a function for turn right, such as:

Table 2. Discriminant analysis for coding attitudes and interests; test of equity of group means

Discriminant analysis results for coding attitudes and interests. Test of equity of group means.

Variables	Wilks' lambda	F	Sig.
SAT Verbal	.847	10.449	.002**
SAT Math	.789	15.479	.000***
SAT Writing	.889	7.266	.009**
Comfort with iPad	.987	.780	.381
Interest in Learning to Code	.963	2.253	.139
Experience with Coding	.994	.333	.566
Comfort in Teaching Coding	.998	.095	.759
Play Instrument	.986	.828	.366
Participate in Art Activities	.991	.540	.466
Uses Functions Task	.926	4.662	.035*
Uses Loops Task	.784	15.937	.000***
Transfer Success	.959	2.479	.121
Uses Loops Transfer	.864	9.115	.004**
Uses Functions Transfer	.996	.229	.634
Background Survey Score	.987	.749	.390

*Statistically significant at ***<.001, **<.01, and *<.05*

```
func turnRight () {
                turnLeft ()
                turnLeft ()
                turnLeft ()
              }
```

Thus, if they created this function, they could just write turnRight () into their code instead of listing turnLeft () three times every time they needed to turn to the right.

Only 38% of pre-service teachers used loops in the end of unit assessment within Swift Playgrounds. A loop is a block of code that is repeated either (1) a certain amount of times or (2) until a defined condition is met. For instance, in the Swift Playground app, pre-service teachers need to move their character, Byte, through a series of movements such as turning, collecting gems, switching on and off sensors, and moving forward. Coders should have noticed that there is was a pattern to the task and could write a loop to have a block of code repeated to make the code more efficient. For instance, pre- service teachers could create a loop for a block of code to repeat three times like this:

```
For I in 1 ... 3 { turnRight () gem ()
 sensors () turnLeft () moveForward () }
```

This code combines functions that pre-service teachers created in a block of tasks so that their character Byte turns right, collects a gem, switches a sensor switch, turns left and then moves forward to run through the series of commands twice more. All of the pre-service teachers who used loops completed the task successfully, and this association was statistically significant (p=.000) (See Table 2).

The authors also asked pre-service teachers to attempt a coding task outside of the Swift Playgrounds environment. Pre-service teachers had more difficulty with this task, with only 23% of pre-service teachers able to successfully complete the transfer task. Completion of the transfer task was not statistically significantly associated with preservice teachers' completion of the initial coding task (p=.121) (See Table 2). Interestingly, pre-service teachers continued their use of functions and loops, with 62% of pre-service teachers using functions and 23% of pre-service teachers using loops in their code for the transfer task. Unlike the task within Swift Playgrounds, only 37% of pre-service teachers who used functions successfully completed the transfer task while all pre-service teachers who used loops in their code found success with the transfer task. Thus, pre-service teachers' use of functions in the transfer task was not statistically significantly associated with their ability to transfer their coding skills from Swift Playgrounds to a new task (p=.634), while pre-service teachers' use of loops in the transfer task had a statistically significant association with their successful completion of the initial coding task (p=.004) (See Table 2).

Background Knowledge

Pre-service teachers' background knowledge was not associated with their success with writing Swift code. In general, pre-service teachers had minimal knowledge of coding languages and vocabulary before participating in the three-unit study. Pre-service teachers who were successful in the end-of-unit coding task answered 8.2 out of 16 questions correctly, while pre-service teachers who were not successful answered 8.3 out of 16 questions correctly. This difference was not statistically significant (p = .390) (See Table 2).

Interests and Attitudes

The authors wanted to assess whether pre-service teachers' success with coding was associated with their comfort with using an iPad, their comfort with the prospect of teaching coding, their interest in coding, and their experience with coding prior to their 300-level educational technology class.

Comfort With iPads

In general, pre-service teachers were comfortable with using an iPad. Our university has an iPad initiative in the College of Education and Social Work, where most pre-service teachers have the opportunity for 1:1 iPad use for several semesters of their training. Pre-service teachers who were successful with the end-of-unit coding task reported comfort with iPads as an average of 4.2 on a 5-point scale. Pre-service teachers who could not complete the task also noted comfort with iPads, rating their comfort as an average of 4.4 on a 5-point scale. This difference between the two groups was not statistically significant (p = .381) (See Table 2).

Preparedness for Teaching Coding

Pre-service teachers reported apprehension about their preparedness for teaching coding in their K-12 classrooms. Both the pre-service teachers who were successful and unsuccessful with the end-of-unit coding task reported their comfort with teaching coding as an average of 1.9 on 5-point scale. The difference between the two groups was not statistically significant (p = .759) (See Table 2).

Interest in Learning to Code

However, pre-service teachers did report some interest in learning how to code themselves. Those who were successful in the coding task reported their interest in learning to code as an average of 3.2 (out of 5), while the pre- service teachers who could not complete the end of unit coding task reported their interest in coding as an average of 2.9 (out of 5). The difference between the two comparison groups was not statistically significant (p = .139) (See Table 2).

Experience With Coding

Pre-service teachers reported minimal prior experience with coding before their 300-level educational technology class. While the pre-service teachers who were successful with coding reported their coding experience as an average of 1.3 (out of 5), pre-service teachers who were unsuccessful with the coding task reported their coding experience as an average of 1.1 (out of 5). This difference between the two groups was not statistically significant (p = .566) (See Table 2).

Musical or Artistic Inclination

Pre-service teachers' experiences with art and music were not statistically significantly associated with their success in learning to code within Swift Playgrounds. Pre-service teachers who played an instrument were no more likely to complete the coding assessment correctly than their peers (p = .366) (See Table

2). Likewise, pre-service teachers who frequently participated in art-related activities such as drawing, photography, ceramics, painting (and more) were no more likely to complete the coding task than their peers (p = .466) (See Table 2).

Discriminant Analysis Model

The structural matrix (See Table 3) suggests that the discriminant function is consistent in predicting group membership. In particular, those variables marked with an asterisk are ones that have the strongest relationship with the discriminant correlation, including the use of loops on both the initial and transfer tasks; SAT mathematics, verbal, and writing scores; and use of functions on the initial task. The canonical correlations show the strength and direction of the correlation of each of the variables with the discriminant function. This discriminant function is statistically significantly able to predict whether a pre-service teacher would be able to complete the initial coding task (p = .027).

This model is able to predict group membership consistently. Of the 16 pre-service teachers who did not complete the initial coding task, this model predicted that 15 of them would fall into that category. Similarly, of the 44 pre-service teachers who did complete the coding task, this model predicted that 35 of them would complete the task (See Table 3). Therefore, this model was able to predict pre-service teachers' likelihood of completing the initial coding task with 83% total accuracy.

In addition to trying to understand predictors for how successful teachers will be in learning to code themselves, the authors also wanted to explore how pre-service teachers who have successfully completed coding units in Tynker and/or Swift Playgrounds in an undergraduate literacy class use their new skills to teach early elementary students beginning coding concepts within a literacy framework.

Table 3. Discriminant analysis results: structure matrix and summary of the function

Discriminant analysis results. Structure matrix and summary of the function.

Structure Matrix Variables	Canonical correlation
Uses Loops Task*	.282
SAT Math*	.484
SAT Verbal*	.431
Uses Loops Transfer*	.282
SAT Writing*	-.170
Uses Functions Task*	.372
Transfer Success	.272
Interest in Learning to Code	.237
Play Instrument	.301
Comfort with iPad	-.199
Background Survey Score	-.056
Participate in Art Activities	-.197
Experience with Coding	.064
Uses Functions Transfer	-.361
Comfort in Teaching Coding	.249

Test of function

Wilks' Lambda	Chi-square	df	Sig.
.583	27.273	15	.027

Classification results

Predicted group membership

		0	1	Total
Original Group Membership (count)	0	15	1	16
	1	9	35	44
Original Group Membership (%)	0	93.8	6.3	100
	1	20.5	79.5	100

The following section shares the stories of two teachers as they implement lessons during a schoolwide "Hour of Code" event.

OBSERVATIONS FROM THE FIELD: HOW PRE-SERVICE TEACHERS EXPLORE CODING WITH KINDERGARTEN AND FIRST GRADERS

At the university, author Heather Schugar teaches a 6-credit Reading Practicum course for pre-service teachers to get extended, real-world experience with literacy instruction and assessment. In recent years, a number of mentor teachers had requested that the pre-service teachers lead lessons that incorporated coding instruction. Thus, to address this trend, Dr. Schugar edited the course to include an assignment that required pre-service teachers to use elements of literacy instruction to teach coding in their classrooms.

In the authors' personal and professional observations in the elementary classrooms, teachers had typically facilitated coding instruction through a platform such as *Code.org*. Students would choose a unit or game to work on and independently practice skills via instructions embedded within the platform. In these instances, the pre-service teacher typically served as technology support for the students, instead of a facilitator of instruction. The authors also noted this trend in their previous literacy-based, educational technology research where they reported that teachers focused instruction on the technology tools (e.g., how to use the app or software program) instead of the intended learning outcomes (e.g., how to use functions or loops) (Schugar, Smith, & Schugar, 2013). By focusing on the specific technology tools students were using to learn to code, our pre-service teachers often missed the opportunity to build on their students' growing literacy foundations through decoding code, identifying coding vocabulary, and comprehending blocks of code.

Thus, using the literacy strategies that the pre-service teachers are already employing to teach their students to read and write, the author encouraged pre-service teachers to transfer their literacy instruction strategies to use when teaching coding languages. For instance, one pre-service, first grade teacher used elements of effective vocabulary instruction when teaching her students to use commands and functions when block coding on the Tynker app:

With a schoolwide, Hour of Code initiative happening later in the week, Ms. Fillani wanted to ensure her students had some background knowledge with coding before they were expected to independently participate in the event. When she informally assessed her students' experiences with coding, she noticed that while most of her first graders had used Tynker before and knew how to move their character around to help him complete obstacles, they did not have the vocabulary to talk about their process nor did they understand the skills they were learning that would help them to become better coders.

In response to her initial assessment, Ms. Fillani decided to focus her lesson on three difficult, but necessary, coding vocabulary terms: command, obstacle, and function. Using videos found on Brain Pop Jr., she engaged students with a brief, entertaining overview of the vocabulary that would be the focus of the lesson. Then, she modeled for students how to use block coding to help the main character complete the task, using the three key vocabulary terms that she introduced in the beginning of the lesson. After modeling, students came up to the projected computer to try their hand at block coding with teacher scaffolding. Ms. Fillani reinforced the students' use of the vocabulary throughout and questioned students on the "why" behind their choices, ensuring the lesson was about the intended learning outcomes and not just the app they were using to learn these skills. After the whole class scaffolding, students were paired to work through a unit together. Students had to communicate to complete the task, including problem solving when there was a bug in their code. With the gradual release of responsibility at the beginning of the lesson, students were able to complete the tasks and communicate using technical vocabulary with minimal teacher support.

As a teacher, Ms. Fillani understood that her students were generally adaptable to new technology and did not need her support to use apps. Instead, she found her students required scaffolding regarding the vocabulary and comprehension of code in order to be able to communicate about code and learn more advanced coding elements. Similarly, in several of our pre-service teachers' Kindergarten classrooms, they found that the Bee-Bot Programmable Robot was an accessible tool for introducing their young learners to coding. For instance, in one classroom, Bee-Bot was used to reinforce letter-sound correspondences:

Ms. Lane, a Kindergarten pre-service teacher, sought an active and accessible way to introduce coding to her students. In the district-mandated literacy curriculum, the students had been working on recognizing lowercase letters and their corresponding sounds. Thus, to relate coding to their current curriculum, Ms. Lane developed a lesson that reinforced students' phonics skills and provided a basic introduction to coding. As her students gathered on the carpet, she laid out pictures on a grid. In her hand, Ms. Lane held some of the letters that they had recently worked on in class. She introduced the goal of the lesson to her students, noting that today they would use "commands" to tell Bee-Bot how to get to the picture that represents the sound that corresponds with the letter card in her hand.

Before starting the lesson, she reviewed the terms "command" and "debug", and also reviewed directional words such as left, right, forward, and backward. After this overview, she modeled for students how she would code Bee-Bot with a series of commands to get it to the picture of "hat" on the far, left side of the grid – as that was the picture that represented /h/. After modeling an example, students worked as a class to decide what commands the Bee-Bot needed to complete the task. In addition, when they ran the series of commands and found they had made a mistake, they collectively worked together to debug the code and determine how they needed to change the series of commands to make it work. Throughout the lesson, students were required to use the language of coding and to explain their decision-making process.

By providing her Kindergarteners with the vocabulary to talk about coding and the comprehension strategies for determining what commands would allow them to complete the task, Ms. Lane focused her lesson on the coding language and not on the technology tool. In this case, the process of developing a list of commands for Bee-Bot to complete was similar to the literacy strategy of "Reading and Writing to Perform a Task". By making connections between what they know about these literacy skills and what they were being asked to do in the coding exercise, students were able to easily adapt to the new task. In addition, in using elements of good literacy instruction, including activating background knowledge, vocabulary development, and monitoring comprehension, Ms. Lane supported her students in learning some basic elements of coding that they can build on in future lessons.

DISCUSSION

The authors suggest that the trend in education to weave programming into the curriculum will continue to grow, evolve, be driven through organizations like Code.org and companies like Apple and Microsoft. However, these one-size-fits-all, anyone-can-do-approaches may be skipping an important step in teaching K-12 students to code: namely an emphasis on teaching coding as a literacy rather than a computer science. Much of the responsibility of implementing programming curricula is falling upon teachers, through no fault of their own, with minimal training in how to code themselves and even less training on teaching coding and computational thinking. Additionally, much of the current, accessible coding curricula lacks real world context and, instead, emphasizes gamifying the content rather than critically thinking through authentic problems. As exemplified in our study, given the association between pre-service teachers' literacy aptitude and their success in learning to code, the authors believe that teaching coding should be taught through the lens of literacy-based practice. Because coding language requires the use of vocabulary, syntax, decoding, and comprehension skills, those with weaker literacy skills may need more explicit support when applying their current set of literacy strategies to reading and writing code.

Studying how to operationalize a literacy-based approach to teaching coding does have its challenges, but inevitably, the gains associated with creativity, imagination, and problem solving outweighs any shortcomings. Even the study described here has its own limitations, namely the lack of any real-world application, but that does not dismiss the authors' findings nor the importance of the contemporary work trying to study this phenomenon. For instance, Falloon (2017) suggested that young learners (ages 5-6) who learn to code will have an increase in higher order thinking (i.e., Bloom's Taxonomy) and creative problem solving which could aid students with computational thinking and debugging. Mak (2014) echoes these sentiments with her experience teaching robotics to third graders, particularly how collaboration assisted with the problem solving/debugging when the students' robots moved off course (see also Marasco & Taranto, 2016). However, when looking at coding education in Finland, Tuomi and her colleagues (2018) addressed the need for research on literacy-based coding instruction, "There is a need for international research that gathers information on the different strategies, in order to come up with a larger framework for today's ICT skills, coding skills, logical thinking, programming competence, and so on" (p. 431). In a sense, how students are learning the programming language is an essential component for learning to code but also a key component to being successful after school and in the workplace.

Further research into coding as literacy includes the development of a curriculum based on sound literacy teaching techniques that build on familiar teaching concepts for literacy teachers. Additionally, teacher education programs should also explore ways to integrate the teaching of coding and computational thinking into their programs. Understanding how professional development can be incorporated into existing schools and districts is also of the utmost importance particularly as programs shift from rudimentary, worksheet-based exercises into transformative (teaching) and learning opportunities.

CONCLUSION

Tom Liam Lynch (2016), in a series of columns for *The English Journal*, explained various reasons why and how to include computer science in the English Language Arts classroom; after all, it is in these spaces that students learn about the subtleties of language. Subsequently, he posits that it seems only natural then to include computational languages in that instruction as well; not because more of our teaching and learning embraces newer technologies, but because literacy is integral to our democracy. Lynch concludes one piece with the following observation, "Integrating programming into public schools is a necessary part of 21st-century democratic education. Not because the business world is in short supply of software engineers, but because our republic is in short supply of participants" (Lynch, 2016, p. 96).

As we try to provide opportunities for our students to gain the skills necessary to be full participants in society, initial forays into unexplored research spaces (such as coding as a literacy) are integral for building a greater understanding of the impact and viability of expanding how coding is taught in teacher education programs as well as demonstrating creative ways to help our students problem solve through participatory literacy practices.

REFERENCES

Apple Developer. (2017). *The Swift programming language (Swift 4) guide.* Retrieved fromhttps://developer.apple.com/library/content/documentation/Swift/Conceptual/Swift_Programming_Language/Closures.html

Baran, D. (2014). A review of research on mobile learning in teacher education. *Journal of Educational Technology & Society, 17*(4), 17–32.

Brennan, K., & Resnick, M. (2012). *New frameworks for studying and assessing the developments of computational thinking.* Paper presented at the American Educational Research Association Meeting, Vancouver, BC.

Cantor, E. [EricCantor]. (2013, December 9). *Becoming literate in code is as essential to being literate in language and math. #hourofcode. VIDEO:* https://youtu.be/Vgn_YbSmHnw [Tweet]. Retrieved from https://twitter.com/ericcantor/status/410080680366727168?lang=en

Dimeo, J. (2017, September 6). *Re-coding literacy.* Retrieved from https://www.insidehighered.com/digital-learning/article/2017/09/06/professor-writes-everyone-should-code-movement-re-coding

Dole, J. A., Nokes, J. D., & Drits, D. (2009). Cognitive strategy instruction. In S. E. Israel & G. G. Duffy (Eds.), *Handbook of Research in Reading Comprehension* (pp. 347–372). New York: Taylor and Francis.

Domingo, M. G., & Gargante, A. B. (2016). Exploring the use of educational technology in primary education: Teachers' perception of mobile technology learning impacts and applications' use in the classroom. *Computers in Human Behavior, 56*, 21–28. doi:10.1016/j.chb.2015.11.023

Faloon, G. (2016). An analysis of young students' thinking when completing basic coding tasks using tasks using Scratch Junior on the iPad. *Journal of Computer Assisted Learning, 32*(6), 576–593. doi:10.1111/jcal.12155

Hughes, A. (2017, December 6). Composing code: Why musicians make great software developers. *HuffPost.* Retrieved from https://www.huffpost.com/entry/composing-code-why-musici_b_10714288

Jenkins, H. (2009). *Confronting the challenges of participatory culture: Media education for the 21st century.* Cambridge, MA: MIT Press. doi:10.7551/mitpress/8435.001.0001

Kennedy, J. (1962). *John Kennedy's Rice stadium moon speech* [Transcript]. Retrieved from https://er.jsc.nasa.gov/seh/ricetalk.htm

Knochell, A. D., & Patton, R. M. (2015). If art education then critical digital making: Computational thinking and creative code. *Studies in Art Education, 57*(1), 21–38. doi:10.1080/00393541.2015.11666280

Literacy Advance of Houston. (2019). *Defining literacy*. Retrieved from https://www.literacyadvance.org/About_Us/Defining_Literacy/

Lynch, T. L. (2016). Soft(a)ware in the English classroom: Letters to the machine: Why computer programming belongs in the English classroom. *English Journal, 105*(5), 95-97.

Mak, J. (2014). Coding in the elementary school classroom. *Learning and Leading with Technology, 41*(6), 26–28.

Manovich, L. (2011). Trending: The promises and the challenges of big social data. *Debates in the Digital Humanities, 2*, 460–475.

Marasco, A., & Taranto, G. (2016). Coding is TOPS in middle school. *Association for Middle Level Education, 3*(8), 11–14.

Melymuka, K. (1998, July 31). Why musicians may make the best tech workers. *CNN.* Retrieved from http://www.cnn.com/TECH/computing/9807/31/musicians.idg/

Obama, B. (2010). *Remarks by the President on space exploration in the 21st century* [Transcript]. Retrieved from https://www.nasa.gov/news/media/trans/obama_ksc_trans.html

Ousterhout, J. K. (1998). Scripting: Higher level programming for the 21st century. *Computer, 31*(3), 23–30. doi:10.1109/2.660187

Papert, S. (1980). *Mindstorms: Children, computers, and powerful ideas*. New York. Basic Books, Inc.

Perkins, D. N., & Salomon, G. (1992). *Transfer of learning. International Encyclopedia of Education* (2nd ed.). Oxford, UK: Pergamon Press. Retrieved from https://pdfs.semanticscholar.org/fb86/245e6623502017940c796c01ed508c3d8208.pdf

Prottsman, K. (2015, March 4). Coding vs. programming – Battle of the terms! *Huffington Post.* Retrieved from https://www.huffingtonpost.com/kiki-prottsman/coding-vs-programming-bat_b_7042816.html

Resnick, M., Maloney, J., Monroy-Hernandez, A., Rusk, N., Eastmond, E., Brennan, K., ... Kafai, Y. (2009). Scratch: Programming for all. *Communications of the AMC, 52*, 60–67.

Robertson, L., Taczak, K., & Yancey, K. B. (2012). Notes toward a theory of prior knowledge and its role in college composers' transfer of knowledge and practice. *Composition Forum*, 26. Retrieved from http://compositionforum.com/issue/26/prior-knowledge-transfer.php

RTL Z. (2016, May 5). *Apple CEO Tim Cook interview at Startup Fest Europe*. Retrieved from https://youtu.be/OHCyMyQ2TAo

Saeli, M., Perrenet, J., Jochems, W. M., & Zwaneveld, B. (2011). Teaching programming in secondary school: A pedagogical content knowledge perspective. *Informatics in Education, 10*(1), 73–88.

Schugar, H. R., Smith, C., & Schugar, J. T. (2013). Teaching with interactive picture e-books in grades K-6. *The Reading Teacher*, *66*(8), 615–624. doi:10.1002/trtr.1168

Schugar, J., Schugar, H., & Penny, C. (2011). A nook or a book: Comparing college students' reading comprehension levels, critical reading, and study skills. *International Journal of Technology in Teaching and Learning*, *7*(2), 116–132.

Sommers, N., & Saltz, L. (2004). The novice as expert: Writing the freshman year. *College Composition and Communication*, *56*(1), 124–149. doi:10.2307/4140684

Tatsuoka, M. M., & Lohnes, P. R. (1988). *Multivariate analysis: Techniques for educational and psychological research* (2nd ed.). New York: Macmillan.

Tuomi, P., Multisilta, J., Saarikoski, P., & Suominen, J. (2018). Coding skills as a success factor for society. *Education and Information Technologies*, *23*(1), 419–434. doi:10.100710639-017-9611-4

Vee, A. (2017). *Coding literacy: How computer programming is changing writing*. Cambridge, MA: MIT Press. doi:10.7551/mitpress/10655.001.0001

Wing, J. (2006). Computational thinking. *Communications of the ACM*, *49*(3), 33–36. doi:10.1145/1118178.1118215

Wing, J. M. (2008). Computational thinking and thinking about computing. *Philosophical Transactions of the Royal Society of London. Series A, Mathematical and Physical Sciences*, *366*(1881), 3717–3725. doi:10.1098/rsta.2008.0118 PMID:18672462

Wohlwend, K. E. (2017). Who gets to play? Access, popular media and participatory literacies. *Early Years*, *37*(1), 62–76. doi:10.1080/09575146.2016.1219699

Yadav, A., Burkhart, D., Moix, D., Snow, E., Bandaru, P., & Clayborn, L. (2015). Sowing the seeds of assessment literacy in secondary computer science education: A landscape study. *Computer Science Teaching Association Report.* Retrieved from https://www.csteachers.org/documents/en-us/78193875-4ed9-42ea-8224-841d13da1f74/1

ADDITIONAL READING

Bers, M. U. (2018). *Coding as a playground*. New York: Routledge.

Castek, J., Coiro, J., Hartman, D., Henry, L. A., Leu, D. J., & Zawilinski, L. (2007). Thinking about our future as researchers: New literacies, new challenges, and new opportunities. *College Reading Association Handbook*, *28*, 31–50.

Grover, S., & Pea, R. (2013). Computational thinking in K–12: A review of the state of the field. *Educational Researcher*, *42*(1), 38–43. doi:10.3102/0013189X12463051

Knezek, G., & Christensen, R. (2016). Extending the will, skill, tool model of technology integration: Adding pedagogy as a new model construct. *Journal of Computing in Higher Education*, *28*(3), 307–325. doi:10.100712528-016-9120-2

Knochell, A. D., & Patton, R. M. (2015). If art education then critical digital making: Computational thinking and creative code. *Studies in Art Education, 57*(1), 21–38. doi:10.1080/00393541.2015.11666280

Manovich, L. (2011). Trending: The promises and the challenges of big social data. *Debates in the digital humanities, 2*, 460-475.

Moreno-León, J., Robles, G., & Román-González, M. (2016). Code to learn: Where does it belong in the K-12 curriculum? *Journal of Information Technology Education: Research, 15*, 283–303. doi:10.28945/3521

Resnick, M. (2017). *Lifelong kindergarten: Cultivating creativity through projects, passion, peers, and play*. Cambridge, MA: MIT Press. doi:10.7551/mitpress/11017.001.0001

Solomon, G. (2015). Hours of code: Past & present. *Tech & Learning, 36*(3), 28–31.

KEY TERMS AND DEFINITIONS

Coding: A basic language-type of scripting used to communicate with computers.

Computational Thinking: An algorithmic, problem-solving mind frame.

Function: A named set of commands that make codes more efficient.

Loop: A block of code that is repeated either (1) a certain amount of times or (2) until a defined condition is met.

Mobile Pedagogy: Using mobile technologies for teaching and learning.

Pre-Service Teacher: A teacher attending a college or university in order to earn their initial teaching certification through both university and field-based experiences.

Programming: Historically situated within the computer science discipline indicating the communication between humans and machines.

Swift Playgrounds: An Apple app used for teaching coding and a precursor to Swift, a programming language.

Chapter 10
Rethinking Writing Pedagogy:
Supporting Preservice and Inservice Teachers' Digital and Multimodal Writing Practices

Melanie Hundley
Vanderbilt University, USA

Robin Jocius
The Citadel, USA

Emily Pendergrass
Vanderbilt University, USA

ABSTRACT

This chapter examines practices, strategies, and assessments used to support preservice and inservice teachers in becoming digital writers who can thoughtfully integrate digital and multimodal writing into their pedagogical practice. The chapter is organized into two sections: (1) a research-based discussion of goals and strategies for integrating digital and multimodal writing into preservice and inservice teacher education courses, and (2) concrete examples of activities and assessments for teacher education courses that can successfully scaffold teachers into becoming digital writers. Findings demonstrate that the thoughtful and purposeful integration of digital, multimodal writing into teacher education courses can shift understandings of writing as a participatory practice and support teachers in successful classroom integration.

INTRODUCTION

Preparing English teachers is in such a state of flux right now. All this social media, digital media, and transmedia doesn't seem to be going away, so I guess we're going to have to address it, Lara, Teacher Educator, 2017.

DOI: 10.4018/978-1-7998-0000-2.ch010

The writing that I did as a student is so different than the writing my students need to do—I was words on paper and they are words on paper, plus words with video and images and so much more. We need to think about what will help students write in thoughtful, complex ways using all the tools available to them, Abbie, Middle School Teacher, 2018

As the above quotes from Lara and Abbie demonstrate, how writing is defined and how it is taught is shifting, transitioning from familiar forms of print to digital and multimodal modes. In order to take advantage of the rapidly expanding repertoire of digital tools that enable new ways of making, communicating, and disseminating meaning in the 21st century, both preservice and inservice teachers need explicit support and opportunities to engage with digital writing practices (VanKooten & Berkley, 2016). In order to shift their thinking and to push on critical understandings of what writing is, it is essential to disrupt teachers' current understandings and to challenge them by providing multiple and varied experiences with writing across 21st century tools and forms. More specifically, to come to understand writing as a set of multimodal, multigenre, and distributed practices that enable participation and communication in an increasingly connected world, teachers must first become digital and multimodal writers themselves.

This chapter examines practices, strategies, and assessments used to support preservice and inservice teachers in becoming digital writers who can thoughtfully integrate digital and multimodal writing into their pedagogical practice. The chapter is organized into two sections: (1) a research-based discussion of goals and strategies for integrating digital and multimodal writing into preservice and inservice teacher education courses; and (2) concrete examples of activities and assessments for teacher education courses that can successfully scaffold teachers into becoming digital writers. Throughout each section, we draw on our work with both preservice and inservice teachers across two universities to demonstrate that thoughtful and purposeful integration of digital, multimodal writing into teacher education courses can both shift understandings of writing as a participatory practice and support teachers in successful classroom integration.

BACKGROUND

As we began thinking about the possibilities and challenges of supporting teachers' development as digital and multimodal writers, we realized that we first needed to surface the kinds of writing that are most prevalent in the classroom experiences of the teachers with whom we work. We began by reviewing the Common Core State Standards (CCSS) (National Governors Association Center for Best Practices & Council of Chief State School Officers, 2010), as well as other state and national curriculum mapping documents, to synthesize the most common types of writing identified as part of these standards. We found that, overwhelmingly, concepts of writing in these standards center on three particular genres: narrative, argument, and informative/explanatory. Additionally, although little explicit attention is paid to digital and multimodal writing, the expectation is that P-12 students will learn to be able to move skillfully among new and print media and to create and remix many different media forms. For instance, as Dalton (2012) argued, the open-endedness of the CCSS offers "wide latitude...to integrate technology and literacy in ways that matter for students' learning and engagement" (p. 333).

Then, in order to gather more information about teachers' perceptions of current practices in P-12 schools and to compare these practices to the standards, we conducted several informal surveys of in-service and preservice English teachers. From 2013-2018, we surveyed approximately 129 preservice teacher candidates enrolled in MAT programs and 98 inservice teachers enrolled in advanced M.Ed. in Literacy Education programs. Of the inservice teachers who responded, 57% said digital media was important, but fewer than 9% taught digital texts and fewer than 7% assigned or allowed digital products to be submitted for assignments. Likewise, the preservice teachers recognized the value of digital media, but fewer than 23% said they felt comfortable creating digital writing assignments and only 21% said they could envision how to use digital writing tasks in their future classrooms. One common theme among the few teachers who did teach digital writing was that they often taught those media formats after standardized testing was over for the year. Similarly, many of the preservice teachers who thought they would use digital writing tasks thought those tasks would likely occur during specific times of the year—before breaks or after testing, for example. One of our major takeaways from this work is that despite rapid shifts in tools and forms for communicating meaning in informal, online, and out-of-school learning contexts, print texts and print practices are still privileged in many classrooms and schools.

In our analysis of the teachers' perceptions of print and digital writing, largely, we found that our teachers still have not embraced expanded definitions that include different modalities and experiences with writing. Inservice and preservice teachers both tend to demonstrate a fixed view that separates print writing from digital writing. Writing is, for them, words on paper or screen; writing that includes images, sound, video, animation, or social interaction is something else. For instance, as one preservice teacher, Ariella, stated, "Writing is writing words on paper, words in rows, neat margins, fixed text. It is the kind of writing that matters. It is also the kind of writing that is tested." The focus on what gets measured in testing or for grades gives the preservice teacher a sense of authority; they can say that schools have to teach print writing because an authority says it is valuable. They can do this without having to rethink what writing is or how it should be taught.

It comes as no surprise, then, that when we asked teachers to list the most common types of writing taught and assessed within their classrooms, the most common assignments were literary analysis essays, text summaries, and persuasive essays, all completed in unimodal (print) forms. Carrie, a 12th grade English teacher, described the writing her students did as "both rigid and fragmented" and further noted that the professional development sessions offered in her school district privileged writing forms like the five-paragraph essay, the "hamburger" model, and RAFT. The few "creative" responses identified by teachers were limited to memoir, short stories, and poetry, and tended to be part of units that happened after testing.

Educators who are beginning to rethink the role of digital writing in classrooms must navigate multiple, competing definitions of what writing is and how it should be assessed. One particular challenge that teachers described in their survey responses was in how to think about, support, and assess writing that looked different from traditional writing. As Erica, an 8th grade teacher, explained, "I know how to give feedback on an essay or a poem but I don't know how to give it on a video. I don't know how to break down the steps a student needs to do to create a video or Twitter poetry."

Interestingly, the types of writing that teachers described as most common in their classrooms were in sharp contrast to their perceptions of the types of writing that students were engaging with in informal spaces. As one inservice teacher, Sara, noted,

My students write so much more than they think they do. I see them tweet, Instagram, and blog all the time. They don't see that as writing; writing is something that they do at school for teachers, not for themselves. What I want to see in my classroom is students recognizing and valuing the writing they do outside of school. I'd like it to help the writing they do in school and vice versa.

As we thought about how to support Sara and others like her, we focused our thinking around the following question: *as teachers of writing, how can we support our preservice and inservice teachers as they learn to write differently for themselves and to teach their current and/or future students? What experiences do they need, as writers, in order to develop a nuanced and flexible writing pedagogy.* In the following sections, we outline how research and theory have guided the ways in which we incorporate and support the development of digital writing pedagogies and practices in our preservice and inservice teachers.

Digital Natives, Digital Writing Novices

The term "digital natives" was coined by Prensky (2001), who used it to describe a generation who had been exposed to technology from birth and who differed from previous generations in terms of the amount and variety of technological tools available to them. While many studies have focused on the experiences of digital natives as students, there is a growing body of research focusing on the characteristics and needs of new generations of teachers who have grown up in a world where technology is ubiquitous (Kirschner & De Bruyckere, 2017; Lei, 2009). These studies demonstrate that despite common perceptions of younger generations of teachers as digital natives—and their proficiency in the use of technologies for social communication purposes—there are many gaps that need to be addressed in order for them to use technology as part of purposeful classroom pedagogies.

Research suggests there are several reasons why teachers are resistant to incorporating technology into the classroom, including a lack of technological expertise with digital tools and a lack of support for the development of new pedagogies involving technology (Doering, Beach, & O'Brien, 2007; Staples, 2010). For instance, Lei's (2009) study of preservice teachers identified as "digital natives" revealed that while these teachers held strong positive beliefs towards technology, they often hold reserved attitudes towards the use of digital tools in a classroom setting and lack experience and expertise in classroom technology integration. Teacher education programs play a key role in providing opportunities to help support the development of new pedagogical approaches as well as shifts in attitudes. As Lei (2009) argued, "teacher preparation programs need to help them gain knowledge and experiences with a wider range of technologies and more advanced technologies that can support their future role as teachers" (p. 92). In short, incorporating ongoing and explicit support for teachers as they experiment with different technological tools can support more complex understandings of pedagogy and practice.

Kirschner and De Bruyckere (2017) further suggested that teacher education programs need to explicitly address the most effective ways of using technology in classroom settings and that knowing how and when to use technology to accomplish particular goals is an often underutilized skill. Specifically, in relation to digital writing, teachers need opportunities to challenge their own preconceptions of what writing is and to explore the expansive and participatory practices afforded by writing in digital, multimodal, and online spaces. As discussed in the next sections, research has demonstrated that both preservice and inservice teachers benefit from participation in theoretical discussions about the possibilities for writing in digital spaces as well as more opportunities to explore and examine specific technological tools as both users and teachers. The side-by-side exploration of both the experiences of writing digitally and the development of pedagogical questions and frameworks allows teachers—both inservice and preservice—to develop digital writing practices and ways of thinking about the teaching of digital writing.

Redefining Digital Writing Practices

The changing and expanding definitions of text require that teachers rethink what counts as writing in schools—a complicated task that involves the conceptual change of teacher beliefs and attitudes towards digital writing (Damico, Panos, & Myers, 2018; Doering, Beach, & O'Brien, 2007; Miller & McVee, 2013; Rish, 2013). As a normative component of the writing instruction they received throughout their educational experience, both preservice and inservice teachers have developed strongly held beliefs about traditional writing techniques (Damico, Panos, & Myers, 2018). Writing is often approached as a singular text output/production of words on paper (see Bezemer & Kress, 2017), not as a complex thought process or participatory literacy practice that can be showcased in numerous ways. Given their firmly established repertoires of repeatable skills and techniques used to accomplish academic purposes, it is often a struggle to help both preservice and inservice teachers reconceptualize what it "means" to write—and to help them specifically understand the affordances of digital and multimodal tools for communicating meaning across genres and media. It is essential to provide opportunities for teachers to reflect on the disciplinary practices that are part of writing within particular genres in either print or digital forms. And even more importantly, teachers must also learn to conceptualize digital writing as existing within a larger context that addresses the navigation of physical, digital, and intellectual spaces.

One way to support teachers in making a conceptual shift is to ask them to explicitly transform traditional written products to digital and multimodal formats. Focusing teachers' thinking on traditional kinds of writing allows them to work within their "comfort zones" while also encouraging them to stretch and grow their thinking. This process also serves to highlight skills and disciplinary practices that are part of writing in a particular genre—and can help teachers think about the potential affordances of communicating in digital and online spaces. For example, in our own classes, in order to spark thinking about practices and skills that can be supported in digital and multimodal contexts, we pose a series of questions: How do we define writing? What is it that we expect a good writer to do? How do we learn what good writing is? Then, as teachers grow more comfortable with thinking of writing as a set of disciplinary practices designed to develop and communicate meaning, we shift to thinking about the particular practices involved in the composition of digital and multimodal texts. For example, we prompt teachers to think about the following questions: What is it that we expect a good writer of digital texts to do? What affordances do digital and multimodal media provide for creating, remixing, and disseminating ideas?

Research has shown that explicit reflection on the affordances of digital media, coupled with opportunities for teachers to become digital writers, can support conceptual understandings that new and digital tools afford for writing. For instance, Johnson and Smagorinsky (2014) described how one preservice teacher, Mara, broadened her perception of what it means to become a writer in the 21st century through multimodal composing. As part of a writing methods course, Mara was tasked with designing a multimodal "I am from" poem that described her personal history and background. Through examination of Mara's composition and reflections on the experience, the authors found that she was able to create emotion through a combination of image, sound, and text, which interrupted traditional written norms for both her and her classmates. This experience allowed the class to develop a "metaknowledge of composing practices" that provided preservice teachers in the class with opportunities to rethink the role of digital and multimodal writing in their future classrooms (p. 276). The authors conclude by cautioning that due to the focus on accountability in many schools and districts, as well as ongoing resistance to multimodal means of communication from teachers, administrators, parents, and even P-12 students, fully incorporating digital and multimodal literacies into the classroom remains a key challenge for teacher education.

Other studies have demonstrated that, when developing writing assessments across both print and digital forms, teachers often focus on the final product, not the discrete skills involved in the process (Henriksen, Mishra, & Fisser, 2016). While thinking deeply about each component of an assessment is an important step for designing both print and digital writing projects, it is especially important for teachers to be able to understand the roles of individual elements of writing and the role that each element plays across digital and print-based forms. In creating an argumentative text, for instance, writers must be able to explain what their argument is, identify the pieces of evidence that can be used to support that argument, incorporate leads and hooks, use key phrases or terms that signal transitions between paragraphs or among ideas, and justify their claims using different rhetorical techniques. All of these elements must be brought together in order to craft an effective argument, and the ways in which they are utilized varies dramatically based on the modes and tools that are used. To unpack and utilize all of the different affordances of digital and multimodal means for communication, teachers need to be able to make their thinking visible to students (Ritchhart, Church, & Morrison, 2011) and to point to specific disciplinary practices and goals within digital formats (Miller & McVee, 2013). In order to support teachers in coming to understand the vast range of meaning-making opportunities in digital, multimodal contexts, Rish (2013) argues for using remediation to consider how to broaden existing pedagogical practices to support digital composition. As Rish notes, taking on a "*remediation* stance involves disrupting the very print-based, school-sanctioned literacy practices that helped define them as successful students of English language arts" (p. 13). As preservice teachers composed print and video versions of "This I Believe" texts, they were also asked to reflect on their composing processes and the unique affordances of each type of media for conveying meaning.

So, as research has demonstrated, an important step for supporting preservice and inservice teachers as they become digital writers involves surfacing, disrupting, and even discarding traditional and firmly held beliefs about what writing is and is not. To scaffold this difficult and important work, several different strategies have been proposed, including leveraging print-based texts and carefully studying the affordances of print and digital media for conveying particular types of messages. However, although it is necessary to engage teachers in deep conceptual thought about the goals and purposes of digital writing as a tool for communication, creation, and knowledge dissemination, it cannot be to the exclusion of practical strategies that address the functionality of technological tools or how to integrate these tools with existing curriculum materials. Nor should it be done at the exclusion of print writing connections. Both print and digital practices must be examined in relation to each other in order to support the development of both digital practices and flexible pedagogy. In the next section, we describe the necessity of hands-on engagement with a wide array of digital composing tools and pedagogical practices.

From Theory to Practice: Exploring Digital Pedagogies and Tools

As Okojie (2011) argued, teachers who implement digital writing pedagogies in the classroom environment must learn to take on numerous, multi-faceted roles that they often have little training for. Teachers who support digital writing must become mentors, information providers, life-long learners, and information technology specialists, all while motivating student learning and making explicit connections to standards that are often rooted in more print-centric concepts. Without direct, hands-on experience with different composing forms, teachers are often unable to fully understand the complexity of digital and multimodal writing—and cannot envision how these skills can be successfully integrated into the curriculum. Their lack of understanding about the complexity of digital and multimodal writing makes it difficult for them to determine how this writing can be used to teach writing concepts and skills.

Research has demonstrated the importance of providing teachers with explicit instruction in various purposes for digital writing. For instance, Albers's (2014) study of preservice teachers' composition of Public Service Announcements demonstrated the value of critical engagement with multimodal media and of positioning teachers as multimodal composers, "capable of expressing ideas about social issues through multimodal tools" (p. 111). As the teachers in this study engaged in the process of composing using multimodal and digital forms, they began to think about how digital writing might allow for greater engagement with distributed audiences and with social action. Their firsthand engagements with multimodal and digital composing allowed the teachers to begin to understand a broader range of communicative forms as well as purposes for composing.

Other researchers (Hundley & Holbrook, 2013; Bruce & Chiu, 2015; Miller & McVee, 2013) have shown that teachers need ongoing and extensive experiences with new digital tools in order to help them explore the myriad possibilities for digital and multimodal writing. For instance, Bruce and Chiu (2015) studied preservice teachers' perceptions of composing with digital video in order to document the experiences and reflections of more than 240 teachers across 15 undergraduate and graduate courses. They found that teachers commonly recognized a number of positive results from their experiences, including freedom in how to conceptualize their work using multimodal modes, pride in their finished products, and more flexibility in their use and manipulation of digital tools. In order for teachers to be successful, Bruce and Chiu (2015) argued that all projects should be grounded in disciplinary practice and include enough time for teachers to thoroughly investigate and explore the affordances and constraints of different technological tools (p. 281). Providing teachers with enough time and space to engage in creative play with technology can enable them to envision how new tools might fit into their classrooms and curricula.

In order to support teachers in transferring their new conceptions of digital writing to classroom pedagogies, teacher educators need to foster bridges and explicit conversations among theory and practice. This work also involves providing opportunities for teachers to experience digital and multimodal writing themselves. Thinking of our preservice and inservice teachers first as writers and then as teachers of writing allows us to provide the necessary scaffolding and guidance as they first develop the skills to create products such as video essays, hypertext poem analyses, kinetic texts, digital memoirs, and other new media compositions. For instance, as Tori, an inservice middle school ELA teacher enrolled in a Literacy M.Ed. program, said,

I knew I had to rethink what writing was, what I wanted my students to be doing, and what the possibilities enabled by technology were. And even then it was only through experiencing the frustration and the joy of writing and creating in new ways myself that I really understood what those possibilities are.

Kevin, another inservice middle school teacher, echoed this idea, explaining, "Creating the digital writing that I did showed me the depth of thought (and frustration) that went into doing the task; it helped me see how different modes allowed for different kinds of expression." Participating in these writing experiences first as writers and then as teachers allowed the teachers to focus on the process of creating the writing from beginning to end—from prompt through product—and pushed them to be explicit about the steps.

In the next section, we offer concrete examples of different strategies to support this dual positioning—to help preservice and inservice teachers come to think of themselves as both digital writers and teachers of digital writing who can adapt their own practices and pedagogies to changing contexts and tools.

RETHINKING NARRATIVE, ARGUMENTATIVE, AND INFORMATIONAL TEXTS FOR DIGITAL CONTEXTS

In this section, we present examples from studies of multimodal and digital writing in preservice and inservice teacher education courses across two universities. Specifically, we describe how we leverage knowledge of three traditional writing genres (narrative, argumentative, and informational) to support teachers in shifting their perceptions of writing from unimodal, one-directional, and print-based forms to writing as multimodal, participatory, and digital. In highlighting the experiences of preservice and inservice teachers through their engagement with four different types of projects (literacy interpretation videos, hypertext literary analyses, infographics, and literacy video projects designed for community audiences), we demonstrate how they came to new understandings of writing as a participatory practice that involves creating with new and digital forms.

Rethinking Narrative Texts: Literacy Interpretation Videos

As evidenced in our review of state and national standards, much of the writing done in secondary ELA classrooms focuses on literary analysis or interpretation of narrative texts such as novels, short stories, or poems. Generally, the preservice and inservice teachers that we work with are accomplished print writers with an established repertoire of print-based practices that they have been able to use, repeat, revise, and reuse in multiple school settings. However, when asked to name or define the specific practices they use when creating a print piece, teachers do not necessarily know how to identify the moves they make as writers. This mindset makes the specific disciplinary practices that writers engage in invisible and therefore makes it difficult for teachers to see the specific practices they need to use with their students when teaching them to write. We have found that both preservice and inservice teachers need ongoing opportunities to practice identifying and breaking down the individual components involved with crafting interpretations of literary texts.

The literary interpretation video assignment asks teachers to explore one possible interpretation of a canonical text. While the task is new, the supports we have designed to prepare them to interpret the text are not. We have redesigned and honed this assignment over the past several years. Before officially introducing the video task to teachers, we instead scaffold them through carefully designed engagements with mentor texts, including the series of Levi's Go Forth ads (Levi's, 2009) that used the text of two of Walt Whitman's poems for the basis of their campaign. In order to support teachers' understanding of recursive cycles of interpretation for multimodal texts, we begin by viewing each ad—the one using "America" and the one using "O Pioneers"—a minimum of five times. With each viewing, we focus on what our preservice teacher candidates notice about the visual text: How is the text used? What kinds of images are included? How is color used? How is movement or sound or transition used? In order to support teachers' understanding of how themes emerge in multimodal texts and how craft elements are used to create meaning, teachers use meaning maps and other graphic organizers to document their ideas.

After teachers have analyzed the text of the ads and can describe how different modes are brought together to create meaning for a particular audience, they are introduced to the literary interpretation video. This assignment requires that teachers read and understand a poem, develop an interpretation of the poem that is supported by the text, and then compose a video that uses image, sound, animation, transition, movement, juxtaposition, and text from the poem to share that interpretation. They must be able to demonstrate their interpretations using the different modes that digital tools enable, rather than stating their interpretation using only words. This shift in modes of expression presents multiple challenges. We've found that as teachers begin thinking about translating their interpretations into video forms, they must engage in a process of examining what it is they do as print writers, which surfaces print practices that they previously had difficulty naming or defining. Additionally, it makes visible the ways in which image, sound, animations, and other digital tools can be used to create meaning. As one preservice teacher, Emma, explained,

I didn't really take video seriously as a way to create literary meaning because video seemed to be an 'entertainment' thing. I had to use it to explore my interpretation of the Frost poem and that made me think about what it could do to make meaning.

The idea of writing as a meaning making process is not new but the ways in which digital writing can make meaning seem to be challenging to preservice teachers.

This task also supports teachers' reexamination of how they understand text and what it takes to create a text in both digital and print forms. Alex, another preservice teacher, argued that he did not believe that "creating a video was as conceptually hard as writing a strong essay was because it didn't require the depth of thought because you just added pictures or sound." This sentiment, echoed by several other preservice teachers, quickly changed as they engaged in the process of creating their literary interpretation videos. After creating his video, Alex articulated the changes he saw in his thinking:

Because I had not actually created a video before, I had no idea the depth of thinking and work that goes into the tiniest decision like where to put a sound or whether the word needed a pause...I can see the intellectual rigor that is here that I didn't see before.

Additionally, teachers pointed out that the shift from one mode of expression to another made them aware of the complexities of composing both print and digital texts and made the tools more visible.

As the teachers share their videos for feedback and assessment, we lead discussions about how to "read" the videos. We ask what they notice about the digital craft the authors used and how they think the interpretation was developed and supported. Questions about how to read and understand the video can draw attention to the ways in which the written word is privileged. For instance, Kim said that she "thought the video was hard to read because it seemed so open to what the reader knows and has experience in where the printed word is so much more explicit." The discussion around whether or not video or print text was more open to varied understandings allows students to recognize how much they relied on the idea that words were not subject to interpretation by the reader. We've found that when teachers talk about the digital craft elements they notice, they frequently refer to what they notice in the video, how different modes and elements create meaning for them and readers, and how these elements may have differed in print interpretations. This back-and-forth of digital and print craft connections helped teachers build their repertoires as writers while also deepening their conceptual understanding of writing practice.

This richer and more nuanced conception of writing is an expectation of the 2012 NCTE Standards for the Initial Preparation of English Teachers (National Council of Teachers of English/International

Reading Association, 2012), which focus on reading and composing digital, multimodal, and print texts. The process of composing, providing feedback, and then examining the interpretation videos allows teachers to experience how to read and create a digital text. Further, the focus on interpretation as a literary tool—using video and image as a new way to represent key ideas in a text—provides a task that is both familiar and different. Teachers come to recognize what they already value as print writers and experience the affordances of current digital media as a tool for thinking and communication.

Rethinking Argumentative Texts: Hypertext Literary Analysis

Literary analysis is a foundational and ubiquitous type of writing assignment in secondary English classrooms. It carries significant weight as a valuable skill and type of writing for P-12 students to learn—for instance, the CCSS foregrounds and highlights analytical and argumentative writing for students in all content areas (National Governors Association Center for Best Practices & Council of Chief State School Officers, 2010). When we ask our preservice and inservice teachers to define literary analysis, they generally focus on two aspects: the thesis and the detailed textual support. One preservice teacher, Kyle, described literary analysis as "an essay where you cut up a text in order to say something really important about how it works." Another preservice teacher, Evan, explained that "literary analysis is where you make a claim that isn't too broad and then find and use only the evidence that supports your claim. Like a treasure hunt that is only looking for one type of treasure."

Before beginning the hypertext literary analysis assignment, our preservice teacher candidates work to create a shared definition of literary analysis based on their own experiences as writers. The familiar literary analysis requires writers to examine a piece of literature, break it into parts for study, and figure out how those parts relate to the whole piece. As a group, the candidates develop a definition of the literary analysis essay as a cohesive written product that has a strong thesis, an argument, synthesis, and textual evidence that also requires the writer to bring in personal experience and literary lenses. For the hypertext literary analysis assignment, preservice teachers use their literary analysis skills but in a digital and multimodal format, which allows for a more open format and a non-linear type of argument structure. Morgan (2000) argues that hypertext and its forms of branching and linking "enable us to think otherwise about the explicit propositional form of chained argument, which seeks to close down positions and to subsume the voices of others in order to effect singularity and closure" (p. 139). A hypertext literary analysis differs from the more conventional print format in that the argument is not developed paragraph by paragraph in a linear chain (e.g., claim, evidence, analysis, transition, claim, claim, evidence, analysis, transition, claim, etc.). Instead, the argument in a hypertext is an exploration of links that builds an argument across the text as the reader clicks and reads, diverging and moving in a click-follow-reveal movement through the text.

This shift in the structure frequently frustrates preservice teachers as they try to determine what they want to say and how to say it. As Allison stated, "It was the lack of control that frustrated me. I wanted to know exactly the path the reader would take. In my first draft, I created a version that rigidly controlled the reader, making the choices very, very limited." What the preservice teachers come to realize is that they are accustomed to analyses that follow a rigid path and, while they express frustration with those texts, they have come to expect that level of authorial control. When they create hypertexts that allow them to explore a text in multiple levels and layers, they begin to unearth a way of thinking that lets their argument accrete over screens rather than develop linearly through paragraphs. Amelia said that she had resisted the idea of hypertexts—even though she was annoyed by what she had to leave out in more traditional analyses—until she "realized the power of following tangents, of exploring single lines and even single words to really dig deeply into a text."

The hypertext literary analysis task challenges preservice teachers to think and compose analysis differently; they can use sound, images, links, juxtaposition, songs, YouTube videos, and other digital affordances as they create the hypertext. They build their hypertext in PowerPoint, using the hyperlinking features of the program, and incorporate multiple forms of media as well as links, commentary, analysis, questions, and movement. The task allows preservice teachers to demonstrate both their abilities to analyze a literary text and their abilities to use digital media to construct and share their work.

The recognition that analysis as a form of argument can take many forms plays a key role in developing preservice teachers' abilities to plan complex instructional tasks. As one preservice teacher, Elise, explained,

I knew that my students could analyze a passage in something other than an essay because of the hypertext assignment we did so I created an Instagram scene analysis for them to do...I just needed to think about what I wanted them to show me and in what format. Once I let go of the essay as the only way to show analysis, I was able to choose widely from a lot of digital tools.

Further, teachers noted that their experiences with creating the hypertexts help them better break down their requirements for students to craft arguments in print-based forms. As digital writers begin to question assumptions of genre and disciplinary practice while making meaning in digital, multimodal environments, they have new opportunities for thinking about the goals and purposes of writing—in any form.

Rethinking Argumentative Texts: Infographics

Like the hypertext literary analysis, the infographic assignment leverages inservice and preservice teachers' knowledge of more conventional forms of argumentative texts. An infographic is a document that is created using graphic design platforms (e.g., Visual.ly, Picktochart, Infogr.am, and Canva) to illustrate information and statistics and to create a visual argument. This assignment challenges teachers to visually communicate a thesis backed by data to craft an argument. This assignment meets several goals: teachers develop valuable skills in synthesis and effective communication of complex topics at the same time as they are developing expertise in bringing together many different modes—such as text, images, graphics, color, and shapes—to craft meaning.

During the process of composing infographics, we lead our teachers in critical discussions of how these tools can enable writers to make particular kinds of arguments. For instance, rather than asking teachers how technology changes writing, we ask questions such as, w*hat does technology allow us to do with writing and communication that we cannot easily do with print writing*? Or, instead of looking specifically at what changes about writing when we shift modes, we look at what is made possible when we shift modes of writing from print to digital. In relation to the infographics, we ask our teachers to attend to how graphics and images can support the development of particular kinds of arguments and can make more effective and efficient cases for their theses.

The process of composing an infographic argument continues with selecting a topic that is comprehensive yet narrow enough to be well represented in a one-page infographic. Teachers then read and synthesize information about their topic to develop a well-crafted argument. In a typical argumentative assignment, details are combined into a written essay; however, in the infographic assignment, teachers must craft their argument by sketching it out on an infographic storyboard and decide how to visually represent their arguments with image and text. Teachers report that their work on their infographics scaffolded them to deeper understandings of how to tailor their writing to the particular affordances of digital and multimodal tools. For example, Zelda, a preservice teacher, reflected on the assignment by writing,

I did face a challenge on the design portion of creating the infographic. I can write about a topic and explain it without much trouble, but when I need to bring the explanation down to the essentials I begin to question my summary and ability to communicate everything that needs to be said.

Other teachers focused on how the assignment supported richer understandings of content. Another preservice teacher, Rebecca, explained, "After making the infographic, I feel like I understand the topic better because of the summarizing and synthesizing I had to do…I also think the final product is representative of the main ideas in a way that someone could easily access." Her recognition that the ways in which she had to think about the work in order to create an infographic demonstrates a common shift in the preservice and inservice teachers who complete this task.

Rebecca's response embodies the essence of the assignment, which is supported by the 2012 NCTE Standards for the initial preparation of English Language Arts teachers (National Council of Teachers of English/International Reading Association, 2012). Specific standards addressed include 2.1 ("Candidates can use contemporary technologies and/or digital media to compose multimodal discourse") and 5.4 ("Candidates select, create, and use a variety of instructional strategies and teaching resources, including contemporary technologies and digital media, consistent with what is currently known about student learning in English Language Arts"). We've also found that as teachers learn more about the potential of multimodal tools for crafting arguments, their design of pedagogical practices around argumentative writing in both print and digital modes becomes more purposeful—they begin thinking about how different components can work with each other or against each other in the process of creating a cohesive and persuasive argumentative text.

Rethinking Informational Texts: Literacy Videos

As our teachers remind us constantly, one of the essential tasks of any teacher educator is to successfully bridge theory and practice—to bring research-based knowledge and strategies to solve authentic problems of practice. One of those problems of practice that has emerged again and again through our surveys, interviews, and informal conversations with teachers is the necessity of finding new ways to communicate with parents, families, and community members. For example, although many of our teachers report connecting with parents and families using email and learning management systems like PowerSchool, Google Classroom and ClassDojo, classroom websites and other 21st century digital tools remain underutilized resources. As one of our inservice teachers, Claire, said, "Every year, my principal tells us to make a classroom website. And every year, I have no idea what to put up there." This is not uncommon. As Olmstead (2013) noted, the vast majority of teachers who have class websites make updates, at most, 1-2 times per month; and, as a result, parents don't find teacher websites to be useful or a good source of information.

The literacy video assessment, which was designed for a mixed class of preservice and inservice teachers, involved designing a short digital video (2-3 minutes) introducing a literacy topic (e.g., inferring, fluency, phonemic segmentation, reader's theater, disciplinary literacy, academic vocabulary) to an authentic audience of parents, guardians, and community members. This assignment meets several professional standards, including NCTE/IRA (2012) Standard 4 and 2017 ILA Literacy Coach Standard 6 (International Literacy Association, 2017). It also addresses several key goals for both preservice and inservice teachers: supporting teachers in developing technical skills in new media production; asking them to demonstrate effective interpersonal, communication, and leadership skills while modeling a positive attitude towards literacy; and developing interactive content to share with a broad audience. During and after the video design process, teachers are required to reflect on the multimodal composing process and to assist in collaborating to refine the project rubric based on their experiences.

As we've continued to develop and refine this project over the years, we've realized that it serves two primary purposes: honing teachers' skills in juxtaposing different discourses, styles, and communicative modes in digital contexts and helping them to think creatively about how they might connect with P-12 students' families and other community members in an increasingly digital world. Both preservice and inservice teachers found the literacy videos to be beneficial in enhancing their knowledge of how to use digital tools to create informational texts, as well as in providing ideas for how they might expand their communicative channels to connect to more parents and families. Jeff, a preservice Social Studies teacher, noted the value of thinking about how to connect to families before ever getting into the classroom:

I think that's one thing that I missed in my classes. I am pretty confident that I got the content down, but figuring out how to talk to parents has stayed above my head—like a theoretical level...I liked this project because it was a real idea of how I can share what my kids and I are doing in the classroom.

Teachers have reported using literacy videos to encourage ongoing communication among teachers, families, and students. Kelly, a middle school ELA teacher, has used monthly literacy videos as a way for students to share their knowledge of key ELA concepts with their parents and community members.

It is important to note that reimagining assignments to incorporate 21st century communication and presentation skills also requires rethinking the supports necessary for student success. For teachers who are reluctant or who have limited experience with using digital tools to communicate information, engaging in a series of incremental response activities using multimodal tools can be a great way to get started. In addition, providing ongoing supports for the literacy videos—such as student-led critique groups, templates, and model lessons—can help teachers be more metacognitive about their emerging digital composing skills and give them ideas of how to support their own P-12 students. Online and digital tools can even serve as spaces for teachers to reflect on their own composing and to participate in metacognitive discussion about how their ideas of writing have changed as they have engaged with digital and multimodal tools.

DISCUSSION AND IMPLICATIONS

The changing and expanding definitions of text afforded by new technologies require that both preservice and inservice teachers rethink what counts as writing in schools. We know that teachers' experiences and their own writing journeys shape how they teach, so it is even more important that they have opportunities to experiment, create, and play with digital forms. This chapter has presented a research-based overview of the need to support preservice and inservice teachers' understanding of writing as a digital, multimodal, and participatory practice; outlined specific strategies for supporting these teachers in becoming multimodal and digital writers themselves; and detailed the importance of this work as teachers help their P-12 students learn how to take advantage of the unique affordances of digital and multimodal tools for crafting meaning.

One of our primary goals was to demonstrate how providing explicit support and opportunities to engage with digital writing practices can shift preservice and inservice teachers' conceptions of digital writing's role in the classroom. Specifically, we examined examples of activities that leverage three traditional writing genres (narrative, argumentative, and informational) to support new understandings of writing as multimodal, participatory, and digital. First, we illustrated how teachers' engagement in cycles of multimodal text interpretation and critique in the literacy interpretation assignment allowed them to build their repertoires as writers of both print and digital texts. Next, in creating hypertext literary analyses and infographics, teachers came to understand how different modes can enhance the development of particular kinds of arguments and can make more effective and efficient cases for their theses. Finally, digital informational texts, such as the literacy video, can enable teachers to juxtapose different discourses, styles, and communicative modes to create meaning for specific audiences.

We believe that focusing on digital and multimodal writing in teacher education courses offers a number of benefits for teachers' abilities to communicate across print and digital media. Perhaps surprisingly, we've found that the vast majority of the preservice and inservice teachers that we work with have spent very little time questioning their own practices or what they do as writers—they see it as just what writers do. This mindset does not serve them well as writing teachers, because it makes it difficult for them to know the elements of writing and its disciplinary practices that they need to make visible and support for their own students. Shifting media formats for familiar writing tasks makes the process and the practices more explicit for them as writers. Just as candidates notice and discuss key craft elements in print writing and focus on the effects those elements create in the text, so too must they notice and discuss key craft elements in digital and multimodal texts.

The necessity of learning how to put words on paper in effective, thoughtful, and meaningful ways is not going to disappear. Therefore, attending to the craft elements of print writing is important and should not be discounted. However, digital and multimodal writing has created new outlets for writing and communication. In order for teachers to take digital writing as seriously as they do print writing, they must engage in writing experiences that position them as both traditional writers and as digital and multimodal writers. When preservice and inservice teachers can engage in the side-by-side positioning of their analysis and composing of print and digital texts, they are more likely to develop a flexible repertoire of print and digital writing practices, scaffolds, and tools which will help them as writers and teachers of writing.

REFERENCES

Levi's. (2009, June 30). *Levi's America (Go Forth)* [Video File]. Retrieved from https://www.youtube.com/watch?v=HG8tqEUTlvs

Albers, P. (2014). Digital writing and the role of critical pedagogy in preservice teacher education. In R. E. Ferdig & K. E. Pytash (Eds.), *Exploring multimodal composition and digital writing* (pp. 98–115). Hershey, PA: IGI Global. doi:10.4018/978-1-4666-4345-1.ch007

Bezemer, J., & Kress, G. (2017). Young people, Facebook, and pedagogy: Recognizing contemporary forms of multimodal text making. In M. Kontopodis, C. Varvantakis, & C. Wulf (Eds.), *Global youth in digital trajectories* (pp. 22–38). London, UK: Routledge. doi:10.4324/9781315303239-3

Bruce, D. L., & Chiu, M. M. (2015). Composing with new technology: Teacher reflections on learning digital video. *Journal of Teacher Education*, *66*(3), 272–287. doi:10.1177/0022487115574291

Dalton, B. (2012). Multimodal composition and the Common Core State Standards. *The Reading Teacher*, *66*(4), 333–339. doi:10.1002/TRTR.01129

Damico, J. S., Panos, A., & Myers, M. (2018). Digital literacies and climate change: Exploring reliability and truth(s) with preservice teachers. In E. Ortlieb, E. Cheek, & P. Semingson (Eds.), *Best practices in teaching digital literacies* (pp. 93–107). Bingley, UK: Emerald Publishing Limited. doi:10.1108/S2048-045820180000009007

Doering, A., Beach, R., & O'Brien, D. (2007). Infusing multimodal tools and digital literacies into an English education program. *English Education*, *40*(1), 41–60.

Henriksen, D., Mishra, P., & Fisser, P. (2016). Infusing creativity and technology in 21st century education: A systemic view for change. *Journal of Educational Technology & Society*, *19*(3), 27–37.

Hundley, M., & Holbrook, T. (2013). Set in stone or set in motion?: Multimodal and digital writing with preservice English teachers. *Journal of Adolescent & Adult Literacy*, *56*(6), 500–509. doi:10.1002/JAAL.171

International Literacy Association. (2017). *Standards for the preparation of literacy professionals 2017*. Newark, DE: Authors.

Johnson, L. L., & Smagorinsky, P. (2014). Writing remixed: Mapping the multimodal composition of one preservice English Education teacher. In R. E. Ferdig & K. E. Pytash (Eds.), *Exploring multimodal composition and digital writing* (pp. 263–281). Hershey, PA: IGI Global. doi:10.4018/978-1-4666-4345-1.ch016

Kirschner, P. A., & De Bruyckere, P. (2017). The myths of the digital native and the multitasker. *Teaching and Teacher Education*, *67*, 135–142. doi:10.1016/j.tate.2017.06.001

Lei, J. (2009). Digital natives as preservice teachers: What technology preparation is needed? *Journal of Computing in Teacher Education*, *25*(3), 87–97.

Miller, S. M., & McVee, M. B. (Eds.). (2013). *Multimodal composing in classrooms: Learning and teaching for the digital world*. London, UK: Routledge. doi:10.4324/9780203804032

Morgan, W. (2000). Electronic tools for dismantling the master's house: Poststructuralist feminist research and hypertext poetics. In E. A. St. Pierre & W. S. Pillow (Eds.), *Working the ruins: Feminist poststructural theory and methods in education* (pp. 130–149). New York, NY: Routledge.

National Council of Teachers of English/International Reading Association. (2012). *Standards for the English language arts*. Author.

National Governors Association Center for Best Practices & Council of Chief State School Officers. (2010). *Common Core State Standards for English language arts and literacy in history/social studies, science, and technical subjects*. Washington, DC: Authors.

Okojie, M. C. (2011). The changing roles of teachers in a technology learning setting. *International Journal of Instructional Media*, *38*(1), 17–26.

Olmstead, C. (2013). Using technology to increase parent involvement in schools. *TechTrends*, *57*(6), 28–37. doi:10.100711528-013-0699-0

Prensky, M. (2001). Digital natives, digital immigrants, part 1. *On the Horizon*, *9*(5), 1–6. doi:10.1108/10748120110424816

Rish, R. (2013). Exploring multimodal composing processes with preservice teachers. In K. E. Pytash, R. E. Ferdig, & T. Rasinski (Eds.), *Preparing teachers to teach writing using technology* (pp. 1–16). Pittsburgh, PA: ETC Press.

Ritchhart, R., Church, M., & Morrison, K. (2011). *Making thinking visible: How to promote engagement, understanding, and independence for all learners*. San Francisco, CA: Jossey-Bass.

Staples, J. (2010). "Does my iMovie suck?": Assessing teacher candidates' digital composition processes. *English Journal*, *99*(5), 95–99.

VanKooten, C., & Berkley, A. (2016). Messy problem-exploring through video in first-year writing: Assessing what counts. *Computers and Composition*, *40*, 151–163. doi:10.1016/j.compcom.2016.04.001

Chapter 11
Complexities of Identity and Belonging:
Writing From Artifacts in Teacher Education

Anna Schick
University of Minnesota, USA

Jana Lo Bello
University of Minnesota, USA

ABSTRACT

Engaging in artifactual literacy as a collective in a teacher education seminar class gives space for objects and texts to bring forth reimagined and alternative ways to be "teacher." An elementary teacher education program utilizes a seminar space to invite teachers to write from artifacts to analyze, deconstruct, and reconstruct their teacher identities. The analysis and discussions of the reconstructed narratives that define, contest, or shape identities give needed distance from traditional and often constricting narratives of "teacher" and "teaching." The investment of this critical identity work in teacher education is depicted in the analysis of two preservice teachers' collective writing in a digital space.

INTRODUCTION

"What started as a critical reading of a children's book became a social justice 'racial equity' purity test full of hypocrisy." -Will

It was that time of year again. The newness of the fall semester had faded and the teacher candidates were several weeks into the licensure program and student teaching at their school sites. This was the time each year we, the Elementary Education Licensure Program Lead and the Elementary Education Academic Advisor, would begin to receive late night emails from students about their challenging

DOI: 10.4018/978-1-7998-0000-2.ch011

relationship with their cooperating teacher, experiences of racial microaggressions from their supervisor, concerns about deficit-based reading curricula, and the inevitable question: "Is this really the right profession for me?". The response to these individual reach outs was often to gather the Elementary Education team and schedule a progress review meeting. We'd meet, make a plan, and then back out into the field they would go.

This introduction aims to tease out the reasons for revising the writing pedagogy of a particular seminar course. As a one year intensive teacher education program, the fall semester balanced site placement and graduate-level methods courses. Entering spring semester, teacher candidates were full time in their public school elementary classroom and returned to campus only one evening a week for a seminar course. Historically, the seminar was utilized as the catch all for any remaining standards, common assignments, or licensure logistics that had not been addressed in earlier courses or communications. This plasticity of interpretation was conducive for differentiated content but also ran the risk of being experienced as a disjointed assortment of "to dos" before teacher candidates completed the licensure program. In recent years, several of the department's common assessments were assigned to the seminar space. These assignments asked teacher candidates to regurgitate their knowledge of theories and understanding of schools, students, and families. As instructors, the tone of analysis felt formally objective versus the nuanced interpretations as an individual who had spent time working in a school community for a year. Attention was brought to this seminar space as the program explicitly articulated a vision towards supporting teacher candidates to be socially and racially-just teacher leaders.

As former classroom teachers, we acknowledge our roles within this complex community of practice surrounding teacher candidates (Lave & Wenger, 1991). As themes emerged from our fall progress review meetings, we noticed the significant value there was in collaborating from our roles as Academic Advisor and Licensure Program Lead. We were granted permission to co-teach the seminar in the spring in an effort to support the program's growing understanding of the relationship between the advising, clinical placements, and methods course instruction from the perspective of the teacher candidates. In this endeavor, we acknowledge how Jana, the licensure program lead, brings the historical context of the program and seminar course while Anna, the academic advisor, brings the individual stories shared within advising appointments, both from prospective and current teacher candidates.

The following script is a recreated dialogue from a planning meeting prior to the start of the seminar. It aims to support the purpose of the introduction to establish the contributing factors to the revision of the seminar. We use a script to draw out our complicated feelings of the purpose of seminar and our desires for collective narratives. This dialogue further emphasizes the histories and ideas we brought to our vision of co-teaching and artifactual critical literacy.

Jana: *I had another meeting with a teacher candidate this morning.*

Anna: *Same. I had one as well.*

Jana: *How do we get them to share these struggles with each other — not just with us?*

Anna: *We could try a writer's workshop. I tried this with first year teachers but it was in an informal space and during the summer. And they really trusted each other.*

Jana: *Did it work?*

Anna: *I think the effects are still in play in their classrooms. In the workshop, teachers selected artifacts to write about their teacher identities. For example, they brought in screenshots of text messages, middle school bathroom graffiti, prescription pill bottles, and items from their classroom. I wonder if we could rework this approach for seminar.*

Jana: *I see such a need for a shift in authentic reflection. I constantly hear feedback from teacher candidates that "All we do is lesson plan and write reflections. We know how to reflect." It concerns me when year after year I basically read the same formal assignments and reflections without certainty that the teacher candidates are doing more than going through the motions of the program.*
Anna: *It could give an opportunity for teacher candidates to write collectivity rather than reflect alone — and perhaps deconstruct or construct their concept of teacher and teaching.*
Jana: *We can adapt existing assignments and still meet the requirements of the seminar space.*
Anna: *Let's try it.*

Our chapter that follows explores how as a result of the revision of the seminar course, teacher candidates engaged in artifactual critical literacy as a means to disrupt traditional reflective practices and take up participatory literacy in digital spaces to collectively (re)narrate teacher and teaching.

Artifactual Critical Literacy

Teachers enter teacher education programs with ample opportunity and expectation to write — to produce lesson plans, essays, and reflections. In our teacher education program, we sought out critical writing pedagogies, primarily writing from artifacts, to give preservice teachers access to ways to deconstruct and reconstruct teacher identity (Lensmire & Schick, 2017). Kamler (2001) reminds us, "Without [these new narratives] none of us has any way of gaining enough distance to make dominant [narratives] visible and thereby to imagine alternatives." (p.77).

This chapter takes up Pahl and Roswell's (2011) proposed "artifactual critical literacy" as a framework for literacy education. In connection to material cultural studies, artifactual critical literacy suggests objects can provide a platform and starting point for text-making. This understanding is grounded in scholars who have used critical literacy pedagogy to interrogate texts as sites of power (Janks, 2010; Nieto, 2002; Richardson, 2006). Rather than regarding material objects as passive or inert, the application of materialism to literacy research argues for objects as performative agents (Hurdley, 2006; Rowsell & Simon, 2017). In the context of the seminar space, teacher candidates were invited to bring in and draw on artifacts related to teaching or teacher identity.

Digital spaces were utilized to analyze understandings of artifacts. The ability to work simultaneously online to contribute to collective understandings necessarily complicated and enhanced multiple understandings of belonging to the identity of *teacher*. We started with utilizing a shared Google document to collectively generate a narrative from an artifact. As we explored our data, we considered other means for artifactual critical literacy to occur in digital spaces. Participatory literary offers the opportunity for students to develop creative responses to artifacts. As we aim to disrupt traditional notions of reflection in teacher education, the creation of multimodal texts in response to artifacts representative of teacher and teaching is essential to critical literacy work. If the classroom itself is an artifact and everyday objects like a closed door or a children's book can be read as texts, the response should continue to expand our understanding of text and critical literacy. Designing and producing texts, including the decisions that are a part of that process, serve a purpose beyond simply creating texts to "practice a skill" (Vasquez, Janks, & Comber, 2019). Digital spaces offer means to design and produce by creating blogs, podcasts, videos, and infographics. Further, as we push the boundaries of academic writing and challenge the goals of reflection, responses to artifacts in digital space could move towards activism through social media, crowdsourcing, or organizing. The move to a digital space provides not only the capacity to collaborate and collectively narrate, but also the opportunity to participate in global and digital cultures (Wohlwend, 2017).

This study explores what happened when preservice teachers met on a google document to respond to an artifact representing a conflict in their school placement site. Partnering digital spaces and artifactual critical literacy emphasizes the need for collective (re)narration and construction of text not only for the sake of reflection but for cracking the dominant discourses of teacher and teaching.

The Study: Context and Questions

This chapter is based on our observations of teacher candidates, subsequent conversations with them, and a discourse analysis of the work products within an interpretive qualitative study (Erickson, 1986). Interpretive ethnographic data (Erickson, 1986) draws from a larger study analyzing our teacher education program's process toward fuller articulation of our mission and vision for racial and social justice. This part of the study draws on the ways in which the activities within a reflective seminar provide space for critical writing pedagogy (Kamler, 2001) and narrative and writing process theory (Park, 2005). Our research study focuses on one cohort of teacher candidates enrolled in their final clinical and instructional year, taking their experience within a reflective seminar course as a single case study that is not only representative and revelatory (Yin, 2009), but also instrumental (Stake, 2005). Our class demographic, primarily white females, contributed to further inquiries on identity construction and the need for deconstruction. These eighteen preservice teachers offer a representative social narrative of teacher candidates, a narrative that began to crack open in digital spaces when collectively writing from artifacts.

The chapter examines the impact of critical literacy practices in addressing the questions: 1) How do we use artifacts to access new narratives of teacher and teaching? 2) What collective narratives of teacher and teaching emerge? 3) How might the praxis of this seminar course provide space for preservice teacher self-advocacy, including around issues of social and racial justice?

Themes from the data suggest that it is necessary to complicate assumptions around writing as solely academic writing (typically perceived as right or wrong answer) and reflection (typically perceived as a summary of experience) within our elementary teacher education program. Instead, engaging in artifactual literacy provides means for teacher candidates to deconstruct and reconstruct their fixed and fluid experiences as graduate students, as student teachers, as teachers, and as complex individuals.

In this next section, we introduce Nora and Will, two teacher candidates who provided insight into the ways in which the program's efforts for social and racial justice was experienced for teacher candidates. The seminar space was a tangible point within the program where both Nora and Will reinscribed and challenged dominant narratives about what it meant to be "teacher".

Nora and Will

Nora

During the first seminar session, we asked the teacher candidates to write us a letter about their relationship with writing. We discussed how this artifact would be a place to return at the end of the semester to note shifts or changes in writing pedagogy. This letter was also an opportunity for us, as co-teachers, to trace the varied relationships with writing and draw on or complicate them in seminar.

Nora's detailed letter made us nod our heads in understanding and bear in mind the navigation of new belongings as a teacher candidate. Further, Nora fulfills our subconscious expectation that future teachers are writers (who love to write):

Writing has always been important to me. I love reading novels and writing creatively. I also do a lot of reflective writing and I have been keeping a journal regularly since I was in sixth grade. I use it to process a lot of big ideas about education, science, religions, philosophies, ideas in books that I have read, and various other ponderings about the universe. I am enjoying writing lesson plans because they help me process and organize my thoughts before teaching.

Nora's letter, lengthy and honest, also opened up a space to share her relationship with her cooperating teacher (CT). She makes a classic move in her letter which was characteristic of her personality, searching for a silver lining. While she is clearly challenged in her relationship with her cooperating teacher, she includes a positive note to maintain the expectation of a balanced letter and possibly a maintenance of disposition:

My placement is also challenging because my CT and I differ on a lot of values, ideas, and our planning/teaching/management styles. There have been many times when I disagree with what and how she teaches. I am often confused by her directions. On a more positive note, we have open communication and I feel confident asking for clarification when I don't understand what she is doing. My CT likes to talk, and I tend toward introversion. It is sometimes hard for me to go a whole day without any down time for myself, even if it is just ten minutes. Some days I am so tired that I go home, eat dinner, and go straight to bed.

Nora, adamant in understanding racial equity and engaging in critical literacy, outwardly mirrors the dominant teacher candidate in our cohort: white, middle class, mid-twenties female. She was both subject to and upheld the stereotypical image of teacher. The "good" teacher, like the "good" woman, is positioned as "self-sacrificing, kind, overworked, underpaid, and holding an unlimited reservoir of patience" (Britzman, 2003, p. 5). This stereotype engenders a static notion of teacher identity; it assumes that *teacher* is a stable and fixed figure that can be assumed. Nora exhibited a maternal nature and boasted the single greatest reason to become a teacher — Nora loved her students:

I had many reservations and debated whether or not to request a new placement. The reason I decided to stay in my placement is the biggest positive about my experience so far: I love the students in my class.

Nora's representation in this study is complex in her dynamic and engaged disposition but also in her tension, conscious or subconscious, to conform to previous conceptions of teacher and simultaneously disrupt her student teaching site with her learning to become a teacher.

Will

Will's introductory letter stood out as a moment of critical reflection for us as co-teachers. We instructed all teacher candidates that this letter could be informal and there was no page length. Unlike Nora and the rest of his classmates, Will's final writing piece was considerably shorter with less detail. His entire letter is below:

Dear Anna and Jana,

First semester was busy between classes, teaching, and working on the weekends. Some of our methods courses were interesting and worthwhile, others were not. I learned a lot from the students in my room.

I don't really enjoy writing, particularly fiction or creative writing. I'll do it when I have to and I'm confident enough in my abilities to serve the purpose of whatever the writing is.

This was one among many moments we, as co-teachers, processed his participation in the class individually and collectively. If we explicitly stated that there was little criteria for this introductory letter, then why was there an initial notice of a particular teacher candidate? We disclosed to each other our conscious disappointment as a result of what we understood to be a subconscious expectation of [more] writing. This led to a program faculty question: what expectations and structures are we (consciously or subconsciously) harboring? Further, what is the role of conflict, dissonance, and multiple perspectives within a teacher education program whose vision is to prepare social and racially just teacher leaders?

Early in the semester, teacher candidates were asked to do a program audit of the coursework they took in order to identify any areas of interest they believe have not been addressed. Will's response was a listing of all the courses and assignments that were "basically the same class." He took a critical read of the program's efforts for equity-based pedagogies in, we argue, really smart ways. For example, using direct quotes from what was claimed as the same few readings over and over again, he used program foundational texts that called for more diverse teacher recruitment by turning the assertions onto the program, calling out the homogeneity of represented professor identities and experiences within this teacher education program. His final sentiment was left as "What does this teacher education program actually have to offer me besides social justice buzzwords?"

Valentine (2006) suggests performance space is the only place certain language or statements are permissible. For example, when working with women in prisons, Valentine observed performance, specifically scripting and role-playing, as the only space in which a statement such as "fuck the guards" is permissible (p. 315). Following in line with Valentine's (2006) notion of ethnodramas, Will utilized opportunities, such as the critical assignments within this seminar space, to say the things he "couldn't say".

We are not elevating Nora or tearing down Will. Rather, we need them both. Nora is necessary in thinking of ways we crack the dominant narrative of teacher and Will calls our attention to falseness in our attempts and continued conformity and participation in the reproductive system of teacher education.

Positionality

Context

As the academic advisor, Anna met with students most often on an individual basis. Across these meetings, she gathered a collection of stories. Teacher candidates brought in challenges from their student teaching site, the teacher education program, and their personal lives. As the licensure program lead, Jana met with supervisors, instructors, and cooperating teachers. The topics of these interactions included logistical workings of the program, enactment of the program vision, and feedback on a range of stories of teacher candidate performance. During the weekly Elementary Education team meetings, Anna and Jana often tried to synthesize these stories to build a collective narrative around struggles such as the schedule, the tense cooperating teacher-student teacher relationships, financial concerns, or feeling alienated or disconnected from their school site. Yet, in our attempt to (re)narrate these stories the problems were elevated and the discussion shifted from teacher identity and belonging to action orientated moves to remedy the individual situations. Anna frequently voiced that we needed a place in our program where teacher candidates could collectively narrate this experience in order to hear alternatives and build counter narratives to oppressive and limiting definitions of teacher and teaching. In their respective roles, Anna and Jana had come to understand that candidates did not view their current seminar space as a processing space; rather, they understood individual meetings with the academic advisor or licensure program lead as the space to raise dilemmas and conflicting ideas of teacher identity.

Enactment

As part of our commitment to co-teaching this course, we planned and reflected on a weekly basis. Keeping our overarching questions in mind, we were aware of the language and mindsets that we articulated during these processing times. In many ways our experience as instructors paralleled the teacher candidates' experiences as elementary teachers in the negotiation of time. We were all bound within the time of one academic calendar year. From our similar teaching roles, the seminar class acknowledged the spatialization of timing as deep experiences yet temporary belonging to our respective educational spaces. For example, the teacher candidates wrestled with time as it relates to the district calendar systems where elementary teacher and student typically have one grade level year together with an assumption of deep relational and academic growth. For us as university instructors, the parallel yearlong program experience carries assumptions that it is possible to construct a solid identity and professionalization of "teacher" at the commencement of this curricular time together.

Yet, as a result of the temporariness in our respective spaces, language tended to be future-oriented as the "next year narrative" for both university instructor and teacher candidate. "Next year, when you have your own classroom." "Next year, when we teach this course again." With this in mind, we wanted to be reflective with our roles and with our own multiple identities in modeling how the process of engaging with artifactual critical literacy and critical writing pedagogies is ongoing. We wrote with the teacher candidates and shared our own journey with the multiple ways that "teacher" is taken up in educational spaces. This constructed a level of trust with us as advisor, instructor, supervisor, licensure program lead, former teachers, and people.

In this research study, our individual relationships with teacher candidates undoubtedly brought trust to the restructure of the seminar space. Our positionality as their academic advisor and licensure program lead meant that we brought in our knowledge of individual stories in the shaping of a collective experience. The implication of this trust was in most cases a willingness to engage in critical writing and further an openness in negotiating and critiquing the school spaces, the graduate licensure program, and their complex understanding of identity and belonging.

Seminar

It was spring semester, snow still on the ground, and the teacher candidates were full-time in schools. During the day, they were in K-6 schools across the St.Paul-Minneapolis metro area. Teacher candidates returned to campus on Wednesday evenings for seminar. On this particular evening, they were prompted to work in their school groups (teacher candidates who were placed at the same school site). We asked the small groups to select an artifact that represented a conflict in their school. On a shared Google Document, they pasted an image of the object. From this artifact, students were encouraged to collectively write a creative response. Forms of poetry, narrative, and script writing emerged. One group for example chose the office door of their principal — a closed door. They co-constructed a poem, utilizing the digital space to add stanzas in between or finish each other's open lines. The words of their colleagues appearing on Google Document prompted their own. The poem in this way took up many perspectives, encouraged juxtaposition, and delved into the tender desire to be welcomed and belong in these "temporary" spaces (Leavy, 2015). This poem exemplified for us, as researchers, how artifactual critical literacy decentered the conversation from solely the university classroom or the student teaching site by using artifacts to interrogate the social, cultural, and historical understandings and underpinnings of the teaching profession. In Saldaña's (2003) emphasis on the potential of participant voices from two or more data sources, we became interested in the ways writing can be juxtaposed, layered, and merged in collective story creation.

Another group consisting of two teacher candidates, Nora and Will, took their computers to a corner table to write in response to an artifact they felt represented a conflict in their school site. In their Google Document, they posted a picture of a banned children's book: "A Birthday Cake for George Washington." The cover of the book is presented in Figure 1. A few days prior, the teacher candidates had joined a staff meeting which focused on the discussion of this banned book. Beneath the image they collectively took to (re)narrating the experience through script and internal monologue.

Staff gathered around while the "leadership team" discussed this book. The 10-12 members sit in a circle while the rest of the staff watches from the outside. We started hearing audio of a staff member reading the book which told the story of George Washington's kitchen staff making him a cake. The head chef creates a chocolate cake from scratch and works diligently to create his dish. The book talks about how the other slaves deeply respect the man and marvel at his skill. His daughter looks on lovingly as he works. In the end, his cake is a hit and the Washington family comes down to thank him. At this point, the "leadership team" had a moderator prompt the staff for their reactions.

For me (this is Will now dog), I immediately thought to myself, "Jesus Christ here we go."

Figure 1.

The conversations started with very fair points and thoughts about portrayals of slavery in books and looking at the text and images from this book, but quickly turned into a gong show. It quickly became a contest to virtue signal and try to see who could show they were the most outraged using the appropriate social justice vocabulary. What started as a critical reading of a children's book became a social justice "racial equity" purity test full of hypocrisy.

I think this meeting and this activity were a perfect metaphor for the mission statement of the school and social justice in general. The intentions are probably good, and may even have some valid points, but overall the goal of social justice is to portray an image to others and fill yourself with smug self-righteousness.

Although we were only spectators in this discussion, the atmosphere was tense as members of the team discussed the portrayal of slaves in media. Someone from outside the leadership circle broke in:

"Where did you even get this book?"

J looked uncomfortable," I bought the book," she said, "and debated over it for a long time. I wanted to know about it immediately after I found out it was banned. I paid $150 dollar for it."

"That's upsetting," said C. "As a black woman, hearing that you paid so much money for this...you are giving power to this author."

"The book has been pulled from shelves," said someone.

"Oh good!" came several murmurs.

"Yes," said K, waving her photocopy of the book in the air, "And these copies will be shredded! We are not letting students see this whitewashing of slavery."

Now, wait a minute! (thought Nora) Aren't we learning how to critically examine texts so that we can teach our students to do the same? Why can we benefit from discussing this book, but it is morally right to shred and burn all the remaining copies so that others can't? Also...giving power to the author by buying it for $150? No...the author is not benefitting from that money in any way, someone who is taking advantage of censorship is.

Curious, I looked up the book following the staff meeting and learned that the author and illustrator of the book were both black women. I was surprised that this was not discussed in the meeting. So much attention was given to taking power away from the author that no one had bothered to look the author up! I read an article by the author about how she had requested the publisher to use different illustrations, but was ignored. This background knowledge may have (should have) changed the direction of the discussion quite significantly! Would we be reading the text differently knowing that it was written by a black woman? Would we be reading it differently with different illustrations?

As observers of this critical writing in the seminar, we witnessed shifts in participation. The engagement in digital literacies gave necessary space to teacher candidates who normally did not participate in large group discussions or even small group conversations. The ability to add and construct a narrative *with* others recognizes that narratives already exist and they are contributors and disruptors rather than inventors of teacher identity.

We returned to writing from Nora and Will across the seminar course including flipgrid video recordings to ground and question our understanding of their positionality. Following, we employed our research questions to analyze the collective narrative in response to the artifact: "A Birthday Cake for George Washington."

How Do Teacher Candidates Use Artifacts to Access New Narratives of Teacher and Teaching?

In seminar, the space was previously defined as reflective, personal, and supportive. We sought to move beyond a surface level of reflective summation where teacher candidates restate their past decisions and actions as future "could have" or "should have" passive wishes. Instead, introducing artifacts into the critical reflection process pulls the teacher candidate necessarily outside of themselves to see how an artifact manifests representations of self as graduate student, student teacher, activist, and so on. The recentering of the critical reflective process on the artifact "A Birthday Cake for George Washington" instead of the self reinforces that teacher candidates are impacted by their space. Further, instead of a repetitive process of reflecting *on* the spaces they enter and experiences they have *in* schools, writing from an artifact repositions them to see themselves in direct relation to something more than a physical object; it places them as active receivers and perceivers of culture, discourse, and representations of *teacher* and teaching. Further, the focus on artifacts and artifactual literacies shifts literacy research from the exclusive focus on individuals or narrative to examining how artifacts manifest aspects of identity, family, history, ideology, and social relationships (Roswell & Simon, 2017).

The use of an artifact provides a space of meaning making between the object and self. The work of Gutierrez, Baquedano-López, and Tejada (1999) has outlined ways in which artifacts can create "third spaces." Consequently, without the use of artifacts, we believe reflective writing in teacher education is bound up internally and draws less on concrete sites of cultural or historical representation. To this end, artifactual critical literacy is active, questioning, and directly concerned with cultural and social constructs. Artifactual critical literacy has also been examined in ethnographic studies in homes and communities. Here the term "habitus" from Bourdieu (1990) provides insight into the function of artifacts. The term habitus is used to describe enduring patterns or dispositions, passed on across generations and manifested in a number of fields such as home, school, and community. What the concept of habitus offers is an account of social reality inside and outside ourselves.

The object of a children's book functions in Will's internal monologue as a place to capitalize on a position on equity and "virtue signaling." Instead of a reflection on the day or week at his student teaching site, this engagement with an artifact localized and contextualized his tension with the display of social justice orientations versus their actualization. Nora turns to questioning by using the artifact as an opportunity to juxtapose her learnings as a graduate student (namely, how to critically examine texts) and the actions of teachers in her school. She notes what she sees as pertinent information about the author of the text. Her judgment of her "colleagues'" ability to critically analyze a text is evident in her "Would we be reading the text differently …" questions. While she emphasizes that she is unable to speak up about her new critical understanding in her school space, she still utilizes writing in seminar to perform and demonstrate her knowledge (from graduate school). She makes the student move of showing us she's critically analyzing; she is still performing [student] in this space despite its intentional design to be a space of negotiation and construction.

Interestingly, both students when given the opportunity to write creatively from an artifact chose to retreat to their internal monologue. Their scripting of the staff dialogue is important in terms of context but what we were most interested in regarding artifactual critical literacy is how the object of the banned book elicited responses of their thinking on teacher identity.

What Collective Narratives of Teacher and Teaching Emerge?

While we preach to move away from deficit thinking, the "becoming a teacher" process feels very much like figuring out what is lacking and from there accumulating the right traits, language, and dispositions. In an effort to remove the stigma of filling out the teacher form, we seek out collective narration: a collective deconstructive and constructive process of writing on teacher identity. Our teacher education program repeatedly asks teacher candidates to reflect on their experiences and consider their "becoming" teacher identity. These forms often ask them to write from the fixed identity of a "student" — an individual learner of teaching. Part of our aim in introducing artifactual critical literacy is to move away from the emphasis on individual thought, individual grades, and the significance of individual action or experience towards acknowledging how a complex identity exists in relation to other complex identities, structures, and beliefs.

In critical writing pedagogy, Anzaldúa (2007) alludes that writing is an extension of self. Kamler (2001) resists this notion by arguing that writing is situated outside the self. When writing is treated as an artifact and separate from the self, it has the ability to combine and be shaped with others in a collective narrative. Nora and Will's writing from the artifact of the children's book is undoubtedly raw and impartial; yet in the intent to write collectively from an artifact, their writing is grounded less in the personal and more in the social and cultural contexts at play. Further, this writing produces multiple definitions and understandings of teacher and teaching. In the ways "we-narratives" (Bekhta, 2017) in fiction builds a collective character narrator, the creative writing from Nora and Will draws on multiple teacher narrator voices. In analysis, we turned to poetic inquiry to collectively write our interpretations of the narrations of teacher and teaching emerging from Nora and Will's writing:

Will says teacher identity is a gong show.

Nora says teacher identity has the potential to be critical.

Will says teaching is proving oneself in an arena.

Nora says teaching is investigating and researching authors.

Nora and Will say student teachers think but are silent —

Unless they are in seminar.

The writing produced by the preservice teachers complicated a singular notion of "belonging" to the teaching profession. This chapter thereby emphasizes how multiple belongings and identities carry a range of hierarchical positions of power and privilege. The negotiations of both fixed and fluid identities, such as teacher, student, and preservice teacher make the call to explore how access and belonging are experienced within spaces of university teacher education programs and school placements. The exploration of the pedagogical and curricular constructions in this final reflective teacher education seminar we believe affect the development of narratives about teacher identity.

Antioppressive education (Kumashiro, 2002) and liberatory practices (hooks, 1994) both disrupt and resist binary discourses, resulting in the ability to hold multiple trajectories and routes of being and learning. Going beyond the language or discourses of counter narratives, these liberatory practices call for reaction and agentic action on the part of educators and the community to be vigilant in reading and rereading educational practices. Space must be made for reflective literacy practices where students have the opportunity to create for themselves their own representations. Participatory literacy not only expands the repertoire of products, but actively works to disrupt the reliance of traditional, dominant writing practices.

How Might the Praxis of This Seminar Course Provide Space for Preservice Teacher Self Advocacy?

To begin, we return to Will: "What started as a critical reading of a children's book became a social justice 'racial equity' purity test full of hypocrisy". His words signal a critique of his staff meeting and also make a call for reflexivity on the part of institutions, including K-12 and university contexts. The precarious position of being a graduate student and a student teacher is highlighted in the teacher candidates' strong critiques of culturally relevant pedagogy [as graduate students] yet simultaneous emphasize the inability to participate as a teacher in the context [as a student teacher]. Regardless if this message is for the elementary education licensure program or K-12 school context, artifactual critical literacy allowed the teacher candidates to construct a new narrative and critique that produced multiple reads of the same object or event. We find it necessary for teacher candidates to experience participatory literacy practices to pushback on fixed forms of reflection and writing in order for them to construct "we narratives" with each other.

Developing the belief and access to integrate and negotiate practices within their own classrooms is necessary in order for teachers to disrupt dominant and existing narratives that are commonplace in K-12 contexts. Artifactual critical literacy moves beyond a singular assignment or static point within a program towards a mindset that teachers must think outside ourselves in order to disrupt the status quo and (re)narrate. Negotiating these practices is what will ultimately breakdown fixed identities. The collective narratives that emerge from seminar, from critical artifactual literacy, need to find a way to inform teacher education as well.

As a teacher education program, it is the hope that we are supporting teacher candidates to be current and future teacher leaders who are committed to disrupting the status quo of educational practices and policies. Our positionality runs parallel to the very time and space constraints of K-12 classroom contexts where expectations and anticipations of student products is part of the package of lesson planning. While anticipated outcomes are the product of thoughtful planning, the content and multiple perspectives of such work must be given space to be something different than was expected by the planner. Pushback then becomes generative rather than punitive or silenced.

We continue to be interested in how teacher education employs literacy practices to examine identities that open the identity of teacher rather than constrict or limit the narrative of teaching. Teachers cannot be enacting critical literacies and pedagogies in a space that is trying to foster and construct identities if they're unwilling to address and construct these identities for themselves. Cultural artifacts as a "site of meaning making" provide space for vulnerability and struggle within the construction of what it means to be student, student teacher, and teacher (Park, 2005). We see teacher education as both a time and space to consider writing for access to understanding community, activism, and belonging in schools.

Within the span of an academic year, we work with cohorts of teacher candidates who are constantly navigating their multiple identities in an effort to construct their conception of what it means to belong to the field of education as both student and teacher. The role of the teacher education program is to consider how to provide space for teacher candidates to take up their own identities within the foundational work of equity-based and racial justice pedagogies. While much of the space in the program considers negotiating the past and present ways that students move beyond an apprenticeship of observation (Borg, 2004), it is necessary to consider the future-focused ways that teacher candidates will use these processes within their upcoming classrooms. It is therefore necessary for teacher candidates to experience critical literacy practices that ask them to see, wrestle, and question the artifacts that represent teacher and teaching.

REFERENCES

Anzaldúa, G. (2007). *Borderlands/La Frontera: The new mestiza.* San Francisco, CA: Aunt Lute Books.

Bekhta, N. (2017). We-Narratives: The Distinctiveness of Collective Narration. Narrative, 25(2), 164-181.

Borg, M. (2004). The apprenticeship of observation. *ELT Journal*, *58*(3), 274–276. doi:10.1093/elt/58.3.274

Bourdieu, P. (1990). *The logic of practice*. Cambridge, UK: Polity Press.

Britzman, D. (2003). *Practice makes practice: A critical study of learning to teach*. Albany, NY: State University of New York Press.

Erickson, F. (1986). Qualitative methods in research on teaching. In Handbook on research on teaching (3rd ed.). New York: Macmillan.

Gutierrez, K., Baquedano-López, P., & Tejada, C. (1999). Rethinking diversity: Hybridity and hybrid language practices in the third space. *Mind, Culture, and Activity*, *6*(4), 286–303. doi:10.1080/10749039909524733

hooks, b. (1994). *Teaching to transgress: Education as the practice of freedom*. New York, NY: Routledge.

Hurdley, R. (2006). Dismantling mantelpieces: Narrating identities and materializing culture in the home. *Sociology*, *40*(4), 717–713. doi:10.1177/0038038506065157

Janks, H. (2011). *Literacy and power*. London: Routledge.

Kamler, B. (2001). *Relocating the personal: A critical writing pedagogy*. Albany, N.Y.: SUNY Press.

Kumashiro, K. (2002). *Troubling education: Queer activism and antioppressive pedagogy*. New York, NY: Routledge Falmer.

Lave, J., & Wenger, E. (1991). *Situated learning: Legitimate peripheral participation*. Cambridge, UK: Cambridge University Press. doi:10.1017/CBO9780511815355

Leavy, P. (2015). *Method meets art: Arts-based research practice*. New York, NY: Guilford Publications.

Lensmire, A., & Schick, A. (Eds.). (2017). *(Re)narrating Teacher Identity: Telling Truths and Becoming Teachers*. New York, NY: Peter Lang. doi:10.3726/b10687

Nieto, S. (2002). *Language, culture, and teaching: Critical perspectives for a new century*. Mahwah, NJ: Lawrence Erlbaum.

Pahl, K., & Rowsell, J. (2010). *Artifactual Literacies: Every Object Tells a Story*. New York, N.Y.: Teachers College Press.

Park, J. (2005). *Writing at the edge: Narrative and Writing Process Theory* (Vol. 248). New York, NY: Peter Lang.

Richardson, E. (2006). *Hiphop literacies*. London: Routledge. doi:10.4324/9780203391105

Rowsell, J., & Simon, R. (2017). Artifactual literacies. The SAGE Encyclopedia of Out-of-School Learning, 1, 40-42.

Saldaña, J. (2003). Dramatizing data: A primer. *Qualitative Inquiry*, *9*(2), 218–236. doi:10.1177/1077800402250932

Stake, R. (2005). Qualitative case studies. In N. K. Denzin & Y. S. Lincoln (Eds.), *Sage Handbook of Qualitative Research* (3rd ed.; pp. 442–447). Thousand Oaks, CA: Sage Publications.

Valentine, K. B. (2006). Unlocking the doors for incarcerated women through performance and creative writing. In D. S. Madison & J. Hamera (Eds.), *The Sage handbook of performance studies* (pp. 309–324). Thousand Oaks, CA: Sage. doi:10.4135/9781412976145.n17

Vasquez, V., Janks, H., & Comber, B. (2019). Critical Literacy as a Way of Being and Doing. *Language Arts, 96*(5), 300–311.

Wohlwend, K. E. (2016). Who gets to play? Access, popular media and participatory literacies. *Early Years: An International Research Journal, 37*(1), 62–76. doi:10.1080/09575146.2016.1219699

Yin, R. K. (2009). *Case study research: Design and methods.* Thousand Oaks, CA: Sage Publications.

Chapter 12

Preservice Teachers Collaborating and Co-Constructing in a Digital Space:

Using Participatory Literacy Practices to Teach Content and Pedagogy

Chrystine Mitchell
York College of Pennsylvania, USA

Carin Appleget
Creighton University, USA

ABSTRACT

Participatory literacy practices include the ways in which individuals interpret, make, and share as a way of connecting in our digitally mediated culture. This chapter is a culmination of an across-university partnership created between the two authors and the pre-service teachers that collaborated online about teaching and learning. Three threads of participatory literacy practices are shared within the chapter including 1) the use of blogging across university settings, 2) the implementation of digital professional learning communities (PLCs) to connect and collaborate with other pre-service teachers, and 3) the formation and participation in digital literature circles to co-construct meaning from children's literature. This chapter includes the authors' attempts at collaboration across university settings using different tools, platforms, and resources. This work is an example for other teachers and teacher educators to consider how we can help pre-service teachers be part of the participatory culture and provide an even wider community of learners.

DOI: 10.4018/978-1-7998-0000-2.ch012

INTRODUCTION

Teaching in the 21st century requires a unique skill-set to address the competencies necessary to be successful in the changing climate of schools. For teachers of literacy in particular, it is considered a requirement to know and be able to teach these specific skills in order for students to be productive citizens. For example, navigating and evaluating website content is a learned aptitude that students must grasp in order to traverse in literacy tasks using digital content (Cho, 2013). As a result, it becomes a professional responsibility for teacher educators to embed 21st century literacy skills into literacy methods coursework (Mitchell, 2017). This includes carving out time for introducing and modeling digital proficiencies, and it also includes varied opportunities for pre-service teachers to take risks and engage in digital content and experiences. The goal of integrating technological experiences into literacy pre-service education programs is to illustrate how authentic and meaningful opportunities with digital tools and content can, with the proper amount of scaffolding and support, transform literacy learning. This transformation requires that pre-service teachers learn to use, and teach students to use, digital literacy practices to represent, construct, create, and explore. These types of experiences can help to create 21st century learners that are productive, experienced with multi-modalities, and connected with a wider audience (Roswell & Wohlwend, 2016).

As a result of social networks and the connected technological landscape of schools, a "participatory culture" has emerged, and new media technologies are making it possible for people to interact with digital tools in new ways. This participatory culture has members who define what is significant in the culture, and develop new technologies that enhance communication and participation in this culture (Jenkins, Purushotma, Weigel, Clinton, & Robinson, 2009; Jocson & Rosa, 2015). Members in a digital culture take up participatory literacies, which offer ways of interpreting, making, and sharing digital multimedia and allows members to participate in it (Roswell & Wohlwend, 2016). As a result, teachers working in schools have an obligation to help youth learn how to use digital literacy tools effectively in multiple participatory cultures (Jenkins, et al., 2009). Again, this responsibility has a ripple-effect that impacts teacher education programs and the preparation of pre-service teachers entering classrooms expected to be ready to teach in tomorrow's schools.

We focus on three threads of participatory literacy practices that are embedded within the examples shared in this chapter. The examples illustrate: a) The importance of a connection to a wider professional learning community (PLC) to address literacy practices; b) Specific ways to connect pre-service teachers to a larger PLC beyond the scope of their own university walls in an online environment; and c) Different tools and experiences that pre-service teachers can "try out" to enhance their own literacy teaching. Specifically, we focus on participatory literacy practices that would be and could be used in schools *with* students. The highlighted practices exemplified in this chapter include: a) the use of blogging across university settings to learn from one another about technology integration; b) the implementation of digital professional learning communities (PLCs) to connect and collaborate with other pre-service teachers; and c) forming and participating in digital literature circles to co-construct meaning from children's literature and share pedagogical practices and ideas. These practices were developed from research conducted between the two authors and the pre-service teachers in the classes with those authors, located at geographically different university settings.

BACKGROUND

Our chapter rests on three important concepts: the use of digital literacy practices, the TPACK, and the use of professional learning communities. These three models work collectively to provide an important foundation for the ways in which teacher educators can and are preparing future teachers for authentic classroom practice with digital literacies.

Digital Literacy Practices

Digital literacies encompass a multi-modal approach to the way we think about literacy and how students' meaning making through technology can be agentive, multimodal, and design-oriented (New London Group, 1996). Although messages transmitted through print and text are traditionally privileged (Kress & Jewitt, 2003), a much more detailed message can actually be communicated through pictures, movement, font size, and images. Therefore, meaning is built through modes of transduction (Kress, 2003). Equally significant, students' digital meaning making is shaped by context, and it is often limited due to the resources available and because of students' own competencies using those resources (Archer, 2013). In consideration of the different ways students use digital tools, it seems necessary to address the issue of digital literacy pedagogies and how they can be situated as various social practices in classrooms (Stein & Newfield, 2006). For instance, some digital literacy practices of students are not valued in schools because it is challenging for new teachers to integrate technology into instructional practices (Turbill & Murray, 2006). Unfortunately, this disconnect illustrates a growing need for better understanding about digital literacy practices and the ways to effectively teach and assess them in schools. To connect differences in age, class, education and limited understanding, Gee (2004) proposes the need for "affinity spaces" where participatory cultures learn from and engage in deep conversations. These spaces offer important lessons about technology integration, suggesting how educators might better organize their work around students' interests and passions to help promote a common language and understanding (Gee, 2011).

To ground the teaching and learning using digital tools and the practices that evolve from their use, the International Society for Technology Education (ISTE) has developed standards of practice for both students and educators. These standards were developed to identify a set group of expectations for the inclusion of digital practices in schools. In particular, one set of ISTE standards *for students* focuses on students being "knowledge constructors," where students curate and use a variety of digital tools to, "construct knowledge, produce creative artifacts, and make meaningful learning experiences for themselves and others" (ISTE Standards, 2017). A similar set of standards *for educators* focuses on providing digital tools and practices that empower students and improve teaching and learning. In consideration of these two ISTE standards, the framework guiding this chapter is built upon the standards because pre-service teachers are at the crux of what it means to be a student and a future teacher. The standards provide an underpinning for what it means to consider meaningful experiences with digital tools that afford K-12 students an opportunity to transform their literacy learning and the meaning-making that can ensue when given the proper exposure and experience.

The TPACK Framework

The second theory grounding this chapter relates to how teacher educators prepare pre-service teachers to use digital literacy practices in classrooms. The TPACK framework (Mishra & Koehler, 2006) illustrates how to integrate digital tools into classrooms while considering the technological, pedagogical and content knowledge necessary to cohesively teach digital literacies. The TPACK helps researchers consider how technology enhances learning. The TPACK was initially developed using Shulman's (1986) conceptualization of pedagogical content knowledge (PCK), the knowledge teachers need to teach content effectively. Mishra and Koehler (2006) built the TPACK, expanding what it means to teach content effectively using technology. In particular, educators should be seamlessly integrating their knowledge of content, pedagogy and technology with the intended goal of successful educational technology integration. The TPACK construct illustrates the need to consider the knowledge necessary to carry out effective instruction along with the personal and social influences integral to make teaching literacy with technology meaningful and sustainable. If pre-service teachers can navigate the technological landscape, they can help their students understand how to draw upon various modes to meet the challenges of the twenty-first century (Borsheim, Merritt & Reed, 2008).

Researchers have demonstrated that the range of exposure that pre-service teachers have in implementing technology into their methods coursework shapes the ways they use digital practices and the way they use technology in the field as practicing teachers (Agyei & Voogt, 2011). This validates the need for teacher educators to include and embed experiences with technology and to include digital tools into the methods content being taught in teacher education programs (Kay, 2006). Currently, very little attention is given to the knowledge that teachers need as they consider how to teach literacy with technology, mainly due to the struggle many teacher educators find in teaching literacy while effectively using technology (Voogt & McKenney, 2017). The TPACK, in particular, needs to be explicitly related to the development of content area teaching (Harris and Hofer, 2011). In the teaching of literacy, research has pointed to the importance of an educator's ability to assess how a particular tool will align with the meaningful use of that technological tool (Bauserman, Cassady, Smith, & Stroud, 2005). The ideas shared in this chapter are examples of how teacher educators can use the TPACK as a guide for embedding technology into coursework and effectively modeling its use.

Professional Learning Communities

Building on the previous two concepts, professional learning communities are a means of connecting professionals to create awareness and understanding about the previous two constructs. Professional learning communities (PLCs) can be defined as groups of professionals that learn from one another to achieve something they would not be able to accomplish through working alone (DuFour, DuFour, Eaker & Many, 2010). PLCs are grounded in social constructivist theory, grounded in the idea that individuals construct their knowledge through the interaction and connections with others (Vygotsky, 1978). PLCs and social constructivism are the theoretical underpinnings that support shared expertise as a means of producing positive outcomes (McLaughlin & Talbert, 2006). Layering technology into professional learning can enhance the work of PLCs. For instance, Martin and colleagues (2014) found that teachers were better able to incorporate digital tools into the work of an educational professional learning community when they were able to collaborate with peers about successes and challenges. By utilizing technology to connect pre-service teachers in a PLC across different spaces and contexts, we can reach a more diverse audience, extending beyond the walls of one school and one experience. Researchers investigated the utilization of technology for PLCs in teacher education and found that a digital PLC provided a forum for teachers to refine their pedagogical approaches and better understand how to use the technology they were using (Delaney, Trapani, Chandler & Redman, 2014). The work of this chapter focuses specifically on pre-service teachers and how they can be connected in PLCs to learn from and with one another.

Researchers have demonstrated that the use of PLCs has a positive impact on pre-service teachers' understanding of teaching methods (Kuehl, 2018; Bond, 2013). Keuhl (2018) used PLCs in a writing methods course and found that the preservice teachers reported new understandings of how to guide individual students toward reasonable writing goals, as well as increased confidence in their ability to teach writing and to differentiate instruction as a result of participating in the PLCs. Furthermore, Bond (2013) found that the use of PLCs with pre-service teachers helped them connect with one another, share their experiences from the university course and connect to the course material. The use of PLCs has resulted in positive outcomes for pre-service students and helped them connect to the pedagogy and content from university settings. To date, there are no studies investigating digital PLCs with pre-service teachers.

One specific example of how the pre-service teachers in our work connected across universities and contexts is with the use of PLCs and also through digital literature circles. Digital literature circles provide a socially-constructed learning opportunity with an expectation of equal participation (Bowers-Campbell, 2011). In this online learning environment, pre-service teachers not only experience literature circles, but evaluate the potential value of multimodal engagement in learning through digital collaboration. In her work with secondary student-led literature circles, Bowers-Campbell (2011) found that when students engaged with text and each other as members of virtual literature circles, group members' responses were well-crafted and meaningful. These threaded online discussions fostered asynchronous interactions that allowed for an easier discussion between discussants.

The literature illustrates that these are not new ideas related to pre-service teacher education. Yet, they have not necessarily been combined to form a conduit for pre-service teachers to connect and to learn how to seamlessly incorporate digital literacy practices.

CONNECTING PRE-SERVICE TEACHERS TO FOSTER DIGITAL LITERACY PRACTICES IN A PARTICIPATORY CULTURE

Providing meaningful experiences for pre-service teachers is a challenging task for individual teacher educators to undertake alone. In the age of technology and with the multiple mediums and platforms that are available to connect one another, teacher educators can collaborate to unpack what it means to adequately prepare pre-service teachers to use participatory digital literacy practices in their own classrooms. The authors of this chapter worked together in just that way to collaborate and learn from their varied experiences. In particular, the focus of much of this work to engage the pre-service teachers in the modeling, practice, and use of different digital and technological tools, attempting to teach in tomorrow's 21st century schools. Although different tools and applications were explored, it is the collaborative practices that are the focus of this chapter. These collaborative practices include blogging across university settings, exploring the use of digital professional learning communities (PLCs), and participation in digital literature circles. Blogging, connecting and collaborating online, and using digital literature circles have the potential to transform the ways teachers engage students in authentic literacy tasks.

Blogging Across University Settings

Blogging provides a forum for discussion that allows students to read, reflect, and think critically. Blogs can help transform a typical discussion among peers by enhancing the experience using hyperlinks, digital documents, images, videos, voice recordings, and music (Larson, 2008). Because blogging can enrich a discussion that begins in class, students have time to walk away and process their thoughts and course applications to later respond to their peers. Integrating blogging into the work of pre-service teachers helps to provide a forum from which they can discuss their questions and ideas. Pre-service teachers can authentically engage in the act of blogging to connect and collaborate with peers and gain multiple perspectives on technology integration. Hutchison and Wang (2012) found that having pre-service teachers blog in university literacy courses helped to emphasize the importance of modeling uses of technologies that promote literacy learning. Similarly, blogging can provide a means for teacher educators to learn more about the ways pre-service teachers are understanding and experiencing technology integration.

Based on research conducted and shared, Mitchell, Friedrich, and Appleget (2018) designed and implemented a collaborative blog where pre-service teachers enrolled in literacy methods coursework could share their experiences about technology integration. The goal of the work was to study how blogging could be a means for teacher educators to learn more about the ways pre-service teachers are understanding and experiencing technology integration. In particular, the sharing of authentic experiences allowed pre-service teachers to note similarities and differences between schools in different regions and think more critically about technology integration. Instructors arranged for online digital discussion between universities by creating blog sites that they then shared with one another and in-turn the pre-service teachers. The platform Kidblog was used. Kidblog allowed for each instructor to create their own private classroom blog and then share the blog link with the other university so that the other participants could read and respond to posts. With an aim of giving pre-service teachers authentic experiences using digital technology, the goal of using Kidblog was to offer the pre-service teachers an opportunity to work with a platform that could be utilized when the pre-service teachers were classroom teachers. The university instructors also met virtually a number of times to clarify purpose, organization, and implementation of the across-university collaboration (Mitchell, Friedrich & Appleget, 2018).

Since the blogging took place over the course of multiple semesters with multiple groups of pre-service teachers, there were lessons learned that helped the instructors to continue to refine their work and the blogging that resulted. For instance, in the initial collaborative model, there was a weekly schedule created to allow each university to take turns posting to a pre-established prompt. When it was not their week to post, pre-service teachers were asked to reply to the other university pre-service teachers' posts. Replies were framed as opportunities to engage in professional conversations by asking questions and noting similarities and differences in technology integration in varying communities of practice. It became apparent that the blogging was haphazard and that the goal for pre-service teachers to develop an online relationship was not achieved. To rectify this, in later semesters the weekly rotation of blogging was abandoned because it lacked the authentic feel of continuous conversations. Additionally, due to the disparity between the number of responses for blog posts the instructors then assigned pre-service teachers to predetermined groups in an effort to create stable and ongoing conversations in a community. Instead of the predetermined prompts, the pre-service teachers were instead encouraged to blog about their own observations and experiences in their field practicum. These changes were made to help create a better sense of community and collaboration (Mitchell, Friedrich & Appleget, 2018).

What makes pre-service teachers blogging unique is that they are writing for a wider audience. Instead of reflecting on what they see and do in the classroom that only the course instructor sees and grades, in a blogging forum the pre-service teachers could then share their ideas with one another and thus learn from others' experiences. In our case, the focus of the blogging was related to technology integration. They were able to address the types of apps, websites, tools and artifacts that were working in elementary classrooms. Figure 1 illustrates an example of one of the pre-service teachers who shared her experience with the Class Dojo website. She described the site and some of the benefits of using it, giving anyone who wanted to try it an idea of what it does and how she thinks it could be used in schools.

Many of the pre-service student responses indicated that they indeed learned from one another and then tried different digital tools as a result of the online sharing. One example of a reply where a student validated another pre-service teacher's technology share is described below in Figure 2.

Figure 1. Example of pre-service teacher posting to Kidblog

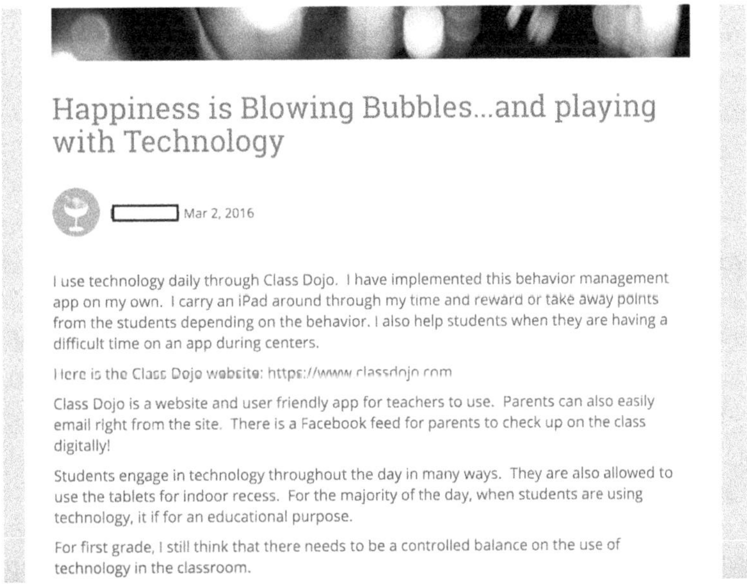

Happiness is Blowing Bubbles...and playing with Technology

Mar 2, 2016

I use technology daily through Class Dojo. I have implemented this behavior management app on my own. I carry an iPad around through my time and reward or take away points from the students depending on the behavior. I also help students when they are having a difficult time on an app during centers.

Here is the Class Dojo website: https://www.classdojo.com

Class Dojo is a website and user friendly app for teachers to use. Parents can also easily email right from the site. There is a Facebook feed for parents to check up on the class digitally!

Students engage in technology throughout the day in many ways. They are also allowed to use the tablets for indoor recess. For the majority of the day, when students are using technology, it if for an educational purpose.

For first grade, I still think that there needs to be a controlled balance on the use of technology in the classroom.

Figure 2. Response to a kidblog post about technology

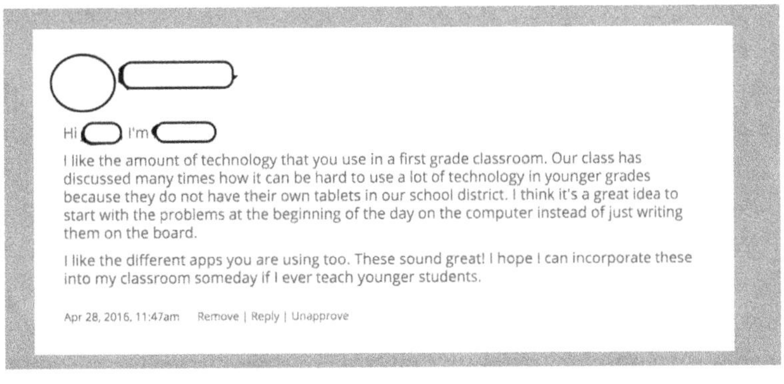

Hi I'm

I like the amount of technology that you use in a first grade classroom. Our class has discussed many times how it can be hard to use a lot of technology in younger grades because they do not have their own tablets in our school district. I think it's a great idea to start with the problems at the beginning of the day on the computer instead of just writing them on the board.

I like the different apps you are using too. These sound great! I hope I can incorporate these into my classroom someday if I ever teach younger students.

Apr 28, 2016, 11:47am Remove | Reply | Unapprove

This pre-service teacher indicated that she was learning from another pre-service teacher about her different classroom experiences, and she also indicated that she learned something about the apps that were shared. The shifting attitudes and development of technology integration pedagogy for pre-service teachers was made apparent by the posts and replies in the pre-service teacher blogs. As noted in the themes, pre-service teachers were more likely to use apps and web-based platforms introduced in the course or by blogging with peers. Authentic collaboration through blogging with peers outside the walls of their own university classroom was a conduit for more meaningful technology integration (Mitchell, Friedrich & Appleget, 2018).

It is also worth noting that the instructor-researchers broadened their own understanding of digital collaboration and of the ways one can grow professionally through ongoing conversations about best practices. It is this emanation that is perhaps most valuable to researchers across disciplines. Digital blogging can provide a vehicle for collaboration with peers in another region to broaden their teaching repertoire beyond the four walls of their own university classroom and practicum. The sharing of authentic experiences allowed pre-service teachers to note similarities and differences between schools in different regions and think critically about technology integration. Similarly, engaging pre-service teachers in the practice of digital citizenship, professional conversations, and meaningful use of 21st Century digital tools might inform their own vision of effective technology integration in a future classroom (Mitchell, Friedrich & Appleget, 2018). As we consider how blogging connects to participatory literacy practices, it is apparent that in this digital age where students are not just reading content, but interacting with it, blogging gives pre-service teachers a forum to actively create their own content from which others can respond and learn.

Digital Professional Learning Communities

The across-university Kidblog blogging connection was an attempt to create a kind of professional learning community (PLC) between groups of pre-service teachers. Yet, no real unity was cultivated although important learning took shape through the blogging process. In order to produce a sense of community and collegiality, a more careful relationship needed to be built. Rather than having pre-service teachers simply disseminate information about *any* type of course content so others could read and respond, a more cohesive dialogue needed to be established. The two course instructors decided to use a different platform and a targeted approach to the partnership. Instead of using a blogging platform, two other digital tools were introduced and implemented. The first of these platforms is Yammer, a free enterprise social networking service used for private communication within organizations. Yammer was introduced and utilized to create a sense of community and enable pre-service teachers to connect in a similar way they would in their personal lives using a platform like Facebook. The second platform, Seesaw, is a digital portfolio tool where teachers can connect students to one another, and they can connect parents with their child's work and progress. Both tools could be used in K-12 schools, so the implementation would mirror what the pre-service teachers could later incorporate into their own classrooms. Another significant aspect of attempting to embody what it means and looks like to be involved in a PLC again meant putting the pre-service teachers in groups. These PLC groups incorporated specific course assignments that were integrated into both university instructors' courses.

One of the most distinguishing aspects of developing a PLC is to get to know the other professionals in the learning community, those with the same professional teaching goals. In this inauthentic context where many of the pre-service teachers did not know one another, it was important to create a sense of kinship. That meant generating an opportunity for them to share a little about themselves: who they are, what they like, what their field placement was like, and what they hoped to gain from the community partnership. The pre-service teachers were asked to create introductory videos about themselves where they could share pictures and showcase their personality. The course instructors shared different apps and websites that could be used. A few of the tools that were introduced and used were tools like: emaze, haiku deck, chatterpix and Adobe Spark video. The videos allowed the pre-service teachers to share details about who they were and what they wanted those in their group to know about them. Then, instead of a prompt-based response protocol or an open-ended discussion forum, specific assignments were embedded into the PLC group work. The artifacts that were included in each of the courses required the PSTs to develop thoughtful, well-developed artifacts worthy of sharing that related to numerous aspects of literacy instruction and assessment, with the focus still being technology integration.

Yammer

The Yammer platform looks almost identical to Facebook, allowing those using it to comment, "like" posts, add multimedia, and create groups. Because the interface is so similar to Facebook, there was a built-in familiarity in using the tool for a majority of pre-service teachers. The course instructors created groups with approximately five pre-service teachers in each group. The pre-service teachers were asked to post assigned content into their Yammer page. The instructors created a schedule so the pre-service teachers from both locations were posting content on Yammer during the same week. Then, each site had the following week to read and respond to the work of the other. Pre-service teachers were encouraged to respond in ways that would further the online conversation. Learning from the work with the blogs, the course instructors modeled what responses should look like to help to promote a rich dialogue among their peers.

A few of the example assignments that were embedded into the course and the Yammer PLCs were: a) a field placement classroom tour, b) a digital storytelling assignment, and c) a group discussion on a shared academic reading. The pre-service teachers were instructed to collect and share images that would help them to tell a story of what it looked like in their field placement classrooms and how that environment would help to teach literacy content. The intent was to "show and tell" the literacy teaching story through images and text. Another shared assignment was the creation of a digital story. Multiple tools and options were shared with the pre-service teachers, and then they had the freedom to use a digital storytelling tool of their choice to share their story. Digital tools such as storybird, bookcreator, and shadow puppet were shared and utilized. Finally, the pre-service teachers read *A Thrice Learned Lesson from the Literate Life of a Five-year-old* by Norton-Meier (2005). This article illustrated one teacher's reflection about her changing views of what it means for a child to be literate, and how teachers can sometimes overlook authentic literacy in the lives of children. This article was chosen to spark online professional conversations between pre-service teachers about what it means to be a teacher of literacy. Along with the introductory videos, the assignments, and the online dialogue, the pre-service teachers met virtually using the Zoom video-conferencing platform. We used class time to allow the pre-service teachers to correspond synchronously in the Zoom meetings and to respond to one another's posts in the Yammer PLC groups asynchronously. The course instructors had access to all the Yammer groups and could post reminders, add to the conversations, and make sure the conversations were effectively developing.

The Yammer PLC conversations led to cohesiveness among the pre-service teachers. The structure of the groups and the embedded assignments enabled PLC groups to do more than just post and reply.

They worked collectively to meet goals, share teaching artifacts, and engage in professional conversations. An example of one of the conversations between two of the pre-service teachers is found below in Figure 3. One of the group members was commenting on a previous post about the learning that transpired between the two colleagues.

Similarly, the university instructors found the digital conversations provided a means to work together, share ideas, and openly discuss the successes and challenges they faced regarding technology integration and teaching. The ability to collaborate in professional learning communities is essential as schools of teacher education attempt to teach pre-service teachers 21st century skills (Hoaglund, Birkenfeld & Box, 2014).

Seesaw

The Seesaw website and app was selected to communicate across groups of pre-service teachers because it is a digital tool being used in elementary classrooms across the country. While it is considered a digital portfolio tool, it also has many other capabilities useful to teachers. Seesaw allows teachers to create activities that can be shared with students, and students can take pictures, draw and record videos. The online content can then be "approved" by the teacher and made available to parents as well as other students within the teacher-created class. The pre-service teachers' names were added to the created "class" and then they scanned a QR code into the app to easily make them a part of the collaborative group. The pre-service teachers were then able to use the digital tool to incorporate video, images, and text while corresponding and collaborating within and across university classrooms. Similar to the Yammer groups, a schedule was created to facilitate posting assigned course content on the Seesaw site/app. The one major difference between these two platforms is the organization and flexibility within and among groups. In Seesaw, the group members' posts were organized in folders, and any other pre-service teacher in the "class" could elect to see that content from others and provide comments. In Yammer, the groups remained separate and were limited to sharing within the group.

A few of the example assignments that were embedded into the Seesaw PLCs were: a) a 360-degree video case study assignment, b) an analysis of a technological tool, and c) a literacy-based, technology-infused lesson plan. The 360-degree case studies were developed from videos taken in local classrooms. After gaining access to classrooms where permission was granted, using a 360-degree video recorder, the videos were filmed across grade levels to provide a means to look at literacy instruction and student engagement. For the 360-degree video case study assignment, the pre-service teachers were given access to seven different 360-degree video case studies and instructed to view them several times. The short

Figure 3. Yammer PLC group post

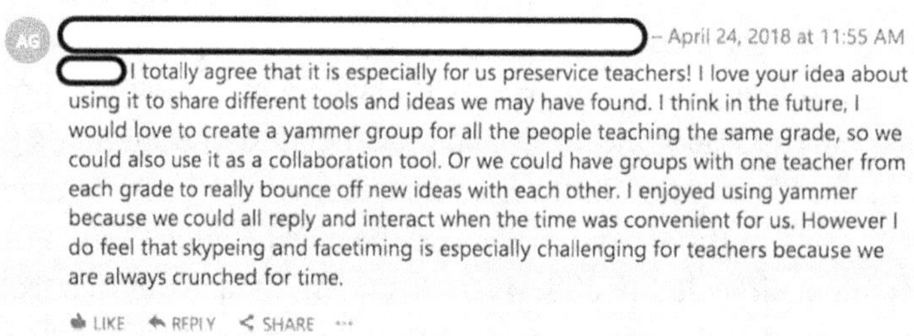

clips focused on some type of instructional content ranging from a shared writing lesson, a guided reading lesson, to a whole-class lesson on CVC words. The videos ranged by grade level as well, allowing pre-service teachers to self-select a lesson they wished to view and then comment on the teaching *and* learning. The unique nature of 360-degree video is that it allows the viewer to look around in all directions, giving them choice and control over what they saw, and thus exposed to a range of educational contexts (Argyriou, Economou, & Bouki, 2017). The pre-service teachers were then able to build online conversations about their observations of the different videos. Subsequently, pre-service teachers were asked to tell the literacy teaching story through images and text. Figure 4 below illustrates an example of one pre-service-teacher's literacy teaching story after viewing a video. It includes important ideas gleaned from the lesson connected to course content and discussions.

This example demonstrates how the use of images and text helped the pre-service teachers share a multimodal response to the observations of the 360-degree videos.

One of the other assignments that incorporated the Seesaw PLC groups was an in-depth analysis of a literacy-focused website or app sharing the strengths, weaknesses, teaching opportunities and threats to the app usage. The final assignment was a literacy-focused lesson plan. These resources became tools that enabled the pre-service teachers to gain ideas about literacy instruction and assessment from one another. Typically, it is the course instructor that "sees" and evaluates pre-service teachers' assignments and reflections, but a learning opportunity for pre-service teachers has been missed. When pre-service teachers can share their important learning with one another and be part of this participatory culture, the artifacts become tools for others to learn from and use. Teachers and educational professionals often find it challenging to find effective apps that meet the needs of their students due to the large number of apps available (Ok, Kim, & Kang, 2016). The underlying goal of the Seesaw PLC was to present a process by which pre-service teachers could analyze literacy instruction and digital tools for specific purposes and have a means to communicate those findings. The outcome was that pre-service teachers shared the uses, challenges, and teaching opportunities associated with their observations among their professional community.

Through these attempts at digital PLCs, pre-service teachers identified that they added to their professional arsenal of teaching tools by clearly articulating useful literacy teaching practices and meaningful technological tools that could be utilized. In consideration of pre-service teachers' developing their TPACK

Figure 4. A pre-service student reflection using the Seesaw app

in relation to learning to use 21st century technologies (Koehler et al., 2011), this work allowed groups to consider the overlapping sets of knowledge necessary to effectively teach literacy with technology. Although limited attention is given to the knowledge that teachers need to foster early literacy through the use of technology (Voogt & McKenny, 2017), we are beginning to prepare pre-service teachers to use the TPACK framework. When attention is given to strategically selecting practical, high-quality digital tools and pairing them with meaningful reading and writing tasks, positive literacy outcomes are more easily achieved (Fitzgerald, 2018). Professional learning across university contexts provided a space for undergraduate students to grow their understanding of literacy and technology pedagogies.

Digital Literature Circles

Building from the previous collaborative experiences, the course instructors aimed to focus specifically on just what it means and looks like for pre-service teachers to both experience and plan for different types of digital literature circle discussions. The purpose was to give pre-service teachers the opportunity to collaborate digitally as participants and planners of digital literature circles. The goal of the work with the across-university digital literature circles was to consider the ways in which the pre-service teachers see the experience of digital literature circles transferring to their future classrooms, engaging with more familiar peers and less familiar peers about books that would conceivably be read in intermediate elementary classrooms.

This work ran across two different cohorts of pre-service teachers during two different semesters. In both semesters, the course instructors designed the groups, similar to what had been done for the digital professional learning communities. By creating the groups, the instructors could ensure that there were equal participants from both classes. During the first attempt at the digital literature circle collaboration, pre-service teachers corresponded after reading the book *Wonder* (Palacio, 2012) and met once using the Zoom video conference platform. They used a reciprocal teaching protocol for their meeting, focusing on the use of different roles such as a discussion director, passage master, clever connector, etc. The pre-service teachers were given preparation assignments to engage them in both reciprocal teaching and literacy circle practices learned in the literacy methods courses (e.g. preparing questions, establishing key vocabulary, highlighting important details). The groups met during a mutual class session to discuss the book and to participate and experience the digital literature circle experience as a student.

The first experience with digital literature circles had one synchronous Zoom video literature circle discussion, but the positive feedback from the pre-service teachers influenced the planning for a second attempt and phase of this work, increasing the number of literature circles to two. For the second digital literature circle collaboration, the pre-service teachers were asked to read and discuss the book, *A Wrinkle in Time* (L'Engle, 2007). The pre-service teachers corresponded two times: once at the midpoint (Lit Circle 1) and once at the completion of the book (Lit Circle 2). For Lit Circle 1 the pre-service teachers connected via the video conferencing tool Zoom. Because Zoom offers a recording feature, each of literature circle meetings were video-recorded for later analysis by both the pre-service teachers and the course instructors. Similar to the first literature circle experience, the Lit Circle 1 guidelines were designed to be a reciprocal teaching protocol with the different literature circle roles. One university was designated to be the leaders for the reciprocal teaching portion of the literature circle. Pre-service teachers were asked to consider the pros and cons of this discussion method from both the teacher and student perspectives. Lit Circle 2 was designed to be more of a "book club" model for discussing the text. The other university led this approach, and facilitated conversations by giving each group member "talking tokens" to spend. They also were instructed to consider the pros and cons of this discussion model from both the teacher and student perspectives. The format for Lit Circle 2 was flexible and dependent on group choice. The pre-service teachers independently planned either synchronous or asynchronous conversations about the book. This allowed them to try other digital platforms (e.g. Flipgrid, GoogleDocs) and make decisions as both students and teachers. Each group was asked to either record the video meeting or share links to any online asynchronous discussions. Figures 5 illustrates two pre-service teachers' responses to one another about the process of engaging in the digital literature circles and their perceptions about the experience.

The ways pre-service teachers authentically engaged in the practice of digital citizenship, professional conversations, and meaningful use of digital tools expected for the 21st century was noticeable through this collaboration. More specifically, the digital literature circles provided an opportunity for the pre-service teachers from different institutions to engage in authentic relationships, have a sense of authentic accountability, model a teaching and learning practice, and engage in pedagogical decision making. They made comments like, "I liked preparing for our lit circle because it felt like a book club, not a real assignment" and, "it was cool to combine different schools in different areas because we were able to share this reading experience." By putting the pre-service teachers in the role of teacher *and* literacy student, they were equipped to view the experiences from multiple lenses and connect it to possible future teaching practices.

Results from the different aspects of the across-university collaborative PLC work illustrates that pre-service teachers from different universities can become a community of learners (Wenger, 1998) in an online environment, co-constructing and collaborating with one another. This work allowed the pre-service teachers to appreciate divergent perspectives, and become familiar with other colleagues that they didn't know inside a typical classroom space. These PLC endeavors utilized pre-service teachers' learning of literacy teaching tasks and particular tools and connected them with other pre-service teachers from learn from and with one another.

SOLUTIONS AND RECOMMENDATIONS

This chapter included multiple examples from the pre-service teachers' conversations that emerged from the digital dialogic opportunities. It summarized specific tools and experiences to address the need and application of digital PLC participatory literacy practices. Participatory literacy practices include the ways in which individuals interpret, make and share as a way of connecting in our digitally mediated culture (Wohlwend, 2017). This work exemplified several different approaches to helping pre-service teachers become part of this culture as they considered how to help future students learn in our con-

Figure 5. Pre-service teacher response to digital literature circles

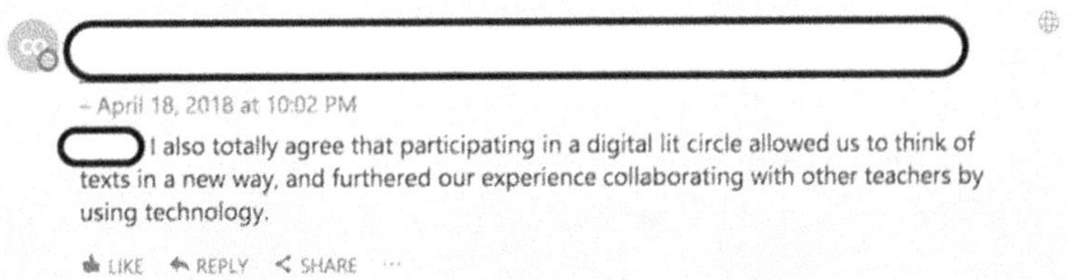

nected society. Different digital tools, applications and platforms were shared to illustrate how they can be used to connect pre-service teachers across geographic regions and to exemplify the types of dialogue that occurred between the pre-service teachers. There was important learning that resulted from the connected encounters. The experiences shared within this chapter are to be used as imperfect examples and attempts to connect pre-service teachers and have them become partners in learning. The goal of these shared experiences was to provide different tools, platforms, experiences and resources for other teachers and teacher educators to accomplish similar goals.

The pre-service teachers learned to work together with different "others" for multiple and varying purposes. Important outcomes of these collaborative efforts included: 1) trying and fusing technology apps and practices into their literacy instruction, 2) learning about teaching literacy in another geographic region, and 3) experiencing digital literature circles from the perspective of a student *and* a teacher. These collaborative experiences positively expanded the pre-service teachers' tool exposure because they were communicating online about and with the different tools. Similar to the work of Delaney, Trapani, Chandler, and Redman (2014) who found that a digital PLC provided the students a forum to refine their pedagogical approaches and better understand how to use the technology they were using, the pre-service teachers in our collaboration also communicated that their own technological, pedagogical and content-specific practices were enhanced. This work revealed the importance of cultivating innovative spaces across university teacher preparation programs that encourage diverse avenues for pre-service teachers' development of TPACK. We believe instructors need to provide transferable learning opportunities that promote productive literacy pedagogies and multimodal experiences that will inspire 21st century literacy practices. This exploration into the use of a shared space to cultivate teacher candidates' ethos of literacy and technology pedagogies in undergraduate preparation programs provided insight into diverse classroom contexts and the conditions necessary to meet the needs of students in different settings.

FUTURE RESEARCH DIRECTIONS

One potential direction for future research includes expanding the collaboration to multiple institutions in an effort to include multiple geographic regions and different viewpoints from varying groups of pre-service teachers. By expanding across the country and into possibly other countries the conversations among pre-service teachers could offer perspectives that would not be foreseeable. Another way for this research to expand is through the use of a fine-tuned protocol for digital collaboration. The authors attempted different aspects of pre-service teacher collaboration and tried to enhance the means and the depth of conversations for each attempt, yet it would be useful to establish an explicit protocol. A protocol for this work could be useful to other researchers and teacher educators.

CONCLUSION

This chapter is important to literacy educators because it contributes to a growing area of interest related to changes in our means of global collaboration and the need for modeled 21st century learning and teaching for pre-service teachers. Given modeling, opportunities for collaboration and a means to learn from one another, pre-service teachers can identify the importance of their role in delivering effective 21st century learning opportunities in classrooms. Through communication and dialogue occurring between groups of pre-service teachers, they can participate in and reflect about issues related to digital literacy practices in classrooms (Mitchell, Friedrich, & Appleget, 2018). These collaborative dialogic opportunities can serve as models for other teachers and teacher educators seeking to elevate digital technology integration and professional dialogue from a single location to a broader audience. Most importantly, these participatory practices illustrated how well university students learn from one another and collaborated professionally in the wider community and culture of learners in a global, connected world.

REFERENCES

Agyei, D., & Voogt, J. (2011). Exploring the potential of the will, skill, tool model in Ghana: Predicting prospective and practicing teachers' use of technology. *Computers & Education*, *56*(1), 91–100. doi:10.1016/j.compedu.2010.08.017

Archer, A. (2013). Power, social justice and multimodal pedagogies. In C. Jewitt (Ed.), *The Routledge Handbook of Multimodal Analysis* (pp. 150–161). Routledge.

Argyriou, L., Economou, D., & Bouki, V. (2017). *360-degree interactive video application for Cultural Heritage Education.* In iLRN 2017: Coimbra workshop, long and short paper, and poster proceedings from the Third Immersive Learning Research Network Conference, Coimbra, Portugal.

Bauserman, K. L., Cassady, J. C., Smith, L. L., & Stroud, J. C. (2005). Kindergarten literacy achievement: The effects of the PLATO integrated learning system. *Reading Research and Instruction*, *44*(4), 49–60. doi:10.1080/19388070509558436

Bond, N. (2013). Developing a professional learning community among preservice teachers. *Current Issues in Education*, *16*(2), 1–14.

Borsheim, C., Merrit, K., & Reed, D. (2008). Beyond technology for technology's sake: Advancing multiliteracies in the twenty-first century. *The Clearing House: A Journal of Educational Strategies, Issues and Ideas*, *82*(2), 87–90. doi:10.3200/TCHS.82.2.87-90

Bowers-Campbell, J. (2011). Take if out of class: Exploring virtual literature circles. *Journal of Adolescent & Adult Literacy*, *54*(8), 557–567. doi:10.1598/JAAL.54.8.1

Cho, B. Y. (2013). Adolescents' constructively response reading strategy use in a critical Internet reading task. *Reading Research Quarterly*, *28*(4), 339–342.

Delaney, S., Trapani, F., Chandler, P., & Redman, C. (2014). *Contemporary practices of technology and its affordances: Perceptions of PSTs on the utilization of technology in teaching and learning practice*, Paper presented at the EDULearn2014 conference, Barcelona, Spain.

DuFour, R., DuFour, R., Eaker, R., & Many, T. (2010). *Learning by doing: A handbook for professional learning communities at work.* Bloomington, IN: Solution Tree.

Fitzgerald, M. (2018). Multimodal knowledge building: Meaningfully using digital tools to foster disciplinary learning. *Literacy Today*, *36*(1), 34–35.

Gee, J. P. (2004). *Situated Language and Learning: A Critique of Traditional Schooling*. New York: Routledge.

Gee, J. P. (2011). Reflections on empirical evidence on games and learning. In S. Tobias & J. D. Fletcher (Eds.), *Computer games and instruction* (pp. 223–232). Charlotte, NC: IAP.

Harris, J., & Hofer, M. (2011). Technological pedagogical content knowledge (TPACK) in action: A descriptive study of secondary teachers' curriculum-based, technology-related instructional planning. *Journal of Research on Technology in Education*, *43*(3), 211–229. doi:10.1080/15391523.2011.10782570

Hoaglund, A. E., Birkenfeld, K., & Box, J. A. (2014). Professional learning communities: Creating a foundation for collaboration skills in pre-service teachers. *Education*, *134*(4), 521–528.

Hutchison, A., & Wang, W. (2012). Blogging within a social networking site as a form of literature response in a teacher education course. *Educational Media International*, *49*(4), 263–275. doi:10.1080/09523987.2012.741197

International Society for Technology in Education. (2017). *ISTE national educational technology standards (NETS)*. Eugene, OR: International Society for Technology in Education.

Jenkins, H., Purushotma, M., Weigel, K., Clinton, K., & Robinson, A. J. (2009). *Confronting the challenges of participatory culture: Media education for the 21st century*. Cambridge, MA: MIT Press. doi:10.7551/mitpress/8435.001.0001

Jocson, K., & Rosa, J. (2015). Rethinking gaps: Literacies and languages in participatory cultures. *Journal of Adolescent & Adult Literacy*, *58*(5), 372–374. doi:10.1002/jaal.368

Kay, R. H. (2006). Evaluating strategies used to incorporate technology into pre-service education: A review of the literature. *Journal of Research on Technology in Education*, *38*, 383–408. doi:10.1080/15391523.2006.10782466

Koehler, M. J., Mishra, P., Bouck, E. C., DeSchryver, M., Kereluik, K., Shin, T. S., & Wolf, L. G. (2011). Deep-play: Developing TPACK for 21st century teachers. *International Journal of Learning Technology*, *6*(2), 146–163. doi:10.1504/IJLT.2011.042646

Kress, G. (2003). *Literacy in the new media age*. London: Routledge.

Kress, G., & Jewitt, C. (2003). Introduction. In J. Jewitt & G. Kress (Eds.), *Multimodal literacy* (pp. 1–18). New York: Peter Lang.

Kuehl, R. (2018). Using professional learning communities to advance preservice teachers' understanding of differentiation within writing instruction. *Teacher Educator's Journal*, *11*, 70–90.

L'Engle, M. (2007). *A Wrinkle in Time*. New York: Square Fish.

Larson, L. (2008). Electronic reading workshop: Beyond books with new literacies and instructional technologies. *Journal of Adolescent & Adult Literacy*, *52*(2), 121–131. doi:10.1598/JAAL.52.2.3

Martin, L. E., Kralger, S., Quatroche, D. J., & Bauserman, K. L. (2014). *Handbook of professional development in education: Successful models and practices, Pre-K-12*. New York: Guildford Press.

McLaughlin, M. W., & Talbert, J. E. (2006). *Building school-based teacher learning communities: Professional strategies to improve student achievement.* Chicago: University of Chicago Press.

Mishra, P., & Koehler, M. J. (2006). Technological pedagogical content knowledge: A framework for teacher knowledge. *Teachers College Record, 108*(6), 1017–1054. doi:10.1111/j.1467-9620.2006.00684.x

Mitchell, C. (2017). Preparing future teachers to teach literacy in the 21st century: Utilizing digital literacies in literacy coursework to foster applicable classroom practices. *37th Edition of the American Reading Forum Yearbook.* Retrieved from http://www.americanreadingforum.org/yearbook/

Mitchell, C., Friedrich, L., & Appleget, C. (2018). Preservice teachers' blogging: Collaboration across universities for meaningful technology integration. *Teaching Education*, 1–17. doi:10.1080/10476210.2018.1486815

New London Group. (1996). A pedagogy of multiliteracies: Designing social futures. *Harvard Educational Review*, *66*(1), 60–92. doi:10.17763/haer.66.1.17370n67v22j160u

Norton-Meier, L. A. (2005). A thrice learned lesson from the literate life of a five-year-old. *Language Arts*, *82*(5), 286–285.

Ok, M. W., Kim, M. K., & Wang, E. Y. (2016). How to find good apps: An evaluation rubric for instructional apps for teaching students with learning disabilities. *Intervention in School and Clinic*, *51*(4), 244–252. doi:10.1177/1053451215589179

Palacio, R. J. (2012). *Wonder.* New York: Random House.

Roswell, J., & Wohlwend, K. (2016). Free play or tight spaces? Mapping participatory literacies in apps. *The Reading Teacher*, *70*(2), 197–205. doi:10.1002/trtr.1490

Shulman, L. S. (1986). Those who understand: Knowledge growth in teaching. *Educational Researcher*, *15*(2), 4–14. doi:10.3102/0013189X015002004

Stein, P., & Newfield, D. (2006). Multiliteracies and multimodality in English in education in Africa: Mapping the terrain. *English Studies in Africa*, *49*(1), 1–22. doi:10.1080/00138390608691341

Turbill, J. B., & Murray, J. (2006). Early literacy and technologies in Australian schools: Policy, research, and practice. In M. McKenna, L. Labbo, R. D. Kieffer, & D. Reinking (Eds.), *International Handbook of Literacy and Technology* (Vol. 2, pp. 93–108). Mahwah, NJ: Lawrence Erlbaum Associates.

Voogt, J., & McKenney, S. (2017). TPACK in teacher education: Are we preparing teachers to use technology for early literacy? *Technology, Pedagogy and Education*, *26*(1), 69–83. doi:10.1080/1475939X.2016.1174730

Vygotsky, L. S. (1978). Mind in society: The development of higher psychological processes (M. Cole, V. J John-Steiner, S. Scribner, & E. Souberman, Eds. & Trans.). Cambridge, MA: Harvard University Press. (Original work published 1934)

Wohlwend, K. E. (2017). Who gets to play? Access, popular media and participatory literacies. *Early Years Journal of International Research and Development*, *37*(1), 62–76. doi:10.1080/09575146.2016.1219699

ADDITIONAL READING

Clark, H. & Avrith, T. (2019). *The google-infused classroom: A guidebook to making thinking visible and amplifying student voice.* ElevateBooksEdu.

Hobbs, R. (2011). *Digital and media literacy: Connecting culture and classroom.* Thousand Oaks, CA: Corwin Press.

Muhtaris, K., & Ziemke, K. (2015). *Amplify: Digital teaching and learning in the K-6 Classroom.* Portsmouth, NH: Heinemann.

Palloff, R. M., & Pratt, K. (2007). *Building online professional learning communities: Effective strategies for the virtual classroom.* San Francisco, CA: Jossey-Bass.

Schaeffer, R., Howard, N. R., & Thomas, S. (2019). *Closing the gap: Digital equity strategies for the K-12 classroom.* Portland, OR: International Society for Technology in Education.

KEY TERMS AND DEFINITIONS

360-Degree Video: Panoramic video that places the viewer in the center of the video, with the capability to focus in on any aspect of the surrounding environment.

Blogging: Posting reflections and ideas in a shared digital space for others to view and where responses are able to respond.

Digital Literature Circle: Moving a traditional literature circles that includes multiple individuals responding to a shared reading of a text to a digital space.

Flipgrid: A website that allows the (teacher) user to post prompts for students to reply to using brief (selfie) videos.

Professional Learning Communities (PLCs): Groups of professionals meeting together with a common goal and with the intention to improve their professional practice.

Seesaw: A digital portfolio app where educators can post student artifacts for others to view and to comment (including other students and parents).

Yammer: An online platform that is similar in appearance to Facebook, yet it is a controlled digital space for educational institutions and professional organizations to connect.

Chapter 13
#TextMeetsTech: Navigating Meaning and Identity Through Transliteracy Practice

Katie Schrodt
Middle Tennessee State University, USA

Erin R. FitzPatrick
University of North Carolina at Charlotte, USA

Kim Reddig
University of North Carolina at Charlotte, USA

Emily Paine Smith
Southwest Christian School, USA

Jennifer Grow
Middle Tennessee State University, USA

ABSTRACT

This chapter addresses the need to make time and space for transliteracy practices in the classroom. University pre-service teachers are used as the primary example as the chapter documents how these students made meaning across a range of platforms, while reading the acclaimed young adult novel The Hate U Give. The university course, titled Language and Literacy, focuses on methods of literacy instruction in the classroom. A lesson plan framework is included in the chapter that is especially user friendly for educator preparation classrooms as well as high school and middle school teachers. The chapter explores the experiences of the college students while reading The Hate U Give, while detailing how the students created meaning through a variety of traditional and modern teaching practices.

DOI: 10.4018/978-1-7998-0000-2.ch013

INTRODUCTION

Literacy in the 21st century is ever changing. The nature of literacy today is continually being revised and adapted as humans make meaning across a range of platforms (Leu, Kinzer, Coiro, Castek, & Henry, 2018). This fluid nature calls for students today to be savvy in both traditional and modern literacy practices. The term "transliteracy" has been coined to define the ways that students must navigate through multiple media, moving in and out of a variety of platforms, and mapping meaning through traditional literacy practices that include orality, handwriting, reading books, and writing, as well as new literacies that include visual and social media (Thomas et al., 2007).

While research shows youth are often intensely engaged in a wide range of literacy practices outside of the school setting, schools often lack the same wide range of literacy taught in the curriculum (Bazalgette, & Buckingham, 2013; Bezemer, & Kress, 2008; Lenters, 2016). In recent years, literacy educators have increasingly recognized the importance of addressing resources other than the textbook in the classroom. The textbook is no longer the sole source of learning. Digital media has become the main resource for learning in the classroom (Rowsell, & Walsh, 2011). Multimodality is now essential to the literacy practices of youth in the globalized communications environment (Cope & Kalantzis, 2000; Faigley, Kress, & van Leeuwen, 2002). Teachers are being encouraged to include various digital media to introduce new literacies to help students make connections between learning in the home and school. Multimodality includes two or more modes of literacy such as, linguistic, visual, audio, gestural, and spatial (Mills, 2010). Although written work is still vital, more is needed to provide students with meaningful communication in all aspects of their life. Adolescents today require a collection of multimodal and digital literacies for social purposes: critical inquiry, creativity, and communication (Kress, & Selander, 2012; Walsh, & Walsh, 2010).

As information and disciplinary literacy become more popular, it is important for teachers and students to not view literacy in compartments or pockets. Transliteracy opens up the idea of working *across*. It effectively bridges isolated spheres of literacy practice and allows students to view and practice making literacy meaning in a variety of methods and through a number of different platforms. As one librarian blogged, "[Transliteracy] is using Wikipedia to find keywords for a search in CINAHL. It's reading an academic journal article and then looking up the author's personal blog for more context. It's comparing hashtags to subject headings and Amazon reviews to abstracts. In a sense, the real force behind transliteracy is encompassed in one little word in the definition: *across*" (Wilkinson, 2010, p. 1). As teachers, it is critical for us to help students see those connections between daily "non-traditional" literacy practices and those more traditional ones. These practices can merge together to create deeper meaning and connections in the classroom.

This chapter will address the need to make time and space for transliteracy practices in the classroom, using as an example university pre-service teachers making meaning across a range of platforms, while reading the acclaimed young adult novel, *The Hate U Give* (Thomas, 2017). A lesson plan framework will be discussed in the chapter that is especially user friendly for educator preparation classrooms as well as high school teachers. The chapter will explore the experiences of the college students while reading *The Hate U Give*, while detailing how the students created meaning through a variety of traditional and modern teaching practices.

The students essentially created a modern and modified text set as they read through the novel. Across time, the students collected a group of related texts, adding in non-traditional texts, such as photographs, social media, YouTube videos, and songs that connected to their personal experiences and meaning making with *The Hate U Give*. Text sets expand comprehension, increase vocabulary and background knowledge, and cultivate a social learning environment (Beck, 2014). The remixed "text set" presented in this chapter provides an opportunity for transliteracy practices that helps students layer and access multiple levels of meaning within the book.

BACKGROUND

The experiences represented in this chapter are from an undergraduate literacy methods course for preservice teachers. Fifteen students took this class as a requirement in their pursuit of becoming elementary school teachers. In this class, teacher candidates gain an understanding of the essential components of effective literacy instruction (phonemic awareness, phonics, fluency, vocabulary, and comprehension) and demonstrate how each component can be taught within meaningful contexts. This course met for 6 hours a week for 15 weeks.

Part of this course includes the personal reading and writing practices of the teacher candidates. The foundation of the class is built on the belief that teachers must view themselves as readers, writers, and critical thinkers in order to best teach reading, writing, and critical thinking to young children (Davis-Duerr, 2015; Karabay, Kuşdemir Kayıran, & Işık, 2015; Parten Gerla, 2010). To better understand the preservice teachers' perceptions of themselves as readers, a short reading survey was conducted at the beginning of the course. Two of the fifteen students identified themselves as current readers, citing they are currently reading a novel for pleasure and regularly read in their free time. A consistent theme from the rest of the students included a love for reading in elementary school that quickly died away once hitting adolescence. One student in particular stated she had never read a novel from cover to cover on her own. With this in mind, regular interaction with modern, high quality young adult and children's literature became a significant goal in the class. The students would be given access to great books that spark discussion and require critical thinking and provided opportunities to think, write, and talk about those books.

The book *The Hate U Give* was selected as a classroom novel based on its award-winning status and multitude of accolades as well as its engaging, thought-provoking content. This book was also chosen for its relevance to true current and historical events, allowing for more room for critical thinking and discussion. The book has also been adapted into a movie, which may serve as a source of reading motivation for students (Lamb, 2018). The movie trailer was played in class as a hook for the students and served as the groundwork for a book talk, selling the students on the worth of the novel and increasing the likelihood of engagement (Fisher & Frey, 2018)

TRANSLITERACY METHODS

Socratic Seminars and Text Sets

Socratic seminar is an inquiry-based discussion method that encourages students to have intentional conversations around a common text (Holden, 2002). Socratic seminars are based on the ideas of Socrates and encourage students to form ideas of their own as well as integrate and collaborate to form new ideas. These seminars set the stage for socially meaningful learning as students learn to listen, ask questions, discuss, form opinions, and create new learning. This traditional teaching practice helps students find their voice through inquiry, discussion-based learning.

In this example, Socratic seminar served as the primary face-to-face discussion for the book *The Hate U Give*. Four Socratic seminars were held across the semester to discuss assigned sections of the text. Traditionally, students come to a Socratic circle with a question to pose to the group as students discuss a common text or theme. In order to make more space for transliteracy practice and movement in and out of traditional and new literacies, each student was asked to come to the seminar with a completed guiding discussion template (See Appendix A). This template served as a scaffold for students as they learned the procedures and dynamics of the seminar. This template helped students layer their thinking about the text, scaffolding them to come to the seminar with a "multimodal text set" of sorts. The text set included the traditional Socratic questions as well as more modern and varied literacies such as a hashtag and a connection to a video, song, current event, or piece of artwork. A text set is a collection of related resources that support a common theme, topic, or issue. These resources can come from different genres, text types, and media. Text sets can help students build content knowledge and vocabulary on a topic, as well as prepare them to continue learning through new texts on the same topic (Cervetti, Wright, & Hwang, 2016).

The first seminar was prefaced with ground rules for listening and speaking. Each participant was given two playing cards to represent the two times they were expected to contribute to the conversation. They could "play their card" when they were ready to speak (Gallagher, 2015).

Hashtags

A hashtag is a word or phrase proceeded by the symbol # that is used on social media platforms to identify, summarize, and categorize topics. A hashtag on social media can identify a keyword or theme of a specific piece of content. The students were asked to use this modern communication method to distill the important information from each section of the reading. Each Socratic seminar ended with everyone going around in a circle and reading off their hashtags. These tags allowed for closure to the seminar that helped summarize the ideas that were discussed as well as aided in comprehension and retention of meaning from the section of reading. The students used this modern communication tool to make meaning, express their feelings, and make connections across texts. *The Hate U Give* hashtag examples from each category can be found in Table 1.

Table 1. Hashtags used in student discussions

Making Meaning	Expressing Feelings	Making Connections
#investigatingorjustifying #dontmove #notanotherstatistic #justiceforkhalil #thekhalilIknow #thuglife #fakeprotests #timetospeakup #lilblackpanther #getyourswirlonbaby #blackfemalewitness	#byehailey #intense #emotional #rollercoaster #pissed #changeofheart #tinybravepartofme	#icantbreathe #handsup #BlackLivesMatter #youwillbefound

Multimedia Connections

At each Socratic seminar, the students were asked to make a connection across media platforms. Students asked themselves if this section of the book made them think of a current event, a song, a video, or a historical event.

Accessing History and Current Events

As an important plot point in the story, Angie Thomas mentions Emmett Till, the 14-year-old African American boy from Chicago whose eyes were gouged out as he was beaten, stripped, shot in the head, and tied to a cotton gin with barbed wire before being dumped into the Tallahatchie River by two white men in Money, Mississippi in 1955. He had been accused of flirting with a white woman. Less than two weeks later an eye witness identified both murderers in court, but in less than an hour, a segregated Southern jury issued a verdict of not guilty. The woman later recanted her story.

The main character in *The Hate U Give*, Starr, posted a disturbing photograph of Till to her Tumblr account. Many students were interested in this section of the text as they began to feel negative feelings toward the character Hailey. Hashtags about Hailey (#byehailey #haileysucks) began to surface in the Socratic seminar conversations. In one seminar, a student brought in a picture of Emmett Till, as well as quotes from Emmett Till's mother, who insisted on an open casket funeral so everyone could see the impact of the horrible things that were done to her son. Many students in the class had not heard of Emmett Till or this significant event in history which sparked a movement in the Civil Rights Era. As the students made meaning across historical documents, they gained a deeper understanding of the feelings Starr and her family might have been having as they continued to face injustice decades after the Civil Rights movement.

In these historical conversations, the title of the book and the word *thug* came up over and over. The history of the word *thug* and what students thought of the word became a topic of conversation. An etymological review of the word shows that throughout history the word *thug* has been used as a general descriptor for a violent person, especially a criminal. Even today, presidents have used it to describe insurgents and rioters. Students debated whether the word *thug* has become a codified slur in and of itself; that is, was the term acceptable in public discourse but covertly carrying the stereotypical, negative connotations inherent in more recognized and eschewed bigoted language? Tupac Shakur brought the word into popular culture and gave it a fresh new twist. Tupac spoke, through his rap music, about THUG LIFE and the unfair treatment of his black brothers and sisters and how that affects everyone. He worked to make it cool and powerful. Since his death in 1996, many people have continued to build on his hopes and writings. The students began to connect Angie Thomas' purpose for naming the book *The Hate U Give* as she chose to give "thug" respect and strength while honoring its definition given by Tupac Shakur. Tupac's words continued as a significant source of conversation as the students began to notice the symbol of Maverick's roses within the novel. Starr's dad Maverick, repeatedly waters his rose garden throughout the book. Despite his efforts the roses seem to be dry and dying. One student stated, "Maverick is continuing to water the dead roses—it is kind of like a symbol for the Carters' life in Garden Heights. They are trying and trying to make it work but things keep happening." A famous Tupac poem titled "The Rose that Grew from Concrete" was discussed as a connection as they deepened their understanding of Starr and her family being those roses.

Black Panther 10-point program was another multimedia connection that accessed history. One student brought in a YouTube video discussing the Black Panther Party and its creation of the ten-point program (History Chapel, 2013). This video explains the ten-point program and contains snippets of speeches given by Black Panther Party leaders as well as real photographs from the time period. This video sparked much discussion as students began to grapple with why they had not heard many positive things about the Black Panther party, but rather associated them only with violence. One student stated, "I felt as if it was always taught to me that Martin Luther King Jr. was good and Malcom X was bad. I am realizing there is more to it than that." Each new historical connection allowed for a new layer of meaning within the book.

At the time of this experience, current events began to mirror some of the events happening in the book. One Socratic seminar included a connection to a shooting of a black man by a white police officer in his own apartment. The student brought in an article as part of the discussion (Jail, 2019). This discussion led to hashtag searches that included some of the most popular and trending hashtags related to the #BlackLivesMatter movement as well as #policebrutality. Some examples included #TamirRice, #handsup, #16times, and #ICantBreathe.

Music and Videos

One of the most moving moments came when a student pulled up a YouTube video of Lin-Manuel Miranda and Ben Platt performing a *Hamilton* and *Dear Evan Hansen* mashup titled *Found / Tonight* (Fierberg, 2018). The lyrics are written out below. The themes of *The Hate U Give* can be directly linked to these lyrics—themes of speaking out, feeling forgotten, telling your story, freedom, rising up, and being "found."

We may not yet have reached our glory
But I will gladly join the fight
And when our children tell their story
They'll tell the story of tonight
They'll tell the story of tonight
Tonight
Have you ever felt like nobody was there?
Have you ever felt forgotten in the middle of nowhere?

Have you ever felt like you could disappear?
Like you could fall, and no one would hear?
Well, let that lonely feeling wash away
All we see is light
'Cause maybe there's a reason to believe you'll be okay
For forever
'Cause when you don't feel strong enough to stand
You can reach, reach out your hand
And oh
Raise a glass to freedom
Something they can never take away
Oh
No matter what they tell you
Someone will come running
To take you home
Raise a glass to all of us
Tomorrow there'll be more of us
Telling the story of tonight
Out of the shadows
The morning is breaking /They'll tell the story of tonight
And all is new
All is new
All is new
It's only a matter of
Time
Even when the dark comes crashing through
When you need a friend to carry you
When you're broken on the ground
You will be found
So let the sun come streaming in
'Cause you'll reach up and you'll rise again
If you only look around
You will be found
And when our children tell their story
You will be found
They'll tell the story of tonight
Whoa
No matter what they tell you
Tomorrow there'll be more of us
Telling the story of tonight
The story of tonight
(Miranda & Platt, 2018).

The students created their own videos through Flipgrid. This website allows students to record and respond to videos in a similar format to Snapchat or Instagram stories; that is, the students can record themselves responding to a particular video, providing a context for a virtual conversation. The video-based discussion topics are organized into a grid fostering user-friendly interaction and facilitating both posts and replies. This platform allowed students to post thoughts and reactions to the text in between Socratic seminar sessions. Students felt compelled to post on Flipgrid when they reached a shocking or significant part in the text. For example, throughout the narrative, tension had been building between the main character Starr and her friend Hailey. In one part of the book, Starr finally punches Hailey. Multiple videos surfaced when this happened with reactions such as, "Starr just straight up punched Hailey in the face. I couldn't be happier. She finally got what's been coming." Another student responded, "Hailey was running her little mouth thinking there would never be any consequences! Find your voice, Starr!" Another significant part of the text inspired deeper thinking, and students considered the multiple sides of the character Iesha. Throughout the book, it seems as though Iesha is not a good mother and does not care for her children. At one point, Iesha puts her own safety and well-being on the line to help her children escape from her abusive boyfriend. At this point, many Flipgrid videos popped up as their perspective of Iesha had changed as the book went on. One student said, "This reminded me of the book *Love* by Matt De La Pena. Love isn't always what we think it is. It shows up in ways we don't always expect. Iesha is a mother. She does love her kids. She sacrificed herself to get Devonte out of harm's way." Another student responded with, "Yes Seven's mom is finally stepping up!" When brought back to the Socratic seminar, students began to speak about the complexity of the characters and situations saying, "Every character has so many layers. I am beginning to understand Kenya more. Khalil and Devante's situations have become more relatable across the book. They both only wanted to help their mothers."

Instagram

At the end of the novel, the students were asked to represent the book through a social media-inspired book review. This assignment asks students to create a #bookstagram photograph for social media that advertises the book and starts a discussion about the meaning of the book. The students curated photographs that contained multiple artifacts to represent themes and important events in the text. The photographs included the cover of the book as well as an impactful quote from the book. Then, students created a caption that gives a book summary and review as well as poses a question for discussion about the book. Lastly, the students were asked to add hashtags and emojis to their post. These photos were posted to Instagram and the students were asked to respond to the photographs and questions online. The Instagram post ended up representing a combination book talk, book review, comprehension assessment, and online Socratic seminar of sorts. See Appendix B for a rubric for the assignment. Examples from other books can be found on www.instagram.com/notasinglestory. If Instagram is unavailable or not an option, the assignment can be adapted by printing the photographs and captions and displaying them in the hallway. Add access to sticky notes and pens for people to make comments.

The students carefully curated their photographs for the Instagram post about *The Hate U Give*, placing items and quotes in the perfect format to represent the meaning they made from the text. Details from two of the photographs are included in Figure 1.

Figure 1. Student Instagram photographs

<table>
<tr><th>Photograph</th><th>Caption</th></tr>
<tr><td></td><td>The Hate U Give by Angie Thomas is an eye opening book that allows the readers to witness the lifestyle of living in a low income African American community, through the lens of a high school student named Starr. Starr's life comes to an unruly halt when she witnesses her childhood best friend, Khalil, get shot by a cop, due to no other reason than the color of his skin, after what was suppose[d] to be a routine traffic stop. Khalil's death follows Starr throughout the book as the community she lives in seeks justice for police brutality, while her white privileged school environment is on the police's side, unaware of who Khalil really is. Starr and her family find themselves in multiple heart-wrenching situations where they see who really supports them and who can't see past the public stereotypes. In the end, despite the protest and the court's decision, Starr decides to never give up and never stop fighting. How will you make a change? #powpow #breakout #wewontforget #notasinglestory</td></tr>
<tr><td></td><td>The Hate U Give, by Angie Thomas, is a must-read for all Americans, especially in our society today. It's a story that resonates with people from all walks of life. The book is the story of a black high school student named Starr who is stuck between two worlds – her affluent, predominately white private school world, and her predominantly black neighborhood that she has lived in her whole life. Starr is the witness of a shooting and it changes her life forever. Her childhood best friend, Khalil, is pulled over by a white police officer and the situation escalates. Khalil is shot and killed. Starr was in the car and saw everything happen. Starr is faced with standing up for justice and at the same time, not wanting to get involved in what will surely be a racially-charged insurgence of hate and anger. She is constantly worried about what other people will think – will her white friends and boyfriend think she's a thug? Will her black friends and neighbors think she sold out? Starr feels different no matter where she is. Starr is brave and resilient. She learns to be honest and to use her voice. The character growth in The Hate U Give is inspiring and will hopefully encourage readers that their voices matter! This book is just as much about a young girl learning to speak up as it is about Americans who are marginalized and oppressed. It's beautifully written and I enjoyed it very much.

#THUG #justiceforkhalil

Have you ever felt like you didn't fit in, or like you weren't meeting anyone's expectations of you?

#notasinglestory</td></tr>
</table>

This assignment offers an opportunity for making meaning across a range of platforms as students carefully chose items and other modes of art to curate a photo. The students featured here chose artifacts that represented a continuum of comprehension as students demonstrated the literal meaning of the text—representing characters and plot points—and also, deeper meanings as they applied, analyzed, and created new layers of understanding with the final photograph and caption. Each photograph contained items that represented important characters in the book, including a Fresh Prince DVD to represent Starr and Chris, and a badge to represent the police officer 115.

The collections in the photographs added another layer of complexity when items represented both a character and a significant plot point or served as an abstract artifact of the culture. The hairbrush symbolized Khalil as a character but also pointed toward the significant plot point in which his hairbrush is mistaken for a gun resulting in his murder by Officer 115. The black hoodie and the black bandana also represented Khalil as a character but moved into a deeper theme of judgment and marginalization. The hoodie has historically been a politically charged symbol of systemic racism as many young black kids are labeled as dangerous when wearing a hoodie. Trayvon Martin, the unarmed 17-year-old fatally and famously shot by a neighborhood watch representative, was wearing a similar hoodie. Students elevated the meaning by making connections to real people like Trayvon, and creating a list of victims of police shootings. The students purposely burned the edges of the list for a two-fold meaning. First, they said because many people wish to ignore and hide the fact that police brutality exists, metaphorically "burning away" their names and memory. Secondly, it represents a significant plot point at the end of *The Hate U Give*, when a fire is set by a fellow black neighbor in Garden Heights. This brings up a significant conversation about a larger theme in the book of how systematic, institutional bias and prejudice serves to fuel more hatred—raising the stakes and decreasing the likelihood of true resolution for everyone involved. This theme is directly linked to the artifact of Tupac's album. The title of the book is named after lyrics from his work and addresses the topic of systemic racism, marginalization, and using your voice to stand up for what is right. In one of the Instagram pictures, each artifact rests on top of a blood-splattered background. This powerful image of blood being shed matched with the quotes from both photographs is a call for action. Both photographs offer quotes that encourage speaking out. "What is the point of having a voice if you're gonna be silent in the times you shouldn't be?" and "I'll never forget. I'll never give up and I'll never be quiet."

Using multiple technology tools: computers, mobile devices, and tablets, as well as social media outlets, allowed students the ability to create projects that are individualized to their personal experiences. When integrated purposefully, media essentials can be powerful and personalized instructional tools (Rao, & Skouge, 2015). Personalizing students' experiences and incorporating culture into reading activities, allows them to deepen their knowledge and comprehension skills and broaden their transliteracy skills.

CONNECTIONS ACROSS ALL PLATFORMS

The goal and eventuality of this process was to move students beyond a traditional reading assignment to further engage, understand, and spur independent literacy practices beyond the classroom. Students read, applying their own lens to understanding the text, then through traditional discussion in Socratic seminars, students encountered the understandings of others and explored the situatedness of their understandings within a more complex timeline of cultural events. Then, they moved their understandings into a technology-based cooperative discussion and the creation of cultural artifacts representing their understandings onto a responsive global platform. In these ways, literacy was demonstrated as a communicative social practice rather than an act of isolation. Classrooms that are home to rich discussion married to challenging academic discourse and instruction support students in internalizing the knowledge and skills to independently carry out literacy tasks (Applebee, Langer, Nystrand, & Gamoran, 2003).

Intertwining meaning and overlapping methods, such as Socratic seminars and multimedia connections, allow students to develop more meaningful, deeper connections to the text. Social interaction and discourse in the classroom create a context which allows for the psychological and semantic growth necessary to support comprehension (Applebee et al., 2003). Incorporating popular culture into the classroom engages students as they encounter and create a variety of multimedia projects bringing the contemporary world into the classroom and fostering connections between reading, technology, and their lived experience. By participating in Socratic seminars, creating hashtags for social media, and relating the book to historical events, music or songs, the students were able to deepen their understanding.

In *Literature as Exploration*, Rosenblatt espoused a philosophy that outlined the relationship between text and the background information a student brings to that text (Rosenblatt, 1938). She argued that social, psychological, and cultural experiences would create differing meaning using the same text. Rosenblatt believes that reading a text is a unique experience and meaning is derived in the transaction between a text and the well of personal experience. "In the interplay between the book and the personality, failures in sensitivity, misinterpretations, and distorted reactions often have their roots in such influences. The effort to help the student arrive at a more balanced and lucid sense of the work thus involves the parallel effort to help him understand and evaluate his personal emphases" (Rosenblatt, 1995).

One meaning does not exist within a text to be mined out like ore by a reader. Rosenblatt valued all of the meanings derived, but held to Dewey's positions of warranted assertions, to justify her position that some meanings were more appropriately aligned with the text than others. She further asserts that students should be given an opportunity to encounter texts that offer them a means to connect, either socially, culturally, emotionally, or otherwise. Then through the process of reading, they can "live through" the characters' lives and operate in a world outside their own, offering them new experiences to fold into their knowledge (assimilation, accommodation, equilibrium). In her view, the aesthetic response to reading encourages students to live through the experience, allowing them to expand their knowledge and understanding of experiences that they may never encounter in their own day-to-day interactions. In this way, students will have a wider view of society, problem-solving, social responsibility, and duties as citizens in the decision-making process.

In Rosenblatt's view, the reason for education is to produce students who are prepared to become citizens active in the decision-making process of moving our country into the future. She was one of the initial theorists to take a social justice stance asserting that, as educators, we have a responsibility to use student responses to literature to help them realize their potential as citizens of a democratic society, to recognize wrongs that are done to people, and to consider methods for righting those wrongs. She also argued for the training of teachers in fields of social sciences to be prepared to better address the psychological and social implications of human nature that are confronted in good literature.

Meaning is not solely in a text but in the individual, who is deciphering the text (Considine, Horton, & Moorman, 2009; Rosenblatt, 1994). Borsheim, Merritt and Reed (2008), stated that a multiliteracy approach promotes a constructivist philosophy of learning in which students gain comprehension through authentic experiences. In this approach, teachers and students play an active role in constructing knowledge, using language as a tool for communication and meaning making (Vygotsky, 1978). Vygotsky's theory promotes learning contexts in which students play an active role in learning. Roles of the teacher and student are therefore shifted, as a teacher should collaborate with his or her students in order to help facilitate meaning construction in students. Learning, therefore, becomes a reciprocal experience for the students and teacher. This reciprocal learning was evidenced in the Socratic seminars and the ways in which new meaning was created throughout the reading of the book based on the knowledge and ideas of the students. They built off of each other, constructing new meaning together.

LAYERED MEANING IN CHARACTER AND THEME

The university students demonstrated a deep understanding of the The Hate U Give and the complexities of the characters and themes. Throughout the book, complex themes and characters are introduced. In many cases, characters in the book show many different sides of themselves, fighting against their inner identities and histories. Characters such as Iesha caught the attention of the students. At first, Iesha continually demonstrated poor judgement and moral character, but throughout the book the students began to see her differently, not judging her decisions and actions so harshly. Students began to connect impact of systemic racism they have been learning about with Iesha's present levels of performance and understanding. Students began to realize that many of the characters had complex identities and were all still learning and growing – or not. One student posed the question, "What different sides of characters do we get to see in this section?" This question sparked one of the most interesting discussions especially about the characters Chris and Hailey. The students were able to see that although both characters possessed white privilege, Chris was trying to understand both his privilege and the perspective of Starr, while Hailey was not. The students were so frustrated with Hailey they began creating anti-Hailey hashtags throughout the Socratic seminars. Two favorite hashtags were #blockdeletereportHailey and #Haileyiscanceled.

The students demonstrated more complex thinking and a deeper understanding of the characters and themes in the books through the discussion and background knowledge cultivated during the updated Socractic seminars. One student connected the tension that all of the characters have been feeling through this quote: "I love the scenes at Seven's birthday party. I think it's the perfect representation of what the book has been building towards. Starr has all the parts of her world in one place, and it's working out okay. I love how we can see Starr grow to learn how to reconcile all the different parts of who she is."

CLASSROOM ADAPTATIONS

University professors or high school teachers who are looking to create space for transliteracy in their classrooms could start by evaluating their own day to day literacy practices, carefully paying attention to practices that require movement across platforms. One effective prompt for both the professor and the university students is to do a one-week log of all literacy practices used throughout the day. People's day-to-day literacy practices are wide, varied, and important. Daily literacy practices can could include art, literacy for a civic duty, participation in community life, structured and unstructured play, formal schooling, or school like learning practices (Purcell-Gates, Perry & Briseño, 2011).

For example, here is a sample morning routine and its intersection with transliteracy.

A young mother quickly checks the refrigerator for the school lunch menu and decides to pack a lunch for her child since he is allergic to the dairy quesadillas being served. She quickly checks Pinterest for the dairy free lunch ideas she pinned yesterday and decides to make turkey wraps. As she adds some sauce to the wraps, she double checks the label to make sure there is no dairy included. Before the mother zips up the lunch box, she writes a love note on a napkin to tuck inside the lunchbox. A text comes in from the neighbor saying her dog is running in the front yard again. In the interest of time she replies with a quick rolling eye emoji text and rushes out before the dog runs into the street. After corralling the dog, she loads up everyone for school. She plugs her first destination into Google Maps to check the traffic and estimated time to arrival. Before she gets everyone in the car, she opens up the Starbucks app and places her order for pick up.

Have all students bring their log to class to discuss and reflect on the similarities and differences among the class in terms of literacy practices. The group may consider the following questions:

How many literacy practices are demonstrated in this simple, but common, morning routine? Which practices were more traditional? Which ones more modern? Did you or your classmates move seamlessly in and out of these practices? Which kind of practices were most prevalent throughout your week?

Additionally, professors and teachers can evaluate their already existing assignments and ask themselves ways to incorporate modern literacy practices into them.

Is there a way to make this assignment multimodal? Can this assignment be adapted to include some of our daily transliteracy practices from our log?

For example, teachers may require students to link a YouTube video through a QR code and paste it into an article normally read for class. *Could traditional article reflections become multimodal as leaving space for student to respond through art, videos, song, or social media? Could students blog about field experiences or post to Flipgrid throughout the week about stories from the field?* Teachers may also consider bringing the assignments to the students, asking for their help on ways to modernize and engage in new literacies. The possibilities are endless.

The assignments presented in this chapter can easily be adapted for different age groups. One fifth grade class adapted the instagram assignment into shared group work while reading the book *Wild Robot* by Peter Brown. The students used Legos to build a robot model and attached a QR code of a video of a real robot. As a group, the students wrote a review of the book that included a summary without spoilers. The students then curated a photo similar to the Instagram photos of the university students. This photo included the book Wild Robot, the Lego robot, and the QR code. The phone was printed to hang on the wall.

The main idea behind transliteracy is for students to fluidly move across a range of technologies, context, and media. This idea can also be adapted into other subject areas like mathematics. For example, students might work with traditional tools such as manipulatives and mathematical equations, while also accessing online coding platforms and blogging about their trials and errors in the process. In science, students might work in nature, logging their observations in a writer's notebook, and then accessing a live stream of a zoo or a documentary clip from YouTube and then post and discuss their thoughts on Flipgrid. Transliteracy work can be done at any age and subject area.

CONCLUSION

This chapter detailed the many ways this assignment can be used and adapted to encourage students to move in and out of various media to create deeper meaning and become a more effective and motivated learner in the 21st century. The example provides teachers with a framework for creating time and space for students as they make meaning within and beyond traditional forms of literacy. The students in this example are seen using language/orality (discussions, linguistics/word history, Socratic seminars); writing and reading (reflections, visual art, curating an Instagram photograph); and social media (photograph, Instagram comments, hashtags, captions, emojis, Flipgrid). By developing transliteracy skills, students are equipped to participate in global conversations, while also having the tools to contribute to in-person classroom discussions. Not only will students be able to communicate with multiple mediums, but they will develop the ability to move seamlessly through various learning and collaboration methods. Having fluency in a wide array of sharing and communication methods provides students with ownership over their reading experience, deepening their connection to the text. The chapter also addressed the importance of incorporating these practices in the college classroom for preservice teachers.

REFERENCES

Applebee, A., Langer, J., Nystrand, M., & Gamoran, A. (2003). Discussion-based approaches to developing understanding: Classroom instruction and student performance in middle and high school English. *American Educational Research Journal, 40*(3), 685–730. doi:10.3102/00028312040003685

Bazalgette, C., & Buckingham, D. (2013). Literacy, media and multimodality: A critical response. *Literacy, 47*(2), 95–102. doi:10.1111/j.1741-4369.2012.00666.x

Beck, P. (2014). Multigenre text set integration: Motivating reluctant readers through successful experiences with text. *Journal of Reading Education, 40*, 12–19.

Bezemer, J., & Kress, G. (2008). Writing in multimodal texts. *Written Communication, 25*(2), 166–195. doi:10.1177/0741088307313177

Borsheim, C., Merritt, K., & Reed, D. (2008). Beyond technology for technology's sake: Advancing multiliteracies in the twenty-first century. *The Clearing House: A Journal of Educational Strategies, Issues and Ideas, 82*(2), 87–90. doi:10.3200/TCHS.82.2.87-90

Cervetti, G. N., Wright, T. S., & Hwang, H. (2016). Conceptual coherence, comprehension, and vocabulary acquisition: A knowledge effect? *Reading and Writing, 29*(4), 761–779. doi:10.100711145-016-9628-x

Considine, D., Horton, J., & Moorman, G. (2009). Teaching and reaching the millennial generation through media literacy. *Journal of Adolescent & Adult Literacy, 52*(6), 471–481. doi:10.1598/JAAL.52.6.2

Davis-Duerr, J. (2015). Planning on preservice teachers' affective domains of reading. *Journal of Reading Education, 40*(3), 17–22.

Faigley, L., Kress, G., & van Leeuwen, T. (2002). Multimodal discourse: The modes and media of contemporary communication. *College Composition and Communication, 54*(2), 318. doi:10.2307/1512155

Fierberg, R. (2018). *Listen to Lin-Manuel Miranda and Ben Platt perform a Hamilton and Dear Evan Hansen mashup*. Retrieved from http://www.playbill.com/article/listen-to-lin-manuel-miranda-and-ben-platt-perform-a-hamilton-and-dear-evan-hansen-mashup

Fisher, D., & Frey, N. (2018). Raise reading volume through access, choice, discussion, and book talks. *The Reading Teacher*, *72*(1), 89–97. doi:10.1002/trtr.1691

Gallagher, K. (2015). *In the best interest of students: Staying true to what works in the ELAclassroom*. Portland, ME: Stenhouse.

History, C. (2013, May 29). *Black Panther Party - Ten point program* [Video File]. Retrieved from www.youtube.com/watch?v=T7ChnjalY-0

Holden, J., & Schmit, J. S. (2002). *Inquiry and the literary text: Constructing discussions in the English classroom. In Classroom Practices in Teaching English*. National Council of Teachers of English.

Jail, K. C. (2018). Dallas cop who killed Botham Jean in his apartment has been indicted on murder. *The Cut*. Retrieved from https://www.thecut.com/2018/09/dallas-police-shooting- botham-jean.html

Karabay, A., Kuşdemir Kayıran, B., & Işık, D. (2015). The investigation of pre-service teachers' perceptions about critical reading self-efficacy. *Eurasian Journal of Educational Research*, *59*, 227–246.

Kress, G., & Selander, S. (2012). Multimodal design, learning and cultures of recognition. *Internet and Higher Education*, *15*(4), 265–268. doi:10.1016/j.iheduc.2011.12.003

Lamb, A. (2018). Digital media Part 2: Energize teen readers with book-film adaptations. *INFOTECH*, *46*, 52–57.

Lenters, K. (2016). Riding the lines and overwriting in the margins: Affect and multimodal literacy practices. *Journal of Literacy Research*, *48*(3), 280–316. doi:10.1177/1086296X16658982

Leu, D., Kinzer, C., Coiro, J., Castek, J., & Henry, L. (2013). New literacies: A dual-level theory of the changing nature of literacy, instruction, and assessment. In D. E. Alvermann, R. B. Ruddell, & N. J. Unrau (Eds.), *Theoretical models and processes of reading* (pp. 1150–1181). Newark, DE: International Reading Association. doi:10.1598/0710.42

Mills, K. (2010). Shrek meets Vygotsky: Rethinking adolescents' multimodal literacy practices in schools. *Journal of Adolescent & Adult Literacy*, *54*(1), 35–45. doi:10.1598/JAAL.54.1.4

Miranda, L., & Platt, B. (2018). *Found/Tonight* [CD]. Warner/Chappell Music, Inc.

Parten Gerla, J. (2010). Madelyn, a preservice teacher becomes a writer. *Southeastern Teacher Education Journal*, *3*(1), 131–140.

Purcell-Gates, V., Perry, K., & Briseño, A. (2011). Analyzing literacy practice: Grounded theory to model. *Research in the Teaching of English*, *45*(4), 439–458.

Roa, K., & Skouge, J. (2015). Using multimedia technologies to support culturally and linguistically diverse learners and young children with disabilities. In K. L. Heider & M. R. Renck (Eds.), *Educating the young child* (pp. 101–115). Boston, MA: Pearson.

Rosenblatt, L. M. (1994). The transactional theory of reading and writing. In R. B. Ruddell, M. R. Ruddell, & H. Singer (Eds.), *Theoretical models and processes of reading* (pp. 1057–1092). Newark, DE: International Reading Association.

Rowsell, J. & Walsh, M. (2011). Rethinking literacy education in new times: multimodality, multiliteracies, & new literacies. *Brock Education: A Journal of Educational Research and Practice, 21*. doi:10.26522/brocked.v21i1.236

Shakur, T. (1999). *The rose that grew from concrete*. New York: Pocket Books.

Sukovic, S. (2017). *Transliteracy in complex information environments*. Cambridge, MA: Chandos Publishing.

Thomas, A. (2017). *The Hate U Give*. New York, NY: Balzer & Bray/Harperteen.

Thomas, S., Joseph, C., Laccetti, J., Mason, B., Mills, S., & Pullinger, K. (2007). Transliteracy: Crossing divides. First Monday, 12.

Vasudevan, L., Schultz, K., & Bateman, J. (2010). Rethinking composing in a digital age: Authoring literate identities through multimodal storytelling. *Written Communication, 27*(4), 442–468. doi:10.1177/0741088310378217

Vygotsky, L. S. (1978). *Mind and society: The development of higher mental processes*. Cambridge, MA: Harvard University Press.

Walsh, M., & Walsh, M. (2010). Multimodal literacy: What does it mean for classroom practice? *Australian Journal of Language and Literacy, 33*, 211–239. Retrieved from http://search.proquest.com/docview/1496986878/

WilkinsonL. (2010, December 21). Why transliteracy? *Libraries and Transliteracy.* Retrieved from https://librariesandtransliteracy.wordpress.com/2010/12/20/why-transliteracy/

ADDITIONAL READING

Fisher, D., & Frey, N. (2018). Raise reading volume through access, choice, discussion, and book talks. *The Reading Teacher, 72*(1), 89–97. doi:10.1002/trtr.1691

Gallagher, K. (2015). *In the best interest of students: Staying true to what works in the ELA classroom.* Portland, ME: Stenhouse.

Ivey, G., & Johnston, P. (2017). Emerging adolescence in engaged reading communities. *Language Arts, 94*(3), 159–169.

Riddell, R. (2018). *Project Lit: How a Nashville educator turned a class project into a nationwide movement.* Retrieved from https://www.educationdive.com/new/project-lit-how-a-nashville-educator-turned-class-project-into-a-nationw/518766/

Thomas, A. (2017). *The Hate U Give*. New York, NY: Balzer & Bray/Harperteen.

Thomas, S., Joseph, C., Laccetti, J., Mason, B., Mills, S., & Pullinger, K. (2007). Transliteracy: Crossing divides. *First Monday*, 12.

KEY TERMS AND DEFINITIONS

Flipgrid: A social media platform created for educators to use for students to share video clips.

Hashtag: A hashtag is a word or phrase proceeded by the symbol # that is used on social media platforms to identify, summarize, and categorize topics.

The Hate U Give: A best-selling, award-winning young adult novel by Angie Thomas.

Instagram: A social media platform used to share photographs and captions.

Multimedia: Using more than one form of communication or expression such as art, text, social media, video, and audio formats.

Socratic Seminar: Socratic seminar is a discussion strategy that allows students to ask questions and engage in discussion about a common text.

Text Set: A collection of related texts that centralize on one theme or topic.

Transliteracy: Transliteracy references the ability for students to make meaning across multiple literacy platforms, including traditional learning methods like discussion and writing, as well as new literacy methods such as social media and art.

APPENDIX A

Socratic Seminar Template

Be prepared to speak at the seminar with some or all of the information below.

One thinking question to pose to the group:

One part that impacted you:

Vocabulary words to think about:

Favorite quote from this section:

Hashtag this section:

Multimedia Connection (did this book remind you of another book, song, photograph, current event, movie, etc):

Writing craft you noticed from the author:

During discussion write one thing you had not thought of:

APPENDIX B

Instagram Book Assignment

In this assignment, you will post a photograph and book review to the Instagram account called "not-asinglestory." This assignment is inspired by a combination of the following: Goodreads book reviews, Instagram book accounts (#bookstagram #booklover #bookworm), the #weneeddiversebooks movement, and Chimamanda Adichie's TED talk titled "The Danger of a Single Story."

Table 1. Rubric

Potential Points	Guidelines
20	**Photograph** • The book is included in the picture and the book title is clearly seen. • The photograph contains at least two artifacts, items, or scenery that is representative of the story. • The photograph includes an important quote from the book. • The photograph contains imagery or explicit depiction of themes representative of the story.
30	**Instagram Caption** When writing your caption consider the following: • What was the author's purpose in writing the book? Did the author accomplish that purpose? • Who is the target audience for the book? • What do you think is the book's greatest value? What makes it special or worthwhile? • Whose voice is heard in this book? Is anyone's voice silenced? • Is the book interesting? Does it hold your attention? • Would it be a useful addition to a school or public library? • How well does the reader relate to the subject? • Is it easy to understand the ideas? • Overall, did you like the book? Would you recommend it to a friend? • Are there any appropriate emojis that might help express your feelings about this book?
10	**Instagram Caption Question** • Pose a question related to themes or characters in the book. This question should serve as a catalyst for future comments and discussion from your classmates.
10	**Hashtag** • Create two hashtags that are representative of the book overall and would be meaningful to someone who read the book. Hashtags can relate to theme, characters, "inside jokes," etc. • Place the hashtag #notasinglestory at the end of your post.
15	**Comment** • Comment on two other pictures on the account. Comments should go beyond "great photo" and address the content in the caption and the question posed by the reader.
10	**Approval and Posting** • Get approval of your picture and caption by your teacher. • Once the teacher has approved, the Instagram posting can be made on your own Instagram account or class Instagram and tag @notasinglestory • If Instagram is not an option, print the photos and hang them on the wall with sticky notes and pens for comments
5	**Length and Mechanics** • Instagram captions can include up to 2,200 characters, including emoji, and up to 30 hashtags. Choose your words thoughtfully when considering the caption. Conventional grammar is not required as long as the message and intention of the post are clear to the reader.

Compilation of References

Ackermann, E., Gauntlett, D., & Weckstrom, C. (2009). *Defining systematic creativity: Explaining the nature of creativity and how the Lego system of play relates to it*. Billund, Denmark: The LEGO Learning Institute. Retrieved from http://www.legofoundation.com/en-us/newsroom/publications

Agyei, D., & Voogt, J. (2011). Exploring the potential of the will, skill, tool model in Ghana: Predicting prospective and practicing teachers' use of technology. *Computers & Education, 56*(1), 91–100. doi:10.1016/j.compedu.2010.08.017

Akçayır, M., & Akçayır, G. (2017). Advantages and challenges associated with augmented reality for education: A systematic review of the literature. *Educational Research Review, 20*, 1–11. doi:10.1016/j.edurev.2016.11.002

Albers, P. (2014). Digital writing and the role of critical pedagogy in preservice teacher education. In R. E. Ferdig & K. E. Pytash (Eds.), *Exploring multimodal composition and digital writing* (pp. 98–115). Hershey, PA: IGI Global. doi:10.4018/978-1-4666-4345-1.ch007

Allor, J., & McCathren, R. (2004). The efficacy of an early literacy tutoring program implemented by college students. *Learning Disabilities Research & Practice, 19*(2), 116–129. doi:10.1111/j.1540-5826.2004.00095.x

Anderson, M., & Perrin, A. (2018, October 26). Nearly one-in-five teens can't always finish their homework because of the digital divide. *Pew Research Center*. Retrieved from http://www.pewresearch.org/fact-tank/2018/10/26/nearly-one-in-five-teens-cant-always-finish-their-homework-because-of-the-digital-divide/

Anzaldúa, G. (2007). *Borderlands/La Frontera: The new mestiza*. San Francisco, CA: Aunt Lute Books.

Apple Developer. (2017). *The Swift programming language (Swift 4) guide*. Retrieved fromhttps://developer.apple.com/library/content/documentation/Swift/Conceptual/Swift_Programming_Language/Closures.html

Applebee, A., Langer, J., Nystrand, M., & Gamoran, A. (2003). Discussion-based approaches to developing understanding: Classroom instruction and student performance in middle and high school English. *American Educational Research Journal, 40*(3), 685–730. doi:10.3102/00028312040003685

Archer, A. (2013). Power, social justice and multimodal pedagogies. In C. Jewitt (Ed.), *The Routledge Handbook of Multimodal Analysis* (pp. 150–161). Routledge.

Argyriou, L., Economou, D., & Bouki, V. (2017). *360-degree interactive video application for Cultural Heritage Education*. In iLRN 2017: Coimbra workshop, long and short paper, and poster proceedings from the Third Immersive Learning Research Network Conference, Coimbra, Portugal.

Arnott, L. (2016). An ecological exploration of young children's digital play: Framing children's social experiences with technologies in early childhood. *Early Years, 36*(3), 271–288. doi:10.1080/09575146.2016.1181049

Aronson, B., & Laughter, J. (2016). The theory and practice of culturally relevant education: A synthesis of research across content areas. *Review of Educational Research*, *86*(1), 163–206. doi:10.3102/0034654315582066

Association for Childhood Education International (ACEI). (2007). *Elementary education standards and supporting explanation.* Retrieved from http://caepnet.org/~/media/Files/caep/program-review/aceielementarystandardssupporting-explana.pdf?la=en

Atwell, N. (1998). *In the middle: New understandings about writing, reading, and learning*. Portsmouth, NH: Boynton/Cook Publishers, Inc.

Baldry, A., & Thibault, P. J. (2006). *Multimodal transcription and text analysis*. London: Equinox.

Bandura, A. (1986). *Social foundations of thought and action: A social cognitive theory*. Englewood Cliffs, NJ: Prentice-Hall.

Bandura, A. (1994). Social cognitive theory of mass communication. *Media Psychology*, *3*(3), 265–299. doi:10.1207/S1532785XMEP0303_03

Bandura, A. (2001). Social cognitive theory: An agentic perspective. *Annual Review of Clinical Psychology*, *52*(1), 1–26. doi:10.1146/annurev.psych.52.1.1 PMID:11148297

Banks, C. A. M., & Banks, J. A. (1995). Equity pedagogy: An essential component of multicultural education. *Theory into Practice*, *34*(3), 152–158. doi:10.1080/00405849509543674

Banks, J. A. (2007). *Educating citizens in a multicultural society* (2nd ed.). New York, NY: Teachers College Press.

Baran, D. (2014). A review of research on mobile learning in teacher education. *Journal of Educational Technology & Society*, *17*(4), 17–32.

Barrett, J., & Cocq, C. (2019). Indigenous storytelling and language learning: Digital media as a vehicle for cultural transmission and language acquisition. In C. Cocq & K. P. H. Sullivan (Eds.), *Perspectives on Indigenous Writing and Literacies* (pp. 89–111). Leiden, The Netherlands: Brill Publishing; doi:10.1163/9789004298507_006

Barton, D., & Hamilton, M. (2000). Literacy as social practice. In D. Barton, M. Hamilton, & R. Ivanic (Eds.), *Situated literacies: Reading and writing in context* (pp. 7–15). London: Routledge.

Barton, K. C., & Levstik, L. S. (2004). *Teaching history for the common good.* Mahwah, NJ: Lawrence Erlbaum. doi:10.4324/9781410610508

Bassey, M. O. (2016). Culturally responsive teaching: Implications for educational justice. *Education in Science*, *6*(4), 1–6. doi:10.3390/educsci6040035

Bauserman, K. L., Cassady, J. C., Smith, L. L., & Stroud, J. C. (2005). Kindergarten literacy achievement: The effects of the PLATO integrated learning system. *Reading Research and Instruction*, *44*(4), 49–60. doi:10.1080/19388070509558436

Bazalgette, C., & Buckingham, D. (2013). Literacy, media and multimodality: A critical response. *Literacy*, *47*(2), 95–102. doi:10.1111/j.1741-4369.2012.00666.x

Beach, R., Hull, G., & O'Brien, D. (2011). Transforming English language arts in a Web 2.0 world. Handbook of research on teaching the English language arts.

Beach, R. (2012). Uses of digital tools and literacies in the English Language Arts Classroom. *Research in the Schools*, *19*(1), 45–59.

Beach, R., & O'Brien, D. (2014). *Using apps for learning across the curriculum: A literacy-based framework and guide*. Routledge. doi:10.4324/9781315769127

Beck, P. (2014). Multigenre text set integration: Motivating reluctant readers through successful experiences with text. *Journal of Reading Education*, *40*, 12–19.

Bekhta, N. (2017). We-Narratives: The Distinctiveness of Collective Narration. Narrative, 25(2), 164-181.

Belshaw, D. (2012, July 12). On the important differences between literacies, skills and competencies [Web log post]. Retrieved from http://www.dougbelshaw.com/blog/2012/07/12/on-the-importantdifferences-between-literacies-skills-and-competencies/

Bevington, R. (Producer) (2018). *What's in a name?* [audio podcast]. Retrieved from https://www.npr.org/podcasts/

Bezemer, J., & Kress, G. (2008). Writing in multimodal texts. *Written Communication*, *25*(2), 166–195. doi:10.1177/0741088307313177

Bezemer, J., & Kress, G. (2017). Young people, Facebook, and pedagogy: Recognizing contemporary forms of multimodal text making. In M. Kontopodis, C. Varvantakis, & C. Wulf (Eds.), *Global youth in digital trajectories* (pp. 22–38). London, UK: Routledge. doi:10.4324/9781315303239-3

Bond, N. (2013). Developing a professional learning community among preservice teachers. *Current Issues in Education*, *16*(2), 1–14.

Borg, M. (2004). The apprenticeship of observation. *ELT Journal*, *58*(3), 274–276. doi:10.1093/elt/58.3.274

Borsheim, C., Merrit, K., & Reed, D. (2008). Beyond technology for technology's sake: Advancing multiliteracies in the twenty-first century. *The Clearing House: A Journal of Educational Strategies, Issues and Ideas*, *82*(2), 87–90. doi:10.3200/TCHS.82.2.87-90

Bourdieu, P. (1990). *The logic of practice*. Cambridge, UK: Polity Press.

Bowers-Campbell, J. (2011). Take if out of class: Exploring virtual literature circles. *Journal of Adolescent & Adult Literacy*, *54*(8), 557–567. doi:10.1598/JAAL.54.8.1

Boyatzis, C. J. (1992). Let the caged bird sing: Using literature to teach developmental psychology. *Teaching of Psychology*, *1*(4), 221–222. doi:10.120715328023top1904_5

Brandes, G. M., & Boskic, N. (2008). Eportfolios: From description to analysis. *International Review of Research in Open and Distance Learning*, *9*(7), 1–17.

Braun, V., & Clarke, V. (2006). Using thematic analysis in psychology. *Qualitative Research in Psychology*, *3*(2), 77–101. doi:10.1191/1478088706qp063oa

Brennan, K., & Resnick, M. (2012). *New frameworks for studying and assessing the developments of computational thinking*. Paper presented at the American Educational Research Association Meeting, Vancouver, BC.

Brenner, K. (2014). Digital Stories: A 21st-Century Communication Tool for the English Language Classroom. In *English Teaching Forum* (Vol. 52, No. 1, pp. 22-29). US Department of State. Bureau of Educational and Cultural Affairs, Office of English Language Programs.

Brenner, A. M., & Brill, J. M. (2016). Investigating practices in teacher education that promote and inhibit technology integration transfer in early career teachers. *TechTrends*, *60*(2), 136–144. doi:10.100711528-016-0025-8

Britzman, D. (2003). *Practice makes practice: A critical study of learning to teach*. Albany, NY: State University of New York Press.

Brown, S. (2017). Building on emergent bilinguals' funds of knowledge using digital tools. In E. Ortileb & E. Cheek Jr., (Eds.), *Addressing diversity in literacy instruction* (pp. 173–193). Bingley, UK: Emerald. doi:10.1108/S2048-045820170000008018

Bruce, D. L., & Chiu, M. M. (2015). Composing with new technology: Teacher reflections on learning digital video. *Journal of Teacher Education*, *66*(3), 272–287. doi:10.1177/0022487115574291

Bruns, A. (2008). *Blogs, Wikipedia, second life, and beyond: From production to produsage*. New York: Lang.

Buck, A. (2012). Examining digital literacy practices on social network sites. *Research in the Teaching of English*, *47*(1), 9–38.

Buckley-Marudas, M. F. (2016). Literacy learning in a digitally-rich humanities classroom. *Journal of Adolescent & Adult Literacy*, *59*(5), 551–561. doi:10.1002/jaal.470

Buckley-Marudas, M. F., & Doerr-Stevens, C. (in press). Critical listening for social change: The possibility of "playback" in English Language Arts. *Ubiquity*.

Burnett, C. (2010). Technology and literacy in early childhood educational settings: A review of research. *Journal of Early Childhood Literacy*, *10*(3), 247–270. doi:10.1177/1468798410372154

Burns, M. K., Senesac, B. V., & Symington, T. (2003). The effectiveness of the hosts program in improving the reading achievement of children at-risk for reading failure. *Reading Research and Instruction*, *43*(2), 87–103. doi:10.1080/19388070409558406

Bushman, B. J., & Huesmann, L. R. (2006). Short-term and Long-term Effects of Violent Media on Aggression in Children and Adults. *Archives of Pediatrics & Adolescent Medicine*, *160*(4), 348. doi:10.1001/archpedi.160.4.348 PMID:16585478

C3 Teachers. (n.d.a). High school Constitution inquiry: Did the Constitution establish a just government? *C3 Teachers*. Retrieved from http://www.c3teachers.org/wp-content/uploads/2015/08/NewYork_11_Constitution.pdf

C3 Teachers. (n.d.b). New York state social studies resource toolkit: 7th grade *Uncle Tom's Cabin* inquiry. *C3 Teachers*. Retrieved from http://www.c3teachers.org/wp-content/uploads/2015/06/NewYork_7_UncleTomsCabin.pdf

Calkins, L., Martinelli, M., Kesler, T., Gillette, C., Cruz, M. C., McEvoy, M. & Collins, K. (2006). *Units of study for teaching writing, grades 3-5* (Vol. 4). FirstHand.

Campbell, D. E. (2007). Sticking together: Classroom diversity and civic education. *American Politics Research*, *35*(1), 51–78. doi:10.1177/1532673X06294503

Campbell, P. (1996). Participatory literary practices: Exploring social identity and relations. *Adult Basic Education*, *6*(3), 127.

Cantor, E. [EricCantor]. (2013, December 9). *Becoming literate in code is as essential to being literate in language and math. #hourofcode. VIDEO:* https://youtu.be/Vgn_YbSmHnw [Tweet]. Retrieved from https://twitter.com/ericcantor/status/410080680366727168?lang=en

Caraballo, L. (2018). Multiple literacies as culturally sustaining pedagogy in English language arts. In *An Authentic English Language Arts Curriculum* (pp. 172–199). Routledge. doi:10.4324/9781351167161-6

Carducci, R., & Rhoads, R. A. (2005). Of minds and media: Teaching critical citizenship to the plugged-in generation. *About Campus: Enriching the Student Learning Experience*, *10*(5), 2–9. doi:10.1002/abc.142

Carspecken, F. P. (2013). *Critical Ethnography in Educational Research*. Abingdon, UK: Routledge.

Center for Information & Research on Civic Learning and Engagement (CIRCLE). (2013). *All together now: Collaboration and innovation for youth engagement: The report of the commission on youth voting and civic knowledge.* Medford, MA: CIRCLE. Retrieved from https://civicyouth.org/wp-content/uploads/2013/09/CIRCLE-youthvoting-individualPages.pdf

Ceraso, S. (2014). (Re)Educating the senses: Multimodal listening, bodily learning, and the composition of sonic experiences. *College English, 77*(2), 102–123.

Cervetti, G. N., Wright, T. S., & Hwang, H. (2016). Conceptual coherence, comprehension, and vocabulary acquisition: A knowledge effect? *Reading and Writing, 29*(4), 761–779. doi:10.100711145-016-9628-x

Chan, E., Narcisee, N., & Moreno, C. (2015). *Medgar Evers College Snapshot, Academic Year 2014–2015.* Medgar Evers College: Office of Institutional Research and Assessment.

Chin, T., Rabow, J., & Estrada, J. (2011). *Tutoring matters: Everything you always wanted to know about how to tutor.* Philadelphia: Temple University Press.

Cho, B. Y. (2013). Adolescents' constructively response reading strategy use in a critical Internet reading task. *Reading Research Quarterly, 28*(4), 339–342.

Choi, Y., Lim, J. H., & An, S. (2011). Marginalized students' uneasy learning: Korean immigrant students' experiences of learning social studies. *Social Studies Research & Practice, 6*, 1–17.

Cochran-Smith, M. (2004). *Walking the road: Race, diversity, and social justice in teacher education.* New York, NY: Teachers College Press.

Cohen, C. J., Kahne, J., Bowyer, B., Middaugh, E., & Rogowski, J. (2012). *Participatory politics: new media and youth political action.* Oakland, CA: Youth and Participatory Politics Research Network. Retrieved from http://ypp.dmlcentral.net/sites/all/files/publications/YPP_Survey_Report_FULL.pdf

Coiro, J., Knobel, M., Lankshear, C., & Leu, D. J. (Eds.). (2014). *Handbook of research on new literacies.* Routledge. doi:10.4324/9781410618894

Coleman, D. (2011). *Bringing the common core to life.* Retrieved June 2019, from http://nysed.gov.rttt/resources/bringing-the-common-core-to-life.html

Colwell, J., & Hutchison, A. C. (2015). Supporting teachers in integrating digital technology into language arts instruction to promote literacy. *Journal of Digital Learning in Teacher Education, 31*(2), 56–63. doi:10.1080/21532974.2014.991813

Comber, B. (2011). Making space for place-making pedagogies: Stretching normative mandated literacy curriculum. *Contemporary Issues in Early Childhood, 12*(4), 343–348. doi:10.2304/ciec.2011.12.4.343

Considine, D., Horton, J., & Moorman, G. (2009). Teaching and reaching the millennial generation through media literacy. *Journal of Adolescent & Adult Literacy, 52*(6), 471–481. doi:10.1598/JAAL.52.6.2

Cope, B., & Kalantzis, M. (2009). "Multiliteracies": New literacies, new learning. *Pedagogies, 4*(3), 164–195. doi:10.1080/15544800903076044

Cope, B., & Kalantzis, M. (Eds.). (2000). *Multiliteracies: Literacy learning and the design of social futures.* New York: Psychology Press.

Council for Exceptional Children. (2015). *What every special educator must know.* Arlington, VA: Author.

Council for the Accreditation of Educator Preparation. (2015). *Standard 2: Clinical partnerships and practice.* Retrieved from http://caepnet.org/standards/standard-2

Cremin, T., Flewitt, R., Swann, J., Faulkner, D., & Kucirkova, N. (2018). Storytelling and story-acting: Co-construction in action. *Journal of Early Childhood Research, 16*(1), 3–17. doi:10.1177/1476718X17750205

Cresswell, T. (2004). *Place: A short introduction*. Oxford, UK: Blackwell Publishing.

Crick, N. R., & Dodge, K. A. (1994). A review and reformulation of social information- processing mechanisms in children's social adjustment. *Psychological Bulletin, 115*(1), 74–101. doi:10.1037/0033-2909.115.1.74

Criscoe, B. L. (1988). A pleasant reminder: There is an established criteria for writing alphabet books. *Reading Horizons, 28*(4), 2.

Croddy, M., & Levine, P. (2014). The C3 Framework: A powerful tool for preparing future generations for informed and engaged civic life. *Social Education, 78*(6), 282–285.

Curwood, J. S., Magnifico, A. M., & Lammers, J. C. (2013). Writing in the wild: Writers' motivation in fan-based affinity spaces. *Journal of Adolescent & Adult Literacy, 56*(8), 677–685. doi:10.1002/JAAL.192

Dalton, B. (2012). Multimodal composition and the Common Core State Standards. *The Reading Teacher, 66*(4), 333–339. doi:10.1002/TRTR.01129

Dalton, B., & Grisham, D. L. (2013). Love that book: Multimodal response to literature. *The Reading Teacher, 67*(3), 220–225. doi:10.1002/TRTR.1206

Damico, J. S., Panos, A., & Myers, M. (2018). Digital literacies and climate change: Exploring reliability and truth(s) with preservice teachers. In E. Ortlieb, E. Cheek, & P. Semingson (Eds.), *Best practices in teaching digital literacies* (pp. 93–107). Bingley, UK: Emerald Publishing Limited. doi:10.1108/S2048-045820180000009007

Davies, B. (2014). *Listening to children: Being and becoming*. New York: Routledge. doi:10.4324/9781315770390

Davis-Duerr, J. (2015). Planning on preservice teachers' affective domains of reading. *Journal of Reading Education, 40*(3), 17–22.

DeJarnette, N. K. (2018). Early childhood steam: Reflections from a year of steam initiatives implemented in a high-needs primary school. *Education, 139*(2), 96–110.

Dejaynes, T. (2018). "What makes me who I am?": Using artifacts as cosmopolitan invitations. *English Journal, 108*(2), 48–54. Retrieved from https://proxy.geneseo.edu/login?url=https://proxy.geneseo.edu:5742/docview/2155618863?accountid=11072

Delaney, S., Trapani, F., Chandler, P., & Redman, C. (2014). *Contemporary practices of technology and its affordances: Perceptions of PSTs on the utilization of technology in teaching and learning practice*, Paper presented at the EDULearn2014 conference, Barcelona, Spain.

Delpit, L. (1995). *Other people's children: Cultural conflict in the classroom*. New York, NY: The New Press.

Deluca, K. (2018). Shared passions, shared compositions: Online fandom communities and affinity groups as sites for public writing pedagogy. *Computers and Composition, 47*, 75–92. doi:10.1016/j.compcom.2017.12.003

Demarest, A. B. (2014). *Place-based curriculum design: Exceeding standards through local investigations*. Routledge. doi:10.4324/9781315795195

Dewey, J. (1934). *Art as experience*. New York, NY: Perigee.

Dimco, J. (2017, September 6). *Re-coding literacy*. Retrieved from https://www.insidehighered.com/digital-learning/article/2017/09/06/professor-writes-everyone-should-code-movement-re-coding

Doering, A., Beach, R., & O'Brien, D. (2007). Infusing multimodal tools and digital literacies into an English education program. *English Education*, *40*(1), 41–60.

Doerr-Stevens, C., & Buckley-Marudas, M. F. (2019). Hearing knowledge into action: Mobilizing sound for multicultural imaginaries. *International Journal of Multicultural Education*, *21*(1), 105–124. doi:10.18251/ijme.v21i1.1735

Dole, J. A., Nokes, J. D., & Drits, D. (2009). Cognitive strategy instruction. In S. E. Israel & G. G. Duffy (Eds.), *Handbook of Research in Reading Comprehension* (pp. 347–372). New York: Taylor and Francis.

Domingo, M. G., & Gargante, A. B. (2016). Exploring the use of educational technology in primary education: Teachers' perception of mobile technology learning impacts and applications' use in the classroom. *Computers in Human Behavior*, *56*, 21–28. doi:10.1016/j.chb.2015.11.023

Dovchin, S., & Pennycook, A. (2017). Digital metroliteracies. In K. A. Mills, A. Stornaiuolo, A. Smith, & J. Z. Pandya (Eds.), *Handbook of writing, literacies, and education in digital cultures* (pp. 211–222). New York, NY: Routledge.

DuFour, R., DuFour, R., Eaker, R., & Many, T. (2010). *Learning by doing: A handbook for professional learning communities at work*. Bloomington, IN: Solution Tree.

Duke, N. K., Purcell-Gates, V., Hall, L. A., & Tower, C. (2006). Authentic literacy activities for developing comprehension and writing. *The Reading Teacher*, *60*(4), 344–355. doi:10.1598/RT.60.4.4

Dunsmore, K., Ordoñez-Jasis, R., & Herrera, G. (2013). Welcoming their worlds: Rethinking literacy instruction through community mapping. *Language Arts*, *90*(5), 327–338.

Dyson, A. (2003). *The brothers and sisters learn to write: Popular literacies in childhood and school cultures*. New York: Teachers College Press.

Edwards, T., & Burnham, C. (2009). The promise of ePortfolios for institutional assessment. In D. Cambridge, B. Cambridge, & K. Yancey (Eds.), *Electronic portfolios 2.0: Emergent research on implementation and impact*. Stylus Publishing, LLC.

Elbaum, B., Vaughn, S., Tejero Hughes, M., & Watson Moody, S. (2000). How effective are one-to-one tutoring programs in reading for elementary students at risk for reading failure? A meta-analysis of the intervention research. *Journal of Educational Psychology*, *92*(4), 605–619. doi:10.1037/0022-0663.92.4.605

Elliot, R. (2009). Using Google my maps for classroom projects. *TESL-EJ*, *12*(4), 1–14.

Ellison, T. L., & Solomon, M. (2018). Digital play as purposeful and productive literacies in African American boys. *The Reading Teacher*, *71*(4), 495–500. doi:10.1002/trtr.1657

Emdin, C. (2016). *For White folks who teach in the hood... and the rest of y'all too: Reality pedagogy and urban education*. Beacon Press.

Erickson, F. (1986). Qualitative methods in research on teaching. In Handbook on research on teaching (3rd ed.). New York: Macmillan.

Esri Story Maps - Harness the Power of Maps to Tell Your Story. (n.d.). Retrieved October 25, 2018, from https://storymaps.arcgis.com/en/

Eynon, B. (2009). Making connection: Laguardia Eportfolio. In D. Cambridge, B. Cambridge, & K. Yancey (Eds.), *Electronic portfolios 2.0: Emergent research on implementation and impact*. Stylus Publishing, LLC.

Faigley, L., Kress, G., & van Leeuwen, T. (2002). Multimodal discourse: The modes and media of contemporary communication. *College Composition and Communication*, *54*(2), 318. doi:10.2307/1512155

Faloon, G. (2016). An analysis of young students' thinking when completing basic coding tasks using tasks using Scratch Junior on the iPad. *Journal of Computer Assisted Learning*, *32*(6), 576–593. doi:10.1111/jcal.12155

Farkas, M. G. (2012). Participatory technologies, pedagogy 2.0 and information literacy. *Library Hi Tech*, *30*(1), 82–94. doi:10.1108/07378831211213229

Fierberg, R. (2018). *Listen to Lin-Manuel Miranda and Ben Platt perform a Hamilton and Dear Evan Hansen mashup*. Retrieved from http://www.playbill.com/article/listen-to-lin-manuel-miranda-and-ben-platt-perform-a-hamilton-and-dear-evan-hansen-mashup

Fingeret, A., & Jurmo, P. (1989). *Participatory literacy education*. San Francisco: Jossey-Bass.

Fisher, D., & Frey, N. (2018). Raise reading volume through access, choice, discussion, and book talks. *The Reading Teacher*, *72*(1), 89–97. doi:10.1002/trtr.1691

Fisher, R. (2010). Young writers' construction of agency. *Journal of Early Childhood Literacy*, *10*(4), 410–429. doi:10.1177/1468798410382407

Fiske, S. T. (2017). *Social cognition*. Reading, MA: Sage Publications.

Fitzgerald, M. (2018). Multimodal knowledge building: Meaningfully using digital tools to foster disciplinary learning. *Literacy Today*, *36*(1), 34–35.

Flewitt, R. (2011). Bringing ethnography to a multimodal investigation of early literacy in a digital age. *Qualitative Research*, *11*(3), 293–310. doi:10.1177/1468794111399838

Frankenberg, E. (2013). The role of residential segregation in contemporary school segregation. *Education and Urban Society*, *45*(5), 548–570. doi:10.1177/0013124513486288

Friere, P. (2005). *Pedagogy of the oppressed* (M. B. Ramos, Trans.). New York, NY: Continuum International Publishing. (Original work published 1970)

Galanis, P. (2013, June 16). The mother of all 'Housewives'. *New York Times*. Retrieved from http://www.nytimes.com/2013/06/16/fashion/the-mother-of-all-housewives.html

Gallagher, K. (2015). *In the best interest of students: Staying true to what works in the ELAclassroom*. Portland, ME: Stenhouse.

Gay, G. (2002). Preparing for culturally responsive teaching. *Journal of Teacher Education*, *53*(2), 106–116. doi:10.1177/0022487102053002003

Gay, G. (2010). *Culturally responsive teaching: Theory, research, and practice* (2nd ed.). New York, NY: Teachers College Press.

Gay, G. (2013). Teaching to and through cultural diversity. *Curriculum Inquiry*, *43*(1), 48–70. doi:10.1111/curi.12002

Gee, J. P. (1996). *Social linguistics and literacies: Ideology in discourses / James Paul Gee*. Bristol, PA: Taylor & Francis.

Gee, J. P. (2004). *Situated Language and Learning: A Critique of Traditional Schooling*. New York: Routledge.

Gee, J. P. (2011). Reflections on empirical evidence on games and learning. In S. Tobias & J. D. Fletcher (Eds.), *Computer games and instruction* (pp. 223–232). Charlotte, NC: IAP.

Gee, J. P. (2017). Identity and diversity in today's world. *Multicultural Education Review*, *9*(2), 83–92. doi:10.1080/2005615X.2017.1312216

Ghiso, M. P., & Low, D. E. (2013). Students using multimodal literacies to surface micro-narratives of United States immigration. *Literacy*, *47*(1), 26–34. doi:10.1111/j.1741-4369.2012.00678.x

Gibson, P., & Smith, S. (2018). Digital literacies: Preparing pupils and students for their information journey in the twenty-first century. *Information and Learning Science*, *119*(12), 733–742.

Gillespie, C. A. (2010). How Culture Constructs our Sense of Neighborhood: Mental Maps and Children's Perceptions of Place. *The Journal of Geography*, *109*(1), 18–29. doi:10.1080/00221340903459447

Ginwright, S. (2004). *Black in school: Afro-centric reform, urban youth, and the promise of hip-hop culture*. New York, NY: Teachers College Press.

Glaser, B., & Strauss, A. (1967). *The discovery of grounded theory: strategies for qualitative theory*. New Brunswick, NJ: Aldine Transaction.

Godsay, S., Kawashima-Ginsberg, K., Kiesa, A., & Levine, P. (2012). *"That's not democracy." How out-of-school youth engage in civic life & what stands in their way*. Medford, MA: CIRCLE. Retrieved from https://civicyouth.org/wp-content/uploads/2012/08/CIRCLE_ThatsNotDemocracy_WebFinal.pdf

Gonzales, A. L. (2017). Disadvantaged minorities' use of the internet to expand their social networks. *Communication Research*, *44*(4), 467–486. doi:10.1177/0093650214565925

González, N., Moll, L., & Amanti, C. (2016). *Funds of knowledge: Theorizing practices in households, communities, and classrooms*. New York: Routledge.

Goodson, L. A., & Skillen, M. (2010). Small-town perspectives, big-time motivation: Composing and producing place-based podcasts. *English Journal*, *100*(1), 53–57.

Google. (n.d.). Google MyMaps mapping application. Retrieved from https://www.google.com/maps/about/mymaps/

Grabe, S., Ward, L. M., & Hyde, J. S. (2008). The role of the media in body image concerns among women: A meta-analysis of experimental and correlational studies. *Psychological Bulletin*, *134*(3), 460–476. doi:10.1037/0033-2909.134.3.460 PMID:18444705

Grossman, D. L. (2017). Global education. In M. M. Manfra & C. M. Bolick (Eds.), *The Wiley handbook of social studies research* (pp. 518–568). Malden, MA: John Wiley & Sons, Inc. doi:10.1002/9781118768747.ch23

Gruenewald, D. A. (2008). The best of both worlds: A critical pedagogy of place. *Environmental Education Research, 14*(3), 308-324.

Guernsey, L. (2014). Envisioning a digital age architecture for early education. *New America-Education Policy Program,* 1-9.

Gutiérrez, K. D., & Jurow, A. S. (2016). Social design experiments: Toward equity by design. *Journal of the Learning Sciences*, *25*(4), 565–598. doi:10.1080/10508406.2016.1204548

Gutierrez, K., Baquedano-López, P., & Tejada, C. (1999). Rethinking diversity: Hybridity and hybrid language practices in the third space. *Mind, Culture, and Activity*, *6*(4), 286–303. doi:10.1080/10749039909524733

Haberman, M. (1996). Selecting and preparing culturally competent teachers for urban schools. In J. Sikula (Ed.), *Handbook for research on teacher education* (2nd ed.; pp. 747–760). New York: Macmillan.

Han, H. (2009). *Moved to action: Motivation, participation, and inequality in American politics*. Stanford, CA: Stanford University Press.

Harris, J., & Hofer, M. (2011). Technological pedagogical content knowledge (TPACK) in action: A descriptive study of secondary teachers' curriculum-based, technology-related instructional planning. *Journal of Research on Technology in Education, 43*(3), 211–229. doi:10.1080/15391523.2011.10782570

Henriksen, D., Mishra, P., & Fisser, P. (2016). Infusing creativity and technology in 21st century education: A systemic view for change. *Journal of Educational Technology & Society, 19*(3), 27–37.

Hicks, T. (2009). *The digital writing workshop*. Portsmouth, NH: Heinemann.

Higdon, J., Reyerson, K., McFadden, C., & Mummey, K. (2011). Twitter, Wordle, and ChimeIn as student response pedagogies. *EDUCAUSE Quarterly, 34*(1).

Hillocks, G. Jr. (2011). *Teaching argument writing*. Portsmouth, NH: Heinemann.

History, C. (2013, May 29). *Black Panther Party - Ten point program* [Video File]. Retrieved from www.youtube.com/watch?v=T7ChnjalY-0

Hoaglund, A. E., Birkenfeld, K., & Box, J. A. (2014). Professional learning communities: Creating a foundation for collaboration skills in pre-service teachers. *Education, 134*(4), 521–528.

Holden, J., & Schmit, J. S. (2002). *Inquiry and the literary text: Constructing discussions in the English classroom. In Classroom Practices in Teaching English*. National Council of Teachers of English.

Hollander, S. (2001). Taking it personally: The role of memoir in teacher education. *Electronic Journal for Inclusive Education, 1*(5). Retrieved 7/3/17 from http://corescholar.libraries.wright.edu/cgi/viewcontent.cgi?article=1034&context=ejie

Hong, C. E., Lawrence, S. A., Mongillo, G., & Donnantuono, M. (2015). Using iPads to support K-12 struggling readers: A case study of iPad implementation in a university-based reading clinic. In H. An, S. Alon, & D. Fuentes (Eds.), *Tablets in K-12 Education: Integrated Experiences and Implications* (pp. 296–309). Hershey, PA: IGI Global. doi:10.4018/978-1-4666-6300-8.ch017

hooks, b. (1994). *Teaching to transgress: Education as the practice of freedom*. New York, NY: Routledge.

Howard, T. C. (2001). Telling their side of the story: African-American students' perceptions of culturally relevant teaching. *The Urban Review, 33*(2), 131–149. doi:10.1023/A:1010393224120

Howard, T. C. (2010). *Why race and culture matter in schools: Closing the achievement gap in America's classrooms*. New York: Teachers College Press.

HP. (n.d.). *Aurasma App now called HP Reveal*. Retrieved from https://www.aurasma.com/

Huang, C. D., & Behara, R. S. (2007). Outcome-driven experiential learning with Web 2.0. *Journal of Information Systems Education, 18*(3), 329–336.

Hughes, A. (2017, December 6). Composing code: Why musicians make great software developers. *HuffPost*. Retrieved from https://www.huffpost.com/entry/composing-code-why-musici_b_10714288

Hull, G. A., & Nelson, M. E. (2005). Locating the semiotic power of multimodality. *Written Communication, 22*(2), 224–261. doi:10.1177/0741088304274170

Hull, G., & Stornaiuolo, A. (2014). Cosmopolitan literacies, social networks, and "proper distance": Striving to understand in a global world. *Curriculum Inquiry, 44*(1), 15–44. doi:10.1111/curi.12035

Hundley, M., & Holbrook, T. (2013). Set in stone or set in motion?: Multimodal and digital writing with preservice English teachers. *Journal of Adolescent & Adult Literacy, 56*(6), 500–509. doi:10.1002/JAAL.171

Hurdley, R. (2006). Dismantling mantelpieces: Narrating identities and materializing culture in the home. *Sociology*, *40*(4), 717–713. doi:10.1177/0038038506065157

Hutchinson, A., & Colwell, J. (2014). The potential of digital technologies to support literacy instruction relevant to the Common Core State Standards. *Journal of Adolescent & Adult Literacy*, *58*(2).

Hutchison, A. C., & Colwell, J. (2014). The potential of digital technologies to support literacy instruction relevant to the common core state standards. *Journal of Adolescent & Adult Literacy*, *58*(2), 147–156. doi:10.1002/jaal.335

Hutchison, A., & Reinking, D. (2011). Teachers' perceptions of integrating information and communication technologies into literacy instruction: A national survey in the United States. *Reading Research Quarterly*, *46*(4), 312–333. doi:10.1002/RRQ.002

Hutchison, A., & Wang, W. (2012). Blogging within a social networking site as a form of literature response in a teacher education course. *Educational Media International*, *49*(4), 263–275. doi:10.1080/09523987.2012.741197

IGI. (2019). *What is participatory literacy.* IGI Global. Retrieved from https://www.igi-global.com/dictionary/participatory-literacy/52242

International Literacy Association. (2017). *Standards for the preparation of literacy professionals 2017*. Newark, DE: Authors.

International Society for Technology in Education. (2017). *ISTE national educational technology standards (NETS)*. Eugene, OR: International Society for Technology in Education.

International Society for Technology in Education. (2019). *ISTE Standards for educators*. Retrieved from https://www.iste.org/standards/for-educators

Ito, M. (2009). *Participatory learning in a networked society: Lessons from the Digital Youth Project.* Presentation for the 2008 Annual Meeting of the American Educational Research Association Presidential Session. Retrieved August 15, 2008, from http://www.itofisher.com/mito/publications/participatory_l.html

Ito, M., Baumer, S., Bittanti, M., boyd, d., Cody, R., Herr-Stephenson, B., & Tripp, L. (2010). Hanging out, messing around, and geeking out: Kids living and learning with new media. Cambridge, MA: MIT Press.

Ito, M., Gutierrez, K., Livingstone, S., Penuel, B., Rhodes, J., Salen, K., Schor, J., Sefton-Green, J, & Watkins, S.C. (2013). Connected Learning: An Agenda for Research and Design. Irvine, CA: Digital Media and Learning Research Hub.

Jackson, A., & Mazzei, L. (2012). *Thinking with theory in qualitative research: Viewing data across multiple perspectives*. New York: Routledge.

Jail, K. C. (2018). Dallas cop who killed Botham Jean in his apartment has been indicted on murder. *The Cut*. Retrieved from https://www.thecut.com/2018/09/dallas-police-shooting- botham-jean.html

Jamil, S., Majoka, M. I., & Sahibzada, H. E. (2018). Investigation of information and communication technology (ICTs) related resources and prospective teachers' competencies in ICTs at university level. *FWU Journal of Social Sciences*, *12*(2), 99–111.

Janks, H. (2011). *Literacy and power*. London: Routledge.

Janks, H. (2013). Critical literacy in teaching and research. *Education Inquiry*, *4*(2), 225–242. doi:10.3402/edui.v4i2.22071

Jenkins, H. (2016). Critical literacy pedagogy. In Literacies (2nd ed.). Port Melbourne, Australia: Cambridge University Press.

Jenkins, H. (2006). *Convergence culture: Where old and new media collide.* New York, NY: NYU Press.

Jenkins, H., Purushotma, R., Weigel, M., Clinton, K., & Robison, A. J. (2009). *Confronting the challenges of participatory culture: Media education for the 21st century.* Cambridge, MA: MIT Press. doi:10.7551/mitpress/8435.001.0001

Jensen, E. (2009). *Teaching with poverty in mind: What being poor does to kids' brains and what schools can do about it.* ASCD.

Jewett, C. (2008). Multimodality and Literacy in School Classrooms. *Review of Research in Education, 32*(1), 241–267. doi:10.3102/0091732X07310586

Jewitt, C. (Ed.), *The Routledge Handbook of Multimodal Analysis.* New York: Routledge.

Jewitt, C., Bezemer, J., & O'Halloran, K. (2016). *Introducing multimodality.* New York: Routledge.

Jia, X., Jung, J., & Ottenbreit-Leftwich, A. (2018). Learning technology integration from a service-learning project: Connecting preservice teachers to real-world problems. *Journal of Experiential Education, 41*(3), 261–276. doi:10.1177/1053825917738269

Jocson, K., & Rosa, J. (2015). Rethinking gaps: Literacies and languages in participatory cultures. *Journal of Adolescent & Adult Literacy, 58*(5), 372–374. doi:10.1002/jaal.368

Johnson, L. L., & Smagorinsky, P. (2014). Writing remixed: Mapping the multimodal composition of one preservice English Education teacher. In R. E. Ferdig & K. E. Pytash (Eds.), *Exploring multimodal composition and digital writing* (pp. 263–281). Hershey, PA: IGI Global. doi:10.4018/978-1-4666-4345-1.ch016

John-Steiner, V., & Meehan, T. (2000). Creativity and collaboration in knowledge construction. In C. Lee & P. Smagorinsky (Eds.), *Vygotskian perspectives on literacy research: Constructing meaning through collaborative inquiry* (pp. 31–48). New York: Cambridge University Press.

Josephson, W. L., & Proulx, J. B. (2008). Violence in Young Adolescents' Relationships: A Path Model. *Journal of Interpersonal Violence, 23*(2), 189–208. doi:10.1177/0886260507309340 PMID:18162636

Jurmo, P. (1993). Participatory literacy education: An update. Columbus, OH: The Ohio State University. Retrieved from the ERIC database. (ED 354298)

KaaSerpent. (2014). *Ira Glass on storytelling, Full* (parts 1 to 4) [video]. Retrieved from https://www.youtube.com/playlist?list=PLE108783228F1E008

Kahne, J., & Bowyer, B. (2017). Educating for democracy in a partisan age: Confronting the challenges of motivated reasoning and misinformation. *American Educational Research Journal, 54*(1), 3–34. doi:10.3102/0002831216679817

Kahne, J., & Middaugh, E. (2012). Digital media shapes youth participation in politics. *Phi Delta Kappan, 94*(3), 52–56. doi:10.1177/003172171209400312

Kamler, B. (2001). *Relocating the personal: A critical writing pedagogy.* Albany, N.Y.: SUNY Press.

Karabay, A., Kuşdemir Kayıran, B., & Işık, D. (2015). The investigation of pre-service teachers' perceptions about critical reading self-efficacy. *Eurasian Journal of Educational Research, 59*, 227–246.

Kawashima-Ginsberg, K. (2013). *Do discussion, debate, and simulations boost NAEP civics performance?* Medford, MA: CIRCLE. Retrieved from https://civicyouth.org/wp-content/uploads/2013/04/CIRCLE_NAEPBechtelFactSheetApril30.final_.pdf

Kay, R. H. (2006). Evaluating strategies used to incorporate technology into pre-service education: A review of the literature. *Journal of Research on Technology in Education*, *38*, 383–408. doi:10.1080/15391523.2006.10782466

Kea, C., Campbell-Whatley, G., & Richards, H. (2006). *Becoming culturally responsive educators: Rethinking teacher education pedagogy*. National Center for Culturally Responsive Educational Systems. Retrieved from: http://www.champaignschools.org/sites/default/files/Teacher_Ed_Brief.pdf

Kellner, D., & Share, J. (2005). Toward critical media literacy: Core concepts, debates, organizations and policy. In Discourse: Studies in the cultural politics of education (Vol. 26, No. 3, pp. 369–386). The University of Queensland, Australia: Routledge.

Kellner, D., & Share, J. (2007). Critical media literacy is not an option. *Learning Inquiry*, *1*(1), 59–69. doi:10.100711519-007-0004-2

Kellner, D., & Share, J. (2009). Critical media literacy, democracy, and the reconstruction of education. In D. Macedo & S. Steinberg (Eds.), *Media literacy: A reader*. New York: Peter Lang.

Kennedy, J. (1962). *John Kennedy's Rice stadium moon speech* [Transcript]. Retrieved from https://er.jsc.nasa.gov/seh/ricetalk.htm

King, L. H., & Allen, A. E. (2018). Beyond preservice special educators: Embedding assistive technology content throughout a teacher education program of study. *Rural Special Education Quarterly*, *37*(4), 228–234. doi:10.1177/8756870518773474

King, L., Hinterland, K., Dragan, K. L., Driver, C. R., Harris, T. G., Gwynn, R. C., ... Bassett, M. T. (2015a). Community Health Profiles 2015, Brooklyn District 8. *Crown Heights and Prospect Heights*, *32*(59), 1–16.

Kirschner, P. A., & De Bruyckere, P. (2017). The myths of the digital native and the multitasker. *Teaching and Teacher Education*, *67*, 135–142. doi:10.1016/j.tate.2017.06.001

Kittle, P. (2008). *Write beside them. Risk, voice, and clarity in high school writing*. Portsmouth, NH: Heinemann.

Knobel, M., & Lankshear, C. (2014). Studying new literacies. *Journal of Adolescent & Adult Literacy*, *58*(2), 97–101. doi:10.1002/jaal.314

Knochell, A. D., & Patton, R. M. (2015). If art education then critical digital making: Computational thinking and creative code. *Studies in Art Education*, *57*(1), 21–38. doi:10.1080/00393541.2015.11666280

Koehler, M. J., Mishra, P., Bouck, E. C., DeSchryver, M., Kereluik, K., Shin, T. S., & Wolf, L. G. (2011). Deep-play: Developing TPACK for 21st century teachers. *International Journal of Learning Technology*, *6*(2), 146–163. doi:10.1504/IJLT.2011.042646

Koenig, S. (Host and Producer). (2014–2019). *Serial* [Audio podcast]. Retrieved from ttps://serialpodcast.org/season-one/about

Kress, G. (2003). *Literacy in the new media age*. London: Routledge.

Kress, G. (2009). *Multimodality: A social semiotic approach to contemporary communication*. New York: Routledge. doi:10.4324/9780203970034

Kress, G., & Jewitt, C. (2003). Introduction. In J. Jewitt & G. Kress (Eds.), *Multimodal literacy* (pp. 1–18). New York: Peter Lang.

Kress, G., & Selander, S. (2012). Multimodal design, learning and cultures of recognition. *Internet and Higher Education*, *15*(4), 265–268. doi:10.1016/j.iheduc.2011.12.003

Kress, G., & van Leeuwen, T. (2001). *Multimodal discourse: The modes and media of contemporary communication*. New York: Oxford University Press.

Kuby, C., & Rucker, T. (2016). *Go be a writer: Expanding the curricular boundaries of literacy learning with children*. New York: Teachers College Press.

Kuby, C., & Vaughn, M. (2015). Young children's identities becoming: Exploring agency in the creation of multimodal literacies. *Journal of Early Childhood Literacy*, *15*(4), 433–472. doi:10.1177/1468798414566703

Kuehl, R. (2018). Using professional learning communities to advance preservice teachers' understanding of differentiation within writing instruction. *Teacher Educator's Journal*, *11*, 70–90.

Kumashiro, K. (2002). *Troubling education: Queer activism and antioppressive pedagogy*. New York, NY: Routledge Falmer.

Kumler, L. M., & Vosburg-Bluem, B. (2014). Climate change in the social studies classroom: A "why" and "how to" guide using the C3 Framework. *Social Education*, *78*(5), 225–229.

L'Engle, M. (2007). *A Wrinkle in Time*. New York: Square Fish.

Ladson-Billings, G. (1994). *The dreamkeepers: Successful teachers of African American children*. San Francisco, CA: Jossey-Bass.

Ladson-Billings, G. (1995). Toward a theory of culturally relevant pedagogy. *American Educational Research Journal*, *32*(3), 465–491. doi:10.3102/00028312032003465

Ladson-Billings, G., & Tate, W. F. (1995). Toward a critical race theory of education. *Teachers College Record*, *97*(1), 47.

Lamb, A. (2018). Digital media Part 2: Energize teen readers with book-film adaptations. *INFOTECH*, *46*, 52–57.

Lankshear & Knobel. (2011). *New literacies: Everyday practices for classroom learning* (3rd ed.). New York, NY: Open University Press.

Lankshear, C., & Knobel, M. (2007). Sampling "the new" in new literacies. In A new literacies sampler (vol. 29, pp. 1-24). New York: Peter Lang.

Lapp, D., & Fisher, D. (2010). Critical literacy: Examining the juxtaposition of issue, author, and self. *Multicultural Perspectives*, *12*(3), 156–160. doi:10.1080/15210960.2010.504494

Larson, L. (2008). Electronic reading workshop: Beyond books with new literacies and instructional technologies. *Journal of Adolescent & Adult Literacy*, *52*(2), 121–131. doi:10.1598/JAAL.52.2.3

Lave, J., & Wenger, E. (1991). *Situated learning: Legitimate peripheral participation*. Cambridge, UK: Cambridge University Press. doi:10.1017/CBO9780511815355

Lawrence, S. A., Donnantuono, M., Mitchell, R., & Johnson, T. (2018, December). The STREAM framework: Integrating literacy, research, and content across disciplines. *Literacy Today*, *36*(3), 28–30.

Leander, K. M., & McKim, K. K. (2003). Tracing the everyday sittings' of adolescents on the internet: A strategic adaptation of ethnography across online and offline spaces. *Education Communication and Information*, *3*(2), 211–240. doi:10.1080/14636310303140

Leavy, P. (2015). *Method meets art: Arts-based research practice*. New York, NY: Guilford Publications.

Lee, C. D. (1992). Literacy, cultural diversity, and instruction. *Education and Urban Society*, *24*(2), 279–291. doi:10.1177/0013124592024002008

Lei, J. (2009). Digital natives as preservice teachers: What technology preparation is needed? *Journal of Computing in Teacher Education*, *25*(3), 87–97.

Lenhart, A. (2015, April 9). *Teens, social media & technology overview 2015*. Pew Research Center. Retrieved from http://www.pewinternet.org/2015/04/09/teens-social-media- technology-2015/

Lensmire, A., & Schick, A. (Eds.). (2017). *(Re)narrating Teacher Identity: Telling Truths and Becoming Teachers*. New York, NY: Peter Lang. doi:10.3726/b10687

Lenters, K. (2016). Riding the lines and overwriting in the margins: Affect and multimodal literacy practices. *Journal of Literacy Research*, *48*(3), 280–316. doi:10.1177/1086296X16658982

Leonard, J., Mitchell, M., Barnes-Johnson, J., Unertl, A., Outka-Hill, J., Robinson, R., & Hester-Croff, C. (2018). Preparing teachers to engage rural students in computational thinking through robotics, game design, and culturally responsive teaching. *Journal of Teacher Education*, *69*(4), 386–407. doi:10.1177/0022487117732317

Leu, D. J. Jr, Kinzer, C., Coiro, J., & Cammack, D. (2004). Toward a theory of new literacies emerging from the Internet and other information and communication technologies. In R. B. Ruddell & N. Unrau (Eds.), *Theoretical models and processes of reading* (5th ed.; pp. 1568–1611). Newark, DE: International Reading Association.

Leu, D. J., Kinzer, C. K., Coiro, J., Castek, J., & Henry, L. A. (2017). New literacies: A dual-level theory of the changing nature of literacy, instruction, and assessment. *Journal of Education*, *197*(2), 1–18. doi:10.1177/002205741719700202

Leu, D. J., O'Byrne, W. I., Zawilinki, L., McVerry, J. G., & Everett-Cacopardo, H. (2009). Expanding the new literacies conversation. *Educational Researcher*, *38*(4), 264–269. doi:10.3102/0013189X09336676

Leu, D., Kinzer, C., Coiro, J., Castek, J., & Henry, L. (2013). New literacies: A dual-level theory of the changing nature of literacy, instruction, and assessment. In D. E. Alvermann, R. B. Ruddell, & N. J. Unrau (Eds.), *Theoretical models and processes of reading* (pp. 1150–1181). Newark, DE: International Reading Association. doi:10.1598/0710.42

Levi's. (2009, June 30). *Levi's America (Go Forth)* [Video File]. Retrieved from https://www.youtube.com/watch?v=HG8tqEUTlvs

Levinson, M. (2010). The civic empowerment gap: Defining the problem and locating solutions. In L. Sherrod, J. Torney-Purta, & C. A. Flanagan (Eds.), *Handbook of research on civic engagement* (pp. 331–361). Hoboken, NJ: John Wiley & Sons. doi:10.1002/9780470767603.ch13

Levinson, M. (2012). *No citizen left behind*. Cambridge, MA: Harvard University Press. doi:10.4159/harvard.9780674065291

Levinson, M., & Levine, P. (2013). Taking informed action to engage students in civic life. *Social Education*, *77*(6), 339–341.

Lewis, C., Enciso, P., & Moje, E. (Eds.). (2007). *Reframing sociocultural research on literacy: Identity, agency and power*. Mahwah, NJ: Lawrence Erlbaum Associates.

Lincoln, Y. S., & Guba, E. G. (1985). *Naturalistic inquiry* (Vol. 75). Newberry Park, CA: Sage Publications.

Lipman, P. (1995). Bringing out the best in them: The contribution of culturally relevant teachers to education reform. *Theory into Practice*, *34*(3), 202–208. doi:10.1080/00405849509543680

Literacy Advance of Houston. (2019). *Defining literacy*. Retrieved from https://www.literacyadvance.org/About_Us/Defining_Literacy/

Luke, A., & Woods, A. (2009). Policy and adolescent literacy. In Christenbury, L.; Bomer, R.; Magnifico, A. M. (2010). Writing for whom? Cognition, motivation, and a writer's audience. *Educational Psychologist*, *45*(3), 167–184.

Lynch, T. L. (2016). Soft(a)ware in the English classroom: Letters to the machine: Why computer programming belongs in the English classroom. *English Journal, 105*(5), 95-97.

Mak, J. (2014). Coding in the elementary school classroom. *Learning and Leading with Technology, 41*(6), 26–28.

Manovich, L. (2011). Trending: The promises and the challenges of big social data. *Debates in the Digital Humanities, 2*, 460–475.

Marasco, A., & Taranto, G. (2016). Coding is TOPS in middle school. *Association for Middle Level Education, 3*(8), 11–14.

Marshall, E., & Sensoy, Ö. (2016). *Rethinking popular culture and media*. Milwaukee, WI: Rethinking Schools.

Marshall, E., & Toohey, K. (2010). Representing family: Community funds of knowledge, bilingualism, and multimodality. *Harvard Educational Review, 80*(2), 221–242. doi:10.17763/haer.80.2.h3446j54n608q442

Marsh, J. (2014). Purposes for literacy in children's use of the online virtual world Club Penguin. *Journal of Research in Reading, 37*(2), 179–195. doi:10.1111/j.1467-9817.2012.01530.x

Marsh, J., Plowman, L., Yamada-Rice, D., Bishop, J., & Scott, F. (2016). Digital play: A new classification. *Early Years, 36*(3), 242–253. doi:10.1080/09575146.2016.1167675

Martin, L. E., Kralger, S., Quatroche, D. J., & Bauserman, K. L. (2014). *Handbook of professional development in education: Successful models and practices, Pre-K-12*. New York: Guildford Press.

McCarthy, A. (2009). "Stanley Milgram, Allen Funt and Me": Postwar social science and the "first wave" of reality TV. In S. Murray & L. Ouellette (Eds.), *Reality TV: Remaking television culture*. New York: New York University Press.

McCulloch, A. W., Hollebrands, K., Lee, H., Harrison, T., & Mutlu, A. (2018). Factors that influence secondary mathematics teachers' integration of technology in mathematics lessons. *Computers & Education, 123*, 26–40. doi:10.1016/j.compedu.2018.04.008

McDevitt, M., & Butler, M. (2011). Latino youth as information leaders: Implications for family interaction and civic engagement in immigrant communities. *InterActions: UCLA Journal of Education and Information Studies, 7*(2), Article 2.

McInerney, P., Smyth, J., & Down, B. (2011). 'Coming to a place near you? 'The politics and possibilities of a critical pedagogy of place-based education. *Asia-Pacific Journal of Teacher Education, 39*(1), 3–16. doi:10.1080/1359866X.2010.540894

McLaughlin, M. W., & Talbert, J. E. (2006). *Building school-based teacher learning communities: Professional strategies to improve student achievement*. Chicago: University of Chicago Press.

McLoughlin, C., & Lee, M. J. W. (2008). The three p's of pedagogy for the networked society: Personalization, participation, and productivity. *International Journal on Teaching and Learning in Higher Education, 20*(1), 10–27.

Melymuka, K. (1998, July 31). Why musicians may make the best tech workers. *CNN*. Retrieved from http://www.cnn.com/TECH/computing/9807/31/musicians.idg/

Merriam-Webster's collegiate dictionary. (2003). (11th ed.). Springfield, MA: Merriam-Webster Incorporated.

Miller, S. M. (2007). English teacher learning for new times: Digital video composing as multimodal literacy practice. *English Education, 40*(1), 61–83.

Miller, S. M., & McVee, M. B. (Eds.). (2013). *Multimodal composing in classrooms: Learning and teaching for the digital world*. London, UK: Routledge. doi:10.4324/9780203804032

Mills, K. (2010). Shrek meets Vygotsky: Rethinking adolescents' multimodal literacy practices in schools. *Journal of Adolescent & Adult Literacy*, *54*(1), 35–45. doi:10.1598/JAAL.54.1.4

Mills, K. A. (2015). *Literacy theories for the digital age: Social, critical, multimodal, spatial, material and sensory lenses*. Multilingual Matters. doi:10.21832/9781783094639

Mills, K., Ulsworth, L., & Exley, B. (2018). Sensory literacies, the body, and digital media. In K. Mills, A. Stornaiuolo, A. Smith, & J. Pandya (Eds.), *Handbook of writing, literacies and education in digital cultures*. New York, NY: Routledge.

Milson, A. J., & Earle, B. D. (2007). Internet-based GIS in an inductive learning environment: A case-study of ninth grade geography students. *The Journal of Geography*, *106*(6), 227–237. doi:10.1080/00221340701851274

Miranda, L., & Platt, B. (2018). *Found/Tonight* [CD]. Warner/Chappell Music, Inc.

Mishra, P., & Koehler, M. J. (2006). Technological pedagogical content knowledge: A framework for teacher knowledge. *Teachers College Record*, *108*(6), 1017–1054. doi:10.1111/j.1467-9620.2006.00684.x

Mitchell, C. (2017). Preparing future teachers to teach literacy in the 21st century: Utilizing digital literacies in literacy coursework to foster applicable classroom practices. *37th Edition of the American Reading Forum Yearbook*. Retrieved from http://www.americanreadingforum.org/yearbook/

Mitchell, C., Friedrich, L., & Appleget, C. (2018). Preservice teachers' blogging: Collaboration across universities for meaningful technology integration. *Teaching Education*, 1–17. doi:10.1080/10476210.2018.1486815

Moll, L. (2014). *L.S. Vygotsky and education*. New York: Routledge.

Morgan, W. (2000). Electronic tools for dismantling the master's house: Poststructuralist feminist research and hypertext poetics. In E. A. St. Pierre & W. S. Pillow (Eds.), *Working the ruins: Feminist poststructural theory and methods in education* (pp. 130–149). New York, NY: Routledge.

Morrell, E. (2012). 21st-century literacies, critical media pedagogies, and language arts. *The Reading Teacher*, *66*(4), 300–302. doi:10.1002/TRTR.01125

Mourlam, D. J., Strouse, G. A., Newland, L. A., & Lin, H. (2019). Can they do it? A comparison of teacher candidates' beliefs and preschoolers' actual skills with digital technology and media. *Computers & Education*, *129*, 82–91. doi:10.1016/j.compedu.2018.10.016

Murray, S., & Ouellette, L. (Eds.). (2009). *Reality TV: Remaking television culture*. New York, NY: New York University Press.

Nagle, J. (2018). Twitter, cyber-violence, and the need for a critical social media literacy in teacher education: A review of the literature. *Teaching and Teacher Education*, *76*, 86–94. doi:10.1016/j.tate.2018.08.014

National association for media literacy education. (n.d.). Retrieved from https://namle.net/

National Association for the Education of Young Children. (2009). *NAEYC Standards for early childhood professional preparation: Position statement*. Retrieved from https://www.naeyc.org/sites/default/files/globally-shared/downloads/PDFs/resources/position-statements/2009%20Professional%20Prep%20stdsRevised%204_12.pdf

National Center for Education Statistics. (2019). *The nation's report card 2017: Reading grade 4*. Retrieved from https://www.nationsreportcard.gov/reading_2017/nation/achievement?grade=4

National Conference on Citizenship. (2009). *America's civic health index 2009: Civic health in hard times*. Washington, DC: Author.

National Council for the Social Studies (NCSS). (1994). *Expectations of excellence: Curriculum standards for social studies*. Washington, DC: NCSS.

National Council for the Social Studies (NCSS). (2013). *The College, Career, and Civic Life (C3) Framework for social studies state standards: Guidance for enhancing the rigor of K-12 civics, economics, geography, and history*. Silver Spring, MD: NCSS.

National Council of Teachers of English. (2018). *Conference Proceedings, Raising Student Voice: 2018 NCTE Annual Convention*. Houston, TX: NCTE.

National Council of Teachers of English/International Reading Association. (2012). *Standards for the English language arts*. Author.

National Council of Teachers of English/International Reading Association. (2012). *Standards for the English Language Arts*. Retrieved from: http://www2.ncte.org/resources/standards/ncte-ira-standards-for-the-english-language arts/

National Governors Association Center for Best Practices & Council of Chief State School Officers. (2010). *Common Core State Standards for English language arts and literacy in history/social studies, science, and technical subjects*. Washington, DC: Authors.

New London Group. (1996). A pedagogy of multiliteracies: Designing social futures. *Harvard Educational Review*, *66*(1), 60–93. doi:10.17763/haer.66.1.17370n67v22j160u

Newell, G., Bloome, D., & Hirvela, A. (2015). *Teaching and learning argumentative writing in high school English language arts classrooms*. New York, NY: Routledge. doi:10.4324/9781315780498

Nielsen. (2005). *Nielsen 2005 Report on Television*. New York: Nielsen Media Research.

Nielsen. (2011, September 21). *10 years of primetime: The rise of reality and sports programming*. Retrieved from http://www.nielsen.com/us/en/insights/news/2011/10- years-of-primetime-the-rise-of-reality-and-sports-programming.html

Nieto, S. (1996). *Affirming diversity: The sociopolitical context of multicultural education* (2nd ed.). White Plains, NY: Longman.

Nieto, S. (2002). *Language, culture, and teaching: Critical perspectives for a new century*. Mahwah, NJ: Lawrence Erlbaum.

Norton-Meier, L. A. (2005). A thrice learned lesson from the literate life of a five-year-old. *Language Arts*, *82*(5), 286–285.

Obama, B. (2010). *Remarks by the President on space exploration in the 21st century* [Transcript]. Retrieved from https://www.nasa.gov/news/media/trans/obama_ksc_trans.html

Ocasio, A. (2014, December 18). Reality TV by the numbers. *ScreenRant*. Retrieved from http://screenrant.com/reality-tv-statistics-infographic-aco-149257/

Ohler, J. B. (2013). *Digital storytelling in the classroom: New media pathways to literacy, learning, and creativity*. Corwin Press. doi:10.4135/9781452277479

Ok, M. W., Kim, M. K., & Wang, E. Y. (2016). How to find good apps: An evaluation rubric for instructional apps for teaching students with learning disabilities. *Intervention in School and Clinic*, *51*(4), 244–252. doi:10.1177/1053451215589179

Okojie, M. C. (2011). The changing roles of teachers in a technology learning setting. *International Journal of Instructional Media*, *38*(1), 17–26.

Olmstead, C. (2013). Using technology to increase parent involvement in schools. *TechTrends*, *57*(6), 28–37. doi:10.100711528-013-0699-0

Orfield, G., & Frankenberg, E. (2014). Increasingly segregated and unequal schools as courts reverse policy. *Educational Administration Quarterly*, *50*(5), 718–734. doi:10.1177/0013161X14548942

Ouellette, L. (2010). Reality TV gives back: On the civic functions of reality entertainment. *The Journal of Popular Film and Television*, *38*(2), 67–72. doi:10.1080/01956051.2010.483347

Ousterhout, J. K. (1998). Scripting: Higher level programming for the 21st century. *Computer*, *31*(3), 23–30. doi:10.1109/2.660187

Pahl, K. (2009). Interactions, intersections and improvisations: Studying the multimodal texts and classroom talk of six-to seven-year-olds. *Journal of Early Childhood Literacy*, *9*(2), 188–210. doi:10.1177/1468798409105586

Pahl, K., & Rowsell, J. (2010). *Artifactual Literacies: Every Object Tells a Story*. New York, N.Y.: Teachers College Press.

Palacio, R. J. (2012). *Wonder*. New York: Random House.

Pantaleo, S. (2015). Language, Literacy and Visual Texts. *English in Education*, *49*(2), 113–129. doi:10.1111/eie.12053

Papert, S. (1980). *Mindstorms: Children, computers, and powerful ideas*. New York: Basic Books, Inc.

Paris, D. (2012). Culturally sustaining pedagogy: A needed change in stance, terminology, and practice. *Educational Researcher*, *41*(3), 93–97. doi:10.3102/0013189X12441244

Paris, D., & Alim, H. S. (2014). What are we seeking to sustain through culturally sustaining pedagogy? A loving critique forward. *Harvard Educational Review*, *84*(1), 85–100. doi:10.17763/haer.84.1.982l873k2ht16m77

Parker, W. C. (2003). *Teaching democracy: Unity and diversity in public life*. New York, NY: Teachers College Press.

Park, J. (2005). *Writing at the edge: Narrative and Writing Process Theory* (Vol. 248). New York, NY: Peter Lang.

Parten Gerla, J. (2010). Madelyn, a preservice teacher becomes a writer. *Southeastern Teacher Education Journal*, *3*(1), 131–140.

Peck, S. M. (2015). Extending school communities through university–school partnerships. In University Partnerships for Community and School System Development (Innovations in Higher Education Teaching and Learning, Volume 5). Emerald Group Publishing Limited.

Perkins, D. N., & Salomon, G. (1992). *Transfer of learning. International Encyclopedia of Education* (2nd ed.). Oxford, UK: Pergamon Press. Retrieved from https://pdfs.semanticscholar.org/fb86/245e6623502017940c796c01ed508c3d8208.pdf

Perrin, A. (2017, May 19). Digital gap between rural and nonrural America persists. *Pew Research Center.* Retrieved from http://www.pewresearch.org/fact-tank/2017/05/19/digital-gap-between-rural-and-nonrural-america-persists/

Pew Research Center. (2012). *Teens fact sheet*. Retrieved from http://www.pewinternet.org/fact- sheets/teens-fact-sheet/

Pozner, J. (2010). *Reality bites back: The troubling truth about guilty pleasure TV*. Berkeley, CA: Seal Press.

Prensky, M. (2001). Digital natives, digital immigrants, part 1. *On the Horizon*, *9*(5), 1–6. doi:10.1108/10748120110424816

Prior, P. (2006). A sociocultural theory of writing. In C. A. MacArthur, S. Graham, & J. Fitzgerald (Eds.), *Handbook of writing research* (pp. 54–66). New York, NY: Guilford Press.

Prottsman, K. (2015, March 4). Coding vs. programming – Battle of the terms! *Huffington Post*. Retrieved from https://www.huffingtonpost.com/kiki-prottsman/coding-vs-programming-bat_b_7042816.html

Pullen, P. C., Lane, H. B., & Monaghan, M. C. (2004). Effects of a volunteer tutoring model on the early literacy development of struggling first grade students. *Reading Research and Instruction*, *43*(4), 21–40. doi:10.1080/19388070409558415

Purcell-Gates, V., Perry, K., & Briseño, A. (2011). Analyzing literacy practice: Grounded theory to model. *Research in the Teaching of English*, *45*(4), 439–458.

Rappaport, D. (2001). *Martin's big words: The life of Dr. Martin Luther King, Jr.* New York, NY: Hyperion Books for Children.

Resnick, M., Maloney, J., Monroy-Hernandez, A., Rusk, N., Eastmond, E., Brennan, K., ... Kafai, Y. (2009). Scratch: Programming for all. *Communications of the AMC*, *52*, 60–67.

Reyes, I., DaSilva Iddings, A., & Feller, N. (2016). Building relationships with diverse students and families: A funds of knowledge perspective. *Journal of Early Childhood Literacy*, *16*(1), 8–33. doi:10.1177/1468798415584692

Rheingold, H. (2008). Using participatory media and public voice to encourage civic Engagement. In W. L. Bennet (Ed.), *Civic life online: Learning how digital media can engage youth* (pp. 97–118). Cambridge, MA: The MIT Press.

Richardson, E. (2006). *Hiphop literacies*. London: Routledge. doi:10.4324/9780203391105

Rideout, V., Foehr, U., & Roberts, D. (2010, January). *Generation M 2: Media in the Lives of 8-to 18-Year-Olds*. Retrieved from https://www.kff.org/other/event/generation-m2-media-in-the-lives-of/

Rish, R. (2013). Exploring multimodal composing processes with preservice teachers. In K. E. Pytash, R. E. Ferdig, & T. Rasinski (Eds.), *Preparing teachers to teach writing using technology* (pp. 1–16). Pittsburgh, PA: ETC Press.

Ritchhart, R., Church, M., & Morrison, K. (2011). *Making thinking visible: How to promote engagement, understanding, and independence for all learners*. San Francisco, CA: Jossey-Bass.

Ritter, G. W., Barnett, J. H., Denny, G. S., & Albin, G. R. (2009). The effectiveness of volunteer tutoring programs for elementary and middle school students: A meta-analysis. *Review of Educational Research*, *79*(1), 3–38. doi:10.3102/0034654308325690

Roa, K., & Skouge, J. (2015). Using multimedia technologies to support culturally and linguistically diverse learners and young children with disabilities. In K. L. Heider & M. R. Renck (Eds.), *Educating the young child* (pp. 101–115). Boston, MA: Pearson.

Robertson, L., Taczak, K., & Yancey, K. B. (2012). Notes toward a theory of prior knowledge and its role in college composers' transfer of knowledge and practice. *Composition Forum*, 26. Retrieved from http://compositionforum.com/issue/26/prior-knowledge-transfer.php

Rogoff, B. (2008). Observing sociocultural activity on three planes: Participatory appropriation, guided participation, and apprenticeship. *Pedagogy and practice: Culture and identities*, 58-74.

Rogoff, B. (1990). *Apprenticeship in thinking: Cognitive development in social context*. New York: Oxford University Press.

Rogoff, B. (1994). Developing understanding of the idea of communities of learners. *Mind, Culture, and Activity*, *1*(4), 209–229.

Rosaen, C. L., Lundeberg, M., Cooper, M., Fritzen, A., & Terpstra, M. (2008). Noticing: How does investigation of video records change how teachers reflect on their experiences? *Journal of Teacher Education*, *59*(4), 347–360. doi:10.1177/0022487108322128

Rosenblatt, L. M. (1994). The transactional theory of reading and writing. In R. B. Ruddell, M. R. Ruddell, & H. Singer (Eds.), *Theoretical models and processes of reading* (pp. 1057–1092). Newark, DE: International Reading Association.

Ross, E. W. (2014). *Social studies curriculum: Purposes, problems, and possibilities* (4th ed.). Albany, NY: SUNY Press.

Rowsell, J. & Walsh, M. (2011). Rethinking literacy education in new times: multimodality, multiliteracies, & new literacies. *Brock Education: A Journal of Educational Research and Practice, 21*. doi:10.26522/brocked.v21i1.236

Rowsell, J., & Simon, R. (2017). Artifactual literacies. The SAGE Encyclopedia of Out-of-School Learning, 1, 40-42.

Rowsell, J., & Harwood, D. (2015). "Let It Go": Exploring the Image of the Child as a Producer, Consumer, and Inventor. *Theory into Practice*, *54*(2), 136–146. doi:10.1080/00405841.2015.1010847

Rowsell, J., & Wohlwend, K. (2016). Free play or tight spaces? Mapping participatory literacies in apps. *The Reading Teacher*, *70*(2), 197–205. doi:10.1002/trtr.1490

RTL Z. (2016, May 5). *Apple CEO Tim Cook interview at Startup Fest Europe*. Retrieved from https://youtu.be/OHCy-MyQ2TAo

Rust, J. (2019). Immobilizing Literacies: Collisions of Difference During the Digital Dialogue Project. In D. Pyles, R. Rish, & J. Warner (Eds.), *Negotiating Place and Space through Digital Literacies*. Information Age Publishing.

Rust, J., & Ballard, S. (2016). I Am/You See: Traversing literacies from page to screen to body. *English Journal*, *105*(5), 61–67.

Sadaf, A., Newby, T. J., & Ertmer, P. A. (2016). An investigation of the factors that influence preservice teachers' intentions and integration of Web 2.0 tools. *Education Technology Research Development*, *64*, 37–64. doi:10.100711423-015-9410-9

Saeli, M., Perrenet, J., Jochems, W. M., & Zwaneveld, B. (2011). Teaching programming in secondary school: A pedagogical content knowledge perspective. *Informatics in Education*, *10*(1), 73–88.

Sakr, M., Connelly, V., & Wild, M. (2016). "Evil cats" and "jelly floods": Young children's collective constructions of digital art making in the early years classroom. *Journal of Research in Childhood Education*, *30*(1), 128–141. doi:10.1080/02568543.2015.1107156

Saldaña, J. (2003). Dramatizing data: A primer. *Qualitative Inquiry*, *9*(2), 218–236. doi:10.1177/1077800402250932

Saldaña, J. (2009). *An introduction to codes and coding. The coding manual for qualitative researchers*. Thousand Oaks, CA: Sage Publications.

Saldaña, J. (2015). *The coding manual for qualitative researchers*. London: Sage.

Sánchez, L. (2011). Building on young children's cultural histories through placemaking in the classroom. *Contemporary Issues in Early Childhood*, *12*(4), 332–342. doi:10.2304/ciec.2011.12.4.332

Saye, J. W. (2017). Disciplined inquiry in social studies classrooms. In M. M. Manfra & C. M. Bolick (Eds.), *The Wiley handbook of social studies research* (pp. 336–359). Malden, MA: John Wiley & Sons, Inc. doi:10.1002/9781118768747.ch15

Schlozman, K. L., Verba, S., & Brady, H. E. (2012). *The unheavenly chorus: Unequal political voice and the broken promise of American democracy*. Princeton, NJ: Princeton University Press.

Schugar, H. R., Smith, C., & Schugar, J. T. (2013). Teaching with interactive picture e-books in grades K-6. *The Reading Teacher*, *66*(8), 615–624. doi:10.1002/trtr.1168

Schugar, J., Schugar, H., & Penny, C. (2011). A nook or a book: Comparing college students' reading comprehension levels, critical reading, and study skills. *International Journal of Technology in Teaching and Learning*, *7*(2), 116–132.

Schug, M., Todd, R., & Beery, R. (1984). Why kids don't like social studies. *Social Education*, *47*(5), 382–387.

Scribner, S., & Cole, M. (1981). *The psychology of literacy*. Cambridge, MA: Harvard University Press. doi:10.4159/harvard.9780674433014

Sefton-Green, J., Marsh, J., Erstad, O., & Flewitt, R. (2017). *Establishing a Research Agenda for the Digital Literacy Practices of Young Children: A White Paper for COST Action IS1410*. doi:10.13140/RG.2.2.10896.30720

Sewell, W. C., & Denton, S. (2011). Multimodal literacies in the secondary English classroom. *English Journal, 100*(5), 61–65.

Shakur, T. (1999). *The rose that grew from concrete*. New York: Pocket Books.

Shanahan, L. (2012). Use of sound with digital text: Moving beyond sound as an add-on or decoration. *Contemporary Issues in Technology & Teacher Education, 12*(3), 264–285.

Shanahan, L. (2012). Use of sound with digital text: Moving beyond sound as an add-on Or decoration. *Contemporary Issues in Technology & Teacher Education, 12*(3), 264–285.

Shanahan, T. (1998). On the effectiveness and limitations of tutoring in reading. *Review of Research in Education, 23*, 217–234.

Share, J., Funk, S., & Kellner, D. (2016, Nov 5). *Critical media literacy framework*. Retrieved from https://www.academia.edu/29786076/Critical_Media_Literacy_Framework_updated_No v._5_2016_

Sheets, R. H. (1996). Urban classroom conflict: Student-teacher perception: Ethnic integrity, solidarity, and resistance. *The Urban Review, 28*(2), 165–183. doi:10.1007/BF02354383

Shulman, L. S. (1986). Those who understand: Knowledge growth in teaching. *Educational Researcher, 15*(2), 4–14. doi:10.3102/0013189X015002004

Shulsky, D. D., Baker, S. F., Chvala, T., & Willis, J. M. (2017). Cultivating layered literacies: Developing the global child to become tomorrow's global citizen. *International Journal of Development Education and Global Learning, 9*(1), 49–63. doi:10.18546/IJDEGL.9.1.05

Siwatu, K. O. (2011). Preservice teachers' sense of preparedness and self-efficacy to teach in America's urban and sub-urban schools: Does context matter? *Teaching and Teacher Education, 27*(2), 357–365. doi:10.1016/j.tate.2010.09.004

Skelley, D. L., Stevens, M. L., & Anderson, R. S. (2016, November). *A university literacy center moving to offsite after-school tutoring: Perceptions of tutors, children, and parents*. Roundtable discussion presented at the 2016 Association of Literacy Educators and Researchers Conference, Myrtle Beach, SC.

Smith, A. (2013, April 25). Civic engagement in the digital age. *Pew Research Center*. Retrieved from http://www.pewinternet.org/2013/04/25/civic-engagement-in-the-digital-age/

Smith, A., Stornaiuolo, A., & Phillips, N. C. (2018). Multiplicities in motion: A turn to transliteracies. *Theory into Practice, 57*(1), 20–28. doi:10.1080/00405841.2017.1390334

Smith, B. (2018). Composing for affect, audience, and identify: Toward a multidimensional understanding of adolescents' multimodal composing goals and designs. *Written Communication, 35*(2), 182–214. doi:10.1177/0741088317752335

Smith, G. A., & Sobel, D. (2014). *Place-and community-based education in schools*. Routledge. doi:10.4324/9780203858530

Smith, K. (2008). *How to be an explorer of the world: portable life museum*. Penguin.

Sofkova Hashemi, S., & Cederlund, K. (2017). Making room for the transformation of literacy instruction in the digital classroom. *Journal of Early Childhood Literacy, 17*(2), 221–253. doi:10.1177/1468798416630779

Sommers, N., & Saltz, L. (2004). The novice as expert: Writing the freshman year. *College Composition and Communication, 56*(1), 124–149. doi:10.2307/4140684

Souto-Manning, M. (2016). Honoring and building on the rich literacy practices of young bilingual and multilingual learners. *The Reading Teacher, 70*(3), 263–271. doi:10.1002/trtr.1518

Stake, R. (2005). Qualitative case studies. In N. K. Denzin & Y. S. Lincoln (Eds.), *Sage Handbook of Qualitative Research* (3rd ed.; pp. 442–447). Thousand Oaks, CA: Sage Publications.

Staples, J. (2010). "Does my iMovie suck?": Assessing teacher candidates' digital composition processes. *English Journal, 99*(5), 95–99.

Starcic, A., Cotic, M., Solomonides, I., & Volk, M. (2016). Engaging preservice primary and preprimary school teachers in digital storytelling for the teaching and learning of mathematics. *British Journal of Educational Technology, 7*(1), 29–50. doi:10.1111/bjet.12253

Stein, P., & Newfield, D. (2006). Multiliteracies and multimodality in English in education in Africa: Mapping the terrain. *English Studies in Africa, 49*(1), 1–22. doi:10.1080/00138390608691341

Stephens, C., & Edwards, S. (2018). *Young children playing and learning in a digital age: A cultural and critical perspective*. New York: Routledge.

Stevens, M. L., Skelley, D. L., & Anderson, R. S. (2016, December). *Exploring cultural responsiveness in afterschool literacy tutoring: "White people don't eat chicken!"* Roundtable discussion presented at the 66th Annual Conference Literacy Research Association, Nashville, TN.

Stornaiuolo, A., Smith, A., & Phillips, N. C. (2017). Developing a transliteracies framework for a connected world. *Journal of Literacy Research, 49*(1), 68–91. doi:10.1177/1086296X16683419

Stornaiuolo, A., & Whitney, E. (2018). Writing as world making. *Language Arts, 95*(4), 205–217.

Street, B. V. (1984). *Literacy in theory and practice*. Cambridge, UK: Cambridge University Press.

Street, B. V. (1995). *Social literacies: Critical approaches to literacy in development, ethnography and education*. London, UK: Longman.

Strudler, N., & Wetzel, K. (2005). The diffusion of electronic ePortfolio in teacher education: Issues of initiation and implementation. *Journal of Research on Technology in Education, 337*(4), 411–433. doi:10.1080/15391523.2005.10782446

Sukovic, S. (2017). *Transliteracy in complex information environments*. Cambridge, MA: Chandos Publishing.

Swalwell, K. (2015). Mind the civic empowerment gap: Economically elite students and critical civic education. *Curriculum Inquiry, 45*(5), 491–512. doi:10.1080/03626784.2015.1095624

Swan, K., Lee, J., & Grant, S. G. (2018). Inquiry design model: Building inquiries in social studies. Silver Spring, MD: National Council for the Social Studies and C3 Teachers.

Task Force on Inequality and American Democracy. (2004). *American democracy in an age of rising inequality*. Washington, DC: American Political Science Association. Retrieved from https://www.apsanet.org/portals/54/Files/Task%20Force%20Reports/taskforcereport.pdf

Tatsuoka, M. M., & Lohnes, P. R. (1988). *Multivariate analysis: Techniques for educational and psychological research* (2nd ed.). New York: Macmillan.

Tatum, B. D. (2007). *Can we talk about race?: And other conversations in an era of school resegregation*. Beacon Press.

Thacker, E. S., Lee, J. K., & Friedman, A. M. (2017). Teaching with the C3 Framework: Surveying teachers' beliefs and practices. *Journal of Social Studies Research, 41*(2), 89–100. doi:10.1016/j.jssr.2016.08.001

The Common Sense Census: Media Use by Tweens and Teens. (2015). Retrieved December 1, 2018, from https://www.commonsensemedia.org/sites/default/files/uploads/research/census_research report.pdf

The global critical media literacy project. (n.d.). Retrieved from gcml.org

Thinglink. (n.d.). *Thinglink App*. Retrieved from https://www.thinglink.com/

Thoma, J., Hutchison, A., Johnson, D., Johnson, K., & Stromer, E. (2017). Planning for technology integration in a professional learning community. *The Reading Teacher, 71*(2), 167–175. doi:10.1002/trtr.1604

Thomas, S., Joseph, C., Laccetti, J., Mason, B., Mills, S., & Pullinger, K. (2007). Transliteracy: Crossing divides. First Monday, 12.

Thomas, A. (2017). *The Hate U Give*. New York, NY: Balzer & Bray/Harperteen.

Tierney, R. J. (2018). Toward a model of global meaning making. *Journal of Literacy Research, 50*(4), 397–422. doi:10.1177/1086296X18803134

Torney-Purta, J., & Wilkenfeld, B. S. (2009). *Paths to 21st century competencies through civic education classrooms: An analysis of survey results from ninth-graders*. Washington, DC: Campaign for the Civic Mission of Schools and American Bar Association Division for Public Education.

Tuomi, P., Multisilta, J., Saarikoski, P., & Suominen, J. (2018). Coding skills as a success factor for society. *Education and Information Technologies, 23*(1), 419–434. doi:10.100710639-017-9611-4

Turbill, J. B., & Murray, J. (2006). Early literacy and technologies in Australian schools: Policy, research, and practice. In M. McKenna, L. Labbo, R. D. Kieffer, & D. Reinking (Eds.), *International Handbook of Literacy and Technology* (Vol. 2, pp. 93–108). Mahwah, NJ: Lawrence Erlbaum Associates.

Unsworth, L. (2001). *Teaching multiliteracies across the curriculum*. Buckingham, UK: Open University Press.

Vadasy, P. F., Sanders, E. A., Peyton, J. A., & Jenkins, J. R. (2002). Timing and intensity of tutoring: A closer look at the conditions for effective early literacy tutoring. *Learning Disabilities Research & Practice, 17*(4), 227–241. doi:10.1111/1540-5826.00048

Valentine, K. B. (2006). Unlocking the doors for incarcerated women through performance and creative writing. In D. S. Madison & J. Hamera (Eds.), *The Sage handbook of performance studies* (pp. 309–324). Thousand Oaks, CA: Sage. doi:10.4135/9781412976145.n17

VanKooten, C., & Berkley, A. (2016). Messy problem-exploring through video in first-year writing: Assessing what counts. *Computers and Composition, 40*, 151–163. doi:10.1016/j.compcom.2016.04.001

Vasquez, V., Janks, H., & Comber, B. (2019). Critical Literacy as a Way of Being and Doing. *Language Arts, 96*(5), 300–311.

Vasudevan, L., Schultz, K., & Bateman, J. (2010). Rethinking composing in a digital age: Authoring literate identities through multimodal storytelling. *Written Communication, 27*(4), 442–468. doi:10.1177/0741088310378217

Vee, A. (2017). *Coding literacy: How computer programming is changing writing*. Cambridge, MA: MIT Press. doi:10.7551/mitpress/10655.001.0001

Villegas, A. M. (1991). *Culturally responsive pedagogy for the 1990s and beyond. Trends and issues paper No. 6.* Washington, DC: ERIC Clearinghouse on Teacher Education.

Voogt, J., & McKenney, S. (2017). TPACK in teacher education: Are we preparing teachers to use technology for early literacy? *Technology, Pedagogy and Education*, *26*(1), 69–83. doi:10.1080/1475939X.2016.1174730

Vygotsky, L. S. (1978). Mind in society: The development of higher psychological processes (M. Cole, V. J John-Steiner, S. Scribner, & E. Souberman, Eds. & Trans.). Cambridge, MA: Harvard University Press. (Original work published 1934)

Vygotsky, L. (1978). *Mind in society: The development of higher psychological processes*. Cambridge, MA: Harvard University Press.

Vygotsky, L. S. (1978). *Mind and society: The development of higher mental processes*. Cambridge, MA: Harvard University Press.

Walsh, M., & Simpson, A. (2014). Exploring literacies through touch pad technologies: The dynamic materiality of modal interactions. *Australian Journal of Language and Literacy*, *37*(2), 96.

Walsh, M., & Walsh, M. (2010). Multimodal literacy: What does it mean for classroom practice? *Australian Journal of Language and Literacy*, *33*, 211–239. Retrieved from http://search.proquest.com/docview/1496986878/

Wasik, B. A. (1998). Volunteer tutoring programs in reading: A review. *Reading Research Quarterly*, *33*(3), 266–291. doi:10.1598/RRQ.33.3.2

White, J. (2016). *Introducing dialogic pedagogy: Provocations for the early years*. New York: Routledge.

Wiggins, G., & McTighe, J. (2005) Understanding by design (2nd. ed.). Alexandria, VA: Association for Supervision and Curriculum Development (ASCD).

WilkinsonL. (2010, December 21). Why transliteracy? *Libraries and Transliteracy*. Retrieved from https://librariesandtransliteracy.wordpress.com/2010/12/20/why-transliteracy/

Windschitl, M. (2002). Framing constructivism in practice as the negotiation of dilemmas: An analysis of the conceptual, pedagogical, cultural, and political challenges facing teachers. *Review of Educational Research*, *72*(2), 131–175. doi:10.3102/00346543072002131

Wineburg, S., McGrew, S., Breakstone, J., & Ortega, T. (2016, November 22). *Evaluating information: The cornerstone of civic online reasoning*. Stanford, CA: Stanford History Education Group.

Wing, J. (2006). Computational thinking. *Communications of the ACM*, *49*(3), 33–36. doi:10.1145/1118178.1118215

Wing, J. M. (2008). Computational thinking and thinking about computing. *Philosophical Transactions of the Royal Society of London. Series A, Mathematical and Physical Sciences*, *366*(1881), 3717–3725. doi:10.1098/rsta.2008.0118 PMID:18672462

Wissman, K., & Costello, S. (2014). Creating digital comics in response to literature: Aesthetics, aesthetic transactions, and meaning making. *Language Arts*, *92*(2), 103–117.

Wohlwend, K. (2011). *Playing their way into literacies: Reading, writing, and belonging in the early childhood classroom.* New York: Teachers College Press.

Wohlwend, K. (2013). *Literacy playshop: New literacies, popular media, and play in the early childhood classroom.* New York: Teachers College Press.

Wohlwend, K. (2017). Chasing Literacies Across Action Texts and Augmented Realities: E-Books, Animated Apps, and Pokémon Go. In *The Case of the iPad* (pp. 49–66). Singapore: Springer. doi:10.1007/978-981-10-4364-2_4

Wohlwend, K. E. (2016). Who gets to play? Access, popular media and participatory literacies. *Early Years: An International Research Journal*, *37*(1), 62–76. doi:10.1080/09575146.2016.1219699

Woolley, G., & Hay, I. (2007). Reading intervention: The benefits of using trained tutors. *Australian Journal of Language and Literacy*, *30*(1), 9–20.

Yadav, A., Burkhart, D., Moix, D., Snow, E., Bandaru, P., & Clayborn, L. (2015). Sowing the seeds of assessment literacy in secondary computer science education: A landscape study. *Computer Science Teaching Association Report.* Retrieved from https://www.csteachers.org/documents/en-us/78193875-4ed9-42ea-8224-841d13da1f74/1

Yahya, R., & Wood, E. A. (2017). Play as third space between home and school: Bridging cultural discourses. *Journal of Early Childhood Research*, *15*(3), 305–322. doi:10.1177/1476718X15616833 PMID:28867965

Yancey, K. B. (2009). Reflection and electronic portfolio. In D. Cambridge, B. Cambridge, & K. Yancey (Eds.), *Electronic portfolios 2.0: Emergent research on implementation and impact.* Stylus Publishing, LLC.

Yang, A. (2010). Engaging participatory literacy through science zines. *The American Biology Teacher*, *72*(9), 573–577. doi:10.1525/abt.2010.72.9.10

Yin, R. K. (2009). *Case study research: Design and methods* (4th ed.). Thousand Oaks, CA: Sage Publications.

Youniss, J. (2012). How to enrich civic education and sustain democracy. In D. E. Campbell, M. Levinson, & F. M. Hess (Eds.), *Making civics count: Citizenship education for a new generation* (pp. 115–133). Cambridge, MA: Harvard Education Press.

Zeichner, K. (2010). Rethinking the connections between campus courses and field experiences in college- and university-based teacher education. *Journal of Teacher Education*, *61*(1–2), 89–99. doi:10.1177/0022487109347671

Zimmer, R., Hamilton, L., & Christina, R. (2010). After-school tutoring in the context of No Child Left Behind: Effectiveness of two programs in the Pittsburgh Public Schools. *Economics of Education Review*, 2918–2928. doi:10.1016/j.econedurev.2009.02.005

Zirkel, S. (2008). The influence of multicultural educational practices on student outcomes and intergroup relations. *Teachers College Record*, *110*(6), 1147–1181.

About the Contributors

Rebecca S. Anderson is a professor and director of the University of Memphis Center for Literacy Research and Practice. Her work focuses on literacy education with specific interests in K-12 literacy instruction for struggling readers, technology integration in reading and writing development, online teaching, and teacher education.

Carin Appleget is an Assistant Professor at Creighton University in Omaha, Nebraska. She teaches elementary education literacy methods and assessment as well as courses focused on critical issues in education. Her areas of research include preservice teacher preparation, elementary literacy instruction, technology integration, and culturally relevant pedagogy.

Sarah Ballard is a teacher at Murrah High School in Jackson, Mississippi, where she has taught English II and AP Literature and Composition for the past thirteen years. She started her teaching career in Belzoni, Mississippi, as a member of the Mississippi Teacher Corps. She was named Teacher of the Year at Humphrey's County High School in 2004 and Murrah High School in 2013. She renewed her National Board Certification in 2018 and was chosen as Star Teacher in 2016. This year she received the Mississippi Excellence in Education award for High School Teacher of the Year. She is most proud of working with students to resurrect The Pleiades, Murrah's prestigious literary magazine, and being awarded Literary Magazine Adviser of the Year in 2017. Sarah resides in the historic Belhaven neighborhood in Jackson with her husband and eight-year-old twins.

Sally Brown is Professor of Reading Education at Georgia Southern University. Prior to teaching in higher education, she taught kindergarten through third grade at public elementary schools for over thirteen years. Her research interests include multilingual learners, early language and literacy development, and integrating technology into literacy instruction. Dr. Brown is the co-editor of Talking Points, a National Council of Teachers of English journal (http://www.ncte.org/journals/tp). She has published articles in several journals including the Reading Teacher, Journal of Research in Childhood Education, and Democracy and Education.

Hayley Bruning, currently employed at Integrated Media Solutions as an Associate Editor, earned a Bachelor's degree in Literature at Ramapo College of New Jersey. She went on to attend West Chester University for its Masters of English program. Her research interests include socioeconomics, writing in higher education, mental health, and technology. She has presented her poetry collection at the 2016

Sigma Tau Delta Convention and an analysis paper on gentrification in the show Shameless at the 2018 Literature and Social Justice Graduate Conference.

Molly Buckley-Marudas is an Assistant Professor of Adolescent and Young Adult English Education at Cleveland State University and a professor-in-residence at Campus International High School in Cleveland, Ohio. Her research interests include adolescent literacy, digital literacies, youth-led research, and English education.

Laquana Cooke is an Assistant Professor at West Chester University. She develops courses in Digital Humanities and Game Design/Development. Her research on critical pedagogy and media criticism, has been published in IEEE, Games Studies, and Changing English.

Tracy Cretelle is an instructional coach for English as New Language teachers in a large urban school district. Tracy earned her Masters Degree in Teaching English for Students of Other Languages from Nazareth College of Rochester. Tracy is a doctoral candidate at the University of Rochester. Tracy's area of study is how multilingual learners leverage their cultural funds of knowledge while engaging in collaborative, creative problem solving and project-based instruction. Tracy teaches English Language Learners, teacher educators and creative writers in urban, rural, and suburban settings. Tracy is a writer, a puppeteer, a teaching artist, and poet.

Charles Ellenbogen is in his 26th year of teaching and his second year of teaching Language and Literature at Campus International High School, a public high school in Cleveland, Ohio.

Erin FitzPatrick is an Assistant Professor at the University of North Carolina at Charlotte in the Department of Special Education and Child Development. She earned her M.Ed. in Literacy from Middle Tennessee State University and a Ph.D. in Students with Exceptionalities from Georgia State University. Prior to working as a professor, Erin served for 11 years as an elementary teacher in Houston and Nashville. She is a 2011 alumna of the Middle Tennessee Writing Project and conducts professional development seminars both nationally and internationally. Erin's research interests include practice-based professional development to support teachers in adopting evidence-based practices as well as self-regulated strategy development to support students with special needs realize writing goals.

Jennifer Grow received her B.A. in K-8 Education from Michigan State University and M.Ed. with an emphasis in reading from Middle Tennessee State University. After teaching 1st and 5th grades, she spent 12 years as a Reading Specialist before returning to school as a student. She is currently pursuing her Ph.D. in Literacy Studies at Middle Tennessee State University.

Casey Holmes received her B.A. in International Studies and M.A. in Teaching secondary social studies from the University of North Carolina- Chapel Hill. She taught high school social studies before beginning her doctoral studies. She is currently pursuing a PhD in social studies education. Her research interests include critical citizenship, global learning, and working with immigrant youth in the social studies classroom.

Melanie Hundley is an Associate Professor in the Practice of Language and Literacy Education at Vanderbilt University's Peabody College; her research examines how digital and multimodal composition informs the development of pre-service teachers' writing pedagogy. Additionally, she explores the use of digital and social media in young adult literature. She teaches writing methods courses that focus on digital and multimodal composition and young adult literature courses that explore race, class, gender, and sexual identity in young adult texts. She has taught both middle and high school English Language Arts and currently co-directs Patterson RAPS, a reading program for middle school students. Her work has been published in the Journal of Adolescent and Adult Literacy, The ALAN Review, Adolescent Literature Today, Innovative Practices in Teacher Preparation and Graduate-Level Teacher Education Programs and Perspectives on Digital Comics.

Robin Jocius is an Assistant Professor and Program Coordinator of Literacy Education in the Zucker Family School of Education at The Citadel. Dr. Jocius earned her Ph.D. in Language, Literacy, and Culture from Vanderbilt University, and her research and teaching interests include critical literacy, digital literacy, teacher learning, and the development of instructional contexts that support culturally and linguistically diverse learners.

Tabora Johnson is an Associate Professor at Medgar Evers College, CUNY. Her extensive education career spans over one decade from middle and high school classrooms to graduate school seminars. Specializing in African-centered pedagogy and culturally responsive education, her research interests include race and identity in education, preparing successful urban teachers, and Black hair and its sociocultural meaning and symbolism.

Margareth Lafontant holds a PhD in Developmental Psychology and a dual Master's degree in Bilingual Special Education from the Ferkauf Graduate School of Psychology of Yeshiva University and Bank Street College of Education, respectively. In addition to Special Education and Child Development issues across the birth - grade 12 span, other areas of expertise include program evaluation and working with English as a New Language learners. Dr. Lafontant's research interests are primarily grounded in the socio-emotional aspects of learning as this relates to both students and teachers.

Salika Lawrence, PhD, is a former middle and high school teacher with the New York City Department of Education. She currently serves as Associate Professor of Literacy and Teacher Education at City University of New York - Medgar Evers College. Her research interests include literacy instruction, teacher professional development, contexts of education, and critical literacy.

Danielle Ligocki is in her third year as a faculty member at Oakland University. Dr. Ligocki is excited about the work being done to change the field of teacher development. Prior to her time at Oakland University, Danielle Ligocki had been a middle school educator for eleven years, circumnavigating the ever-changing standards and values of public education, while putting the needs of her students above all else. Her time spent in a low-income school sparked the fire for her now fervent interest in social justice issues in education. Currently, her research focuses on youth identity and the ways in which media -- specifically reality television -- affects the ways in which youth view themselves and others. This is studied through the lens of liquid modernity, a time in which Zygmunt Bauman argues that all things and people are disposable. Additionally, the framework of critical media literacy is a common thread throughout much of her work.

Jana Lo Bello Miller is the Elementary Teacher Education Licensure Program Lead in the department of Curriculum and Instruction. Her scholarly interests include elementary teacher education, equity-based pedagogies as well as identity constructions within formal and informal educational spaces. She has taught in both elementary and special education contexts where culturally responsive pedagogies informed both her teaching and learning.

Meghan McGlinn Manfra is an Associate Professor in the College of Education at North Carolina State University. She is a former high school teacher, has a master's degree (MA) in history and received her doctorate (PhD) at the University of North Carolina Chapel Hill. Her research focuses on teacher education, teacher professional learning, and the integration of digital technologies into instruction. She is the editor of the Handbook of Social Studies Research and has written numerous journal articles. She has extensive background in educational research and evaluation, including serving as primary investigator and evaluator for federal grants. Dr. Manfra is the past chair of the Executive Board of the College and University Faculty Assembly of the National Council for the Social Studies.

Chrystine Mitchell is an Assistant Professor at York College of Pennsylvania, working with pre-service teachers to help integrate best practices in literacy instruction and assessment. Her area of research and passion is embedding digital technologies in her coursework to help prepare future teachers for the changing landscape in schools. This project was an extension of that work.

Sharon Peck, PhD, received her Ph.D. in Reading and Literacy from The University at Albany. She is an associate professor at the State University of New York College at Geneseo in the School of Education. She studies place-based pedagogy, language arts, play, games in education, and English Language Learning. She runs an urban literacy clinic and strives to support teachers to meet the diverse needs of urban students. For six years she directed a Teacher Leadership Quality Partnership Grant focusing on Reading and Writing in the Community. Sharon is also a puppeteer, storyteller, clown, and teaching artist.

Emily Pendergrass is an Associate Professor of Literacy at Vanderbilt University where she teaches courses in Teaching Reading with struggling readers and directs the Reading Education Graduate Program. Additionally, Emily works closely with the local public schools in literacy coaching and facilitating professional development workshops. Her research interests revolve around the complexities of teaching readers who struggle and new literacies in middle school classrooms.

Chris Penny is an Educational Technology Professor in the College of Education and Social Work at the West Chester University of Pennsylvania. In 2011 he won the Lindback Distinguished Teaching Award for his excellence in the classroom. In 2007 he became an Apple Distinguished Educator, and Google Certified Teacher in 2009. His efforts in teaching and research have the focus of technology integration in K-20 education. He has published a book titled Technology Leadership in Teacher Education: Integrated Solutions and Experiences. Has published articles on reading on electronic devices, eMentoring, 24/7 laptop access for teacher candidates, and digital portfolios. Mobile Pedagogy and Perspectives on

Teaching and Learning is the title of the book which he edited in 2013. His most recent research revolves around the topics of teaching and learning spaces, and teachers teaching coding.

Kim Reddig is a doctoral student in Special Education at the University of North Carolina at Charlotte. She earned her Bachelor's Degree in Special Education from Coker College in Hartsville, SC., and her M.Ed. in Special Education from the University of North Carolina at Charlotte. Prior to becoming a doctoral student, she served as a Special Education teacher in the public and private sector for 32 years. Kim's research interest include diversity, culturally responsive teaching, and inclusive practices for diverse students with disabilities.

Julie Rust began her career teaching ELA in middle and high school. After receiving her Ph.D. in Literacy, Culture, and Language Education at Indiana University, she served as Assistant Professor of Education at Millsaps College in Jackson, MS. She is now working at St. Andrew's Episcopal School as Associate Head of the Middle and Upper School: Teaching, Learning, and Innovation. Her research interests revolve around new media in ELA classroom spaces, dialogue across difference, and the practice turn in teacher education.

Anna Schick is the co-editor of (Re)narrating Teacher Identity: Telling Truths and Becoming Teachers and a doctoral student in Literacy, Language, and Culture at the University of Minnesota. Her scholarly interests include secondary English teacher education, artifactual critical literacy, critical writing pedagogy, and teacher well being and mental health. Her teaching and learning in elementary and secondary classrooms has fostered the desire to disrupt dominant and oppressive writing practices.

Katie Schrodt is an Assistant Professor at Middle Tennessee State University. Katie's 12 years in education have brought her from teaching in the elementary classroom to literacy coaching across Tennessee. Katie serves as a co-director of the Middle Tennessee Writing Project, and spends her time teaching literacy methods to pre-service and serving teachers as well as conducting literacy professional developments both nationally and internationally. Her research interests include reading and writing motivation.

Heather Schugar is a professor of Literacy at West Chester University of Pennsylvania. Her current research interests center on the role of mobile technologies in reading instruction, with a particular focus on students' comprehension when reading from these devices. Her work has been presented widely and published in journals such as The Reading Teacher and The Journal of Technology in Teaching and Learning. In addition, Dr. Schugar's research has been featured by media outlets such as The New York Times, NPR, Education Week, NBC News, Real Simple magazine, and Men's Fitness.

Jordan Schugar, an Associate Professor of English at the West Chester University of Pennsylvania, teaches courses in literature, writing, and educational technology. His research interests include the literacy associated with mobile pedagogies and emerging technologies, digital storytelling, and active learning spaces. He has published articles in journals such as The Reading Teacher, The California Reader, The Journal of Technology, Teaching and Learning. Additionally, he edited Mobile Pedagogy and Perspectives on Teaching and Learning in 2014. Additionally, he has presented his work at a variety of local, state, national, and international conferences like the National Council of Teachers of English (NCTE), the International Literacy Association (ILA), and the American Educational Research Association (AERA). His research has also been featured in the New York Times, USA Today, CNN, The Atlantic, Real Simple Magazine, and Education Week. In 2013, Dr. Schugar was also named an Apple Distinguished Educator.

Dana Skelley began her career in education teaching middle school and is currently an Assistant Professor of Literacy Education at the University of Alabama in Huntsville. Her research interests include digital literacies, critical literacy, and teacher education.

Emily Smith teaches American and English literature and Journalism at the secondary level at a private, college preparatory school in Fort Worth, Texas. She has a Master of Liberal Arts from Texas Christian University (Fort Worth, Texas) and a Bachelor of Arts in English Literature from the University of North Texas (Denton, Texas). She has led sessions at conferences for English educators at both the national and state levels, including the National Council of Teachers of English (NCTE) and the Texas Council of Teachers of English Language Arts (TCTELA). In addition to her classroom experience, Emily created a New Teacher Mentorship program to help struggling new teachers. Emily is passionate about mentoring her students and fellow educators to help them succeed in life beyond the classroom. She believes that teaching literature ultimately helps others understand the human experience, therefore increasing empathy and a desire to connect with others.

Margie Stevens is a researcher at the University of South Carolina School of Medicine-Greenville. Her work focuses on cultural differences in education and addiction education.

Martha Wilkins is a passionate educator who has a heart for student success. For over ten years, she was a classroom teacher in the Chicago Public School system where she was recognized numerous times for her accomplishments with student's academic performance. Most notably getting nominated for the Golden Apple Award for Excellence in Teaching and recognition for outstanding student performance on local, state, and national assessments. Although theses acknowledgements were appreciated, Dr. Wilkins cites her greatest accomplishment as the impact that she has had on the lives of her students and their families. Currently, Dr. Wilkins is an Assistant Professor of Elementary Education at Lewis University in Romeoville, Illinois. There she helps to prepare the next generation of educators who will impact and educate our youth. Wilkins is not only an educator but also a researcher who has presented her research at a number of national conferences and forums. Her research focuses primarily on Students of Color, giftedness, media, and the informal learning process.

Index

T

Y

www.ingramcontent.com/pod-product-compliance
Lightning Source LLC
LaVergne TN
LVHW062146300926
849161LV00010B/2645